"In crisp and engaging prose, Harden charts the birth, life, and (one hopes) death of a big American lie, exposing along the way a century-long list of willing collaborators: missionaries, Indian agents, newspaper editors, politicians, historians, plain old con men, and a university president. *Murder at the Mission* is narrative history that matters, made all the more necessary because the lie's consequences for the Cayuse people are today as real, and raw, as ever."

—Scott W. Berg, author of *38 Nooses: Lincoln, Little Crow, and the Frontier's End*

Praise for *Murder at the Mission*

"Terrifically readable."   —*Los Angeles Times*

"A richly detailed and expertly researched account of how a concocted story . . . became a part of American legend . . . Harden's deeply researched book, often from the letters and words of the principle figures themselves to rebuke lies told on their behalf, is not history revised. *Murder at the Mission* is history revealed."

—*Spokesman Review*

"A fascinating, well-written exposé . . . Harden skillfully brings to life the collision of myth and reality. He has managed to write a fittingly timely book that fits well into the post-Donald Trump era of false narratives, conspiracy theories, and cries of fake news."

—*New York Journal of Books*

"A well-written, fast-paced account . . . [that] succeeds in bringing often-forgotten history front and center . . . Highly recommended."

—*Library Journal* (starred review)

"[A] lively history . . . Enriched by dramatic storytelling and candid interviews with contemporary Cayuses, this immersive account illuminates how the tragedies of the past inform the present."

—*Publishers Weekly*

"Harden's vivid reconstruction illustrates the process of Western mythmaking, beloved of Americans when it paints them in a heroic light; and of cultural collision, with the Whitmans almost willfully ignoring the Cayuse worldview. . . . A boon for those who like their history unadorned by obfuscation and legend."   —*Kirkus Reviews*

"Harden meticulously outlines how one bitter minister crafted an out-landish lie out of the Whitmans' deaths, promoting a narrow vision of heroic white Christians destined to conquer the land, a vision that persisted into the twentieth century, echoing far beyond the Pacific Northwest."
—*Booklist*

"A gifted writer and a tenacious sleuth, Blaine Harden has hit the reset button on a troubling cluster of myths that lie at the foundation of the Anglo-American settlement of the Pacific Northwest. Elucidating, captivating, skeptical of conventional assumptions, and doggedly on the scent of the truth, *Murder at the Mission* is narrative history at its very best." —Hampton Sides, *New York Times* bestselling author of
Blood and Thunder: An Epic of the American West

"In this remarkable history of dishonesty, greed, and perseverance, Harden exposes the chauvinistic and fictitious story that rests at the foundation of U.S. expansion in the Pacific Northwest. He shows how the lionizing of missionaries and mountain men created a triumphant, self-serving narrative that justified the dispossession of the region's native inhabitants. And in the book's indispensable conclusion, he describes how the Cayuse Indians survived the onslaught and are now working to rebuild their communities and restore their traditional homelands."
—Claudio Saunt, author of *Unworthy Republic: The Dispossession of Native Americans and the Road to Indian Territory*

PENGUIN BOOKS

MURDER AT THE MISSION

Blaine Harden is a contributor to *The Economist*, PBS *Frontline*, and *Foreign Policy*, and formerly served as the *Washington Post*'s bureau chief in East Asia and Africa. He is the author of *The Great Leader and the Fighter Pilot*, *Escape from Camp 14*, an international bestseller published in twenty-seven languages, *A River Lost*, and *Africa: Dispatches from a Fragile Continent*, which won a Pen American Center citation for a first book of nonfiction.

ALSO BY BLAINE HARDEN

Africa: Dispatches from a Fragile Continent

A River Lost: The Life and Death of the Columbia

*Escape from Camp 14: One Man's Remarkable Odyssey
from North Korea to Freedom in the West*

*The Great Leader and the Fighter Pilot: The True
Story of the Tyrant Who Created North Korea and the
Young Lieutenant Who Stole His Way to Freedom*

King of Spies: The Dark Reign of America's Spymaster in Korea

MURDER
AT THE
MISSION

A FRONTIER KILLING,
ITS LEGACY OF LIES, AND THE
TAKING OF THE AMERICAN WEST

BLAINE HARDEN

PENGUIN BOOKS

PENGUIN BOOKS
An imprint of Penguin Random House LLC
penguinrandomhouse.com

First published in the United States of America by Viking,
an imprint of Penguin Random House LLC, 2021
Published with a new epilogue in Penguin Books 2022

ISBN 9780525561682 (paperback)

THE LIBRARY OF CONGRESS HAS CATALOGED THE
HARDCOVER EDITION AS FOLLOWS:
Names: Harden, Blaine, author.
Title: Murder at the mission: a frontier killing, its legacy of lies, and
the taking of the American West / Blaine Harden.
Other titles: Frontier killing, its legacy of lies, and the taking of the American West
Description: [New York] : Viking, [2021] | Includes bibliographical references and index.
Identifiers: LCCN 2020053152 (print) | LCCN 2020053153 (ebook) |
ISBN 9780525561668 (hardcover) | ISBN 9780525561675 (ebook)
Subjects: LCSH: Whitman, Marcus, 1802–1847. | Spalding, Henry Harmon, 1803–1874. |
Whitman Massacre, 1847. | Cayuse Indians—Missions—Northwest, Pacific. |
Cayuse Indians—Columbia Plateau—History—19th century. | Nez Percé Indians—
Missions—Northwest, Pacific. | Nez Percé Indians—Columbia Plateau—History—
19th century. | Missionaries—Northwest, Pacific—History—19th century. |
Northwest, Pacific—History—19th century. | Columbia Plateau—History—19th century.
Classification: LCC F880 .H266 2021 (print) | LCC F880 (ebook) |
DDC 979.5/030922—dc23
LC record available at https://lccn.loc.gov/2020053152
LC ebook record available at https://lccn.loc.gov/2020053153

Printed in the United States of America

Designed by Alexis Farabaugh

For the Tribes of the
Columbia Plateau

What mattered was not so much whether a particular story was factually true, but rather, what it signified. Though it was also the case that the more a story circulated, the truer it became.

—JULIAN BARNES, *THE NOISE OF TIME*

CONTENTS

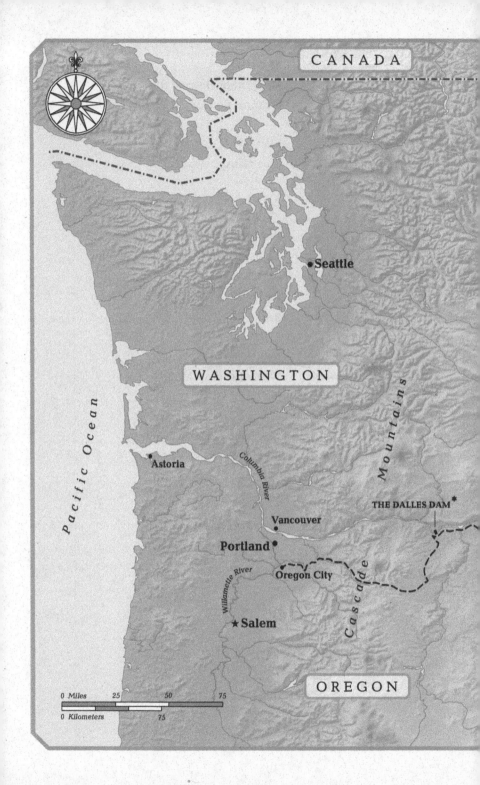

THE PACIFIC NORTHWEST
IN THE NINETEENTH CENTURY

*Locations built in the twentieth century

GRAND COULEE DAM*

Spokane •

Moses Lake*

Columbia River

NORTH-
WEST
IDAHO

HANFORD SITE*

Snake River

Spalding
Mission at
Lapwai

Walla Walla
(Whitman College)

Whitman Mission at Waiilatpu

Columbia River

Umatilla Reservation today
(172,000 acres)

Umatilla River

Pendleton

Blue Mountains

Snake River

Aboriginal Territory
of Cayuse, Umatilla,
Walla Walla Tribes
before 1855 treaty
(6.4 million acres)

OREGON TRAIL

Snake River

© 2021 Jeffrey L. Ward

AUTHOR'S NOTE

Following the conversational usage of the people I am writing about, this book often uses the word "Indian" to refer to Indigenous people in the Pacific Northwest and across the United States. Elders and leaders of the Confederated Tribes of the Umatilla Indian Reservation use "Indian" to refer to themselves, their land, their history, and their way of life. Based on my interviews with them on their reservation in northeastern Oregon, they also describe themselves as Tribal people, Native people, Indigenous people, and Native Americans—or by their tribal affiliations as Cayuses, Walla Wallas, Umatillas, and Nez Perces. Still, the most common self-descriptive term is "Indian," which is also used in an official tribal history of the reservation. But language is alive and changing—and usage of the word "Indian" is generational. Among those under thirty, many prefer to use "Native" or "Indigenous" or their tribal affiliation, and some strongly reject "Indian." It is a matter of personal identity, and Native identity is changing.

David Treuer, an Ojibwe author writing in *The Heartbeat of Wounded Knee*, his landmark history of Native America since 1890, advises that "a good rule of thumb for outsiders" is to "ask the Native people you're talking to what they prefer." This has been my guiding principle in determining the proper terminology for this book.

I am indebted to elders and leaders of the Umatilla Reservation for their participation in this book. It began for me as an effort to explain one of the great hoaxes in the history of the American West. It ended with a new understanding of the power of white racism to sow a century and a half of misery among the Native people of the Columbia River Plateau. I also came to revere their resilience. On the Umatilla Reservation they have engineered a great American comeback.

THE GOOD DOCTOR

My descent into the looking-glass legend of Dr. Marcus Whitman began in elementary school when I performed in a class play about the good doctor. It was the early 1960s and I lived in the tumbleweed outback of the Pacific Northwest, where Whitman had been killed by members of the Cayuse tribe in 1847 and where he lived on as a much-in-demand martyred ghost.

Besides school plays, he had appeared in an opera, poems, hymns, children's books, radio plays, movies, and the stained-glass windows of churches from Spokane to Seattle. His name was on high schools, middle schools, highways, hospitals, banks, churches, nursing homes, a national forest, a county in Washington State, and a glacier on Mount Rainier. Near the Walla Walla River, where his mutilated body had been buried in a mass grave, the National Park Service presided over the Whitman Mission National Historic Site. The tallest building in nearby Walla Walla was a twelve-story luxury hotel called the

This granite shaft, erected fifty years after the 1847 killing of Marcus and Narcissa Whitman, stands on the grounds of the mission the Whitmans built in Cayuse country near the Walla Walla River, in what is now southeastern Washington State. Remains of the Whitmans and eleven others are buried nearby; in the southern distance are the Blue Mountains in Oregon.

Marcus Whitman. It looked down upon the campus of Whitman College, an excellent liberal arts college. Boosters in Washington State raised money in 1953 to send a bronze statue of Whitman—clad in buckskin, carrying a Bible, and bearing a slogan that read "My plans require time and distance"—to Washington, D.C., for display in the Capitol's National Statuary Hall.

The statue received a welcoming speech from Supreme Court Justice William O. Douglas, the most prominent graduate of Whitman College—with the possible exception of Adam West, the actor who played Batman on television in the sixties. Douglas condemned the "treachery" of the Indians who killed Whitman and said that the doctor's example should "fill the hearts of our people with pride and teach them that courage and devotion can overcome even the impossible."

Whitman and his wife, Narcissa, were Presbyterian missionaries from upstate New York. They traveled west—into what Narcissa called "the thick darkness of heathenism"—during a peak season of godliness in the United States. Called the Second Great Awakening, it transformed millions of unchurched Americans into ardent, evangelical, conversion-focused Protestants. Before the revival took off, around 1800, just one in ten Americans attended church; by 1836, when the Whitmans headed west, nearly eight in ten did. As Protestant evangelism surged, it locked arms with nationalism. The result was Manifest Destiny, an imperialist theology of God-ordained exceptionalism and continental expansion that seized the popular imagination just as the federal government was figuring out how to exploit one and a quarter million square miles of newly acquired land that stretched from Texas to California and up to what is now the Canadian border. Manifest Destiny justified almost anything Americans wanted to do in this vast new landscape. It was God's will, after all, for these chosen people "to overspread and to possess."

The Whitmans were at the missionary vanguard of the land grab. Their quest, as they described it, was to convert the "benighted Indians" to Christianity and civilize them so that they might survive a looming stampede of westbound white people. The Whitmans focused their salvific attentions on the Cayuses, a small tribe of expert horsemen and aggressive traders on the Columbia Plateau. When the missionaries arrived in Cayuse country—straddling what would become the state line of southeastern Washington State and northeastern Oregon—tribal elders were intrigued. They hoped that a few white people and their white God might be helpful, augmenting the spiritual power of their own religion. For eleven years, albeit with mounting disappointment and bitterness, the Indians allowed the Whitmans to preach, teach, farm, and build on their land.

On November 29, 1847, a handful of Cayuses ended the experiment. They killed the Whitmans, tomahawking, shooting, knifing, whipping, and stomping them into the mud outside their mission house. Their fury was such that they used one of Dr. Whitman's surgical saws to cleave open his skull and the skull of his wife. Eleven other white men were also killed. Remains of all the victims were buried in shallow graves, where scavenging animals got to them.

As word of the atrocity spread east, it became a tipping point in the history of the West. Within a year, Congress made the Oregon Country—which had been shared for decades with Great Britain under a treaty of joint occupation—an official territory of the United States. The killings also horrified East Coast Protestants, whose Sunday offerings financed missionaries. The mass murder became infamous as the Whitman Massacre.

M y grade school's play about Marcus Whitman did not reenact his violent death, which adults viewed as too grisly for grade schoolers. (The massacre, though, was often acted out in high school and college productions.) The stage productions celebrated Whitman as a patriot, a Christian role model, and a frontier hero who, like Lewis and Clark, possessed undaunted courage. He was depicted preaching on Sundays, curing illnesses, teaching the Cayuses to read, and showing them how to grow wheat, grind flour, and make bread.

Thrillingly, as many of the productions depicted it, Whitman also stopped a British attempt to steal the Pacific Northwest away from the American people. Five years before his murder, Whitman grabbed a Bible, jumped on a horse, and rode alone through terrible winter snows across the continent to Washington, D.C. There, he warned President John Tyler of British scheming and begged him to build a road for wagons rolling west. The dialogue went like this:

TYLER:
You have some farsighted ideas, Dr. Whitman.

WHITMAN (*ENTHUSIASTICALLY*):
What I want to see is the American flag wave from ocean to ocean. Put that road through, build the supply depots and the settlers will come in such vast numbers that we'll forever route the British lion from Oregon Territory! We'll win that country for the United States!

After securing presidential support, Whitman raced back west. He stopped off in St. Louis, Missouri, from where, in 1843, he led what was then the largest-ever wagon train bound for Oregon.

In the years that followed, thousands upon thousands of American settlers rolled west over the Oregon Trail. An unstoppable force, they elbowed the British into Canada, forced Indians off their land, and opened up the Oregon Country for white Protestants, who would eventually include my mom and dad, my two sisters, my brother, and me.

Whitman's story was a real-life Old West passion play—or so it seemed. Violent death at the hands of tomahawk-slinging hostiles gave the story a stirring shiver of last-stand martyrdom. It linked Whitman to General George Armstrong Custer at Little Bighorn, to Davy Crockett at the Alamo, even to Christ at Calvary.

What no one told me at the time was that the Whitman story was largely a pack of lies.

Protestant clergymen had cooked up most of it decades after the Whitmans were murdered. Its principal author was the Reverend Henry Harmon Spalding, a New York–born Presbyterian missionary who himself just barely managed not to be killed by the Cayuses.

Spalding was fiery-eyed, scraggly-bearded, and endlessly aggrieved. He had a poisonously strange relationship with Marcus and Narcissa Whitman. When they were alive, he tormented them. When they were dead, he—with the help of his ordained collaborators—made up the great patriotic whopper that transformed them into legends.

His behavior was rooted in jilted love. In upstate New York, he had fallen for Narcissa Prentiss, then in her early twenties and regarded by those who knew her as attractive, gregarious, and deeply religious. She had golden hair and light blue eyes, a clear soprano voice, and a manner that was both pious and lively. Her parents were well-to-do. When Spalding proposed marriage, she turned him down cold. She later married a broad-shouldered, blue-eyed doctor—Marcus Whitman. Although Spalding found another bride, he could never quite quit Narcissa, nor could he forgive the doctor who won her hand. The reverend's jealousy was inflamed by his intimate proximity to the Whitmans when they were newlyweds. Spalding and his wife joined the Whitmans on their honeymoon trek to the Oregon Country. The two young missionary couples often shared the same tent. It could not have been easy on Spalding's mental stability—never that stable even in the best of times—to bed down so near to Narcissa. She conceived her only child during the journey. She later told her father in a letter that she and Marcus should never have gone west with Spalding, whose "wicked jealousy" tainted their lives.

Spalding was as paradoxical as he was volatile. He frequently used a whip on Indians who did not comport themselves according to his notions of Christian behavior. But he could also be persuasive and empathetic; he was the Northwest's most productive Protestant missionary, as measured by his total lifetime tally of willing Indian converts.

Prone to self-pity and despondency, he was an inventive self-promoter who churned out blood-chilling pulp fiction, which he persuaded newspaper editors to print as eyewitness frontier history from a truth-telling man of God.

He was president of the Oregon chapter of a secret nativist society that demonized Catholics and immigrants. He was most productive—and far less irritable—while living among Indians.

His fellow missionaries wrote countless letters about his erratic, spiteful, and annoying behavior. One said Spalding "seems unable to control himself and . . . has a disease in the head which may result in derangement." Yet a peevish personality and periodic bouts of irrationality did not stop him from collaborating for decades with ministers, writers, and politicians from all across the United States in creating and popularizing the Whitman lie. Nor did a life of lying wreck his posthumous reputation. In 1936, a century after Spalding arrived in Oregon, President Franklin D. Roosevelt recognized his achievements as a missionary and pioneer. A small unincorporated community is now named after him in northern Idaho, where the U.S. National Park Service honors his memory and where his grave dominates Spalding Cemetery, a tribally owned burial ground that serves the Nez Perce people.

Spalding's big break—credibility-wise—came twenty-four years after the Whitman killings. On a visit to Washington, he persuaded the U.S. Senate to print his version of Whitman's heroics in an official pamphlet. It quickly spread—as authentic, government-approved western history—to the pages of the *Encyclopaedia Britannica*, *The New York Times*, *The Ladies' Home Journal*, and most of the American history textbooks in public and private schools across the country.

On a Sunday morning in Chicago half a century after Whitman's death, more than forty Protestant ministers sermonized simultaneously about his "heroic patriotic Christian work." The story was taught in Sunday schools and published in bestselling books. *The Detroit News* described Whitman's journey on horseback to Washington as "the most famous ride in American history!" While it was less well known than Paul Revere's ride, many columnists and editorial writers claimed it was more patriotically magnificent.

Not long after my grade school performed the Whitman play, the history of the American West was given a thorough rewrite. Revisionist scholars—many of them young, non-male, non-white, non-Protestant—shredded the triumphalist view that the frontier had been "tamed." Settlement of the West, they wrote in the 1970s and '80s, had not been an edifying exercise in Jeffersonian democracy or an uplifting application of Christian values. Rather, it was "conquest"—a forced taking of territory that was often brutal, greed-driven, racist, ecologically disastrous, even genocidal.

American Indians were the frontline victims, losing their lands, their cultures, their languages, and often their lives. They were decimated by diseases, defeated in wars, deported from their homelands, and corralled on reservations, and several generations of Indian children were taken away to government-run schools, which tried to turn them into little white boys and girls, sometimes with devastating results. Over time, Indian Country became the poorest part of the West. The Cayuse tribe—branded for generations as the irredeemable demons who murdered the Whitmans—was nearly exterminated.

The "great energizer" of western conquest, as historian Wallace Stegner explained it, was the eagerness of Americans to be lied to—by railroad tycoons, timber interests, mining companies, and the corrupt politicians who served them all. "Too many times," Stegner wrote, settler expectations were "exaggerated, uninformed, unrealistic, and greedy" when it came to understanding what it would take to prosper in the West. Railroad publicists promised that rain would follow the plow, newspapers printed it, and farmers believed what they read.

Settlers might have been more sensible about risk if they had known what federal experts already knew about the bulk of western land. Investigation by the government's most important geologist, John Wesley Powell, had concluded that much of it was too dry for conventional farming. But Powell's report was buried by members of Congress beholden to the railroads. Lies about the land persisted into the Great Depression, when the topsoil of the southwest plains rose into the Dust Bowl wind, asphyxiated farm kids, and darkened skies from Chicago to New York City.

Revisionist historians also exposed what conquest did to major rivers, transforming them into fish-killing plumbing systems that left dirty bathtub rings in canyons all across the West. Agencies of the federal government—the Bureau of Reclamation and the Army Corps of Engineers—built the big dams that generated electricity, diverted water for irrigation, and turned rivers into sluggish stretches of slack water. One of these revisionist tracts was my own book *A River Lost*. It recounts how federal dams on the Columbia, which flows through eastern Washington, not far from my hometown of Moses Lake, have pushed several salmon species to extinction, dispossessing and demoralizing Indians (including the Cayuses) who for centuries had built their nutritional, social, and spiritual existence around salmon. Decades of Cold War plutonium production made the Hanford Nuclear Reservation (on the west bank of the Columbia) the single most polluted place in the Western Hemisphere. Some of its super-poisonous and radioactive toxins dribbled underground into the river; some of it threatened to explode. The federal government is still struggling to defang and contain the deadly mess.

The legacy of conquest, as revisionist historian Patricia Limerick has written, is as fundamental to understanding the West as the legacy of slavery is to understanding the South. Both "have tested the ideals of the United States," and both demand "sober national reflection."

Yet Americans did not see it that way. "The legacy of slavery was serious business, while the legacy of conquest was not," Limerick wrote. She said the unsightly and undemocratic realities of the West had "dissolved into stereotypes of noble savages and noble pioneers struggling quaintly in the wilderness."

To correct these perceptions, Limerick and legions of other revisionist historians took an ax to the story of how the West was won. Their efforts were influential in academia and popular culture, stripping feel-good nonsense out of books, paintings, movies, and television shows. Consider Clint Eastwood's 1992 film *Unforgiven*. It cut false sentiment from every aspect of life in the nineteenth-century West, especially the supposed romance of gunfighting. Eastwood played a destitute pig farmer and washed-up gunfighter who was no longer a sure shot. He went to work for vengeful "whores" who wanted their abusers dead. At close range, so he did not miss, he coldly murdered for money.

In the same somber spirit, filmmakers Ken Burns and Stephen Ives rounded up a sizable herd of revisionist historians in the mid-1990s. Using eight episodes of prime-time public television, they told an unvarnished and uncomfortable story of the West. Compared with what had been on television in the four previous decades (*Bonanza*, *Gunsmoke*, *Little House on the Prairie*), the series was "more frank about our failures and more clear-eyed about the cost of even our greatest successes."

One episode focused on Marcus and Narcissa Whitman, explaining that cultural misunderstandings caused their deaths. The documentary, though, did not bother to debunk the story of Whitman riding a horse to the White House to save Oregon. Echoing the no-more-hokum consensus that typified the work of revisionist historians, the filmmakers simply omitted the Whitman lie—never mind that millions of Americans learned about it in Sunday school, in the pages of their schoolbooks, and in *The New York Times*—and believed it for decades.

L eaving out lies does not get at the truth, especially in the West, where lies have been essential tools for getting rich, going broke, and glorifying the grim business of conquest. Had railroads and banks and newspapers not lied to sodbusters, far fewer of them would have rushed to the arid West to suffer, fail, and plow up land unsuited for row crops.

Brazen falsehoods about the West have always sold briskly—far more than footnoted tomes of scholarly truth. For a century and a half, readers in the United States and Western Europe bought dime novels that delivered golden sunsets, squinty-eyed cowboys, and long-suffering women. Zane Grey banged out sixty-eight of them, Louis L'Amour more than a hundred. A Frenchman named George Fronval published six hundred. Not just city folk were addicted. As western writer Larry McMurtry, who wrote the bestselling neo-pulp classic *Lonesome Dove,* noted: "Dirt farmers too . . . the very people who ought to have known better, preferred fable to fact."

The West was mythologized—that is, lied about—at the same time it was being settled. Indian chiefs and Indian fighters ranged back and forth between flesh and fantasy, between the real West and its dime-novel doppelgänger. Sitting Bull, leader of the Sioux, used the break between the Battle of Little Bighorn, in 1876, and the Massacre at Wounded Knee, in 1890, to tour Europe and the United States while performing for pay in Buffalo Bill's Wild West Show. Kit Carson, an actual Indian fighter, failed in 1848 to save a white woman from Apaches. But near her arrow-riddled corpse he discovered a dime novel about the fictional Kit Carson, who never failed to save a good white woman from Indian peril. Having stumbled upon his better, more marketable mythical self, the real Kit Carson decided to cash in on it, writing (or rather dictating, since he couldn't read) an autobiography.

The "Whitman Saved Oregon" story was a similarly surreal western confabulation. Two decades after running for his life from the Cayuses who killed the Whitmans, the middle-aged Henry Spalding massaged his fading frontier memories, spiced them with hysterical resentments, and colluded with other Protestant ministers to fabricate an utterly original American icon. Pious, fearless, and handy with a horse, he was Marcus Whitman, the martyred missionary doctor who galloped across America, sweet-talked the president of the United States, and added three stars to the red, white, and blue.

Warren G. Harding, a forgettable American president but a wily American demagogue, explained it best. After delivering a speech in 1923 that celebrated the Whitman lie in all its horse-riding, flag-waving, God-fearing glory, Harding observed, "If it isn't true, it ought to be."

This book tracks the long and unlikely arc of a great American lie. An unemployed and embittered Presbyterian minister created it as catnip for churchy countrymen who like their politics—and their history—to be simple, action-packed, hero-driven, patriotic, self-congratulatory, and ordained by Almighty God. Spalding's fraud helped him get a job. It sanctified and encouraged conquest of the West. It transformed a mediocre missionary doctor into a martyred American hero. And it all but exterminated an Indian tribe.

Spalding's story was so "thrilling"—an adjective invariably used in handbills promoting church lectures about Whitman's ride—that even after it was shown to be a deliberate falsehood and self-contradicting nonsense, many white Americans, particularly in the Pacific Northwest, refused to let it go. They couldn't help but retell the story—in Sunday sermons, outdoor summer spectacles, and public-school plays.

The Whitman lie is a timeless reminder that in America a good story has an insidious way of trumping a true one, especially if that story confirms our virtue, congratulates our pluck, and enshrines our status as God's chosen people.

MURDER

AT THE

MISSION

ACT ONE

———◆———

KILL

CHAPTER ONE

"DO NOTHING TO IRRITATE"

Marcus Whitman had promises to keep in the West. On a scouting trip to the Rockies in the summer of 1835, he had met Indians who told him they would welcome missionaries to their tribal lands in the Oregon Country. Whitman vowed to return within a year.

Six months later, he was back home in upstate New York, struggling to keep his word. To get across the continent in time for the planned Indian meetup in the Rockies in the summer of 1836, he needed to marry Narcissa Prentiss by February and head west by March. He also needed to find a second missionary couple for the journey, a couple that included an ordained Protestant minister and a minister's wife who could provide female companionship for Narcissa. This was at the insistence of the American Board of Commissioners for Foreign Missions, the Boston-based organization that would be footing the missionary bills. The American Board, created in the early

1800s by young graduates of Williams College, was the country's largest and most important sponsor of missionaries to foreign lands and to Indians across America. It was controlled by Calvinist ministers, most of whom had been trained at elite colleges and seminaries in New England, where they had been drilled in the teachings of Jonathan Edwards, the Puritan theologian and revivalist preacher who instigated America's religious awakening. Nearly all of the board's leaders—and many of the missionaries they selected in the first half of the nineteenth century—were members of Congregational and Presbyterian churches in the Northeast.

The supply of road-ready East Coast missionary couples was low in the winter of 1835–36. What few candidates Whitman could locate in New York and New England had turned him down. That left him with no alternative but to try to wrestle a commitment out of Henry Spalding.

By the late summer of 1835, the American Board had accepted Reverend Spalding and his wife, Eliza, as missionaries. It planned to send them to the Osage Indians in what is now eastern Kansas. They were supposed to leave in the fall, but Eliza gave birth in October to a stillborn child, and their departure was delayed until she was strong enough to travel.

It was Narcissa who told Marcus they might be available. Having been born and raised in the middle-class Protestant establishment of upstate New York, she was plugged into the comings and goings of local Christians, especially those who had been chosen by the American Board as missionaries. Narcissa's willingness to point her fiancé in the direction of the Spaldings suggested that she had no feelings one way or the other for Henry Spalding. It had been about eight years since she turned down his proposal of marriage. She took for granted that his marriage to Eliza, combined with the passage of time and the recent loss of their first baby, had extinguished his animosity toward her.

When Whitman first asked Spalding to travel with them to Oregon, his reply was lukewarm. "If the Board and Dr. Whitman wish me to go to the Rocky Mountains with him, I am ready. Act your pleasure," he wrote in a late-December letter to the American Board. Within weeks, however, Spalding apparently had changed his mind. He began bad-mouthing Narcissa. He said he would not travel with her because he questioned her judgment. It is not known whether Whitman heard about this; Narcissa's well-connected family certainly did.

Still, Whitman desperately needed a commitment from Spalding. Without it, he would be forced to postpone his missionary dreams for at least another year. Under deadline pressure, he failed to investigate— or chose to ignore—evidence that Spalding held a grudge against Narcissa and that he was all but certain to become a liability in Oregon.

After an early-February snowstorm, Whitman chased after Spalding as the reverend and his wife traveled by sleigh to a nearby village to speak at a Presbyterian church. "We want you for Oregon," Whitman shouted from his horse. The three went to a nearby inn, where they prayed together and Whitman pleaded his case. In a letter, Spalding summarized the argument he heard from Whitman: "All the other attempts to obtain a clergyman have failed and if I refused, the Mission to the Rocky Mountains must be abandoned. . . . I felt it my duty to consent to his request."

Whitman had successfully secured an ordained minister for Oregon and found a female companion for Narcissa. But he expressed his regrets almost immediately. He wrote to the American Board, "I am willing to accompany Mr. Spauldin as an associate yet I know little of his peculiar adaptedness to that station."

Far more worried was Narcissa's father. Judge Stephen Prentiss, a businessman and landowner in central New York, questioned the rationality of Narcissa's traveling across the breadth of North America with a minister who had publicly and repeatedly slurred her character. Judge Prentiss summoned Spalding to his home, where, with Narcissa in attendance, he interrogated the minister about his criticism of his daughter, as well as any feelings he might still be nursing toward her. Spalding somehow managed to mollify Prentiss, who did not object when the Spaldings and the Whitmans went west.

He had clearly been taken in by Spalding: Four years later, in a letter from Oregon to her father, Narcissa wrote, "This pretended settlement with father, before we started, was only an excuse, and from all we have seen and heard, both during the journey and since we have been here, the same bitter feeling exists."

Narcissa Prentiss, Marcus Whitman, and Henry Spalding had come of age in a part of upstate New York that would become famous as the "Burned-Over District," a term that referred to the spiritual flames of revival evangelism. They were fanned by charismatic preachers, and they flared up repeatedly in more than a dozen "burned-over" counties of central and western New York, an area bordered on the east by the Finger Lakes and on the west by Lake Erie. Traveling revivals were the spark, spiritually speaking, for the Second Great Awakening, the movement that built churches, trained ministers, and converted rural Americans to Protestantism at a breakneck pace in the first half of the nineteenth century. The awakening took an especially strong hold in booming factory towns along the Erie Canal, which moved industrial goods between the Hudson River and the Great Lakes. The towns were bursting with young people from farm and shopkeeping families—and many of them turned to evangelical Christianity to organize their lives, mold their values, and regiment their social interactions.

Although Narcissa Prentiss was born six years after Whitman, and five years after Spalding, she was the first to embrace the evangelical movement. In early 1819, when she was just eleven, a revival came to her Steuben County hometown of Prattsburgh, population 1,387. It packed the Congregational church, where parishioners trembled, wept, groaned, and confessed their sins. In June, in an overflow ceremony that had to be held out of doors, Narcissa joined 59 of her neighbors in making a public confession of faith.

Five years later, a few days shy of her sixteenth birthday, Narcissa had a religious epiphany that would be far more consequential. She announced to her family and to her church that she wanted to be a missionary. In a letter to the American Board a dozen years later, she remembered the exact day that her vague teenage yearnings to convert unbelievers became a firm lifelong commitment.

"I frequently desired to go to the heathen, but only half-heartedly— and it was not until the first Monday of Jan. 1824 that I felt to consecrate myself without reserve to the Missionary work."

Although Narcissa was unusually young when she pledged to become a missionary, her vow was no surprise. As the eldest daughter in a prominent Presbyterian family of nine children, she had been groomed for it from birth. Her mother, Clarissa, was a ferocious evangelical force in Prattsburgh. A Presbyterian convert who insisted that her children spend most of every Sunday in church or in prayer, Clarissa helped found the Female Home Missionary Society of Prattsburgh in the front parlor of the Prentiss house. Clarissa encouraged Narcissa to teach Sunday school, read turgid church histories, and sing in the church choir.

Narcissa was intoxicated by the romance and risk of mission work. She devoured books about missionary women who died young while laboring in foreign lands. She also loved the social aspect of Presbyterian life, becoming a popular participant in church-related parties, concerts, and sleigh rides. She needed little encouragement to show off her fine voice.

For Narcissa, her mother, and legions of American women in the early nineteenth century, church activity was a morally sound and socially sanctified way to break the chains of patriarchy and get out of the house. In the name of God, temperance, and Christian charity, women could travel, entertain, and learn about the world without the permission of a husband or a father. Evangelism also gave prosperous families a means and an excuse for imposing their values on others, especially those who did not have as much money. Narcissa's father, for example, belonged to a church committee that investigated sinful behavior among members of the Prattsburgh Congregational Church.

Because Narcissa was a devout young woman of good family, her missionary ambitions opened doors to more formal education than was typical for girls at the time. At sixteen, her parents sent her to a religious academy in nearby Auburn, New York. At nineteen, she enrolled at the private Franklin Academy, in Prattsburgh, where she studied for three years, developing skills that helped her become an affecting diarist and graceful writer of entertaining letters. Her education also put her in a position to take teaching jobs in nearby towns, sometimes spending several months away from home.

Yet her escape from patriarchy went only so far. When it came to winning an appointment as a missionary, she had a disqualifying liability. She lacked a husband.

Dr. Marcus Whitman began his urgent search for a missionary wife after hearing an evangelical minister tell an astonishing story: four Indians from beyond the Rockies traveled to St. Louis in 1831, supposedly in search of missionaries who could teach them about the white man's God.

The story upended Whitman's life in late November 1834. He had gone to an evening lecture at the Presbyterian church in Wheeler, a small Steuben County town where he had been practicing medicine for two years and riding on horseback to treat patients across the Burned-Over District. His practice included Narcissa Prentiss's home-town, just seven miles from Wheeler.

Whitman was then thirty-two, never married, and growing tired of his life as a small-town doctor. He had chosen a career in medicine because relatives convinced him it would pay better than his first choice—the ministry. He had been a committed Christian since he was sixteen, having converted at a revival, like so many others during the Second Great Awakening. His father died when he was seven, and his mother sent him away from the family home in Rush-ville, New York, to his father's family in Massachusetts. There he lived for a decade with his grandfather and uncle, whom he later de-scribed as "pious" and who, he said, gave him "constant religious in-struction and care." Like Narcissa, Whitman attended a private academy that encouraged students to consider careers in the church. When he returned to New York at age seventeen to live with his mother and stepfather, his family actively discouraged his plans to be-come a minister.

At twenty-one, Whitman became an apprentice doctor, learning his profession by riding rounds with an older doctor for two years. Over the next decade, he took a total of eight months of classroom training at a medical college in Fairfield, New York, which at the time was sufficient to earn him a medical degree. He then moved to Wheeler, where he practiced medicine and became active in the Pres-byterian church, teaching Sunday school and serving as a church elder.

But boredom and a sense of religious duty made him restless. He wanted to teach "knowledge of the true God" to "the Heathen," as he told the American Board in a letter written in the summer of 1834. It concluded, "My mind has long been turned to the missionary subject. For the last six months I have been more intent upon it than before. I wish soon to have a definite course."

He found it in church that November night in Wheeler. The story he heard—about Far West Indians seeking the Gospel in St. Louis—was told by the Reverend Samuel Parker, a Presbyterian minister from Ithaca, New York, who was traveling across the Burned-Over District, giving lectures and raising money for a missionary expedition to the West. Although he added a few fictional embellishments of his own, Parker had lifted most of his story from the front page of the *Christian Advocate and Journal and Zion's Herald,* a Methodist newspaper printed in New York. The story, published in March 1833, had become an evangelical sensation. It energized believers all across the United States for several years, and historians later credited it with setting off a chain reaction that added the Pacific Northwest to the United States.

The single source for the newspaper's big scoop about Indians searching for Christian enlightenment in Missouri was a letter from William Walker, a white Christian married into a Great Lakes tribe called the Wyandots. Walker claimed that the four Indians were from the Flathead tribe, located in what is now western Montana. To illustrate what a Flathead looked like, editors at the *Christian Advocate* helpfully placed a drawing of one on the front page. It showed an aboriginal male in profile with a spectacularly flat forehead. Walker said he saw the Flatheads while visiting the St. Louis office of William Clark, the explorer of Lewis and Clark Expedition fame who had since become superintendent of Indian affairs for the federal government. According to Walker's account, the Indians in question called Clark their "great father" and told him this story:

It appeared that some white man had penetrated into their country, and happened to be a spectator at one of their religious ceremonies, which they scrupulously perform at stated periods. He informed them that their mode of worshipping the supreme Being was radically wrong, and instead of being acceptable and pleasing, it was displeasing to him; he also informed them that the white people away toward the rising of the sun had been put in possession of the true mode of worshipping the great Spirit. They had a book containing directions how to conduct themselves in order to enjoy his favor and hold converse with him; and with this guide, no one need go astray, but every one that would follow the directions laid down there could enjoy, in this life, his favor, and after death would be received in the country where the great Spirit resides, and live for ever with him.

Upon receiving this information, they called a national council to take this subject into consideration. Some said, if this be true, it is certainly high time we were put in possession of this model, and if *our* mode of worshipping be wrong and displeasing to the great Spirit, it is time we had laid it aside, we must know something more about this, it is a matter that cannot be put off, the sooner we know it the better. They accordingly deputed four of their chiefs to proceed to St. Louis.

The Flatheads had had many questions about Christianity, Walker claimed, and Clark answered them all by delivering a "succinct history of man," as well as an account of "the advent of the Savior, his life, precepts, his death, resurrection, ascension, and the relation he now stands to man as a mediator—that he will judge the world, etc."

To make sure that Protestant readers understood the earthshaking significance of the Indians' visit, editors at the *Christian Advocate* included on their front page an exclamatory editorial from G. P. Disosway, a New York businessman known for his Methodist piety.

"The [St. Louis] story has scarcely a parallel in history!" he proclaimed. "May we not indulge the hope that the day is not far distant when the missionaries will penetrate into these wilds where the Sabbath bell has never yet tolled since the world began! Let the Church awake from her slumbers, and go forth in her strength to the salvation of these wandering sons of our native forests."

The *Christian Advocate*'s coverage of the Indian visitors in St. Louis was built around a kernel of truth and calibrated for viral popularity. It was especially irresistible to passionate young converts, like Marcus Whitman and Narcissa Prentiss, who ached to become missionaries. Like the lie that Spalding would craft thirty years later about how Whitman saved Oregon, the St. Louis story was only tangentially about the behavior, values, and aspirations of Indians. It was mostly a celebration of white people and the transcendent value of their beliefs.

The story also traded on prevailing prejudices against Indians: that they were, as Disosway put it, "savages" and "simple children of nature" bound in "chains of error and superstition." It demonstrated that even Indians were smart enough to understand that their best shot at eternal life was to find white people who could show them "the true mode of worshipping the great Spirit." The story was perfectly timed, appearing at the zenith of the Second Great Awakening, when unprecedented numbers of Americans were being born again in Christ and giving Sunday offerings to pay for missionaries to travel to and live in remote corners of the earth.

The St. Louis story was larded with wishful thinking, deftly twisted facts, and obvious lies. There is mixed evidence as to whether Walker ever even saw the Indians he described. Three of the four Indians who turned up in St. Louis—Black Eagle, a distinguished elder, and two younger men, No Horns on His Head and Rabbit Skin Leggings—were not Flatheads. They were members of the Nez Perce tribe, headquartered in what is now Idaho. The fourth visitor was Speaking Eagle, also a distinguished elder, who was part Nez Perce, part Flathead. None of them had a flat head of the kind shown in the newspaper drawing. More problematic for the veracity of Walker's claims was the barrier of language. No one in St. Louis at the time (except the four visiting Indians) spoke Nez Perce or Flathead. White trappers had by then been in contact with the Nez Perce people for about fifteen years, so the multilingual tribal visitors to St. Louis would perhaps have been able to speak some broken English and French. They were also likely to have been able to participate in rudimentary conversations using Chinook Jargon, a trading language, as well as sign language and possibly a few phrases from another Native language that Clark understood. Still, it is ludicrous to suggest that Clark could have found a common language that would have enabled him to lecture the Indians on the history of man or elucidate Christian theology.

Of course, Marcus Whitman never learned these conflicting details. He heard an entirely credulous Protestant-centric version of the Indian visit, one intended to help drum up donations. Parker's lecture described the Indians as "four wise men from the West." It explained how Indians beyond the Rockies were being condemned to everlasting torment for lack of Protestant teaching. When Parker concluded his lecture, he announced that he needed someone to go west with him to scout out how to find and save their souls.

Whitman jumped at the offer. He also began searching in earnest—

and in haste—for a wife. The American Board strongly encouraged its missionaries to marry, as a cost-effective way of doubling the number of Christian emissaries it dispatched into the world. Marriage also reduced the likelihood that young male missionaries, lonely and far from home, would take Native wives.

A few days after Parker recruited Whitman, he delivered his lecture in another small Presbyterian church in rural New York. It was in the town of Amity, where the family of Narcissa Prentiss had recently moved. When Parker finished speaking and asked for volunteers to travel west, Narcissa approached him and asked, "Is there a place for an unmarried female in my Lord's vineyard?"

Parker promised to find out and immediately wrote to the American Board: "Are females wanted? A Miss Narcissa Prentiss of Amity is very anxious to go to the heathen. Her education is good—piety conspicuous—her influence is good. She will offer herself if needed."

A reply soon came from the Reverend David Greene, the Boston-based secretary for Indian missions at the American Board and an evangelical bureaucrat who would become a destiny-altering figure in the lives of Marcus Whitman, Narcissa Prentiss, and Henry Spalding. Greene's reply was discouraging: "I don't think we have missions among the Indians where unmarried females are valuable just now."

A solution became clear to Reverend Parker. His prize missionary recruit, Dr. Whitman, needed a missionary wife. Narcissa Prentiss, a young woman with missionary promise, needed a husband. Parker connected their needs. When Whitman traveled to Ithaca to visit him in January 1835, Parker told the doctor to go see Narcissa and propose. Whitman had previously met members of the Prentiss family at a prayer meeting at their home, but Narcissa was not there at the time, having gone to another town for a temporary teaching post. It seems likely that Whitman had at least seen Narcissa before, since they lived near each other and moved in the same circles of the faithful. The best guess is that they may have known each other slightly.

In any case, the die was cast. When Whitman traveled to Amity on the third weekend of February 1835 to call on Narcissa, the imperatives of missionary travel fast-tracked their courtship. He proposed. She accepted. They were engaged. Negotiations were finished by Sunday.

They planned to marry sometime after Whitman returned from his scouting trip to the Rockies with Parker. Before leaving for that nine-month journey the next day, Whitman told Narcissa to write to the American Board and formally request a missionary appointment. She wrote the letter Monday morning. In Boston two weeks later, Secretary Greene looked upon Narcissa's application with pleasure, for it included a letter of recommendation that mentioned she was engaged to be married. The wedding took place a year later, after Whitman's highly successful trip to the Rockies, where he made contact with white mountain men and Indians from the Nez Perce, Cayuse, and several other tribes.

For reasons never explained, Narcissa chose to wear black to her wedding and persuaded her entire family to do the same. Her choice of a dress—more suited to a funeral than a wedding—was perhaps influenced by her obsessive reading about young missionary women who perished in service to the Lord. The historian Bernard DeVoto wrote that Narcissa wanted to be "robed as the bride of death" and that her choice revealed the character of "this full-blooded woman who had been deflected from marriage until what was for the period a late age, and who since childhood had longed to immolate herself converting the heathen." After the exchange of vows and a sermon, the ceremony ended with a hymn. Her soaring soprano filling the church, Narcissa sang its final stanza as a solo for a family she would never see again:

In the deserts let me labor,

On the mountain let me tell,

How he died—the blessed Savior—

To redeem a world from hell!

Let me hasten, let me hasten,

Far in heathen lands to dwell.

The day after the wedding, the Whitmans departed for the Oregon Country, hurrying to catch up with the Spaldings, who had already traveled to Cincinnati. As the two couples made their way west, their missionary commander in Boston, Reverend Greene, composed long letters to Whitman and to Spalding (he wrote nothing to their wives), outlining what the American Board expected of them and giving guidance on how they should behave.

He warned Whitman not to act in a way that might be viewed by Indians as uppity or materialistic: "Let yr single aim be seen to be the benefit of the Indians; especially the introduction of Christian knowledge among them and the salvation of their souls. . . . Avoid any establishment which shall be in that country deemed ostentatious and extravagant. Let all yr worldly and secular concerns be limited."

As for how Spalding would behave as a missionary, Greene had more reason to worry. He had read a disturbing assessment of Spalding's temperament in a letter of recommendation that accompanied his application to become a missionary. It said that, while Spalding was physically strong, ardently pious, and inordinately hardworking, "his mental powers are not remarkable" and he was "not remarkable for judgment & common sense." The letter added that Spalding was often jealous of other Christians and prone to denounce those who were "not as zealous or ardent as himself." The only unequivocal praise in the letter was for Spalding's wife. It said Eliza was "highly respected & loved by a large circle of friends. She is one of the best women for a missionaries wife."

Spalding had himself sent disquieting signals. His letters to the American Board, written from the Burned-Over District before he departed for Oregon, were censorious and petulant. He accused rural New Yorkers of "criminal stupidity" in their failure to understand the needs of American Indians. In response to a query from the American Board about his expenses, Spalding shot back that if the board did not trust him, it "should send me notice immediately that I am recalled from the missionary field." In his 1835 application to be appointed as a missionary, Spalding sent the American Board an autobiographical letter that was rich in self-pity but poor in specifics.

"I was from infancy separated from all friends, bound out to strangers at the age of 16 months, lived a very wicked life among wicked men till the age of 22 when God in great mercy rescued me from the depths of sin, & brought me, as I hope, into his kingdom, ignorant indeed & poor & with feeble health."

Spalding was born out of wedlock (to a mother who had been born out of wedlock) in 1803 near Wheeler, New York, the town where Whitman would later practice medicine. Shortly after his first birthday, his mother gave him up to a local couple. They raised him in circumstances that are not well documented until he was seventeen, when the man in the house violently forced the boy to leave. As Spalding described what happened in a letter written late in his life, "he kicked me out after whipping my mother and me." He went on to describe himself as "sad, destitute, 17, crying, a cast off bastard wishing myself dead."

A schoolteacher in nearby Prattsburgh took Spalding in. The boy worked for his board for four years while attending the public school where his guardian taught. Spalding's teenage education was slipshod: he read with difficulty at age twenty-one and could write only by copying out of a book. Still, he found a way up and out. He embraced Christianity, joined the Prattsburgh Presbyterian Church, and was baptized by the Reverend James H. Hotchkin, who led that church throughout the teenage years of Narcissa Prentiss. With Hotchkin's help and guidance, Spalding enrolled in 1825 at the Franklin Academy in Prattsburgh, where he studied for the next six years while taking periodic leaves to teach at regional schools. Spalding came to know Narcissa at the academy, where she enrolled in 1828, at age twenty. He also knew her through the church, where she sometimes led services in prayer and in song.

In his diary, Spalding described himself as a "bashful" student who avoided public speaking and struggled to write papers. At the academy, he had good reason to feel insecure. While most students, including Narcissa, were sons and daughters of the town's elite, Spalding was poor, parentless, probably ill-dressed, and certainly unpolished. Photographs taken when he was a middle-aged man show that Spalding was bald, burly, and frizzy-bearded. At the beginning of his studies at the Franklin Academy, he was barely literate, an embarrassment amplified by his age: he was several years older than his academic peers.

Out of bashfulness or shame, he wrote nothing in his diary or surviving letters about meeting Narcissa at the academy, falling in love with her, or proposing marriage. There is nothing in Narcissa's letters, either, that details exactly what happened between her and Spalding at the school. Spalding's rejection, though, is confirmed in a letter written by Narcissa's youngest sister, Harriet. She wrote that when Spalding was a student at the academy, "he wished to make Narcissa his wife, and her refusal of him caused the wicked feeling he cherished toward them both"—meaning Narcissa and Marcus.

Spalding was a dogged, if uninspired, student. He invested nearly a decade of his life in higher education, mostly studying Calvinist theology. In the process, he became a prolific writer and a vigorous sermonizer. Like many evangelical ministers of his era, he could be stupendously long-winded. He differed from his ordained peers, though, in the often hysterical quality of his rhetoric. It would become more graphic, more sanguinary, and more stomach-churning as he aged, making frequent and extended allusions to shattered skulls, blood-red hands, and gory death.

He paid for most of his studies by working as a printer and by winning scholarships from the American Education Society, a church-funded group based in Boston that supported students studying for the ministry. After getting the equivalent of a junior college degree from the Franklin Academy, he briefly attended Hamilton College, in Clinton, New York, before moving to Ohio, where he graduated from Western Reserve College and entered Lane Theological Seminary.

Between college and the seminary, Spalding married Eliza Hart, a seminary student four years younger than him. Marrying Eliza, as Spalding often said, was the smartest decision of his life. Eliza Spalding would become an effective—and beloved—Protestant missionary in the Pacific Northwest. A superb linguist who had studied Greek and Hebrew, she became fluent in the Nez Perce language. Within two months of her arrival in the Oregon Country, she could communicate meaningfully with the Indians in their language—an accomplishment never achieved by Narcissa Whitman.

For all her gifts as a helpmate, Eliza could do little to tame the character of her husband. Spalding's ornery righteousness would endure, metastasize, and make him a laughingstock in Oregon.

Back in Boston in the spring of 1836, Reverend Greene of the American Board sensed the tumult that Spalding would cause. In his letters of guidance, he repeatedly advised Spalding to keep his cool:

"Be patient, mild, forbearing, in meekness & love reproving, if called to it," Greene wrote. "Show forth under all circumstances the loveliness of the Gospel."

Greene's instructions boiled down to a single sentence, a four-word mandate that would prove impossible for Henry Spalding.

"Do nothing to irritate," Greene wrote.

The order could not be enforced. It would never be obeyed.

CHAPTER TWO

"WHAT A DELIGHTFUL PLACE"

It started off surprisingly well. The journey over the Rockies was safe, on schedule, and elaborately escorted by American mountain men, British fur traders, and gracious Indians. The caravan consisted of two wagons, twelve horses, six mules, and seventeen head of cattle, including four milk cows. The travelers brought along far too much baggage, struggled with broken-down wagons, and exhausted themselves fording swollen rivers. Yet as Marcus Whitman informed his Boston sponsors, the missionaries enjoyed "much more comfort than we antisipated."

In heavy boots and voluminous skirts, Narcissa Whitman and Eliza Spalding rode sidesaddle or sat on the spine-mashing seat of a springless wagon. They traveled about twenty miles a day, rarely bathed, cooked with buffalo dung, washed their clothes only three times, and subsisted for weeks on dried buffalo meat. Still, by their own accounts, they had a splendid time. Eliza was sick for part of the journey and often unable to ride a horse. But she recovered while traveling and arrived in the Oregon Country feeling better and looking more robust than when she left New York seven months earlier. Along the way, after the missionary party was joined by a welcoming escort of nearly two hundred Nez Perces, she began learning their language.

The newlywed Narcissa also thrived. "I never was so contented and happy before," she wrote to her family from what is now western Nebraska. Within a few days of writing those words, she and Marcus conceived a daughter. With her golden hair, blue eyes, and pleasure in being admired, Narcissa also became the object of a "gazing throng" when the missionaries arrived in July at South Pass, in what is now Wyoming, where they crossed the Continental Divide, entered the Oregon Country, and became the featured attractions at the high-summer rendezvous of white fur traders and Indian trappers. These annual meetings, where furs were swapped for horses, saddles, clothing, tobacco, and whiskey, were festivals as well as trading fairs. Mountain men and Indians danced, gambled, drank, feasted, brawled, competed in footraces and target shooting, and told one another elaborate lies about their trapping prowess. White trappers sometimes paid in beads or yards of cloth to have sex with young Indian women who attended the meetups.

This particular rendezvous, with two white women in attendance, was different from all those that had come before. Indians and white men were curious and intrigued. Nez Perce women pressed near Narcissa for sisterly kisses. Mountain men, who had not seen a white woman in years, paraded outside her tent. One of them, Joe Meek, would later entrust his daughter to Narcissa for schooling at the Whitman mission. Still later, Meek would be the hangman, executing five Cayuse men convicted of killing Marcus and Narcissa. But at the rendezvous in July 1836, Meek was made dizzy by the "striking figure" and "affably attractive manners" of the fair-skinned Mrs. Whitman.

He told her that someday he would like to stop fighting grizzly bears and "settle down."

Narcissa's prose would make a similarly dazzling impression on American readers when her journal and letters were published in newspapers and in books. During her first year away from home, Narcissa wrote evocatively and optimistically about the landscape, the Indians, the birth of her daughter, and the middle-class comforts she left behind. Famously, she soliloquized about a piece of luggage. It was a gift from her sister Harriet, and she abandoned it in what is now southern Idaho. "Poor little trunk, I am sorry to leave thee," she told her family. "I thank thee for thy faithful services and that I have been cheered by thy presence so long. Thus we scatter as we go along. . . . Husband thought it best to lighten the wagon. . . . The custom of the country is to possess nothing & then you lose nothing while traveling."

Narcissa and Eliza were the first white women to travel overland to the Pacific Northwest. The relative ease of their passage over the Rocky Mountains, as word of it spread in Narcissa's writings, would change the way Americans perceived the geography of the West, dilute the perceived menace of crossing the Rockies, and unlock the Oregon Trail for hundreds of thousands of pioneer families. "Thus has vanished the great obstacle to a direct and facile communication between the Mississippi Valley and the Pacific Ocean," Senator Lewis Linn of Missouri said in Congress two years after the Whitmans and the Spaldings arrived in Oregon.

Over the coming decades, annual caravans of settlers—whose wagon wheels still scar the prairie—would trek more than 2,100 miles from embarkation points along the Missouri River to Oregon City, now a southern suburb of Portland. Most would settle in the Willamette Valley, about a hundred miles from the Pacific, where the weather is mild, the soil fertile, and rain abundant. First as a farm region, then as a cluster of cities and towns, the region would become the heart of Oregon. Portland, at the confluence of the Willamette and the Columbia, would emerge as the principal city. Today about three-quarters of the state's population lives in the Willamette Valley.

The Whitmans and the Spaldings, though, were not bound for that wide and temperate valley. Methodist missionaries and their families— about seventy-five easterners in all—had beaten them to the Willamette by two years. (A handful of the Methodist men had traveled overland, while women and the rest of the missionary party had arrived by sea after sailing around Cape Horn.) The Whitmans and the Spaldings would settle much farther inland—among the Cayuses and the Nez Perces. Leaders of both tribes believed that the white man's God might give them good fortune and a leg up against rival Indians and encroaching white trappers; they had sent emissaries to the midsummer rendezvous in the Rockies to greet the missionaries, escort them west, and persuade them to establish missions on their respective tribal lands.

By then, after a long summer of sharing a tent, bad blood between Marcus Whitman and Henry Spalding was boiling over. The two missionaries—one expecting a child with Narcissa, the other unable to get Narcissa out of his heart—squabbled in front of witnesses at least three times. As they traveled west, they agreed to split up their missionary efforts. The Spaldings would settle among the Nez Perces and the Whitmans with the Cayuses. Spalding would soon blame his and his wife's isolation (in what is now northern Idaho) on his fraught relationship with Marcus and Narcissa: "Do you suppose I would have come off here all alone, a hundred and twenty miles, if I could have lived with him and Mrs. Whitman?"

Both the Nez Perces, the largest of the Columbia Plateau tribes, and the much smaller Cayuse tribe occupied lands that were several days' travel from the coast. The Cayuses were about 300 miles inland, the Nez Perce an additional 120 miles to the east. Those miles meant that the missionary couples would settle in landscapes as different from the Willamette Valley as the plains of Nebraska are from the forests of upstate New York.

The Cascade Mountains slice the Pacific Northwest into two distinct climatic worlds. The jagged, snowcapped range, running south from what is now British Columbia to southern Oregon, scrapes rain from clouds that roll in off the Pacific. This soaks the west side for several months a year, giving it dense evergreen forests of Douglas fir, Sitka spruce, and western red cedar. The east side—with semi-desert river basins and mountains patchily forested with Ponderosa pine and red alder—is dry and hot in summer, cold and snowy in winter. Land on this side is fertile, but much of it needs irrigation to produce reliable and profitable crops.

The two sides are connected by the West's largest and most powerful river, the Columbia. As it roils west to the sea, the river passes through a canyon it has been gouging through the Cascades for more than ten million years. The Columbia River Gorge is three miles wide, seventy-five miles long, and up to four thousand feet deep.

On the morning of September 1, 1836, Marcus and Narcissa Whitman had all but completed their overland journey. They had crossed the Blue Mountains and were riding west together on horseback—two days ahead of the Spaldings—when, for the first time, they saw the Columbia. They began to gallop.

It was not the big river that excited them. It was civilization such as they had not seen in many weeks—in the form of Fort Walla Walla. The Hudson's Bay Company, the royally chartered British monopoly that had built a network of fur-trading stations along the river, maintained the fort as its most easterly outpost on the Columbia. It was built on a sandy patch of land near where the Walla Walla River flows into the Columbia. (The site is now flooded by a reservoir that backs up behind McNary Dam, one of more than a hundred hydroelectric dams on the Columbia and its tributaries.)

The Whitmans arrived hungry and in time for breakfast. Pierre Pambrun, a French Canadian who ran the fort, ushered them to cushioned armchairs in a dining room where they ate fresh salmon, potatoes, tea, bread, and butter. Later, they lunched on melons. Still later, they dined on roast pork and, for the first time in several months, slept on beds in a room with a roof. Narcissa celebrated her sated appetite and her comfort in her journal, saying that she felt "remarkably well & rested."

At Fort Walla Walla, the Whitmans and the Spaldings had hoped to buy supplies to build and furnish mission houses for the winter. They were told, however, that those supplies could be purchased only at Fort Vancouver, the headquarters in Oregon for the Hudson's Bay Company. The fort was another 240 miles downstream through the Columbia Gorge, on the north bank of the Columbia, just across the river from what is now Portland.

There, Dr. John McLoughlin, a Canadian physician turned fur-trading potentate, presided over a domain that extended from Alaska to what is now Northern California, from the Pacific to the Rockies. He alone would decide whether the HBC should sell its wares to American missionaries. In that decision—and in many others over the next eleven years—McLoughlin loomed large in the lives and deaths of the Whitmans.

In his early fifties, Chief Factor McLoughlin was a physical giant: six feet, four inches tall, heavy-browed, with a shock of shoulder-length white hair. He was brilliant, commanding, and without peer as a manager. Fearing his temper but respecting his judgment, Indians of the Northwest called him "White-Headed Eagle." He had put white men in shackles for abusing Indians. His wife, Marguerite, was part Swiss, part Cree. History would judge McLoughlin as a compassionate, farsighted,

Dr. John McLoughlin was the chief factor of the Hudson's Bay Company in the Oregon Country when the Whitmans arrived there in 1836. He befriended the missionary doctor and his wife, sold them supplies at bargain prices, and advised them not to live among the Cayuses. Over the years, he often urged them to abandon their mission, warning that the Cayuses killed failed medicine men.

and fair-minded man who made the best of an almost impossibly complicated job.

When the missionaries came downriver, McLoughlin had been at his post for twelve years. In that time, he had built a multiethnic workforce of English, Scottish, Canadian, and American fur traders who worked with Iroquois, Hawaiians, and Northwest Indians. The company traded ammunition, kettles, blankets, and guns for beaver pelts that were shipped to England to make felt hats. Treating Indians as business partners, the company under McLoughlin made no effort to change their way of life or their religious beliefs. Many of the company's white traders lived and had children with Indian women.

McLoughlin embodied the law in Oregon, a region that had no formal laws, no government, and no courts. Instead, a joint occupation treaty signed in 1818 by the United States and Britain had created a stateless frontier zone. It gave citizens of the two countries equal rights to claim land and start businesses—but no rules by which they could sort out their differences. The governing vacuum and the absence of laws had been workable at first, because there was so much land and so few white people. But by the mid-1830s—as Americans filtered in from beyond the Rockies and saw the bounty of the Willamette Valley—McLoughlin's empire was becoming much trickier to rule.

When he learned that two American missionary women had safely crossed the continent, he recognized it as an "extraordinary event," one that was likely to lure large numbers of American families west and tip the balance of political power in Oregon in favor of the United States. He knew, too, that his bosses in London did not approve of his neighborly attitude toward Yankees, be they laymen or missionaries. But in letters to his home office he said American settlers were an inescapable fact of life. If the HBC did not do business with them, he wrote, competitors would.

"Can we prevent Missionaries dispersing themselves Among these Indians?" McLoughlin wrote to his bosses. "I say we cannot even if we were so Inclined. . . . We ought in policy to secure their Good Will and that of those who support them in their Laudable Endeavours to do Good."

After a week's rest, the Whitmans and the Spaldings left Fort Walla Walla. They boarded a Hudson's Bay Company boat and floated downstream on the Columbia, heading west through the Cascades to collect the supplies they would need to build and furnish their planned missions among the Nez Perces and the Cayuses. Traveling with them was a problematic young lay missionary, William H. Gray, a Presbyterian who had joined their party back in Missouri as a carpenter and mechanic. Gray would become a chronic malcontent and a notably unreliable historian of the Pacific Northwest. He wrote letters back to the American Board complaining about the other missionaries and rarely spoke well of anyone but himself. He did not like Narcissa, calling her stern and condescending, apparently because she paid little attention to him on the journey over the Rockies. He would later write one of the first histories of Oregon—a volume that vilified Catholics, smeared the HBC, and popularized the claim that Marcus Whitman saved Oregon.

When the boat carrying the American missionaries arrived at Fort Vancouver on September 12, 1836, McLoughlin walked down to his company's dock on the Columbia to greet them in person. He enjoyed conversation with newcomers, especially on the very rare occasions when they were well educated and articulate white women. He stepped forward on the dock and offered his arm to Narcissa, who was about three months pregnant.

"We are in Vancouver. The New York of the Pacific," Narcissa wrote. "What a delightful place. . . . What a contrast this to the barren sand plains through which we had so recently passed."

McLoughlin welcomed the missionaries as honored guests, with the exception of William Gray, whom he regarded as support staff and did not allow at his table. Gray never forgave or forgot the slight. For the rest of his life, he would disparage McLoughlin.

Servants pampered the Whitmans and the Spaldings, feeding them from the bounty of the Columbia and of the fort's two-thousand-acre farm: fresh sturgeon and salmon, roast duck, peaches, cheese, grapes, melons, and apple pie. McLoughlin gave tours of his gardens, orchards, and yards full of livestock. He did not approve of missionaries settling on the east side of the Cascades, where he considered the Indians to be unpredictable and dangerous. He said as much to the missionaries, warning them repeatedly not to settle there. He urged Narcissa to, at the very least, spend the winter at his comfortable home, arguing that she should not return to the east side of the Cascades until after she had given birth.

Still, he sold them provisions, housewares, and building supplies at prices lower than what they would have paid back in the States. He also gave Marcus Whitman and Henry Spalding use of a company boat, which allowed them to make the treacherous upstream journey on the Columbia. They left Fort Vancouver on September 21 to scout for sites where they could build mission homes in Cayuse and Nez Perce country.

The Cayuses allowed Whitman to establish his mission on land along the Walla Walla River, about twenty-five miles east of Fort Walla Walla. Cottonwood and birch trees clustered near the river. The soil was fertile, and wild rye grass grew higher than a man's head. The Cayuses called it Weyfilet, the "place of waving grass," and the mission that Whitman established there came to be known to white settlers as Waiilatpu, a transliteration of the Cayuse name for the site. Rounded humps of the Blue Mountains rose in the near distance to the southeast. In the far distance to the west, the peaks of the Cascades could be seen, black against the low autumn sun. It was a restful and verdant place—and it was not far from the favorite winter camping ground of a local Cayuse leader. The Cayuse people as a whole did not have one dominant chief, but rather several leaders who presided over bands of Indians spread from the Walla Walla River to the Blue Mountains. In this respect they were like the Nez Perces and many other tribal nations in the West. The notion of a king-like chief with sovereign authority over a sprawling tribe was more a white American invention than a political reality among Indians.

When the Cayuses permitted Whitman to occupy the three-hundred-acre site on their land, he was already planning a substantial farm operation, with fencing for livestock, irrigation ditches, and fields of grain and vegetables "for ourselves, and our friends that shall come to take part with us." Waiilatpu was along the route of travelers bound for the Willamette Valley that would soon become the Oregon Trail. Many thousands of settler families would roll by the mission.

As mutually agreed, Spalding looked farther to the east—out of easy arguing range with the Whitmans. It was a four-day ride from Waiilatpu, in the heart of Nez Perce country. The mission that the Nez Perces allowed him to build was about twelve miles east of the confluence of two major western rivers, the Clearwater and the Snake. It was near Lapwai Creek and came to be known as Lapwai. Unlike at the Whitman mission, there was plenty of nearby timber. It was also well off the beaten track for settlers, trappers, and other travelers.

The Nez Perces welcomed Spalding with an openness that the Whitmans would never receive from Cayuses. Spalding was astonished by their hospitality, writing that he would be "happy to spend the rest of our earthly pilgrimage" with the Nez Perces.

The Nez Perces were disappointed that Marcus Whitman and his wife had declined to live among them. When they learned they would settle among the Cayuses, Nez Perce leaders prophetically warned that it was a bad and dangerous choice. "The Nez Perce do not like my stopping with the Cayous; and say that the Nez Pierces do not have difficulties with white man, as the Cayous do; and that we will see the difference," Whitman wrote. He ignored their counsel.

A hundred years before the Whitmans settled among the Cayuses, the tribe had engineered a remarkable rise. They became rich and powerful, intimidating and feared, with influence that was disproportionate to their numbers.

"They are fond of domineering & troublesome characters," chief trader Samuel Black of the HBC wrote of Cayuse warriors from Walla Walla in 1829, nearly a decade before Marcus Whitman arrived on the tribe's land. Black described the Cayuses as "excelling in bravery, hunting & athletic exercise" and said that they were the first Indians in the region "to procure guns and ammunition. . . . This tribe [is the smallest on the Columbia Plateau] but have great influence over the others."

A reputation for sharp-elbowed behavior has endured in the tribe's oral traditions. "We were always small in numbers, but we feared no one," said Chuck Sams, whose ancestors were Cayuse and who is now a tribal leader on the Umatilla Reservation, in eastern Oregon. "We were arrogant and haughty and proud of it. I'd be happy to go back to the old ways: conk you on the head and take your fish."

Before they had extended contact with actual white people, the Cayuses built their power and their pushiness on white people's technology. They were early and aggressive adopters of rifles and steel knives. But their signature success came from a sleek European import that was fast, highly maneuverable, and self-reproducing: the horse.

It arrived in the American West before 1600, brought by Spaniards to what is now New Mexico. For nearly a century, Spanish colonists would not allow Indians to ride horses, and they became a symbol of white domination. When the Spanish Empire weakened, around 1680, so did its monopoly on horses. Bought, stolen, bartered for, and bred, they spread north among Indians on both sides of the Rocky Mountains.

First among the tribes of the Columbia Plateau, the Cayuses began riding, herding, trading, and selectively breeding horses around 1730. By the turn of the nineteenth century, they had vast herds and had become trading partners with many of the tribes that lived between the Cascades and the Rockies. Horses made it possible for the Cayuses to travel as far south as present-day Northern California, where their raiding parties took slaves from the Shasta Indians. Wealth and political influence within the tribe were calibrated in horses, with important leaders having as many as a thousand or more. The Cayuses helped introduce horses to the Nez Perces, which strengthened a long-standing commercial, military, and cultural alliance with the larger tribe. That alliance, which included intermarriage and adoption of the Nez Perce language, helped the Cayuses maintain their regional status and power, even as their numbers dwindled.

Horses perfectly suited Cayuse country, where the Blue Mountains descend westward in rolling foothills and broad grasslands to the Umatilla, Walla Walla, and Columbia rivers. In the high country during summer and in riverine pastures during winter, there was nutritious bunchgrass and plenty of water. Horses became so much a part of Cayuse identity—and of western culture—that by the mid-nineteenth century an Indian pony anywhere in the West came to be known as a cayuse. The name persisted into the twentieth century. The tribe even found pop culture immortality in a Cole Porter song, "Don't Fence Me In," sung by Roy Rogers and then by Bing Crosby:

> *Underneath the western skies*
>
> *On my cayuse, let me wander over yonder*

The Cayuses, who rarely numbered more than eight hundred men, women, and children during the nineteenth century, used horses to expand their geographic range. As middlemen on horseback, as sharp traders, as well-armed warriors, Cayuses rode to coastal Oregon to exchange buffalo robes for beads and copper kettles, and to the Great Plains to hunt buffalo and acquire guns and ammunition. Along the Columbia, where their neighbors used spears and conical baskets to catch huge numbers of migrating salmon and steelhead, the Cayuses were both traders and raiders, bartering for and sometimes stealing what they needed for regional trading and winter eating. Members of the tribe also caught salmon themselves on the Umatilla River and its smaller tributaries in their territory.

The first fur trappers—Iroquois and Algonquins who had worked in eastern Canada and the northeastern United States with the HBC and American fur outfits—began filtering into the Oregon Country in the late 1700s. From those peripatetic Indian traders and from white trappers, the Cayuses were quick to pick up the ways of a new barter economy. They began trapping beaver and trading for arms. From their trading, traveling, and slaving, the Cayuses learned that white people from different countries and speaking different languages were all around them—and more were surely on the way.

When Lewis and Clark traveled down the Columbia in 1805, heading toward the Pacific, the American explorers found European goods and clothing in nearly every Indian village along the river. Lewis wrote that they heard Indians "repeating many words of English, as mesquit, powder, shot, nife, damned rascal, sun of a bitch &c." They saw English muskets and Spanish coins, steel cutlasses and coffeepots, trousers and jackets. "The Plateau Indians who stepped from their teepees and mat houses to greet Lewis and Clark knew far more about Europeans than any European knew of them," wrote Larry Cebula, a history professor at Eastern Washington University.

By then, Indians also knew—from catastrophic personal experience—that contact with white people could trigger mass death from invisible forces. A smallpox epidemic in 1770 and another in 1800 killed about a third of all the Indians in the Pacific Northwest. The disease—against which none of the Indians had immunity—was probably transmitted by contact with Spanish sailors on the Oregon coast or by Plateau Indians riding back from trading and hunting expeditions on the Great Plains.

In 1805, Lewis and Clark found ghost villages up and down the Columbia. They talked to an old woman—her face pitted by the pox—who said the disease had killed everyone she knew when she was a young girl. A third wave of deaths occurred in 1830, this time from malaria transmitted by British sailors. It killed as many as 90 percent of Indians living along the coast and in the lower reaches of the Columbia. Dysentery killed many others. "Depopulation here has been truly fearful," wrote John K. Townsend, an American naturalist who traveled along the Columbia in 1834–35. "The thoughtful observer cannot avoid perceiving that in a very few years the race must, in the nature of things become extinct. . . . It seems as if the fiat of the Creator had gone forth, that these poor denizens of the forest and the stream should go hence, and be seen of men no more."

Starting in the late 1700s, when people of European descent began to visit the Pacific Northwest, there was a century-long "unremitting across-the-board decline in population among Northwest Native people." At a minimum, about 80 percent of the pre-contact population disappeared.

The mass death of Indians from disease was quicker and more devastating in the Northwest than on the Eastern Seaboard or in the Great Plains, and it explains the relative ease and speed with which whites would come to dominate the Oregon Country. "From an imperialist standpoint, this was literally the best of all worlds," historian Elliott West wrote, noting that whites usually survived the diseases they introduced, even "as they cut terrible swaths through Indian peoples." In the Northwest, so many Indians died so quickly that many white settlers were never bothered by them.

Oregon politicians and historians, well into the twentieth century, celebrated the beneficial cleansing effect of bringing highly infectious contagions from Europe to the Native people of the Oregon Country. "Always it will be a source of thanksgiving that the destruction of the Indians of the Pacific Northwest by diseases spared the pioneer settlers the horrors of the strong and malignant foe," Leslie M. Scott, the acting governor of Oregon as well as a newspaper editor and regional historian, wrote in 1928 in the *Oregon Historical Quarterly*. "Throughout the entire West the Indians were victims, but perhaps nowhere else so badly as in the Pacific Northwest; and nowhere else were the results so good for the whites."

By the late 1830s, when the Whitmans arrived, the Cayuses had weathered the white man's epidemics rather better than most other tribes in the Northwest. They had lost about a third of their population to smallpox, but slave raiding and intermarriage with the Nez Perces had kept their numbers from collapsing. They had escaped malaria because the cold and arid climate of the Columbia Plateau was not hospitable to the mosquitoes that carry the disease. Still, disease had severely weakened the foundations of Cayuse culture, killing off their aged medicine men and eroding confidence in traditional spiritual treatments for physical illness.

Like the Nez Perces, the Cayuses were keen to reinforce their spiritual and material defenses in a strange new world filling up with guns, white men, and mysterious lethal plagues. The Indians wanted to survive, using whatever military hardware and spiritual power whites had to offer. Since 1816, the tribes had been in regular contact with white mountain men, most of whom were British or French Canadian. The Nez Perces and the Cayuses first heard about Christianity from these contacts and from several Indian boys who had gone from the Oregon Country in the 1820s to an Anglican school in Canada and returned with the Bible and other Christian books. The Indians associated Christianity with the potent white technology they were already benefiting from—including horses, guns, wool blankets, cooking pots, and other objects made of metal.

The consensus view of historians and anthropologists—shared by many Nez Perce and Cayuse elders today—is that the four Nez Perces who traveled to St. Louis in 1831 were looking for a competitive edge against other tribes, a mix of spiritual insight and material goods that could increase the well-being of their people. (It was that same search for competitive advantage that motivated the Nez Perces and the Cayuses to help the Whitman party cross the Rockies in 1836 and establish missions on their tribal land.)

Besides meeting William Clark on that celebrated trip to St. Louis, the Indians visited a church. It was Roman Catholic, not Protestant. The Catholic bishop of St. Louis, Joseph Rosati, met the Indians and reported in a letter that they seemed to like his church but that it was impossible to know for sure, because "there was no one who understood their language." Shortly after the Indians came to the city, two of them fell ill. Before they died, Rosati said, priests visited the Indians and saw them make the sign of the cross—a signal that they might be Catholics. None of the Indians ever asked for a Bible. None asked for Protestant missionaries. All of which suggests that Marcus Whitman's decision to go west to spread Protestantism among Bible-starved "heathens" was based upon an almost entirely invented story—composed of wishful thinking, ethnocentrism, and evangelical fervor.

While their husbands were staking out mission sites on the Columbia Plateau, Narcissa and Eliza stayed on at Fort Vancouver, as McLoughlin had suggested. McLoughlin asked Narcissa—entering her fifth month of pregnancy—to help his wife tutor their daughter and listen to her recitations. In the evenings, she sang for McLoughlin, his wife, and some of their four children, who ranged in age from fifteen to twenty-four. She also revised and polished entries in her journal, consolidating into it letters that she had been unable to mail since crossing the Rockies. She celebrated how civilized and comfortable her life had become in McLoughlin's domain.

"I think every time I look into the glass if Mother could see me now she would not think my cheek bones were very prominent. We have every comfort we can ask for here, enough to eat & drink & are as well provided for as we should be in many boarding houses in the States."

In her ode to the trunk she left behind on the trail, Narcissa had written that "the custom of the country is to possess nothing." But that was not how she and Marcus would choose to live their missionary lives. In Vancouver, she stocked up on household goods that would furnish her mission home with many of the comforts she had known in New York. She bought white blankets, bleached linen, coffeepots, and teapots, rounded up enough fowl feathers for a feather bed, and ordered cooking tinware from HBC artisans. Marcus would soon see to the acquisition of glass windows, a wood-burning stove, and chairs with deer leather seats. The Whitmans would almost always have domestic servants—mostly orphan teenage girls from the Oregon Trail and Hawaiians who had come to Oregon as laborers.

Over McLoughlin's strong protests, Narcissa and Eliza returned to the east side of the Cascades in mid-November—escorted by Spalding, who traveled down the Columbia to pick them up. A week later, Spalding took his wife from Fort Walla Walla to his rugged and freezing mission under construction at Lapwai. Narcissa stayed at Fort Walla Walla until her husband, assisted by William Gray and several Indians, had nearly completed the new residence at Waiilatpu. Soon after moving into the mission house in mid-December of 1836, she described her frontier life to her mother in a long series of letters: "My heart truly leaped with joy as I alighted from my horse, entered and seated myself before a pleasant fire (for it was now night). . . . [There is] a good chimney & fireplace & the floor laid."

Glass windows and a table built by the HBC arrived a week later. Narcissa celebrated her newlywed domesticity: "Thus I am spending my winter as comfortably as heart could wish & have suffered less from excessive cold than in many winters previous in New York. . . . My object is to show you that people can live here & as comfortably as in many places east of the mountains."

Winters in Walla Walla, it turned out, were generally shorter, warmer, less snowy, and far less punishing than those in upstate New York. As for what was supposedly the all-consuming purpose of their presence in Oregon—converting Indians to Christianity—the Whitmans found that task to be surprisingly easy. That is, at first.

CHAPTER THREE

CAYUSES IN THE KITCHEN

I n cold and dismal weather that winter, the Cayuses were willing to attend daily worship services, where they sang Christian songs and recited prayers they had already learned from Catholic traders. Although Marcus and Narcissa barely spoke a word of Nez Perce (which had become the most commonly used language among the Cayuse), they were greatly encouraged by what they saw and heard from the Indians. After a song-filled Sunday evening service in her kitchen, Narcissa assumed that "a strong desire is manifest in them all to understand the truth and be taught." Marcus persuaded himself that the Cayuses understood many tenets of Christianity, writing that their familiarity with church services "has had a favorable influence upon them in rendering them more civil & little addicted to steal. Some of the leading truths of Revelation have been taught them."

Still, Narcissa was quick to condemn the character of the Cayuses and of all Indians. Based on letters, neither she nor her husband showed interest or found value in the traditional teachings and spiritual practices of the Cayuses. Less than a month into her stay, she accused the elderly local chief, Hiyumtipin, on whose land they had built their mission, of being "full of all manner of hypocrisy deceit and guile. He is a mortal beggar as all Indians are. If you ask a favor of him, sometimes it is granted or not just as he feels, if granted it must be well paid for."

Narcissa soon began to insist upon physical separation from the Cayuses, who, she wrote, had fleas and occasionally shed them in her kitchen. Less than three weeks after moving into her house, she wrote that she and Marcus were taking measures to make some of their rooms off-limits to the Cayuses. "We have just finished a separate room for ourself with a stove in it," she wrote on January 2, 1837. In the same letter she wrote that she had made her first visit to nearby Indian lodges; it made her uneasy. She felt "widely separated from kindred souls, alone, in the thick darkness of heathenism." At the end of January, she reported that she and Marcus had decided to keep the Indians completely out of their living space. "As soon as we are able to prepare a seperate room for them they will not be allowed to come in any other part of the house at all."

On March 14, 1837, Narcissa gave birth to a healthy baby girl, Alice Clarissa Whitman. Labor lasted just two hours, and Narcissa, who became a mother on her twenty-ninth birthday, recovered in a week. Alice was the first white American baby born in the Oregon Country, and her arrival was celebrated by the Cayuses as a favorable omen. It reduced distrust and eased suspicion of the Whitmans. Narcissa explained it all to her mother:

The Little Stranger is visited daily by the Chiefs & principal
men in camp & the women throng the house continually
waiting an opportunity to see her. Her whole appearance is so

new to them. Her complexion her size & dress & all excite a
deal of wonder. . . . She is plump & large, holds her head up
finely & looks about considerably. She weighs ten pounds. . . .
The whole tribe are highly pleased because we allow her to be
called a Cayuse Girl.

Narcissa often mentioned a Cayuse chief who took a warm personal interest in Alice's birth. His name was Telokite, and he led the band of Cayuses who lived near the Walla Walla River. Narcissa told her mother that Telokite was "a kind friendly Indian" who told her that Alice's "arrival was expected by all the people of the country."

Despite this initial favorable description, Telokite would threaten Marcus and Narcissa Whitman on several occasions over the coming decade. In 1850, he would be hanged, along with four other Cayuse men, for murdering them.

In Nez Perce country, the mission and ministry of Henry and Eliza Spalding got off to an even more hopeful start. Eliza gave birth to a healthy baby girl in November 1837. Before and after the birth, she taught large classes in English and in Nez Perce literacy and instructed Indian women in weaving, spinning, and sewing. Like the Cayuses, the Nez Perce tribe was already familiar with Christian rituals, liturgy, and hymns, having learned them from white trappers and Christianized Indians. But there were hundreds more Nez Perces living near the Lapwai mission, and they eagerly joined the Spaldings in song, prayer, and Sunday services.

The Spaldings were not as finicky as the Whitmans when it came to physical proximity to Indians. Without hesitation, they allowed most of the space in their mission house (in total, eighteen feet wide and forty feet long) to be used by the Nez Perces as a schoolroom and place of worship.

Henry Spalding was overwhelmed by what he perceived as the

near-miraculous success of his mission during its first year. He soon became a missionary sensation on the East Coast by boasting about his achievements—and the splendor of the Pacific Northwest—in a series of letters to the American Board that were prominently published in *The Missionary Herald.*

"I am astonished," he wrote, "at the correctness and rapidity with which several [Nez Perces] will go through with many events recorded in the scripture. But no history is listened to with such profundity as the story of the cross of Christ."

He claimed that his wife's success as a teacher had been almost instantaneous:

> On the 27th of January, Mrs. S. opened her school, and here a
> scene commenced, more interesting, if possible, than any we
> had before witnessed. Nothing but actual observation can give
> an idea of the indefatigable application of old and young,
> mothers with babes in their arms, grand-parent and grand-
> child. Having no books, Mrs. S., with her numerous other
> cares, is obliged to supply the deficiency with her pen, and
> print her own books; consequently, she can spend but a short
> time each day in school. But her absence does not close the
> school. From morning till night they are assembled in clusters,
> with one teaching a number of others. Their progress is
> surprising. Today a stranger will enter the room, not knowing
> a letter, tomorrow he will be teaching others.

Spalding compared the land around his mission to the "garden of Eden," praising its fat cattle, beautiful horses, and superior grass. He wrote that the Nez Perces were "remarkably kind, possess industrious habits, with scarcely the appearance of the savage or heathen about them. . . . We are very much attached to our Indians. . . . We are now comfortably located among a people with whom we shall be happy to spend the remnant of our earthly pilgrimage."

As for his prowess as a preacher, Spalding often exaggerated his evangelical effect on Indians. He claimed that when he traveled for supplies, "multitudes" of Indians insisted that he deliver evening sermons: "Of course I must preach. . . . I shall probably be followed by hundreds, and perhaps thousands, for several days on my way home, to hear something about Jesus Christ every night."

These early dispatches from the fields of the Lord would later be ridiculed—by other Presbyterian missionaries—as examples of Spalding's habitual dishonesty and self-aggrandizement. But when they were published, at stupendous length, in 1837—one filled five pages of *The Missionary Herald*—they excited considerable evangelical passion, especially among the missionary managers at the American Board. With Spalding suggesting that entire Indian tribes were on the brink of committing their lives to Jesus, the American Board decided to expand its evangelical work in Oregon.

In the spring of 1838, three new missionary couples and a single missionary man joined the misanthropic carpenter-missionary William Gray, who had returned east the previous autumn to marry, on his journey back to Oregon. They arrived in late August.

It was then—with twice as many missionaries on the ground—that the Protestant endeavor in Oregon began to fall apart.

One event stands out as the tragic symbol of this shift. It occurred on a lazy Sunday afternoon in June 1839, at the Whitman mission. Alice Clarissa Whitman, age two, was sitting and reading with her father. She was a precocious toddler, strong and rambunctious, chatty in English and in Nez Perce, constantly singing hymns in both languages, and much inclined to read. She was "blooming in health," her mother said, "cheerful and happy in herself."

As Sunday afternoon wore on, Alice climbed down from her father's lap, grabbed two empty water cups from the table, amused herself for a while in the yard, and then walked alone to the nearby Walla Walla River. She intended to fill up the empty glasses—something she had never done before. But she never came back.

Occupied with their books, Marcus and Narcissa did not notice their daughter's absence. While they continued to read, Alice tumbled into the river.

Unable to find their daughter, they asked the Cayuses for help. An elder in the tribe dove into the river and found the little body. Marcus carried the girl home, where Narcissa wrapped her in a shroud. The

The Whitman mission in the mid-1840s—as depicted a century later by artist William Henry Jackson—became prosperous, with herds of livestock, irrigated fields, and a mill for grinding grain. Some of the Cayuses came to resent the prosperity of the missionaries and wanted rent payments.

Whitmans kept the corpse in their mission house, where Narcissa anesthetized her grief by stroking her daughter's face.

"This proved to be a great comfort to me," Narcissa wrote to her mother. "For so long as she looked natural and was so sweet and I could caress her, I could not bear to have her out of my sight."

The body started to decompose after four days.

"When she began to melt away like wax and visage changed I wished then to put her out of my sight, and felt it a great privilege that I could put her in so safe, quiet and desirable a resting place as the grave—to see her no more until the morning of the resurrection."

It was then that Narcissa began to panic. She had been raised in the Calvinist belief that eternal life was not available to the unconverted. She feared that Alice, who had been too young for a conscious and voluntary conversion to Christianity, would not make it to heaven and could be bound for hell.

"For a moment," Narcissa wrote, "I felt all the horrors of the reflections that perhaps it might not be well with my precious child."

Narcissa quickly came up with a rationale for believing her daughter would reach heaven. She told herself that she and Marcus had earnestly prayed for Alice's salvation before she drowned. What's more, Alice had been a prayerful girl with a "thoughtfulness and relish for worship." Therefore, her mother reasoned, Alice would surely "rest in the bosom of the blessed Jesus." Narcissa worked her way through all this in an agonized letter of nearly four thousand words, which she wrote to her mother four months after the drowning.

Confidence in Alice's salvation, however, did little to ease her guilt for allowing her toddler to wander alone to the bank of a swift river. Narcissa soon descended into a severe and long-lasting depression. "The trial was upon me which I dreaded more than anything else. . . . What I went through I cannot describe," she wrote, describing herself as "a poor, weak female . . . alone among the heathen."

Her parents and sisters were a continent away. Her husband traveled constantly, tending to sick Indians and missionaries, often leaving the mission for weeks at a time. And her vivacious little Alice, who "had always been my relief in such lonely hours," was gone—although Narcissa, as she wandered around the mission, continued to hear Alice's voice and footsteps.

The Whitmans would never have another child. Narcissa soon lost the insouciant charm that had beguiled white mountain men. Gone, too, was the optimistic sense of purpose that had drawn her west. Unexplained illnesses, probably related to depression, confined her to her bedroom. Ten months after Alice drowned, Narcissa complained in a letter to her mother about the filth the Cayuses left behind in her house. She found the Indians to be "proud, haughty, and insolent." She made certain that when her flood-damaged mission house was rebuilt in 1838–39, it had the long-planned separate room for visiting Indians.

As the years went by, she devoted less and less time to missionary work with the Cayuse people. Her daily contact with the "heathen" she had journeyed west to save dwindled to almost nothing. She focused instead on white and mixed-raced children who turned up at the mission after losing their parents to accidents and illness on the Oregon Trail.

Narcissa periodically admitted she was losing hope.

"To be a missionary in name and to do so little or nothing for the benefit of heathen souls, is heart-sickening," she wrote a half year after Alice's death. "I sometimes almost wish to give my place to others who can do more for their good."

As the farm operation at the mission became prosperous—with herds of fat livestock, irrigated fields bursting with corn and wheat, mills for grinding wheat and for sawing lumber—Narcissa sometimes viewed herself as a fraud and a failure. She wrote that she was "astonished" that the American Board had found her competent enough to send west as a missionary. In the second year after the death of her daughter, she told her parents, "I am entirely unfitted for the work."

Yet her husband had no desire to give up on missionary work, and she had convinced herself that she could not leave.

As a young girl she had dreamed of becoming a missionary. She knew that her artful and compelling letters to her family and friends were being read aloud in gatherings back home, making her a missionary heroine in the Burned-Over District. She believed that her God, her parents, and her husband expected nothing less of her. She was duty bound to stay.

Protestant missionaries who found their way to Oregon in the 1830s demonstrated an astonishing aptitude for failure. They failed as evangelists, converting only a handful of Indians. They failed one another as Christian colleagues, endlessly quarreling and mercilessly tattling on each other in letters to the American Board. Even when it came to managing tragedies in their own lives, as Narcissa's struggles suggest, they often failed themselves.

Part of the reason for all this failure was the excruciating rigor of their Calvinist faith—and its total incompatibility with what Indians were seeking in their worship of the white man's God. The more the Indians of the Columbia Plateau learned about religion from the Calvinist missionaries, the more they found it to be useless, insulting, and—most of all—incomprehensible.

Back in New England and New York, the Presbyterian and Congregationalist missionaries had been indoctrinated in a Calvinist interpretation of Christ's teachings that was hard to understand, harder to teach (especially to Indians who spoke little or no English), and all but impossible to live by. The missionaries believed in the "natural depravity" of all human beings, including themselves. This meant that everyone was going to burn forever in hell, except the faithful. And even the faithful had to keep a constant focus on self-denying usefulness, lest they slip into sin and damnation. (Paradoxically, this made an arduous life among the Indians attractive to Calvinist missionaries, as it required a commitment to self-denying usefulness that seemed sure to guarantee their own salvation.)

The missionaries believed that each person bore primary responsibility for the outcome of his or her life. But they also believed that God alone controlled all events as part of his inscrutable plan. To reconcile these seemingly irreconcilable positions, the missionaries tried to take comfort in the concept of God's forgiving grace, which allowed flawed but prayerful people to lead lives pleasing to him.

There were still more complications: the missionaries believed that no adult could escape hell merely by going to church and following the teachings of Jesus Christ. Marcus Whitman scolded Indians who believed "that worshipping would save them," telling them that they were "lost ruined + condemned." He and the other missionaries insisted that a true convert had to undergo "a saving faith experience"— a personal epiphany that brought home the miracle of Jesus dying on the cross. Whitman's standards were so high that in his eleven years as a missionary, only two Cayuses were admitted to the church, according to tribal records.

The American missionaries demanded more than just religious conversion. Assuming that their way of life was superior in every way to the centuries-old spiritual beliefs and cultural practices of the Indians, they sought to transform them into "copies of their white neighbors."

To that end, the missionaries insisted that the Indians learn English, cut their hair, wear white people's clothes, abandon their traditional nomadic lives, forsake collective ownership of land, accept private property, settle down as farmers, embrace "hard work," learn to plow, and raise row crops—all while obeying the Ten Commandments and re-nouncing polygamy, drinking, gambling, dancing, and horse racing.

As ethnocentric and downright impossible as all these demands may seem at a distance of nearly two centuries, there was an additional, more laudable motive behind the Protestant effort to assimilate the Indians. Many devout Christians on the East Coast were horrified by the U.S. government's increasingly brutal policy toward Indians. After passage of the Indian Removal Act of 1830, federal troops had forced about a hundred thousand Native people to leave their homelands. They had to march, sometimes in shackles, to what the U.S. government called "Indian Country," territory west of Arkansas and Missouri.

When the Whitmans were setting up their mission in Oregon in 1837, President Andrew Jackson used an Indian uprising as an excuse to forcibly remove the entire Creek tribe from Alabama. Marching west in the 1830s along their various trails of tears, thousands of Choctaws, Creeks, and Cherokees died of disease, starvation, and exhaustion.

By rushing to Oregon ahead of federal troops enforcing Indian removal—and ahead of white American settlers, many of whom would come to believe that "the only good Indian is a dead Indian"—the missionaries intended to teach the Cayuses, the Nez Perces, and other tribes how to survive the inevitable coming of white control. If the Indians spoke and acted and believed in God like white Americans did, perhaps settlers would not steal their land and order them elsewhere.

"What we most fear," Reverend Greene, head of missionary affairs for the American Board, told Whitman in a letter, "is that, should the [Oregon] country come under the United States, there will immediately be a rush towards it by speculators & adventurers, making it a theatre for all kinds of wickedness, leading to the corruption and oppression of the Indian tribes beyond anything that has yet been seen on our borders."

Greene concluded the letter by telling Whitman that he and his fellow missionaries could, with the help of the Lord, preserve the Indians "from utter extinction."

D espite the many obstacles to Calvinist conversion, Henry Spalding claimed stupendous progress among the Nez Perces. "We might as well hold back the sun from his march, as hold back the minds of this people from religious inquiry," Spalding wrote after just three months at his mission.

His boasts were believed—and widely published in Christian newspapers—until the missionary reinforcements arrived in Oregon in 1838. After that, there was a foul eruption of fact-checking, gossip, and discontent. The new missionaries soon saw for themselves that Spalding was full of hot air. They were also offended by his abrasive personality and presumed spiritual superiority. They began to express their disapproval in letters to the American Board.

The most toxic and verbose of them was the Reverend Asa Bowen Smith. He was a brainy, Vermont-born, twenty-nine-year-old graduate of Yale Divinity School. He had never wanted to come to Oregon, but rather had hoped to become, along with his new bride, Sarah, the first Protestant missionary in Siam (now Thailand). The board had other ideas. After its leaders had read Spalding's accounts of Oregon Indians who he claimed were clamoring for Christ, they redirected Smith to the Pacific Northwest to be one of several junior ministers taking orders from Spalding and Whitman. Smith and his wife arrived in Oregon in the late summer, along with two other newlywed missionary couples from New England: the Reverend Cushing Eells and his wife, Myra, were from Maine, while the Reverend Elkanah Walker and his wife, Mary, were from Massachusetts.

The entire party, which included the newly married William Gray and his wife, had bickered and picked at one another during their five-month trek across the United States. By the time they arrived at the Whitman mission, where the New Englanders spent most of the winter crowded into Narcissa's kitchen, the missionary couples were barely speaking to one another.

Historians have described the behavior of these missionaries as "envious and complaining," "smug and unbearably self-righteous," and poisoned by "crabby jealousies." These descriptions are documented by a mountainous paper trail—a million words' worth of missionary letters written between 1836 and 1847. Mary Walker, one of the missionary wives and a sharp-witted writer, said of her fellow Protestant travelers, "We have a strange company of missionaries. Scarcely one who is not intolerable on some account."

In the running for most intolerable of all was Reverend Smith's wife, Sarah, who was often sick from unknown ailments. As historian Alvin M. Josephy Jr. described her in his book about the Nez Perces, she was "a small, prudish soul [who] in Oregon proved to be a vicious gossip and troublemaker, constantly bursting into tears and complaining about her miserable lot." The Nez Perces remembered her as the "weeping one."

Her husband, though, was the principal saboteur of the Protestant missionary enterprise in Oregon. His sabotage took the form of staggeringly long letters—one ran to ten thousand words—to Greene in Boston. While the claims in Smith's letters were twisted by his insecurities and jealousies, as well as by his whiny discontent at being posted in Oregon, there was much in them that was true. The early letters exposed and ridiculed Spalding's exaggerations; the later ones eviscerated him as a fraud and a liar, a thief and a madman.

With the exception of Eliza Spalding, Smith was the only Protestant missionary in Oregon who quickly mastered the Nez Perce language. He did so in just a few months. Soon he wrote a dictionary, systematized Nez Perce grammar, and conducted a census of the tribe. All this allowed him to demolish Spalding's earlier accounts—many of which had been published—of the Nez Perces' understanding of English and their acceptance of Calvinist dogma.

"Not a child can be found who can read a single sentence of English intelligibly," Smith informed Greene. Furthermore, Smith wrote that the Nez Perces find it "very offensive" to be taught the "great truth" that all unconverted men are damned to eternal fire. According to Smith, the Nez Perces were calculating liars who professed interest in Christianity only in order to get their hands on the seeds and hoes that Spalding was all too willing to give away.

The Spaldings, the Whitmans, and all the American Board missionaries in Oregon found Smith and his wife to be insufferable—and the dislike was mutual. So the Smiths went to live in a remote community in the heart of Nez Perce country. Called Kamiah, it was about sixty miles southeast of Spalding's mission and nearly two hundred miles from the Whitmans'. In his isolation, Smith had plenty of time to brood and churn out letters of complaint. He argued that it was a waste of time and money for the board to try to convert the few thousand Indians who lived on the Columbia Plateau. "The more we do to encourage their selfish desires," he wrote, "the more difficult will it be to bring them under the influence of the gospel."

Mostly, though, Smith presented a damning picture of the reverend: Spalding did not understand the Nez Perce language. Spalding used board money to buy Indian horses he intended to keep for himself. Spalding was "much in the habit" of whipping Indians and of ordering Indians to whip each other, which caused one Indian "woman to be whipped 70 lashes." Other visitors to Spalding's mission confirmed reports that he sometimes whipped Indians.

Smith also accused Spalding of baptizing Nez Perces before they had proven themselves worthy of the privilege—an accusation that showed Smith's puritanical blindness to Spalding's one great strength as a missionary: he understood the Indians' struggle to grasp the intricacies and convolutions of Calvinist-style Christianity. More than any other Protestant missionary in Oregon at the time, Spalding was willing to cut the Indians some theological slack. He believed that if they tried to practice the ethical teachings of Christ while slowly adapting to white American ways, they would eventually become Christians. Unlike other Protestant missionaries—especially Smith, but also Whitman—Spalding was willing to baptize Indians in the early stages of their search for salvation. This would give Spalding, more than any of his missionary peers, enduring influence over the affairs of the Nez Perces. He baptized and trained men who would become devout, lifelong Christians and influential tribal leaders in the second half of the nineteenth century.

None of this penetrated Smith's zealotry. After little more than a year among the Nez Perces, his letters became venomous. He clearly intended to destroy Spalding. In a letter to the board, Smith said he had consulted with Marcus Whitman and that the doctor concurred that Spalding had "a disease in his head which may result in derangement." The board would be wise, Smith wrote, to bring Spalding "back to his native land and dismiss him."

A week before Smith's accusation, William Gray—the resentful carpenter—wrote a similarly vicious letter to the board. It painted a nightmarish portrait of group dynamics among the missionaries. Whenever they met for a conference, Gray wrote, Spalding ruined everything by sniping and sneering at Marcus Whitman. Spalding could not get over his feelings for Narcissa, Gray wrote, nor would he forgive Whitman for marrying her and bringing her to Oregon. Even after the drowning of little Alice Clarissa Whitman, Gray wrote, Spalding refused to behave himself: "The same jealous and unsubdued disposition burst forth. . . . Duplicity is a trait in his character that never in all probability will change."

Gray closed his letter by "hoping and earnestly praying" that the American Board would send an agent to Oregon to investigate the turmoil among the missionaries. "I now feel that nothing short of a removal of some members of this Mission will restore harmony."

CHAPTER FOUR

"WANT OF CHRISTIAN FEELING"

I t took a year for the explosive letters from Smith and Gray to find their way to Reverend Greene's desk in Boston, and five more months for the American Board to digest the charges and rule on the future of the Oregon mission. The letters of response Greene wrote to explain the board's decisions then took eight months to reach the missionaries in Oregon.

The two-year delay seemed to amplify the impact of the board's decision. Like land mines that explode long after the end of a war, Greene's letters, when they finally reached Oregon, were as unexpected as they were destructive.

During the two-year interval, an unusual calm had fallen upon the lives of the Oregon missionaries. By September 1842, when the secretary's letters were opened, the ministers and their wives had mostly stopped bickering.

The principal troublemaker, Asa Smith, was gone. He and his

sickly wife, Sarah, had fled in 1841 for a more commodious assignment in Hawaii. William Gray had also announced that he was leaving the mission. Most significantly, Henry Spalding had finally—after
six years of unremitting spite—apologized to Marcus Whitman, securing a long-term truce between the two men. Spalding joined with
missionaries Eells and Walker in signing a letter to the American
Board that said there was cause "to hope for permanent peace & harmony." Missionary wife Mary Walker noted in her diary, "The minds
of all were relieved."

Then they opened Greene's letters.

The greatest shock was Spalding's. While he had suspected that
Smith and Gray had written unflattering letters about his behavior, he
was unaware of just how mercilessly lacerating they had been. And, in
the intervening years, he had earnestly tried to be a better colleague.

Now, as he read Greene's letter, he discovered that the American
Board regarded him as a cancer to be excised. Board members judged
his continued presence in Oregon as a "reproach" to "the progress
of Christianity."

"The Committee have been pained & perplexed by the want of
harmony and the despondency which seem to pervade your branch of
the mission," the secretary wrote. The committee had "voted to recall
you, expecting that you will return to the United States at the earliest
opportunity. . . . Should you decide to continue in the country, you
will, of course, cease on the receipt of this, to draw on the treasury of
the Board."

He was fired. His mission was ordered closed. It was the worst
humiliation of Spalding's adult life. Nothing so devastating had happened to him since he was seventeen, when his adoptive father whipped
him and threw him out of the house, when Spalding became, as he
described it, "a cast off bastard wishing myself dead."

This time, though, Spalding's humiliation was shared—with Marcus

Whitman. The letter Greene sent to Dr. Whitman was longer than the one he wrote to Spalding. It was also worded more acidly.

> The Committee have been deeply grieved [at] the want of confidence in each other & the want of fraternal intercourse, which have prevailed in your branch of the mission. . . . They are pained at the thought too that the alienation & strife which have prevailed among your number have been known to the traders and others in the country & thus religion and missions dishonored before them & perhaps their own souls ruined through the want of Christian feeling and action which they have witnessed in your number. . . .
>
> Your company can not live & labor together. . . . The mission must either be abandoned or new men must be sent into the field to take your places. This is to the Committee extremely painful and humiliating. It is an alternative to which they have never been brought by any other mission & which for the honor of the cause, they trust may never occur again.

Whitman was to be demoted and marginalized, but, unlike Spalding, he was not sacked outright or ordered home. Greene told him to dispose of the Waiilatpu mission as speedily as possible and move north to assist other missionaries who had settled in Colville, north of the present-day city of Spokane, Washington. Greene's letter made no mention of Narcissa, other than to wish her his "Christian regard."

Finally, Greene ordered Marcus Whitman to be extremely wary in his dealings with Spalding, who Greene seemed to suspect was mentally ill.

"In everything that relates to Mr. Spalding you will need to act with much discretion and kindness," Greene wrote. "If he remains in the country, it would not be expected that all in his possession should be taken from him."

For a missionary, Whitman was not an especially contemplative man. In school, he had struggled with theological abstractions. He did not keep a diary. When he was emotionally overwrought, he did not write deeply felt letters to family or friends. "He could never stop to parley," wrote one of Whitman's missionary peers, a Methodist minister in Oregon. "He was always at work."

Whitman's response to the American Board's order was to try to overturn it as fast as possible.

He called an emergency meeting of the missionaries, including Henry Spalding, Cushing Eells, and Elkanah Walker. At his mission on September 27, 1842, he stunned them all: he was riding to Boston. He would persuade the American Board to change its decision regarding him and Spalding. The next day the missionaries agreed "that Dr. Marcus Whitman be at liberty & advised to visit the United States as soon as practicable to confer with the Committee . . . in regard to interest of this mission."

This, then, in Whitman's own handwriting, was the explicit motive for his famous winter ride across the continent. Completely contradicting the claim authored by Spalding that endured well into the twentieth century—the tale of a pious patriot riding east to save Oregon from the perfidious British—Whitman's ride was driven by self-interest. He did not want to lose the mission that he and Narcissa had worked so hard to build. He did not want to become a subordinate on a smaller mission run by a minister who had once been his junior. He was determined that the American Board should know that he, Spalding, and the other missionaries in Oregon had settled their differences—and that they must be allowed to continue their work.

Spalding, of course, approved of Whitman's impulsive decision to ride east. More than anyone, he had a gut-level understanding of what was at stake. If Whitman succeeded, Spalding would not be sacked or publicly disgraced. He would not have to acknowledge in public that he—and his incessantly aggrieved personality—had been the primary cause of what Reverend Greene described as a "catastrophe" among Christians in Oregon.

For Spalding, it was a fateful—and ironic—turning point. For nearly seven years, his entire career as a missionary, he had needled, derided, and sniped at Marcus Whitman. For nearly twenty years, ever since Narcissa had rejected his romantic overtures, he had resented and disrespected the woman who became Whitman's wife. As she explained to her father, "My dear husband has suffered more from [Spalding] in consequence of his wicked jealousy, and his great pique toward me, than can be known in this world."

Now Spalding needed Whitman more than he had ever needed another man. Assuming he did not freeze to death crossing the Rockies, Whitman just might be able to salvage Spalding's career.

The winter ride that began in the late fall of 1842 was miserable, risky, almost fatal. Whitman organized it in a single week. For part of the journey, he was accompanied by an Indian guide and a freshly arrived newcomer to Oregon, a young lawyer named Asa Lovejoy. Crossing the ice-choked Colorado River, Whitman and his horse disappeared underwater—before popping up like corks and scrambling to the far bank. To avoid Indian attack, Whitman took a southerly route toward Taos, in what is now New Mexico. Along the way, the three men ran out of food. They ate their pack mules and their pet dog, Trapper, once a pet of his daughter, Alice Clarissa. Later, after separating from his companions and while traveling alone on his way to St. Louis, Whitman made a wrong turn at the Arkansas River and was delayed for several days.

Dressed in greasy buckskins, Whitman turned up in March of 1843 in St. Louis, where his presence generated intense interest among westbound pioneers. The city was bustling with "Oregon fever." A few weeks before his arrival, a bill written by Missouri senator Linn had been approved in the U.S. Senate. It sought to extend federal jurisdiction over the Oregon Country and offered 640 acres of land to any American who settled there. Though that bill did not get through Congress—it failed to win approval in the House of Representatives—the prospect of free land in the Willamette Valley had drawn hundreds of prospective settlers to several Missouri towns, including St. Louis, where a wagon train bound for Oregon was being assembled for departure in May. Whitman made arrangements to return with it to his mission, assuming he could get back from Boston in time.

First, though, he hurried east, by steamboat up the Ohio River to Cincinnati and then overland to Washington, D.C., where he appears to have stayed for two or three days in mid-March. Why Whitman did not travel directly to Boston is not known, and what he did in the nation's capital has never been established with documented certainty.

The Washington visit is at the core of the Whitman Saved Oregon myth that would surface two decades later. As will be explained in greater detail, accounts written by Spalding and his many disciples and imitators describe nation-changing encounters between Whitman and President John Tyler and his famous secretary of state, Daniel Webster, even going so far as to include verbatim quotations from supposed conversations in the White House.

There is a consensus among historians that Whitman went to Washington in March of 1843 because of the existence of one document: a letter dictated later that year by Whitman and written in Narcissa's hand. It was found fifty-two years later in the archival records of the War Department. Addressed to Secretary of War James M. Porter, it begins, "In compliance with the request you did me the honor to make last winter while at Washington." The long letter goes on to outline a proposed bill to protect settlers traveling to Oregon. It was never acted upon. And though it does place Whitman in Washington, it does not make clear whether he actually met with the war secretary or merely tried to.

There are no other known government records of any meetings Whitman may have had in Washington. No references to Whitman have been found in the papers or letters of Tyler, Webster, Porter, or their aides. Nor are there any contemporaneous newspaper or magazine accounts of any encounters between the three most powerful men in the United States and an almost penniless, roughly attired missionary doctor from Oregon.

When Whitman left Washington and traveled to New York City in late March, he did stir up a considerable fuss in the press. America's most famous newspaper editor, Horace Greeley of the *New York Daily Tribune*, judged the missionary to be newsworthy, mostly for his shabby clothes, his lack of money, and his having been cheated by a Manhattan cabbie. Whitman seems to have said nothing to Greeley (who certainly would have included the scoop in his newspaper) about meetings with President Tyler and other higher-ups in Washington. Greeley's account of his conversation with Whitman ran at the top of the *Tribune*'s second page:

ARRIVAL FROM OREGON

We were most agreeably surprised yesterday by a call from Dr. Whitman from Oregon, a member of the American Presbyterian Mission in that Territory. A slight glance at him when he entered our office would have convinced any one that he had seen all the hardships of a life in the wilderness. He was dressed in an old fur cap that appeared to have seen some ten years' service, faded and nearly destitute of fur; a vest whose natural color had long since fled, and a shirt—we could not see that he had any—an overcoat every thread of which could be easily seen, buckskin pants, etc.—the roughest man that we have seen this many a day—too poor, in fact, to get any better wardrobe! The Doctor is one of those daring and good men who went to Oregon some years ago to teach the Indians religion, agriculture, letters, etc. A noble pioneer do we judge him to be—a man fitted to be a chief in rearing a moral empire among the wild men of the wilderness. We did not learn what success the worthy man had in leading the Indians to embrace the Christian faith, but he very modernly remarked that many of them had begun to cultivate the earth and raise cattle. . . .

We give the hardy and self-denying man a hearty welcome to his native land. We are sorry to say that his first reception, on arriving in our city, was but slightly calculated to give him a favorable impression of the morals of his kinsmen. He fell into the hands of one of our vampire cabmen, who in connection with a keeper of a tavern house . . . fleeced him out of two of the last few dollars which the poor man had.

From New York, Whitman traveled by steamship to Boston, arriving six months after he had left Oregon. Without an appointment, nearly broke, and still dressed in the stained buckskins he had been wearing since crossing the Mississippi, he walked into the offices of the American Board, where he startled and discomfited the Reverend David Greene.

Clearly unhappy to see Whitman, Greene asked the missionary

why he abandoned his post in the West. Another board member gave Whitman some cash and told him to go buy decent clothes.

The next day, looking far more presentable, Whitman started over. He told Greene that the many letters he had read about discord and disarray in the Oregon mission were now out of date: Spalding had begun to behave himself. The pot-stirring tattler, Asa Smith, and his wife had gone to Hawaii. The other missionaries and their wives were no longer at one another's throats. Whitman also pointed out that the large and productive farm at his mission was helping to feed all the missionaries in Oregon.

Whitman's arguments proved persuasive. Greene and other members of the American Board changed their minds. They concluded that the "difficulties between Mr. Spalding & the others were apparently resolved. Mr. S. promises to pursue a different course. . . . Resolved, That Doct. Marcus Whitman and the Rev. H.H. Spalding be authorized to continue . . . as they did previous."

But Whitman wanted more than merely a return to the status quo. He wanted to increase missionary outreach to the Indians while expanding farm operations. To give himself and other missionaries more time for proselytizing, he asked the board to hire and send to Oregon five or ten men "of piety and intelligence" to take over the demanding physical labor of growing crops and running mills on lands near the missions. The board was not interested in expanding white colonies near the missions and flatly refused to hire anyone to go west with Whitman. But it did want to know more about the character and culture of the Indians among whom Whitman was living. On April 4, 1843, when the board officially authorized continued support for Whitman, it asked him for a report on the Cayuses.

Three days later, while still in Boston, Whitman wrote a report of 2,500 words that described the customs and superstitions of the tribe—and also presciently provided a rationale for his own murder.

He described the extraordinary personal risk of practicing medicine among the Cayuses. If a spiritual conjurer, a medicine man, or a doctor failed to cure a disease that was killing members of the tribe, he wrote, the Cayuses hunted down the man responsible for bad medicine—and killed him.

"The number + horror of the deaths of this kind that have come under my observation + knowledge have been great," Whitman wrote. "Very often in cases of this kind nothing can save the Conjurer."

CHAPTER FIVE

"A THOUSAND LITTLE HARASSING EVENTS"

T he day after her husband left for the East Coast, an Indian forced his way into Narcissa Whitman's bedroom. She awoke around midnight as the intruder raised the latch on her bedroom door. As it inched open, she remained in bed, listening and silently panicking. Then, shrieking for help, she bounded out of bed and tried to force the door shut. The intruder shoved back, muscling his way into the bedroom. With Narcissa still screaming and others in the house beginning to stir, he disappeared.

"A saucy Indian got into the house," Narcissa wrote later. "I got dreadfully frightened. . . . Had the ruffian persisted, I do not know what I should have done."

By the autumn of 1842, six years into the American Board's evangelical effort in Oregon, the relationship between missionaries and Native people was falling apart. By and large, the Cayuses had lost interest in the white man's God, whose supernatural favors had been much anticipated but never seen. Attendance at mission schools and church services was falling. Many Indians were fed up with the missionaries, viewing them as squatters on tribal land who behaved in a way that was increasingly bossy, arrogant, and selfish. The Cayuses and the Nez Perces had watched with mounting resentment and anger as the Whitmans and the Spaldings built handsome houses and expanded their fields and herds—all while refusing to pay any rent to tribal elders.

They noticed, too, that more white people kept showing up. Just before Marcus Whitman rushed away to the East in the autumn of 1842, another 125 American settlers appeared out of the east, their wagons rolling through Cayuse land on their way to the Willamette Valley.

After the midnight break-in at the mission, Narcissa's mysterious illnesses worsened. She took to her bed. Soon she left the mission, staying away during much of her husband's yearlong absence. She lived with a minister and his wife at a mission to the west, on the Columbia River, and in Vancouver with Dr. McLoughlin's family. After she fled the mission, which foundered as a working farm during Dr. Whitman's travels, Indians burned down its gristmill, destroying hundreds of bushels of wheat and corn, as well as lumber and flour.

The Spaldings had trouble with the Nez Perces, too. What started as "a thousand little harassing events" escalated into serious threats to their lives. The mill dam at their mission was demolished. Indians pummeled the mission house with rocks. Spalding, who had sometimes whipped Indians who disobeyed him, was himself threatened with a whip on several occasions. When he objected to Indians burning a cedar fence near his house, several Nez Perces tossed him into their fire. Only a thick buffalo skin coat kept him from being burned.

"I have had a gun cocked & presented at my head for 15 or 20 minutes while 4 of the principle men stood & looked on with as much indifference as if a dog were to be shot down," Spalding told Greene in a letter that described a pattern of threats at his mission over several years.

He wrote that a mob of five hundred angry Nez Perces had gathered near his house and threatened to "tie & whip my wife." Eliza had complained to a chief about two naked men painted with "horrible figures" who showed up at her school, made indecent gestures, and refused to leave.

Though Henry Spalding had convinced himself that the Nez Perces were hungry for the Gospel, and had been successful in converting a few Nez Perce chiefs, he was also aware that most members of the tribe did not care if he lived or died. In a letter written in early 1843, while Marcus Whitman was still away, Spalding said that, "should a reckless fellow from [the tribe], or even a stranger, make an attack on my life and property, I have no evidence to suppose but a vast majority of them would look on with indifference, and see our dwelling burnt to the ground and our heads severed from our bodies."

American law did not protect missionaries in the Oregon Country. It remained semi-foreign, governed loosely, if at all, by the decades-old joint occupation treaty between the United States and Britain. There were no police, courts, or jails. But in the late autumn of 1842, about a month after Whitman rode away to Boston, a newly appointed U.S. government official decided unilaterally—and illegally—to fill the jurisdictional vacuum and impose law and order on the Nez Perces and the Cayuses.

Dr. Elijah White, a New York physician, minister, and former missionary, had a dodgy record in Oregon. On his first outing to the territory, with Methodists in the mid-1830s, he had clashed with other missionaries in the Willamette Valley. Ultimately, he had to resign amid charges of taking church money and sporting with Indian women. Prior to his second trek to Oregon in 1842, he persuaded clueless bureaucrats in Washington that he was an expert on what he called Far West aboriginals and won a job as the federal subagent for Indians in the Northwest.

White had been back in Oregon a few weeks when he learned of disturbances at the Whitman and Spalding missions. He hired six armed men, found a couple of interpreters, and headed up the Columbia River to restore calm. When his party arrived at the Whitman mission, Narcissa was gone and there were few Indians around. He traveled on to the Spalding mission, where, he later recalled, the missionary couple greeted him and his bodyguards with "joyful countenance and glad hearts. Seldom was a visit of an Indian agent more desired."

The Spaldings needed help controlling what they saw as unruly young Nez Perce men. At the same time, they still had reliable relationships with many older leaders of the tribe. When White and his posse showed up at the mission, Spalding seized the opportunity. He asked Nez Perce headmen to gather for an important meeting. In the two days it took for them to assemble, he worked with White to draft eleven "Laws of the Nez Perces."

The first two laws called for the execution of anyone who took a life or burned a house. Other laws prescribed fines, imprisonment, and flogging for theft, breaking into a house, or burning crops.

White tried to make the laws palatable to the tribe by including a provision that said, "If an Indian break these laws, he shall be punished by his chiefs; if a white man break them, he shall be reported to the agent, and be punished at his instance." Nez Perce elders were given an opportunity to accept or reject each law, White later said. But after long conversation, he claimed, they agreed to all of them and "were greatly pleased."

The Indians may have willingly accepted the laws. More likely they felt pressured to do it, and they probably did not understand the full meaning of what they were accepting. In any case, agreeing to the laws was a grave mistake. It compromised the tribe's independence and gave white men a legal loophole that they would energetically exploit to plunder Indian land. "The Indians would discover that the laws could not be made to apply to white men," historian Alvin Josephy wrote. The laws "would give whites liberty to exploit, rob, persecute, and murder Indians, for no Indian agent would ever have the power or authority to bring a white man to justice."

The Nez Perces numbered about three thousand men, women, and children, and their peaceful acceptance of White's laws put pressure on smaller regional tribes to do likewise, especially their closest ally, the Cayuse tribe. For a time, the Cayuses resisted the pressure. White's legal code was a trick, their leaders complained, one that would destroy the tribe and take its land. The Cayuses began meeting with leaders of other small tribes, including the Walla Wallas, discussing resistance tactics that included attacks on settler caravans. "The principal cause of the excitement," Narcissa wrote to her husband in the spring of 1843, was that "the Kaiuses do not wish to be *forced* to adopt the law recommended by the Agent."

But the Cayuses were a much smaller and more geographically vulnerable tribe than the Nez Perces, with land exposed to the predations of white newcomers. The Oregon Trail, which funneled more settlers into the territory every year, cut through the heart of Cayuse country. In the end, under pressure from White and his armed men, as well as from their Nez Perce neighbors, the Cayuses backed down. In May 1843, with Marcus Whitman still absent from Oregon, they agreed to abide by White's code.

This, too, was a fateful mistake. The first law in that code would, in less than a decade, threaten the very existence of the Cayuses. It would give armed white men an excuse to take much of their land. The law said, "Whoever willfully takes life shall be hung."

W hen Marcus Whitman first traveled to Oregon, his responsibilities as a missionary could not have been explained more
clearly. "Let yr single aim be seen to be the benefit of the Indians,"
Greene instructed him by letter in 1836. Greene told Whitman to forsake all worldly interests and focus on "the salvation of their souls."

But after seven hard years in Oregon, Whitman was ignoring those
orders. By the time he returned from Boston to his mission, he had
reinvented himself as an agent of white settlement. His letters show
that his transformation was conscious and deliberate. The missionary
doctor not only became a champion of Manifest Destiny but did so
with his eyes wide open to the potentially catastrophic consequences—
for the Cayuses and for himself.

He knew the Indians feared white settlement. He knew, too, that
they were likely to respond to it with violence, and that he and his wife
were at risk. As he wrote to his mother on the way west, "it will be
strange if the emigration does not cause us much trouble." But for
reasons that he never spelled out in any letter, Whitman did not take
precautions to protect his wife and himself from the rage he knew was
growing among the Cayuses.

The westbound wagon train that left Missouri in 1843 was seven
times larger than any previous Oregon-bound assemblage of settlers,
mules, horses, and farm equipment. Including Marcus Whitman, there
were about a thousand people, four thousand head of livestock, and at
least 120 wagons. This was the first great emigration to Oregon, and
it would tip the balance of geopolitical power in the territory. Within
three years, the joint occupancy of Oregon would come to a negotiated end as Great Britain acceded to demographic reality and re-
linquished its claims to land south of what is now the U.S.-Canada
border. It was the unstoppable increase in the number of American

feet on the ground—not Whitman's three-day trip to Washington, D.C.—that wrested Oregon away from the British and made the political calculus right for creating the states of Oregon, Washington, and Idaho.

Those feet, when they showed up en masse as part of the great emigration of 1843, had a second powerful effect: they panicked the Cayuses and the Nez Perces. The number of new settlers that year was equivalent to about a third of the entire Nez Perce tribe. As historian Elliott West has noted, "An equivalent for Bostonians would have been about twenty-eight thousand western Indians passing through the city toward settling on Cape Cod, announcing that even more were sure to follow."

Sure enough, fifteen hundred more white settlers showed up the next year, and there were twenty-five hundred more in 1845. The Indians were fast becoming a minority in their own country.

Whitman had nothing to do with organizing the wagon trains or recruiting the hordes of settlers who joined them. Professional boosters of western expansion—politicians, business interests, and the press—did that job. Missouri's senator Linn pushed a bill that offered free land in Oregon, and newspapers across America celebrated the Willamette Valley as paradise on earth. The Cleveland *Plain Dealer* called it "a land of pure delight."

It was happenstance that placed Whitman in Missouri in the late spring of 1843, when he joined settlers bound for Oregon. But once the big wagon train was under way, he seized the moment and helped make history. Using his experience as a long-distance traveler in the West, he became a pilot on horseback, searching out the safest routes for prairie schooners and finding fordable sites for river crossings. At the Continental Divide, when a Hudson's Bay Company official told settlers their wagons could not negotiate the remaining mountain passes, Whitman dismissed the warning as nonsense. He said wagons had done it before and many more could do it again. Speaking from experience, he was able to persuade most of the settlers not to give up. He helped keep the wagon train from disintegrating. He delivered babies and doctored the sick.

Before the trip was over, Whitman had impressed the hard-bitten pioneers who would, in coming decades, become the founding fathers of Oregon. He did so not as a soul-saving missionary but as a trail-blazing guide, energetic physician, and jack-of-all-trades. His "great experience and indomitable energy were of priceless value to the migrating column," wrote Jesse Applegate, one of the settlers. "To no other individual are the emigrants of 1843 so much indebted."

When the journey ended, Whitman enthusiastically embraced his new identity as an impresario of American land acquisition.

"If I never do more than to have been one of the first to take white women across the Mountain & prevent the disaster & reaction which would have occurred by the breaking up of the present Emigration & establishing the first waggon road across to the border of the Columbia River, I am satisfied," he wrote Greene about a month after his return to his mission.

Five months later, Whitman convinced himself that his efforts should be rewarded. He felt he deserved a land grant from the U.S. government.

"As we have so eminantly aided the government," he wrote to Greene, "not least as I brought the last Emigrants to the shores of the Columbia with waggons contrary to all former assertions of the impossibility of the route; we may be allowed the rights of private Citizens, by taking lands in the country."

Whitman also claimed credit for weakening Great Britain's hold on Oregon, telling Narcissa's parents in a letter, "As I hold the settlement of this country by Americans rather than by an English Colony most important, I am happy to have been the means of landing So large an

Imigration onto the Shores of the Columbia with their Waggons Families and Stock all in Safety."

In that letter, Whitman abandoned all pretense that he and his fellow missionaries could—or even should—protect the Cayuses from losing their land. He made it clear that he believed Indians were doomed and that his primary responsibility as a missionary was to the white people replacing them.

"I have no doubt our greatest work is to be to aid the white settlement of the Country + help to found its religious institutions," he wrote, noting that soon "the White Settlers will demand the soil + seek the removal" of the Indians.

Good Christians need not be "anxious" about the demise of the Indians, Whitman assured his pious in-laws, because the Indians had "refused or neglected" to fulfill the "designs of Providence."

"The Indians have in no case obeyed the command to multiply and replenish the earth," he wrote. "They cannot Stand in the way of others in doing so."

About a year before Whitman hurried back to Boston, Cayuses who lived near his mission had made it clear that they no longer trusted him. They were angry about bumper crops he was raising on Cayuse land; they wanted some kind of rent or other payment. Failing that, they wanted Whitman and his wife to clear out of Cayuse country.

To enforce their demands, Telokite, the chief whom Narcissa had once regarded as friendly, released tribal horses inside Whitman's fenced-in cornfields. When the doctor complained, Telokite punched him twice in the chest and commanded him to stop talking. A few days later, Telokite ordered Whitman and Narcissa to leave the mission. In an ensuing quarrel, the chief again punched Whitman, tossed his hat in the mud, and pulled on both his ears. Not long after that, Telokite and a few of his men barged into Narcissa's kitchen, menaced her with a hammer, and threatened Marcus with an ax. "I did not challenge them nor did I want to suffer pain but still I did not fear to die," Whitman wrote a few weeks later.

Whitman's return from Boston in 1843, which ushered into Oregon more white people than the Cayuses had ever seen, deepened Indian resentment. "They fear the Americans are going to overrun the country," Whitman told Greene the year after he came back to Waiilatpu. "It is not strange at such a time that they are agitated."

Indian agitation, though, did not change Whitman's loyalties. He continued to support mass American migration into Oregon. In the autumn of 1845, when yet another wagon train neared the mission— this one the biggest yet—Whitman and his wife rushed out to meet the new arrivals with a wagon full of flour, cornmeal, and potatoes. By then, Whitman seems to have convinced himself that the Cayuses had outgrown their fear of white invaders.

"An important change for the better has taken place in regard to the conduct and disposition of the Indians," he wrote Greene. "They have shown a special spirit of forbearance toward white men in general which gives strong hope of permanent quiet."

Whitman was mistaken to the point of delusion. Less than a month after discovering a "special spirit" of restraint among the Cayuses, his life was threatened by Young Chief, one of the tribe's most powerful leaders. Whitman trembled when he wrote about it in a letter to his fellow missionaries. "I am so nervous that I cannot govern my hand So that you will excuse me," he wrote. "I might be killed on the most slight or sudden occasion."

The Cayuses had discovered an American plot to steal tribal land, Young Chief told Whitman, adding that he knew the Americans were "prepared with poison and infection to accomplish their purpose."

What's more, the chief accused Whitman of "conniving at these things" with his own secret kit of poisons and infectious agents. When Whitman pleaded ignorance of any such plans and denied owning any poisons, Young Chief calmly and curtly replied, "It is not to be expected that you would confess it even were it true."

As threats and harassment from the Indians grew more frequent and more frightening in the mid-1840s, both Whitman and Spalding began to consider abandoning their missions. After Young Chief's blood-chilling threat in October 1845, Whitman said he might move in the spring. When Spalding's mission was vandalized repeatedly in 1846, he, too, seemed to lose heart, writing that the Nez Perces were making impossible demands: "We are now called upon to pay for the water we use, the wood we burn, the trails we travel in, and the air we breathe."

But neither Spalding nor Whitman ever gave up on their missions. In large measure, it was because their Protestant blood was up. They blamed their Indian troubles on "papists."

Demonizing Catholics and discriminating against them was a time-honored American tradition. Before the First Amendment wrote religious freedom into the U.S. Constitution, all the American colonies, save Rhode Island, had laws that discriminated against Catholics, in part because they were thought to be loyal to a foreign master, the pope.

Spalding and Whitman came of age in this tradition as zealous evangelical Presbyterians in the Burned-Over District of New York. There and across New England, the pope was referred to as "the Man of Sin," and adoration of the Virgin Mary was perceived as idolatry. Violence against Catholics was not uncommon. In August 1834, a mob, acting on a rumor that a priest had imprisoned a nun, burned a Massachusetts convent to the ground.

Catholic priests had arrived in Oregon in the late 1830s and were competing aggressively with Protestant missionaries for Indian souls. More upsetting than their arrival was their effectiveness. Catholic clerics were converting Indians at a pace that far exceeded their Protestant counterparts. Compared with Spalding and Whitman, the "black robes" were much lighter on their liturgical feet. They baptized first and dispensed dogma later. They did not demand that Indians become farmers or give up their nomadic ways.

Competition for Indian converts was not gentlemanly. In their letters, priests sneered at the Protestants, calling them "selfish professors of false doctrines" and preachers of "principles of error and corruption."

Priests used visually alluring rites and rituals to win the attention of Indians. They also used an innovative teaching device called a Catholic ladder. It showed Indians a pictorial stairway to heaven while warning them to avoid the hellish errors of Protestantism. The ladders were scrolls made of durable yellow wrapping paper and inscribed with simple drawings. One ladder included the Ten Commandments, the Crucifixion, and a withered tree branch that veered away from heaven and died—this was the path of Protestants like Whitman and Spalding. A later version of the Catholic ladder was even more explicitly insulting to American Board missionaries. It included a good road from the Garden of Eden straight to redemption via the Catholic Church. The bad road led to the "pretended" Protestant reformation, the devil, and eternal damnation.

"Perhaps one-fourth of this tribe [Nez Perce] have turned Papists, and are very bitter against the Protestant religion," Spalding complained in 1847. The Cayuses, too, were susceptible to Catholic conversion, especially in tribal leadership, with some prominent families that included both Catholic and Protestant converts.

Spalding, who had an artistic wife and expertise in the printing trade, fought back by creating a Protestant ladder. For a Nez Perce to get to heaven following the Spalding ladder, he had to hew to a narrow and virtuous path. As for the broad and easy road of the papists, it was a highway to perdition, a place where the pope burned in eternal fire.

Blaming Catholics for all manner of evil would become the defining obsession of Spalding's long and angry life. Whitman was also obsessed. In nearly every letter he wrote in the 1840s, he complained that his mission was being undermined by papists. He worried, too, about white Catholic converts in Oregon and often demanded that Greene dispatch pious Protestants from New England to turn back the rising Catholic tide. After Dr. McLoughlin of the HBC converted to Catholicism in 1842, Whitman called his trusted old friend "a zealous advocate for Papacy." Anger blinded Whitman to growing danger at his mission as he ignored McLoughlin's repeated warnings that he and his wife should move immediately to safer ground.

In 1847, the last year of Whitman's life, a Catholic bishop took up residence in Fort Walla Walla, a few miles from the Whitman mission. The encroachment on his territory incensed Whitman, and he confronted Bishop Augustin-Magloire Blanchet soon after his arrival from Montreal.

"I know very well," Whitman told Bishop Blanchet, "for what purpose you have come."

"All is known," Blanchet replied. "I come to labor for the conversion of the Indians, and even of Americans, if they are willing to listen to me."

The conversation deteriorated from there. Whitman threatened never to sell any provisions to the bishop or his priests, saying that he would not feed a Catholic missionary unless he was starving. Whitman also condemned the conversion strategies of papists, especially their use of Catholic ladders. He warned the bishop that he intended to deface one with blood, to symbolize "the persecution of Protestants by Catholics."

Soon he made good on the threat, smearing blood from a butchered steer on one of the scrolls and giving it to Edward, a Cayuse leader and son of Telokite. "You see this blood!" Whitman shouted at the time, according to an account that Edward later gave to priests. "It is to show you that now, because you have the priests among you, the country is going to be covered with blood!! You will have nothing now but blood!"

While the presence of Catholic priests made Whitman and Spalding apoplectic, they were not a fundamental cause of unrest among the Cayuses. Rather, it was the endless arrival of white settlers from the United States. And Whitman was their most visible champion. Every year brought more. They appeared in Cayuse country on the road Whitman had helped to establish. He and his wife welcomed the settlers, most of whom passed through on their way to the Willamette

By 1847, there were seventy-five people living at the Whitman mission, forty-five of them children, many of whom attended a school run by Narcissa Whitman. Large numbers of white settlers arrived in Oregon every summer in wagon trains. "The poor Indians are amazed by the overwhelming numbers of Americans coming into the country," Narcissa wrote.

Scholars believe these pencil sketches are the only authentic likenesses of Narcissa and Marcus Whitman. They were drawn by Canadian artist Paul Kane at the Whitman mission in late July 1847, about four months before a small group of Cayuse warriors killed the Whitmans and eleven others.
STARK MUSEUM OF ART, ORANGE, TEXAS

Valley, by feeding them, doctoring them, and allowing orphaned children to attend school at the Whitman mission. Spalding also became a promoter of white settlement. In an 1846 letter to a wagon train leader in Indiana, he wrote this advertisement for Oregon: "Were I to select for my friends a location for a healthy happy life, and speedy wealth, it would be this country."

In the late summer of 1847, more than a thousand wagons rolled past the Whitman mission, bringing four thousand more Americans to Oregon and setting a new annual record for settlement. The white people in that one wagon train outnumbered the population of the Cayuse tribe by at least two to one.

By then, Narcissa Whitman had stopped interacting with the Cayuses. There was so much else to do. Seventy-five people lived at the mission, forty-five of them children. They had found places to sleep in the main mission house, in a nearby house for immigrants, in the black-smith shop, in a sawmill cabin, and in a small Indian lodge. Narcissa had become the foster mother of eleven children who had lost their parents on the Oregon Trail. But even she noticed the effect the biggest-ever wagon train was having on the Cayuses.

"The poor Indians are amazed by the overwhelming numbers of Americans coming into the country," she wrote in her final letter to her parents. "They seem not to know what to make of it."

CHAPTER SIX

"BEASTLY & SAVAGE
BRUTALITIES"

I n the fall of 1847, Cayuses began to die in terrifying numbers, which seemed to confirm Young Chief's intelligence. By the end of November, nearly half were dead. It was measles, still the most contagious of all human viruses. Then (as now) nine out of ten non-immune people who came into close contact with the disease got infected. In the 1840s, most white settlers had some natural resistance; they got sick but most often survived. Indians had virtually no resistance; once infected, they usually died. Their mortality rate was especially high because many had been weakened by malnutrition before the epidemic started. The previous winter had been unusually long and severe, killing large numbers of Indian horses and cattle, making game scarce, and causing widespread meat shortages.

The measles epidemic was probably not introduced to Cayuse country by that year's surge of white settlers. A raiding party of Cayuse horsemen, who in midsummer rode south on a failed mission to rebuild the tribe's cattle herd, had become infected with measles in Northern California. Some scholars believe they brought the virus back to Oregon.

None of these epidemiological details, of course, was understood at the time by Indians or by whites. What the Cayuses believed—for a constellation of reasons, some old and some new—was that Marcus Whitman was responsible for the rising number of dead Indians.

As a nineteenth-century doctor who believed in bleeding his patients and who had zero understanding of what caused measles, Whitman was treating all its victims—Indians and whites—with equal ineffectiveness. Yet many of his white patients survived, while most of his Indian patients did not.

As Whitman had described in his 1843 report to the American Board, traditional Cayuse law was clear about what should happen next. Whitman was a failed medicine man. He needed to be killed.

If there was any hesitation on the part of the Cayuses, it didn't help that, as the measles epidemic worsened, a new conspiratorial story spread among them, twisting and amplifying their long-standing suspicions and resentments. It came from Joe Lewis, an emigrant from Maine who arrived in Oregon in early November of 1847 on that year's wagon train. Part Delaware Indian, part French Canadian, he had found work at the Whitman mission and lived in a lodge a few hundred yards from the main Whitman house. He claimed to have overheard Marcus and Narcissa Whitman making a plan with Spalding to poison the Cayuses and take their horses and land.

Lewis was not the only mixed-blood immigrant stirring the pot. For many months, men of Iroquois and Delaware ancestry had been telling stories about a continent-wide, white-led pattern of murder, land theft, and forced Indian deportation that alarmed the Cayuses. These stories were not fiction, of course; they depicted the genocidal reality of official U.S. government policy toward Indians.

Now the aggrieved and mendacious Joe Lewis was convincing some tribal leaders that another vicious scheme was afoot, this one at the instigation of Spalding and the Whitmans. The proof was everywhere, Lewis said. In November, as many as five Cayuses were dying every day. If the Whitmans were killed, Lewis told the Cayuses, "the evil would be removed."

MASSACRE OF REV. DR. WHITMAN OF THE PRESBYTERIAN MISSION.

This artist's conception of the killing of Marcus Whitman was published in 1870, twenty-three years after the event.

On November 29, a cold and foggy Monday, several Cayuse men called on Whitman after lunchtime. They asked for medicine. Once inside the doctor's kitchen, some of the Indians spoke with Whitman as he sat near the cookstove. As they talked, another Cayuse, Tomahas, walked behind the doctor and pulled a tomahawk from beneath his blanket. He drove it into the back of Whitman's head. A second blow knocked him to the floor, splitting the top of his skull. Another Indian shot him in the neck.

The entire Whitman mission, on that gray November day, was

Tomahas was one of five Cayuses hanged in 1850 for the Whitman killings. Some witnesses said he struck the first tomahawk blow, which fractured Marcus Whitman's skull and started the killings at the mission. The Cayuse tribe believes the painting was completed after the Whitman killings, which accounts for the fierceness of the image.

Chief Telokite knew the Whitmans for many years and initially welcomed them. Narcissa Whitman called him a "kind friendly Indian." But he became angry with the missionaries for their refusal to pay rent and resented their role as champions of white settlement. He was one of five Cayuses convicted for killing the Whitmans and was hanged in Oregon City.

suddenly as helpless as the bleeding doctor. Waiilatpu had become a kind of refuge hospital for Narcissa's wards, orphaned students, a few hired hands, and several families recently arrived off the Oregon Trail. Many of them were sick with the measles or just beginning to recover. Besides Whitman, there were sixteen white adult men. Their arsenal consisted of a couple of rifles and a pistol, along with a few knives and axes. None of the men were trained or equipped to repel an Indian attack.

With Whitman mortally wounded, there was an eruption across the mission grounds of gunfire, war whoops, and bloodshed. The attack was on. Cayuses killed and dismembered three white men who that afternoon were butchering a steer. A schoolteacher, a gristmill operator, and a tailor were killed.

Inside the main mission house, Narcissa was in the living room—behind a closed door—when she and several of her foster children first heard shouting and gunfire. As the commotion shifted outside, she opened the door to the kitchen and found Marcus on the floor, severely wounded, bleeding profusely but not yet dead. With help, she dragged him into the living room, locked the door, and put a pillow under his head. She tried and failed to stop the bleeding from his neck wound.

Narcissa was standing near a shattered window, looking out, when a bullet struck her in the right shoulder. She stumbled backward. Surrounded by her adopted children, she began praying, saying again and again, "Lord, save the little ones." She prayed for her parents, too, saying, "This will kill my poor mother."

After panicked negotiations with the Indians and after Narcissa had become weak from loss of blood, she consented to be carried outside on a kind of sofa, supposedly for transport to a safer place.

But it was a ruse. Once she was out of doors, several Indians shot her. Others struck her in the face with a whip. They rolled her off the sofa into the mud, where she died. While the Indians were killing Narcissa, Chief Telokite found the mortally wounded Dr. Whitman and mutilated his face beyond recognition with an ax. The missionary doctor was forty-five when he died.

Narcissa, dead at thirty-nine, was the only white woman the Cayuses killed that day. She was not murdered by mistake. They spared the other white women and all the children. The other twelve victims, including Marcus Whitman, were adult white men. In the next two weeks, three others at the mission died of illness or neglect or from exposure while trying to escape. One of them was a child, Helen Mar, the daughter of Joe Meek, the mountain man who had been smitten with Narcissa when she first arrived in the Oregon Country.

The Cayuses took forty-seven hostages, including Henry Spalding's daughter Eliza, who was twelve and had recently come to the mission to attend school.

The Indians were determined to find and kill her father, who was not at the mission on Monday when the bloodletting began.

Two days later, Spalding, who happened to be in Cayuse country when the attack occurred, decided to ride to the Whitman mission. Unaware of the killings and unaware that the Cayuses wanted him dead, he sought news about the measles epidemic and the welfare of his daughter.

Three miles from the mission, he happened upon a black-robed priest. It was Father Jean-Baptiste Abraham Brouillet, one of the newly arrived Catholic missionary priests. Spalding, who had first met the priest a few days earlier, reined in his horse. The priest reached out and held Spalding's extended hand.

Brouillet had just left the mission. He had gone there the previous morning and found corpses and body parts strewn across the grounds. He also met with hostage women and children who, as he later wrote, were "in a situation deplorable beyond description." The Cayuses allowed him, as a Catholic priest from Canada, to collect the corpses and bury them in a common grave inside the mission grounds. While he was there, the priest and his Indian interpreter heard the Cayuses raging against Americans. In particular, they wanted Spalding.

Risking his own life, Brouillet left the mission with his interpreter on Wednesday morning, hoping to find Spalding and warn him. To the priest's consternation, he had a second traveling companion that day—an armed Cayuse warrior. His name was Edward (Narcissa had named him), and he was the eldest son of Chief Telokite. Edward had participated in the massacre, and he was tagging along with Brouillet in the hope that he might be able to kill Spalding, should the minister show up on the road.

Before Brouillet dared tell Spalding what had happened inside the mission, he attempted to defuse the imminent threat posed by Edward. Through the interpreter, the priest begged Edward—as a "special favor"—not to kill Spalding. The Indian hesitated, uncertain what he should do. Finally, he said he could not take responsibility for sparing Spalding. He needed to return to his camp to ask his elders for advice.

Twenty lifesaving minutes elapsed between Edward's departure for consultations and the thundering arrival on horseback of three armed Cayuses who came gunning for Spalding. During those minutes, Brouillet detailed the bloodletting that had taken place and the desire of the Cayuses to take Spalding's life.

"You have no time to spare," the Catholic told the Presbyterian.

Overwhelmed and terrified, Spalding was unsure what to do next. He asked about his daughter. The priest said she had not been harmed but was among the hostages. When Spalding asked Brouillet to look after her, the priest said he would do his best. He offered boiled beef and bread to Spalding, promised to pray for him, and once again urged him to run for his life. Spalding turned on his horse and disappeared before the Cayuse warriors arrived.

When they learned that Brouillet had warned Spalding to flee, the warriors were seriously displeased. "The priest ought to have attended to his own business, and not to have interfered with ours," they told him through the interpreter.

Brouillet began to tremble. Fearing death, he struggled to stay atop his horse. The Cayuses, in the end, did not take time to punish the priest. They raced off in search of Spalding.

ACT TWO

HANG

CHAPTER SEVEN

"PRIESTS WET
WITH THE BLOOD"

H enry Spalding called his escape "wonderfully miraculous." And it was, especially for a forty-four-year-old missionary who was not much of a horseman. He had fallen off his horse a few days before the Whitman killings, badly wrenching a knee. His Cayuse pursuers, by contrast, were superb young horsemen and experienced trackers.

As it turned out, the afternoon of December 1, 1847, was tailor-made for a mediocre rider who knew where he was going and how to get there. With heavy fog blanketing the hills, the early darkness of late autumn in the Pacific Northwest arrived even earlier that day. From countless journeys, Spalding had expert knowledge of the terrain separating the Whitman mission from his home among the Nez Perces.

Still, he barely made it.

Spalding and his horse crossed the Walla Walla River and galloped east for the foggy hills. As he later told the story—and almost certainly dramatized and distorted it—he rode all night, following the braid of a shallow stream called the Touchet. At dawn, he rested under cover of riverine bushes. Riding the second night along a streambed, he heard the snort of horses and the crack of whips. He wheeled his horse out of the water, made the animal lie down, and "seized him by the nose to prevent him from calling out to the passing horses." In the darkness, the Cayuses missed him.

The next morning, exhausted and out of food, Spalding forgot to hobble his horse before collapsing into fitful asleep. When he awoke, the animal was gone. He had well over fifty miles still to go, and he walked. His boots were too tight, and eventually he threw them away, wrapping his feet in his leggings. His blanket, soaked by rain, was too heavy, and he left it behind as well. With a bad knee, he limped and lurched the rest of the way, somehow managing to cover twenty to thirty miles a night. He hid during daylight but rarely slept, shaking "to the center of every bone with cold," he wrote. "I wanted sleep, but could get none."

It took six days—avoiding trails, walking in streambeds, yanking thorns from his mangled feet—for Spalding to make it back to Nez Perce country.

About twelve miles from home, he had to cross the Snake, the second-most-powerful river in the Pacific Northwest. It was too cold and swift to swim. He did not have the strength to gather logs for a raft. On a windy night, he searched the riverbank for a canoe and soon found several that belonged to the Cayuses. He stole one and pushed out into the wind-tossed river, which was boiling with whirlpools. To his astonishment, the canoe cut a course straight across the Snake. Spalding had to paddle only a third of the way. He suspected divine intervention.

"Ah, it is the Lord," he wrote the following year in a front-page article in the *Christian Observer*, a Philadelphia newspaper owned by the Presbyterian Church. "He knows my weak state, and has sent his angel in the storm to waft me over this river."

Among the Nez Perces, Henry and Eliza Spalding had far more friends than enemies. Those friends had rescued Eliza and her three young children in the crazed aftermath of the Whitman Massacre, when other Nez Perces and some Cayuses, riled up by the murders, surrounded and looted the Spalding mission.

By the morning of December 6, 1847, Spalding had stumbled to within two miles of his mission, where he stood on a high bluff and looked down upon his house. Nearly catatonic with fatigue, he had no idea whether his family was still alive. "Anxiety prevailed over reason," and he was overcome by morbidly detailed thoughts about Indians killing his wife. He shared those thoughts in the *Christian Observer:* "The bloody tomahawk which buried in the head of my dead sister Whitman, may have done the same dreadful work on the sacred head of my dear wife. [Ravens] may have made their last meal on the flesh of her mangled body."

After descending into a ravine and hiding for most of the day, Spalding emerged in the afternoon before the early dusk of late autumn. A Nez Perce woman who knew him and his family spotted a ragged white man. She failed, at first, to recognize the mud-caked, barefoot, near-comatose interloper as Reverend Spalding. Eventually, perhaps after getting a good look at his pale bald head, she realized it could only be him. She went for help and returned with Nez Perce Christians who were close to his family. Soon Spalding was reunited with his wife and children in a friend's cabin, under the protection of Nez Perce friends.

But they were not free to go.

News of "the horrible massacre committed by the Cayuse Indians" soon reached white settlers in the Willamette Valley, where they began to bay for Indian blood. Nez Perce leaders, who had had nothing to do with the killings, feared indiscriminate American retaliation; they held Spalding and his family as "hostages of peace." They also compelled Spalding, who feared for himself and for the lives of his family, to write a letter to Bishop Blanchet at Walla Walla begging whites not to come up the Columbia River to avenge the mission killings. Spalding asked in the December 10 letter that his plea be passed on to the Americans who were trying to raise a militia.

Blanchet, of course, was the recently arrived Catholic prelate with whom Whitman had squabbled in the months before the massacre—the "papist" whose very presence on the Columbia Plateau had infuriated Spalding. But in his letter, Spalding addressed the bishop as a "dear friend" and praised him as a kindhearted agent of peace. "I know that you will do all in your power for the relief of the captives" at the Whitman mission, Spalding wrote, and "you will spare no pains to appease and quiet the Indians." Spalding also thanked Father Brouillet, the priest who had warned him to run for his life, as "my dear friend [who] furnished me with provisions" for a successful escape.

Given his hysterical hatred of priests, it was perhaps the most insincere letter Spalding ever wrote. And the Catholics soon seized upon it as proof that they had helped save Spalding and assisted in the release of the American captives. When the letter was published the next month in the *Oregon Spectator,* the territory's principal newspaper, Spalding was embarrassed and enraged. He would quickly denounce every conciliatory and Catholic-friendly sentiment he had written in it.

S palding's ferocious disavowal of his own letter marked a turning point in his life. It signaled a profound shift in his role in making—and making up—the history of the American West. Before he wrote it, Spalding had been an exceptionally irritating, notably cantankerous, but mostly conventional Protestant missionary who by and large adhered to the doctrines and strictures of the Presbyterian Church.

In the aftermath of the letter, however, he became a conspiracy peddler, a publicity-savvy fabulist in the garb of a pioneer preacher. He began to twist and embroider his own experiences—and those of Marcus and Narcissa Whitman. He dramatized and reimagined his escape from the Cayuses. He insisted that Roman Catholic priests had instigated the killings at the Whitman mission. Spalding owed his life to a priest who—at great personal risk—warned him to run from the Cayuses. But less than a year later, in a national Protestant newspaper, Spalding published a riveting and salacious account of the massacre that blamed the murders on "Romish priests, who have lately come into the country."

As decades went by, he dreamed up new and dramatically improved versions of Marcus Whitman and his courageous wife, Narcissa.

A number of historians have speculated that Spalding lost his health, his judgment, and even his sanity after the Whitman Massacre and his harrowing flight from the Cayuses. They suggested that his rants and grievances—especially against Catholics—were symptoms of post-traumatic stress disorder of a kind typical of many American pioneers who had near-death encounters with Indians. Frances Fuller Victor, the Portland-based historian who interviewed Spalding and exchanged letters with him in the 1860s, wrote that "Mr. Spalding lives, but wrecked in health and spirits."

Yet there was a deliberate, consistent, and sustained method to Spalding's madness. After the Whitman killings, he kept at it for a quarter century, successfully marketing his exaggerations and lies to newspapers, churches, politicians, and even the U.S. Congress. His ginned-up versions of history were provocatively written, emotionally seductive, effectively timed, and cleverly demagogic. Like all successful populists, he exploited the divisions of the day: against Catholics, against Indians, against foreigners. All the while, he celebrated the courage and patriotism of white Protestants—himself, the martyred Whitmans, and his wife, Eliza, chief among them.

T he last thing the Hudson's Bay Company wanted was an all-out Indian war in the Pacific Northwest. Managers of the London-based company knew that a war would sink their decades-long investment in the region's fur trade and stir up xenophobic resentments among the Americans who kept streaming into the country. An Indian war, the company feared, would almost certainly arouse the U.S. Congress and trigger deployment of American soldiers along the Columbia.

From its regional headquarters at Fort Vancouver, on the north bank of that river, the company was now operating on land officially controlled by the United States. A treaty signed in 1846 by Britain and the United States had ended decades of joint occupancy by the two nations. It gave all the Oregon Country (up to the forty-ninth parallel, the current Canadian border) to the Americans. The treaty did guarantee continued ownership of the existing properties of the HBC, along with its rights to continue trading and navigating on the Columbia. But those rights would mean nothing if the region exploded in a war of vengeance, especially if Americans viewed the British as collaborating with the Indians.

On December 6, 1847, when a courier first brought word of the Whitman killings to Fort Vancouver, the new chief factor of the HBC moved decisively. He was James Douglas, a stout, capable, and experienced company man who had recently replaced John McLoughlin, now a landowner, miller, and merchant in Oregon City. Anticipating that Americans in Oregon would respond to the massacre by mobilizing a militia, Douglas beat them to the punch.

He dispatched three boats up the Columbia on December 7 with seventeen men who were employed by the HBC. They were led by a white-haired fur trader, Peter Skene Ogden, who had long experience with the Cayuses and with Indians across the region. Ogden's mission was limited. In an effort to forestall the Americans' rage, he was to obtain release of the hostages—the forty-seven women and children at the mission—as well as Spalding and his family and fetch them back to Fort Vancouver by boat.

Outmaneuvering the Americans was easy—at least in the short term. The provisional government of Oregon was a three-year-old, seat-of-the-pants creation of Willamette Valley settlers. It had no legal standing with the federal government in Washington, and Congress had dithered in passing legislation that would officially create an Oregon Territory. In addition, the provisional government was broke. It had $79.74 in its treasury, against debts of $4,079.74.

Once its boats had started up the Columbia to try to rescue the hostages and avert more bloodshed, the HBC released news of the Whitman killings to settlers in the Willamette Valley. As the company had feared, it triggered American fear, fury, and demands for vengeance. Within two days, Oregon's legislative assembly had voted to raise and equip fifty riflemen and send them up the Columbia. Within three days, it had voted to send another five hundred armed men "for the purpose of punishing the Indians." A week later, the assembly voted to send a messenger to Washington, D.C., to demand federal money and men in arms for the conflict with the Indians. Oregon settlers had been pleading for recognition and various kinds of help from Washington for years. Now they dared hope that the Whitman killings would finally concentrate minds in Congress.

"Having called upon the government of the United States so often in vain, we have almost despaired of receiving its protection. . . . We have the right to expect your aid [and] you are duty bound to extend it," the settlers stated in their rather petulant instructions to the messenger.

As chief messenger for Oregon, the legislative assembly picked Joe Meek, the former mountain man. A teller of tall tales who wore leather pants and had a rough-around-the-edges charisma, Meek also happened to be kin to the wife of President James K. Polk.

The man who once had been intoxicated by Narcissa Whitman was now a family man in the Willamette Valley. His daughter, Helen Mar, had been attending school at the Whitman mission when the killings occurred. She was not physically harmed, but in the ensuing days she died of measles while a hostage of the Cayuses. Her body, like many others, had been pulled by scavenging animals from a shallow grave and mutilated. On his way east to alert President Polk and Congress about the massacre, Meek visited the mission, where he identified and reburied his daughter's remains. He also helped rebury scattered pieces of Narcissa's body, whose head had been completely severed. While doing so, Meek collected tresses of her "golden hair," which have since been preserved and periodically displayed in at least six museums, university archives, and state historical societies across the Pacific Northwest.

To raise money for a war of vengeance, the provisional government of Oregon was not content to wait around for help from Washington. Settlers knew it would take a year, at best, for Meek to bring back news—and money and soldiers—from Washington. For immediate satisfaction, the Americans turned to the only outfit in the Northwest with serious reserves of money. They asked the HBC for an emergency loan of nearly $100,000—about $3.5 million today.

The answer was immediate and definitive: No. The HBC did not want war. But it also had no desire to antagonize the Americans. Responding to the loan request, Chief Factor Douglas explained that his seventeen peacemakers were already on the ground in Cayuse country, serving "the calls of humanity," working to "prevent further aggression," and certain to rescue the American women and children still being held hostage.

In a remarkably short time—before vengeful Americans in Oregon could kill a single Indian—the HBC delivered on its lofty promises, with invaluable assistance from the Catholics.

On December 20, Bishop Blanchet called five Cayuse chiefs to a mission house on the Umatilla River, a few miles south of the site of the Whitman killings in what is now the state of Oregon. The chiefs included Telokite, who took part in the mission killings, and his son Edward, who had hesitated to kill Spalding. The bishop began by explaining to the chiefs the purpose of the meeting: "avoiding war, which is always a great evil."

By the time of this gathering, Blanchet had already learned—from the soon-to-be-infamous friendly letter that Spalding had written to him—that the region's most powerful tribe, the Nez Perce, was desperate to avoid a war with whites. The bishop asked the Cayuses under what conditions they would be willing to join with the Nez Perces in making peace. After long deliberations, the chiefs instructed the bishop to inform the Americans that the Whitmans had been killed for an important reason: Dr. Whitman, his wife, and Henry Spalding had been systematically poisoning them. Nevertheless, the Cayuses said they would release their white hostages if "two or three great men" would travel from the Willamette Valley to Cayuse country and negotiate a peace.

Three days later, the HBC made its own appeal for the hostages.

Peter Ogden, leader of the company's rescue party, called Cayuse chiefs to Fort Walla Walla for a parley. Two Nez Perce chiefs also attended. The Indian leaders viewed traders like Ogden much differently than they viewed Americans, having traded amicably with him and the HBC for several decades. The Indians, in fact, wondered why the company was even involved in a fracas between them and the Americans.

Ogden was blunt with the Cayuses, much more so than Bishop Blanchet had dared to be. He made certain the Indians understood that his company's strategic interests were altogether separate from those of the Americans'. But he also cautioned the Cayuses that they had foolishly ventured to the edge of an abyss.

> We have been among you for thirty years without the shedding of blood; we are traders, and of a different nation from the Americans; but recollect, we supply you with ammunition, not to kill Americans, who are of the same color, speak the same language, and worship the same God as ourselves, and whose cruel fate causes our hearts to bleed.
>
> Why do we make you chiefs, if you cannot control your young men? . . . Your hot-headed young men plume themselves on their bravery; but let them not deceive themselves. If the Americans begin war they [the young Cayuses] will have cause to repent their rashness; for the war will not end until every man of you is cut from the face of the earth!
>
> I am aware that many of your people have died; but so have others. It was not Dr. Whitman who poisoned them; but God who commanded they should die. You have the opportunity to make some reparations. I give you only advice, and promise you nothing should war be declared against you.

The company have nothing to do with your quarrel. If
you wish it, on my return I will see what can be done for
you, but I do not promise to prevent war.

Deliver me the prisoners to return to their friends, and I
will pay you a ransom; that is all.

Cayuse chiefs wanted to hold their strongest cards—the hostages—
until American leaders agreed to a favorable peace, one that did not
demand punishment of the killers of the Whitmans. Yet the chiefs did
not want to anger the HBC, their primary source of weapons, ammunition, and gunpowder. In the end, after much argument, the Cayuses
accepted the ransom—sixty-two blankets, sixty-three shirts, twelve
guns, six hundred loads of ammunition, thirty-seven pounds of tobacco, and twelve flints. The two Nez Perce chiefs agreed to release
Spalding and his family in exchange for a similar ransom.

The Cayuses soon brought all their hostages, including Spalding's
now emaciated daughter Eliza, to Fort Walla Walla. A few days later,
the Nez Perces escorted Spalding, his wife, and their young children
to the fort. On January 2, 1848, all of the hostages and eleven other
anxious whites at the fort left by boat for Fort Vancouver, where they
arrived safely after six days on the river.

They got away in the nick of time. A few hours after the boats with
the hostages disappeared down the Columbia, fifty armed Cayuses on
horseback thundered up to the gates of Fort Walla Walla. They had
heard that armed Americans were on their way to Cayuse country.
Before riding to war, the Cayuses had come to kill Spalding.

T he rescue mission organized by the Hudson's Bay Company—
with a timely assist from Bishop Blanchet—was a complete and
astonishing success. It saved at least four times as many American

lives as were lost in the Whitman killings. But settlers in Oregon were in no mood to give credit to the British fur company or to foreign-born priests. Nor were they willing to accept the obvious and tragic cause of the Indian killings: a handful of Cayuses, panicked by an epidemic that spared whites and killed their own people, had lashed out in a spasm of violence that most members of the tribe had nothing to do with and deeply regretted.

The real story behind the killings, as settlers saw it, had to be darker and more conspiratorial.

"Where else could it be looked for except in the natural depravity of barbarians, incited, of course, by some influence not American—the French priests, or the English fur company, or both together?" wrote Frances Victor, the Oregon historian who was one of the few regional writers of her era to criticize racism and jingoism among American pioneers.

Release of the hostages failed to calm white settlers; indeed, it made them crazy with anger. For hostages told tales not only of murder but of rape. Three young white women from the Whitman mission said they had been raped by Indians during their captivity. Following the newspaper fashion of the day, the *Oregon Spectator* would not use the word "rape." It could only allude to sexual assault by speaking of "the painful intelligence that a portion of [the hostages] have been subjected to further outrage and insult—the basest—the deepest that can be conceived, and from which our mind recoils with horror."

As in the American South, where accusations of Black men raping white women often led to lynching, accounts in Oregon and across the West of Indians raping white women led to a fevered and near-universal demand for punitive war. Vengeance became a Christian obligation and a patriotic duty. "Oh, how terrible should be the retribution," the *Oregon Spectator* howled on its front page after the hostages were returned. "For the barbarian murderers . . . let them be hunted as beasts of prey; let their name and race be blotted from the face of the earth."

The alleged rape of Lorinda Bewley was a particular lightning rod. When the twenty-two-year-old blond-haired woman told her story, she implicated Catholic priests as co-conspirators.

Twelve days after the Whitman killings, Bewley was separated from the other hostages at the mission by order of Five Crows, a powerful Cayuse chief in his mid-forties. He had been schooled and baptized by Spalding, making him one of the few Cayuses to have been formally converted as a Protestant. To complement his white religion, he wanted a white wife—and the pool of young women among the hostages at the Whitman mission gave him the chance to grab one.

Bewley was sick (still recovering from measles) when she arrived at Five Crow's lodge, where she adamantly refused to have sex with the chief. At first he did not force the issue. He dropped her off at the nearby Catholic mission house, where Bishop Blanchet lived with three other priests, including Brouillet, who had saved Spalding.

In a deposition, Bewley said that when she went to the Catholic mission, she "begged and cried to the bishop for protection," but he told her that she "had better go [to bed with the chief], as he might do us all an injury" if she did not.

After allowing her three quiet days and nights in the home of the priests, Five Crows came for the young woman.

"The bishop finally ordered me to go," Bewley said. "My answer was, I had rather die. After this, he still insisted on my going as the best thing I could do. I was then in the bishop's room; the three priests were there. I found I could get no help, and had to go, as he told me, out of his room. The Five Crows seized me by the arm and jerked me away to his lodge."

The young woman's story is disputed by descendants of Five Crows, who say she willingly became his wife and reluctantly left him. At a time when white Christian society regarded such a union as an abomination, the Bewley story would seed decades of animosity and suspicion in Oregon between Protestants and Catholics—and, of course, between white and Native people.

A fter arriving in the Willamette Valley with Bewley and the other hostages, Spalding became the self-appointed expert on and national spokesman for the Whitman Massacre. His credentials for that job were impeccable. He had come west with the Whitmans, spoke an Indian tongue, and probably knew as much about the Nez Perces as any white man. He had run for his life from the Cayuses, and they still wanted to kill him. He was also among the most senior of the Protestant clerics in the Oregon Country, where white settlers were overwhelmingly Protestant.

In the first days of his new and highly visible life in the Willamette Valley, Spalding was uncharacteristically measured, even careful. He gave credit where credit was due, politely thanking Peter Ogden for saving him and the other hostages. In a letter to Greene that January, he informed the American Board that the HBC had provided "timely, prompt, judicious & Christian efforts in our behalf." Spalding also provided the board with an accurate description of the help he received from Father Brouillet in escaping the Cayuses.

But there was a limit to his fact-based gratitude. In the very same letter, Spalding said that Brouillet had baptized Cayuse children at the Whitman mission "while the hands of their parents were yet wet with the blood of their Protestant teachers"—something he could not have personally observed.

As the oracle of the massacre, he became a letter-writing, article-publishing, lecture-giving dynamo, explaining the violence at the mission to the American Board, to the families of Marcus and Narcissa

Whitman, to the people of Oregon, to the militia commanders who would soon go forth to kill Indians, and to the American people at large. In sermons, letters, and newspaper articles, he described the Whitman killings as if he had been an eyewitness.

As time went on, those accounts only grew darker, gorier, and more lurid. He let his imagine run wild: "The heavens & earth were black with ravens hovering over dead bodies." He ignored the measles epidemic as a trigger for the massacre and demonized the Cayuses, calling them "bloody savages who, without the least provocation, murdered their devoted missionaries."

Always alert to mob sentiment, he weaponized Lorinda Bewley's rape accusation, using it as an anti-Catholic bludgeon. Describing her as "an ever-to-be-pitied, amiable" victim whose rape was "the most brutal crime upon a helpless young woman ever committed," he railed against Bishop Blanchet for forcing her "into the hands of the savages." Spalding conveniently neglected to mention that he himself had baptized Five Crows.

T he commander of the Oregon people's army was Colonel Cornelius Gilliam, a veteran of wars against the Seminoles in Florida and an ordained Baptist minister. Gilliam made no secret of his dislike of Catholics, the HBC, and Indians of all tribes. In a letter to Gilliam, Spalding encouraged the colonel, as he organized the Oregon militia and prepared to wage war, to trust his prejudices while stealing as many Cayuse horses as possible. "I think but few of the Cayuse are innocent," Spalding wrote.

As for Catholics, Spalding urged the colonel to expel them from the region.

"Ask any Indian in the upper country & he will tell you the Catholic priests caused this Massacre. . . . Behold what a war in religion has done. I need not call the mind to the fact who was first on the ground. But I have said too much, though I could fill volumes with facts. But permit me to beg of you not to hurt these priests for my sake, for the sake of the interest of this country, for the honor of our holy religion.... You will doubtless require them to leave the country."

In January of 1848, as Spalding was presenting himself to Colonel Gilliam and to Oregon settlers as a stalwart champion of a vengeful war, the letter he had written to Bishop Blanchet while being held captive in Nez Perce country was published in the *Oregon Spectator*. The letter had not only pleaded with settlers not to avenge the Whitman killings but also acknowledged Spalding's debts to his "dear friend[s]" the bishop and Father Brouillet.

Embarrassed, Spalding falsely claimed he had written the letter under papal duress, while "the Bishop's foot was on my neck.... I saw my life, under God, in the hands of the Bishop and his priests."

At the same time, Spalding invented a criminal role for the Catholic clergy in the Whitman killings. Now it was not just the hands of the Cayuse warriors that were wet with blood. "I seemed to see the hands of these priests wet with the blood of my murdered associates," he wrote in February 1848.

The *Oregon Spectator* refused to publish his false and libelous claims. So Spalding published them himself, in the *Oregon American and Evangelical Unionist*, a splenetic and short-lived weekly that he helped create after shipping his printing press from Nez Perce country to the Willamette Valley.

When the Hudson's Bay Company refused to loan Oregon settlers money to fund their war, merchants and farmers decided to self-finance. Using loans and gifts, they armed and outfitted about four hundred volunteer soldiers. Spalding pledged $500 (about $16,000 today) of the American Board's money. To justify his unauthorized donation, he told board members in Boston—falsely—that many Indian tribes were uniting against whites in the Willamette Valley. "May the Lord spare this infant colony from universal massacre, but the clouds are gathering fast," he wrote to Greene.

The Oregon militia soon crossed the Cascades and moved up the Columbia. They initiated a series of skirmishes that killed more Cayuses than white soldiers and forced the Indians to retreat again and again.

Even so, Colonel Gilliam and his makeshift militia were not particularly good at soldiering. Gilliam accidentally shot himself with his own gun and soon died. For nearly two years, holdouts among the Cayuses would elude capture in the mountains of eastern Oregon, where they refused to surrender. Nor would they turn over those responsible for the murder of the Whitmans.

A fundamental problem for the Cayuses was lack of allies. Their chiefs failed to persuade the tribe's most important ally, the Nez Perce tribe, or any of the large tribes on the Columbia Plateau to join their cause. Only one small tribe, the Palouse, was willing to fight. After three months of losses and retreat, the Cayuses themselves were divided about the war, with some eager to give up the killers of the Whitmans, even as others held out in the Blue Mountains.

"I did not give my consent to the murder, neither will I protect or defend the murderers," said Chief Camaspelo of the Cayuse, at a March peace conference with Oregon militia leaders.

The Americans, however, wanted much more than to arrest, try, and hang a few Indians for murder. They wanted Cayuse land. At the meeting with Chief Camaspelo, they explained why they were entitled to take it. The Cayuses had "bad hearts," said Joel Palmer, one of the negotiators representing the provisional government of Oregon. Because of murderous and warlike behavior, Palmer said, the Cayuses had forfeited their right to live on land they had occupied for centuries.

By summer the land seizure was formalized into an official statement that alarmed the Cayuses and all the Northwest tribes that heard about it. It said that "in consideration of the barbarous and insufferable conduct of the Cayuse Indians," their land was "forfeited by them, and is justly subject to be occupied and held by American citizens."

The statement had no basis in common law or in any treaty with the Indians. A pure expression of might makes right, it enforced collective punishment for individual crimes. A century later, such an action would be characterized as a violation of the laws of war and of the Geneva Convention. But in 1848, the land seizure sent a clear message. It signaled to Indians in the Pacific Northwest that there were no rules when it came to fighting the Americans. They would take what they wanted.

CHAPTER EIGHT

A PROPER TRIAL

Nothing accelerated the settlement of the Pacific Northwest more than the killing of Marcus and Narcissa Whitman. Indeed, all across the West, a clear pattern would emerge in the wake of massacres of whites by Indians—especially if a white woman was among the victims: racial hatred was inflamed, armies were launched, and Indians were pushed off their land. Vengeful responses to white killings stirred up East Coast press coverage of the West, aroused settler interest in free western land, extended the reach of the federal government, and validated the God-wants-us-to-take-it precepts of Manifest Destiny.

Earlier than most, Henry Spalding intuited all of this. Just weeks after the Whitmans were killed, he began to write, privately and publicly, about the opportunities their deaths presented. The "tears & blood" generated by Indian killings, Spalding wrote in a letter to Reverend

Greene at the American Board, had "laid the foundations of those institutions civil & religious of which we are justly proud."

By the late spring of 1848, less than six months after the Whitmans were killed, the foundations of a new all-American Oregon were being laid. Joe Meek, who now called himself "Envoy Extraordinary and Minister Plenipotentiary from the Republic of Oregon to the Court of the United States," had arrived in Washington, D.C., aiming to bring the situation to the attention of Congress and President Polk, who was married to his second cousin.

Meek showed up at the White House "ragged, dirty, and—lousy." But he cleaned up nicely. He was tall (six feet, two inches), handsome, and amusing at dinner. He entertained Washington elites with stories

about eating his mule, marrying three Indian women, and ending a wrestling match with a grizzly bear by sinking a tomahawk in its skull.

The first meeting between Meek and the president lasted two hours, mixing family chitchat with sober discussion of Indians on the loose in the distant Northwest. The president invited Meek to stay on as a guest in the White House.

"Meek was not the sort of man to be long in getting used to a situation however novel or difficult," writes his biographer. "In a very short time he was *au fait* in the customs of the capital.

Joe Meek was a mountain man and fur trapper in the Oregon Country when Marcus and Narcissa Whitman arrived there. His daughter, Helen, was attending the Whitman mission school in 1847, when the Cayuses killed the Whitmans, and she later died there of measles. Meek became the first U.S. marshal in Oregon and presided over the hanging of the Cayuse Five.

His perfect frankness led people to laugh at his errors as eccentricities; his good looks and natural *bonhomie* procured him plenty of admirers; while his position at the White House caused him to be envied and lionized at once."

By all accounts, Meek was a mesmerizing talker. But it was the substance of his message—the awful particulars of the Whitman killings—that triggered a fundamental shift in U.S. government policy toward Oregon. In addition to detailing how the missionaries had been killed, Meek could describe how his own daughter had died as a result of the massacre. He could speak from twelve years of personal memory about how much he had admired Narcissa Whitman, whose golden hair he carried. And he could also provide an eyewitness description of the looted and burned Whitman mission, where he had reburied his daughter's remains.

In his conversations with the president of the United States, Meek had a receptive audience; the two men's interests dovetailed. An aggressive expansionist, Polk had campaigned in 1844 on a promise of ending British claims to Oregon, saying he would use force if necessary. After he won the presidency, Polk cut a deal with Britain that gave the United States nearly everything it wanted in the Pacific Northwest. But Polk's other expansionist ambitions—the annexation of Texas, in 1845, and war with Mexico, in 1846–48—had distracted Congress from acting to make Oregon an official part of the United States.

Meek's reports about the massacre and a looming Indian war gave Polk new ammunition to take to Congress. He could report that good Christian white folk were dead out west, and that more would surely die unless members of Congress stopped sitting on their hands.

The day after he spoke with Meek, Polk sent that message to Congress, declaring that Americans in Oregon were in a "perilous and distressed situation." Any delay in coming to their aid and protection, he said, "may prove destructive to the white settlements."

Congress did delay for a number of weeks, however, and Meek grew impatient. In June, he made a personal appeal to lawmakers on the front page of *The Washington Union*. Apologizing for his "uncouth bluntness," he warned, rather wildly, that Oregon was about to become "a charnel-house."

"We are at the mercy of an enemy, whose ruthless passions, drunken with blood, are too well known, in common with the most unheard-of violence, to admit the hope of peace returning once more to our borders, unless that protection is afforded us by the United States."

On August 14, 1848, Congress at last approved legislation establishing Oregon as a territory of the United States and authorizing military action against the Indians. Six hundred riflemen who had fought in the Mexican War were dispatched to Oregon from Kansas. A year and a half later, the Whitman killings continued to influence U.S. government policy, opening up a land rush for white settlers that fundamentally transformed Oregon. Congress passed the Donation Land Claim Act, a revamped version of the Oregon land claim bill that had failed to get through Congress in 1842, when Whitman rode east to save his mission. The new law gave 640 acres to white settler couples then in Oregon and 320 acres to those who could get there before the law expired in 1855. Farming families soon flooded into the territory, more than quadrupling its population within a decade. The law was racist in its language and its consequences, excluding Blacks, Hawaiians, Asians, and Indians (except "half-breed" males) from claiming land. It laid a legal foundation for many decades of racial exclusion in Oregon and sparked what amounted to a race war in the early 1850s, as white militias drove Indians off their lands.

Polk appointed his yarn-spinning distant cousin as the first U.S. marshal in the new territory. Marshal Meek arrived home in the spring of 1849, along with Oregon's newly appointed territorial governor,

Joseph Lane, a segregationist general from Kentucky who had won Polk's admiration during the Mexican War. Polk also appointed three federal judges and a U.S. attorney.

By the spring of 1850, two and a half years after the Whitman killings, all the pillars of American justice stood ready in Oregon. A proper trial in a federal territory could begin. The officers of the court lacked only for perpetrators.

D uring the intervening eighteen months, the hunt for the Cayuses had been put on hold. The primary reason: gold fever. In 1849, about two-thirds of Oregon's white male population had decamped for California, where the military governor had declared that gold in abundance could be acquired by any man with a pick, a shovel, and a tin pan. Crops rotted in the ground throughout the emptied-out Willamette Valley. The legislature did not have enough members for a quorum. Newspapers could not be printed, for lack of men to operate the presses. The ragtag fighters who had raced east to punish the Cayuses in early 1848 had turned south by 1849, racing other forty-niners from all across the country to the gold fields.

The Cayuses, meanwhile, were desperate and isolated. Before the measles epidemic ended in the spring of 1848, it had killed 197 people, about half the tribe. Those who survived on their traditional land were shunned by neighboring tribes that did not want a war with the Americans. The Cayuses were also turning on one another. Many wanted nothing to do with the handful of warriors who had taken part in the Whitman killings. Those men, still led by Chief Telokite, were hiding out in the Blue Mountains.

The stalemate ended in September 1849, when federal troops that had been dispatched nearly a year earlier arrived from Kansas and rode through Cayuse country on their way to the Willamette Valley. It was a sobering sight for the Indians: six hundred mounted riflemen and thirty-two officers in a vast wagon train with twelve hundred mules.

Suddenly the new territorial government was armed and ready for war. Governor Lane had the means to enforce collective punishment for the Whitman Massacre. In his first message to the territorial legislature, he announced that he would do just that. "The whole tribe will be held responsible," he said, until those involved in the "melancholy and horrible affair, are given up for punishment."

Governor Lane was also the federal Indian agent for the new territory, which meant he was responsible for protecting Indians and preventing whites from stealing their land and livestock. But his actions suggest that he saw it as his primary duty to show the Cayuses and all other Indians the awful price of killing white people. He told the secretary of war that if "the guilty be not punished, they will construe it as a license for the most atrocious outrages."

Once federal troops were in place in Oregon, Lane did not need to use them. The Nez Perces, the Walla Wallas, most of the Cayuses, and, after one fight with the American troops, the Palouses decided it was in their best interests to avoid all-out war by producing the culprits. In January 1850, Nez Perce and Cayuse chiefs led eighty-five warriors into the Blue Mountains to find the murderers of the Whitmans and turn them over to Lane. After a shootout that killed two of the outlaw Cayuses and led to the capture of four others, Telokite and his men fled higher into the mountains. But their horses and livestock were dying. They were low on food and ammunition. Without allies, they faced starvation.

Telokite, Tomahas (accused of fracturing Whitman's skull with a tomahawk), and about ten others surrendered to Young Chief, the Cayuse leader who had decided to cooperate with the Americans. He transported them to The Dalles, a village on the Columbia River east of the Cascade Mountains, where he turned them over to Lane and federal riflemen in April 1850. The suspects probably did not understand that they were going to be arrested and put on trial in an American court. A priest who spoke with them said they "consented to go down [the river], not as guilty, but to have a talk with whites and explain all about the murderers." They told the priest that all the other Cayuses involved in the massacre were already dead.

Lane, however, viewed his prisoners as "guilty barbarous murderers." His certainty about their guilt foreshadowed what awaited the Indians when they arrived in the Willamette Valley.

Just five Cayuses—out of the dozen or so who were believed to have taken part in the massacre—were turned over. They included Telokite and Tomahas. It is not clear why the others suspected in the killings were released. The prisoners did not include a prime suspect: Joe Lewis, the mixed-race Indian from the East Coast who had helped instigate the killings by convincing the Cayuses that the Whitmans and Henry Spalding were poisoning them to steal their land.

Lewis had been with Telokite and his men when they fled to the Blue Mountains, and had told them to stand and fight against the Americans. But Lewis had other, more profitable plans. Along with two of Telokite's sons, he had taken off for Salt Lake, bringing with him many of the tribe's best ponies. Before leaving, he promised to find Mormons in need of horses and trade for ammunition. Instead, he stole all the horses and murdered one of the chief's sons. Twelve years later, he was reported killed while trying to rob a stagecoach in southern Idaho.

For Lane, it was a shame not to have apprehended Lewis, but the newly appointed federal bosses in Oregon were happy to have five Indians in hand. Lane informed the secretary of war that he had rounded up all the living culprits. The arrests gave whites in the Willamette Valley a focus for their vengeance, and tensions eased across Oregon. Travel east of the Cascades became safer. The Indian war had been won—at least for the time being.

As Telokite traveled down the Columbia to face trial for murder, he was asked by an American guard why he and his men had surrendered. The chief understood the question, having served as an English–to–Nez Perce interpreter for Marcus Whitman's sermons at the mission. Telokite's reported reply made it clear that he had been paying careful attention during those sermons.

"Did not your missionaries tell us that Christ died to save his people? So die we, to save our people."

The trial was held in Oregon City, the territorial capital at the time. A town of seven hundred inhabitants, it squatted on the east bank of the Willamette River, beside one of the most powerful waterfalls in North America. Willamette Falls coated Oregon City in a cold mist, and the din of crashing water was sometimes so loud that people on the streets had to go indoors to make conversation. The Willamette River was flood-prone and periodically deadly, especially in the late spring and early summer, when snowmelt coursed down from the Cascades.

The territorial capital would soon be moved south to Salem, and Portland, a few miles to the north, had already become a bigger and more important center for trade, but in late May of 1850, Oregon City was still booming. Willamette Falls powered five sawmills and two gristmills. Factories made plows, bricks, saddles, and tinware. There were three large hotels, three dozen stores, more than twenty lawyers, six doctors, and the *Oregon Spectator*, the first newspaper in America west of the Rockies. Settlers rolled into the territory every year on the

Oregon Trail, which terminated in Oregon City. Six thousand more would show up that year, after the trial concluded in the late summer.

The trial of the Cayuses was held in 1850 in Oregon City, then the territorial capital and a boomtown with seven hundred residents. Built on the east bank of the Willamette River, Oregon City stood beside Willamette Falls and was often sprayed by the cold mist from the river, which powered mills in town.

Some of the settlers who had run off to California's gold fields were by now filtering back into Oregon City; a few came back with fortunes, but most came back with next to nothing. The wealthiest man in town was John McLoughlin, the Canadian-born former chief factor of the HBC. He had moved to Oregon City, where he owned most of the land, in 1845. He laid out the town's streets, built many of its mills, and lived in its grandest house, not far from the falls. He was sixty-five in the spring of 1850 and had applied to become an American citizen. He would soon be called to testify as a witness for the Cayuses in the murder trial.

The Indians still respected him as the White-Headed Eagle, and some whites honored him as the Father of Oregon. But powerful Protestant merchants resented McLoughlin for being a rich foreign-born convert to Catholicism and a known "Indian lover." They were undermining his fortune. Using legal trickery in Oregon and in Washington, D.C., they defrauded him of land he rightfully owned in Oregon City. Some of that land, including a valuable island in the Willamette River that was home to a sawmill and a gristmill, had been deeded to Joe Lane soon after the newly appointed governor arrived in Oregon in 1849. Lane was part of a generation of politicians and judges in Oregon who used government service as a launching pad for getting rich.

The rowdiest and most disruptive inhabitants of Oregon City in 1850 were the federal troops who had been dispatched by President Polk to protect it. Far from home, with no Indians to fight, young riflemen and bored officers roamed the streets of the town, drinking to excess, harassing settlers, and brawling with one another and with strangers. The *Oregon Spectator* noted their "abounding drunkenness." An inebriated major was reported to have tried to kill himself by slitting his own throat. Several dozen riflemen deserted and rode south in search of gold. When the Mounted Rifle Brigade was transferred out of Oregon City, relieved residents burned down their quarters to make sure they would not return.

At the same time, Henry Spalding was stirring up more trouble. He continued to write anti-Catholic and anti-Cayuse screeds for local newspapers and national Protestant publications. What he could not place in more established outlets, he published in the *Oregon American and Evangelical Unionist*, the notably mean-spirited newspaper he secretly co-owned.

In a territory where nine out of ten settlers were Protestant, Spalding found a receptive audience. His articles, published in the anxious months leading up to the arrest and trial of the Cayuses, spread suspicions throughout the Willamette Valley—and across the United States—that Catholic priests and HBC executives had conspired in the mission murders.

Spalding pushed so hard on these baseless conspiratorial claims that he offended and alienated his own friends. Protestant ministers who knew him were put off by his obvious lies and gore-drenched rhetoric. A number of them wrote him letters saying he was wrong to claim that the Catholics had "any direct agency" in the Whitman killings. They told him to his face that a missionary had no business "passing judgment" on the causes of the massacre. Spalding ignored their advice, claiming that "the public demanded an explanation of the matter and he was compelled to publish."

Though it was the boomtown capital of a newly established U.S. territory with a nascent justice system, Oregon City did not have a jail that could accommodate the five Cayuse prisoners. To the acquisitive new governor of the Oregon Territory, this dilemma presented a business opportunity. Joe Lane imprisoned the five Indians in a one-room house he owned. It was near Willamette Falls on the one-acre island he had recently taken off John McLoughlin's hands, thanks to his political connections. After the trial ended, Lane and his Oregon Milling Company collected a payment on the proceedings. For feeding, housing, and supplying lumber for gallows and coffins, the U.S. government paid Lane's company $98.52, about $3,000 today.

Oregon City also lacked a courthouse, so the four-day trial took place in a hotel saloon. A spectacle of a kind that had never occurred in Oregon, it drew a massive audience of nearly three hundred people. The crush of spectators, which packed the saloon and spilled out into the streets, included aging mountain men and young farm wives, military officers and local merchants, Governor Lane himself, and several Cayuse elders, including Young Chief. He had traveled to Oregon City with fifty Cayuse horses, which were to be traded to pay defense lawyers and other court costs.

Young Chief, a leader of the Cayuses, traveled to Oregon City in 1850 to observe the trial of his kinsmen. He and his men brought along fifty horses to pay defense lawyers and other court costs. Young Chief and his party left town before the hanging.

Joe Meek, in his capacity as U.S. marshal, had taken charge of the prisoners. He transported the Cayuses, shackled in chains, back and forth to the saloon courtroom from their island prison, where twenty soldiers guarded the only bridge. There were fears that free Cayuses in Oregon City for the trial might attempt a jailbreak. They never did.

The five defendants, seated at a table with their lawyers, heard the proceedings through the slow filter of two interpreters. The first translated English into Chinook Jargon, a kind of commercial language developed by whites and Indians for trade. The second interpreter converted the jargon into the Nez Perce language, which the accused Cayuses understood better. The complicated translation process often left the suspects confused, if not utterly in the dark, about what was going on around them.

There had been a handful of murder trials in the Oregon Country before it officially became a territory of the United States, but none remotely as proper as this. The principal officers of the court had been named to their jobs by the president himself. The trial observed the rituals and procedures of big-city courtrooms on the East Coast.

Everyone had to stand when the judge entered and departed the court-room. Clerks and attorneys kept detailed records of motions, witnesses, and testimony. The local newspaper provided comprehensive coverage.

The pomp and formality of the trial sent a reassuring message to white settlers from the States. They were once again living under the protection of American law. The trial sent a different message to Indians, one that was not nearly as comforting: from now on, they would be helpless pawns governed by inscrutable rules made by the same white men who were busily taking their land.

Judge Orville C. Pratt, just thirty years old, a lawyer trained in New York and Illinois, presided over the trial. He ran a tight ship, demanding silence from trial spectators. He was also pompous and greedy. Like the new governor, Pratt would use his authority and connections to get rich in the West. The judge soon acquired a multi-million-dollar fortune in real estate in California. He would go on to an infamous career as a gambler, investor, philanderer, and scandal-scarred opportunist. One contemporary in Oregon wrote that Pratt's "moral character stands very low here, it otto be rubbed up a little." As a federal judge in Oregon, Pratt was alert to the prevailing political winds. During the Cayuse trial, he bent the law—and the U.S. Constitution—to those winds.

The prosecutor was Amory Holbrook, whom Polk had named the first U.S. attorney in Oregon. Holbrook shared Spalding's rabidly anti-Catholic views. He would later join the minister as a member of the Oregon chapter of a secret nativist group: the Supreme Order of the Star-Spangled Banner, often called the Know-Nothings. It opposed and vilified Catholics, Blacks, and immigrants while supporting exclusion laws that for many years banned African Americans from living in Oregon.

Judge Pratt personally selected defense counsels for the accused.

He had a number of experienced and well-trained lawyers to choose from, including one whose father had been a law partner in Illinois with Abraham Lincoln and another who had recently defended Puget Sound Indians accused of murder. But the judge looked elsewhere.

As lead defense counsel he selected Kintzing Pritchette, who had been appointed by Polk as secretary of the Oregon Territory and was the number-two government official in the region. Pritchette had been trained as a lawyer in Pennsylvania, but his two junior defense counsels had no legal training. They were military officers stationed in Oregon City with the Regiment of Mounted Riflemen. Major Robert B. Reynolds barely spoke during the trial. Captain Thomas Claiborne made a noisy fool of himself. Both wore military dress uniforms in the courtroom, which could not have been reassuring to the Cayuses.

"Captain Claiborne led off for the defense," Joe Meek later recalled. "He foamed and ranted like he war acting a play in some theatre. He knew about as much law as one of the Indians he war defending; and his gestures were so powerful that he smashed two tumblers that the Judge had ordered to be filled with cold water for him."

In keeping with Meek's description, Claiborne was by all accounts a highly emotional champion of the Cayuses—in the courtroom and on the streets of Oregon City. He had traveled up the Columbia with the governor to arrest the Indians and apparently befriended some of them. He would not tolerate anyone who spoke ill of them in his presence.

In an "outdoor incident" that occurred while the murder trial was under way, Claiborne confronted and cursed out Spalding, who had been summoned to Oregon City as a trial witness. Spalding had "used his liberty to talk with the free Cayuses about town," the *Oregon Spectator* reported. It is not difficult to guess what Spalding might have said to the members of the tribe that had pursued him for a week after the massacre and still wanted to kill him. When he overheard Spalding's words, Claiborne told the minister to shut his mouth. As the *Spectator* described the encounter: "Captain C. disputed [Spalding's] right to converse with the free Indians, and meeting Mr. Spalding on the street, addressed him in language at once severe, profane, and improper."

The management of the newspaper, which had recently refused to publish Spalding's anti-Catholic venom, was offended that Claiborne would swear at a man of the cloth. "We wish it to be understood by all," an editorial said, "that tirades of ill feeling towards the religious teachers of the country, and especially to cast a shade over the memory of the dead, shall not pass unnoticed."

For Spalding, what did not pass unnoticed was his growing power to influence public opinion. He was a frontier celebrity, a founding father of Oregon, and a grieving friend to the martyred dead at the Whitman mission. He could make headlines whenever he wanted, shape the country's understanding of Oregon's most infamous killing, invent a heroic persona for Marcus Whitman, and vilify the Catholic clergy as criminals who took their orders from Rome.

In a prophetic letter he wrote to a Protestant friend soon after the well-publicized shouting match, Spalding embraced his new powers:

"While the public mind is awake to know the history of the Massacre & the probable causes that led to it may we not with great advantage throw before them the thrilling fact of the subject of Romanism. . . . Our beginning is small but we may be able to do better in a few years."

J udge Pratt ordered Marshal Meek to round up a few dozen "good and lawful" men as candidates for a twelve-man jury. Many settlers, though, did not want to serve. It took Meek several days and much effort to locate the twenty-four jury candidates he ushered into the courtroom. Within a few hours, defense lawyers dismissed twenty as unacceptable, and the prosecution dismissed two. Running out of potential jurors, Meek had to improvise: he grabbed men who had wandered into the saloon as spectators.

One of them was Anson Sterling Cone, age twenty-three. A native of Indiana, he had arrived in Oregon by wagon train in the autumn of 1846, a year before the Whitmans were killed. The first man Cone met in Oregon was Marcus Whitman, when Cone went to his mission to ask for a job. Instead of employment, Dr. Whitman gave the young man a packhorse, food, and provisions for a new life in the Willamette Valley. He told Cone he could pay it back later.

"He was a good man," Cone recalled. "He had a heart like an ox!"

His high opinion of Whitman did not—in the eyes of the court— disqualify Cone from judging Indians accused of murdering the missionary.

With a jury impaneled, it was time to begin calling witnesses. But before the prosecution could call its first witness, Judge Pratt had to deal with what to him must have seemed an irritatingly clever defense motion. It claimed that no American court had jurisdiction over the Whitman Massacre, because the killings had occurred on land that at the time was not subject to the laws of the United States.

The defense argued that the Whitman mission was outside the vast region of the West that Congress had designated as "Indian Country" and over which the U.S. government claimed sovereignty. The western edge of Indian Country, under federal law, stopped at the Rocky Mountains.

This meant that the killings had occurred in a North American no-man's-land, as far as the U.S. legal system was concerned. Therefore, the defense argued, the accused murderers should be "subject to the laws and usages" of the "free and independent Cayuse nation," where the killings occurred. The defense also argued that those laws and usages allowed Cayuses to kill medicine men deemed to be incompetent, as tribal chiefs had deemed Dr. Whitman. (To this day, the Cayuse people believe this argument was historically sound and should have led to the acquittal of the accused men.)

In response to the defense motion, Pratt delivered what a newspaper reporter described, rather ambiguously, as "a labored and very lucid opinion of the whole matter." Then he dismissed the motion and moved forward, aware, no doubt, that if he freed the Cayuses on a legal technicality, the people of Oregon would probably have hanged the Indians anyway and forever regarded the judge as an overeducated fool.

In the weeks leading up to the trial, prosecutor Holbrook had summoned more than twenty witnesses. Seven gave testimony before the grand jury that indicted the Cayuses. But Holbrook decided to call only four of them as witnesses in the public trial. He did not call Eliza Spalding, the reverend's daughter, even though she was the only white survivor of the massacre who was fluent in Nez Perce. She would have been able to tell the court what the Indians were saying before, during, and after the massacre. Holbrook decided, too, against calling fifteen-year-old Catherine Sager, whose detailed writings about the massacre would prove helpful to generations of historians. The prosecutor also chose not to call an adult woman, Mary Saunders, who had witnessed much of the killing and helped calm the Cayuses so they would not kill more women or any children.

In his book about the trial, Ronald B. Lansing, a law professor and historian, speculated that these three potential witnesses—and former captives—were kept off the witness stand because they were all somewhat sympathetic toward the Cayuses: Eliza Spalding thought of the Indians she had grown up with as human beings. Catherine Sager said she felt sorry for Telokite and his collapsed world. Mary Saunders said the Indians had always treated her "with decency and respect."

The four witnesses Holbrook called to the witness stand were less sympathetic to the Indians. But their testimonies proved vague, inconclusive, and contradictory.

The first witness was Eliza Hall, a widow whose husband had drowned trying to escape the Cayuses on the day of the massacre. She testified that she saw Telokite—from a distance that was later measured at about 120 yards—strike Marcus Whitman three times in the face with a hatchet as the doctor lay on the ground outside his mission house. Under cross-examination, however, she acknowledged that her view of the hatchet attack was obstructed by other Indians moving around in her line of sight.

Hall's testimony differed from that of Lorinda Chapman (the former Lorinda Bewley, who said she had been raped by Cayuse chief Five Crows). She was upstairs in the Whitman house, sick with the measles, when she said she heard gunfire and other noises coming from the kitchen. That's where she believed Marcus Whitman was attacked and mortally wounded. She said she saw the bleeding doctor dragged from the kitchen to the living room, where she last saw him alive, though mortally wounded. She added that she believed she heard Telokite's voice but did not see him during the attack.

A third witness, Elizabeth Sager, a younger sister of Catherine who was ten at the time of the killings and was inside the Whitman house during the attack, also said she had not seen who killed Marcus Whitman. She testified that she saw one of the Cayuse defendants, Isiaasheluckas, shoot a white man on the mission grounds.

The fourth witness for the prosecution was Josiah Osborne. He had survived, along with his wife and three children, by hiding under the loose floorboards in a ground-level room of the Whitman house. Since he was hiding at the time of the attack, he saw little of it. He could not link any of the accused Cayuses to any murder.

Osborne's testimony, in fact, seemed to help the defense's claim that the massacre was a tragedy caused by fear, panic, and cultural misunderstanding. Osborne said that on the morning of the murders he had talked with Dr. Whitman about the worrisome number of Indians who were dying of measles. During their conversation, Whitman had said that the Cayuses believed he was a "sorcerer" and that he was giving the Indians "different medicines from those he gave whites." Whitman also said that he had been explicitly warned by the Cayuses that he "would be killed at some time."

One of the five Cayuse defendants, Kiamasumkin, was not mentioned in the testimony of any witnesses, except that of Lorinda Bewley Chapman, who remembered seeing him at the mission on the day of the killings. She did not, however, see him hurt or threaten anyone. Marshal Meek's own brother, Stephen, believed that Kiamasumkin was completely innocent and that he had been handed over by Cayuse tribal leaders merely to satisfy white demands for culprits.

Judge Pratt hurried the trial along, packing all witness testimony into a single afternoon. The first of three witnesses for the defense was John McLoughlin, the white-haired eminence who had lived in Oregon longer than any other white person in the courtroom.

McLoughlin testified that when he was in charge of the HBC at Fort Vancouver, he had frequently warned Marcus and Narcissa Whitman about the risks of living with the Cayuses. He said he had invited the missionaries to come and live with him at Fort Vancouver. He wanted them to stay away from the Cayuses for at least two years, he said, until the Indians calmed down and invited them back. Finally, McLoughlin said he had specifically warned Dr. Whitman not to give any medicine to the Cayuses, because "they killed their medicine men."

The second defense witness was Chief Stickus, an elderly Cayuse leader who had known the Whitmans for a decade and had remained friendly with them. Through the two interpreters, Stickus said he warned Dr. Whitman the night before the murders that the Cayuses were "talking bad" about him and that he was in extreme danger.

Before Stickus left the witness chair, defense attorney Pritchette asked him if it was "the Custom and usage of the Cayuse nation to kill their bad medicine men."

The prosecution strenuously objected to the question, and Pratt did not allow the witness to answer it. The judge apparently did not want the jury to conclude that the Indians who killed the Whitmans had acted in accordance with the laws and traditions of their tribe.

The final witness for the defense was Reverend Spalding. As nearly every white settler in Oregon would have known, the minister had been fulminating for months in the newspapers and from the pulpit about the Whitman Massacre. At the end of a very long day in the courtroom, neither the defense counsels nor the prosecutor dared ask open-ended questions of Spalding, who was righteously long-winded even while being sworn in by Judge Pratt. When asked if he would promise to tell the truth, he replied, "I do so swear upon the Holy Evangelists of Almighty God."

The defense and prosecution asked tightly focused questions of Spalding. In response, he said only that he had been with Dr. Whitman on the night before the killings and that he heard about the Cayuse plan to kill the missionaries. He offered no evidence against any of the five individuals on trial for murder.

On the morning of the final day of the trial, Judge Pratt gave extraordinary—indeed, outrageous—instructions to the jury. He said that since the five suspects had been turned over to the court by the Cayuse people, the jury could properly conclude that those suspects were guilty of murdering the Whitmans. "The Cayuse people know best who were the perpetrators of the massacre," Pratt said.

The defense strongly objected—and for sound legal reasons. Pratt's instructions to the jury ignored the Sixth Amendment to the Constitution, ratified in 1791, which guarantees defendants the right to confront witnesses against them. Pratt's instruction also ignored the common-law prohibition against using hearsay as evidence in a criminal case.

In a motion for a new trial, the defense said that "there was no evidence before this court that the Cayuse nation had surrender[ed] the Defendants as the murderers." The defense also said that Pratt had no right to communicate this claim to the jurors as an "official fact."

The motion went nowhere.

The jury returned a verdict after deliberating for an hour and fifteen minutes. It found the five Cayuses guilty.

CHAPTER NINE

FIVE AT ONCE

J udge Pratt did not waste time. On May 24, 1850, the day the jury found the five Indians guilty of murder, he sentenced each one to be "hung by the neck until you are dead." Besides being swift, his sentence was exacting. It instructed Marshal Meek to guard the Indians "until Monday the 3d day of June A.D. 1850, and on that day at the hour of two o'clock in the afternoon" Meek was to hang all five of them at once. When interpreters explained the sentence, two Cayuses showed no reaction. But the other three, as Meek described the scene, "were filled with horror and consternation they could not conceal."

As warrior horsemen, the Cayuses were aggressive, violent, and proud of it. To acquire horses, slaves, and other wealth, they killed and risked being killed. They shot, knifed, and tomahawked their enemies. But they did not hang them. Nor were they hanged by their enemies. The idea of being choked to death at the end of a rope struck the convicted Indians as inhumane, terrifying, and insulting. In the days after the judge's sentence—indeed, all the way to the gallows—they complained bitterly about the indignity of hanging to anyone who would listen.

"They grew very much excited when told their doom," remembered Eliza Spalding, the reverend's daughter, who attended the Cayuse trial and the hanging. "They said they wouldn't mind being shot, but to die by the rope was to die as a dog and not as a man."

The ten-day delay between Pratt's sentence and the hanging was a matter of logistics. The handful of previous court-ordered hangings in Oregon had been of the rope-and-tree-limb variety. Proper gallows, with a scaffold and a trapdoor, had never been built in the territory. Carpenters needed time to design and build one large enough for five simultaneous executions.

The delay, though, has proved illuminating for historians. It gave the Cayuses, who by then had nothing to lose, an opportunity to explain the fundamental reason for the Whitman killings. One of their confessors was their jailer, the ubiquitous Joe Meek.

> At Oregon City, Meek had many conversations with [the convicted Indians]. In all of these they gave but one explanation of their crime. They feared that Dr. Whitman intended, with the other whites, to take their land from them. . . .
>
> And they were told by Jo Lewis, the half-breed, that the Doctor's medicine was intended to kill them off quickly, in order the sooner to get possession of their country. None of them expressed any sorrow for what had been done.

The Cayuse belief that the Whitmans were colluding with other whites to steal Indian land is at odds with how history—white history, at least—would remember the missionary couple.

During the trial and for nearly a century afterward, the Whitmans were portrayed as selfless martyrs who sacrificed everything to bring God's love to heathens.

But some of the Indians' harshest judgments of the couple were affirmed in a letter written six months before the trial by a white Protestant missionary who knew the Whitmans well.

The letter's author was the Reverend Henry Kirke White Perkins, originally from Maine. During the late 1830s and '40s, Perkins and his wife, Elvira, were stationed at a Methodist mission near the Columbia River, about 160 miles west of the Whitmans. Reverend Perkins met Dr. Whitman in 1838, and the two remained friends until the massacre. Narcissa moved in with Perkins and his wife in 1842, when Marcus rode to the East Coast. For nearly a decade, Narcissa exchanged letters with Elvira Perkins. Narcissa's sister Jane Prentiss later wrote to Reverend Perkins, asking him if he could shed light on the causes of the killings. His reply must have shocked her.

Narcissa had been ill-suited for missionary work, Perkins wrote, and the Cayuses deeply resented her. Perkins said the Indians judged her as "proud, haughty, as far above them. . . . She wanted something exalted. . . . She loved company, society, excitement & ought to have always enjoyed it. The self-denial that took her away from it was suicidal."

His critique of Marcus Whitman was more detailed and much harsher. And it eerily foreshadowed statements the five condemned Cayuses made to Meek as they waited for the gallows: Perkins insisted in his letter that if Marcus Whitman had been more of a loving missionary to Indians and less of a boosterish land agent for whites, the Cayuses would not have killed him.

Dr. Whitman in pursuing his missionary labors never so identified himself with the natives as to make their interests paramount. He looked upon them as an inferior race & doomed at no distant day to give place to a settlement of enterprising Americans. . . . Indeed it might almost be doubted whether he felt half the interest in the natives that he did in the prospective white populations. He wanted to see the country settled. The beautiful valley of the Walla Walla he wanted to see teeming with a busy, bustling white population. Where were scattered a few Indian huts, he wanted to see thrifty farm houses. Where stalked abroad a few broken-down Indian horses, cropping the rich grasses of the surrounding plain, he wanted to see grazing the cow, the ox, & the sheep of a happy Yankee community. With his eye bent on this he was willing meantime to do what he could incidentally, for the poor, weak, feeble doomed [Cayuses]. . . .

And in meeting death in the way he did, it might be said with more truth that he died a martyr to the progress of American civilization than to the cause of Missions.

Had Dr. Whitman given himself up wholly to the interests of the natives, with all his natural unfitness for the place he occupied, he no doubt would have been safe, as safe as anywhere in Christendom.

After the trial but before the hangings, Protestant and Catholic clerics visited the condemned Indians. Henry Spalding ventured out to their island jail, offering to pray with them. They told him to go away. Spalding did not mention the rebuke in his writings, but as a man sensitive to slights and prone to resentment, he surely never forgot it.

The prisoners were more welcoming to Catholic archbishop Francis Norbert Blanchet, brother of the bishop who had established a mission in Cayuse country. The archbishop visited the Cayuses twice daily, from the sentencing to the morning of the execution, trying to teach them the meanings of Catholic sacraments and preparing them for death. On the morning of the hangings, Blanchet and another priest conducted mass, baptized the Cayuses, confirmed them as members of the church, and christened them with names for the afterlife— Andrew, Peter, John, Paul, and James.

The archbishop's obsessive focus on the condemned Indians suggests that they had become pawns in a sectarian fight. By the time of the hangings, Spalding's wild claims that priests had conspired to kill the Whitmans had persuaded many Protestant settlers to blame papists for Indian trouble. The Catholic clergy, meanwhile, was profoundly offended by Spalding's writings. In his memoirs, Archbishop Blanchet seems to gloat when describing how the condemned Cayuses refused to meet and pray with Spalding. Blanchet saw it as a telling measure of the failure of Protestant missionaries like Spalding and Whitman to convert Indians or secure their loyalty. "Such were the fruits of the eleven years of the doctor's teaching," Blanchet wrote.

T he afternoon of the hanging was unusually hot, with no wind. Between one and two thousand spectators—as much as a sixth of the twelve thousand whites in the territory—pressed into Oregon City under a cloudless sky. Amid fresh rumors that Indians might attempt a rescue, men from the countryside brought rifles. To maintain an appearance of calm, many hid their guns on the edge of town.

Carpenters had erected the gallows at the far south end of Main Street, near the river and the roar of Willamette Falls. The scaffold was close enough to John McLoughlin's mansion that his family could watch the hanging from their windows. Meek, riding a white horse and carrying a tomahawk in his belt, led the condemned Indians off their island prison in a procession that included soldiers from the Regiment of Mounted Riflemen and the archbishop. They walked across the bridge and into the noisy crowd that surrounded the gallows.

Conspicuously absent were the free Cayuses who had traveled to Oregon City to observe the trial. Young Chief and others who had helped arrest the five defendants had returned home. They are believed to have been alarmed by the death sentences and afraid that they might be next.

According to Meek, only one defendant claimed innocence to the end: Kiamasumkin. The evidence against him was particularly thin. No witness identified him as a participant in the massacre. On the gallows, he begged Meek to kill him with a knife rather than allow him to hang. His final plea of innocence, made on the eve of his death, was heart-wrenching: "I was not present at the murder nor was I any way concerned with it. I am innocent—it hurts me to talk about dying for nothing. . . . The priest says I must die tomorrow. . . . This is the last time that I may speak."

According to the *Oregon Spectator*, Chief Telokite pleaded "earnestly to be shot, as hanging, in his view, was not only an ignominious fate, but not in exact accordance with the true principle of retributive justice." Telokite and the others had argued—to no avail—that since they had not hanged any white people at the Whitman mission, white people should not hang them.

Standing on the gallows, Telokite refused for a time to allow his hands to be tied. He acquiesced only after the archbishop held up a crucifix. The only Indian who spoke loudly enough from the gallows to be heard by the crowd was Tomahas, the tallest and most physically imposing of the group. He was the one, witnesses said, who first struck Marcus Whitman. Even before the killings, Tomahas had a reputation as a ferocious warrior and a dangerous man. Some in his tribe called him "the Murderer." On the day of his death, Tomahas took a turn at peacemaking.

"*Wáaqò láwtiwaama*," he said, "*wáaqò láwtiwaama*": "Now friends, now friends." The sacrifice he and the other Cayuses were about to make, he seemed to be saying, should satisfy white demands for vengeance and signify the start of a new chapter of friendship between Indians and settlers. It was a laudable, if desperately vague, sentiment from a doomed man. And it would not prove prophetic.

After Meek fitted the five nooses, he gave an impromptu benediction: "The Lord have mercy on your souls," he said. Then he swung his tomahawk, cutting the rope that secured the trapdoor beneath the Indians' feet. Meek watched as the five Cayuses "hung in the air." Three died instantly, their necks broken, as the priests together prayed: "Onward, onward to heaven, children: into thy hands, O Lord Jesus." The other two thrashed about on the ends of their ropes for about fourteen minutes, when the fourth finally died.

Meek assisted in speeding the death of the last Cayuse. It was Tomahas, who Meek believed "had been cruel to my little girl at the time of the massacre. So I just put my foot on the knot to tighten it, and he got quiet."

T he white victims of the Whitman Massacre had played a pivotal role in the creation of a continental United States. Their deaths helped bring Oregon into the union.

The five Cayuses who died on the gallows in Oregon City were collateral casualties of nation-building. As Frances Fuller Victor explained, they were "martyrs to a destiny too strong for them, to the Juggernaut of an incomprehensible civilization."

Their execution was like a carnival event. Many in the crowd in

Oregon City reportedly enjoyed watching them die. The Indians were "hanged, greatly to the satisfaction of the ladies, who had traveled so far to witness the spectacle," according to the *New York Tribune*. Some spectators got drunk and created a disturbance.

But others were depressed, even disgusted, by what they saw. In a diary entry on the evening of the hanging, a local minister in Oregon City described the event as a "sad spectacle. I was not near, but saw the people coming away. Not much levity manifest." Samuel L. Campbell, a mountain man who knew the Indians who died that day, was among the dispirited. "I truly hoped after seeing this execution," he wrote, "that I would never see another hanging."

The execution of the Cayuse Five, however, would mark a beginning, not an end.

Mass public hangings of Indians would proliferate across the West. As a response to Indian attacks on settlers, they were viewed as smart policy and good politics: calming white folks down, slaking public thirst for vengeance, and celebrating white Christian dominance over savagery. They also won votes for politicians and increased local faith in army commanders. Hanging Indians—and sometimes leaving them to decompose on the rope—was believed by some to be a teaching event. It supposedly showed Indians who was in charge and demonstrated to white Americans that it was becoming safer to settle in the West. In the decade after the executions in Oregon City, white settlers flooded into the Pacific Northwest, vastly outnumbering the Indigenous people. By 1860, when the U.S. Census first counted the population of the new state of Oregon, it made a desultory attempt to include American Indians but found just 177 and 52,160 whites. In fact, there were several thousand Indians in the state, but the census did not count them unless they were paying taxes. Most had been or soon would be moved to reservations, where they did not qualify for enumeration.

There was a consistent pattern to white conquest in the West over the next four decades—and the Whitman Massacre helped establish the template. The process began with white provocations of Indians—land seizures, bullying treaty agreements, and broken promises about compensation. This, in turn, provoked Indian attacks on whites, which provoked government-sanctioned white vengeance, the scale of which was often grossly disproportionate to any Indian violence. Then, once the Indians were neutralized, ever larger waves of white settlers poured in.

The pattern was particularly brutal in California, where the Indian population plummeted from about 150,000 in 1846 to about 30,000 in 1864. Disease caused many of the deaths, but so did a policy of "extermination," which included state-funded murder of men, women, and children of the Yuki tribe in Northern California. In twelve years, by the most conservative estimates, the tribe's population was reduced by 90 percent, from 6,000 to 600. After California became a state, in 1850, its residents lynched at least 141 Indians across the state. Lynching increased when Indians resisted white efforts to take their land. Instead of finding and punishing an individual Indian suspected of killing a white person or stealing his cattle, a group of white settlers would go after the band or tribe of an accused Indian—and hang one or more of its members, regardless of the individual's guilt or involvement. A temporary eruption of idealism in the California State Legislature in 1855 gave Indians the right to testify against whites in criminal trials, but this was crushed beneath the reality of extralegal Indian removal in 1863, when the legislature banned Indians—along with Chinese and "Mongolians"—from testifying against whites.

In Texas, in the name of protecting white women and children, settlers refused to allow Indians to live anywhere in the state, including reservations. By 1850, vigilantism and lynching had chased most Indians out of the state. The 1900 census showed only 470 Indians in all of Texas.

But it was in Minnesota that the rituals of white conquest turned into a one-of-a-kind pageant of death and revenge. There, the body count would set records—both for the number of whites murdered and for Indians hanged—and an explicit policy of Indian extermination and removal would find expression in state and federal law, and be rigorously enforced.

The federal government began the provocations in Minnesota in the 1850s with a series of treaties that dispossessed and infuriated the Dakota Indians (also called the Eastern Sioux). The treaties forced them to give up most of their land. In return, the government promised annual payments of cash, food, and other supplies. But the payments were rarely made, mostly because they were stolen by corrupt agents of the federal Office of Indian Affairs.

Like the Cayuses, the Dakotas were expected by whites to give up their mobile culture of hunting and gathering to become farmers of row crops. They were ordered to live on ever smaller tracts of land, where they could not find enough game to hunt, where they could not gather or grow much food, and where white settlers kept grabbing parcels for themselves. Malnutrition and starvation spread among Dakota women, their children, and the elderly. Rage spread among young Dakota men.

In May 1862, President Abraham Lincoln, consumed by the Civil War, then in its second catastrophic year, heedlessly ratcheted up the sense of panic and desperation among the Dakotas when he signed the Homestead Act. For a $10 fee, it offered 160 acres of land to every adult American not fighting for the South in the Civil War. All they had to do was travel west, grab land other whites had not previously taken, put up a structure, and maintain a presence on their homestead for five years. Thousands of American families headed for Minnesota.

In early August, as ever more whites poached Indian land, as federal Indian agents continued to steal annual payments, and as starvation increased, the Dakotas struck back. They attacked white family farms and small towns. During a month of raids, they killed between 625 and 800 people, most of them unarmed civilians. About a third of them were children under the age of ten, many of them from newly arrived settler families. It was the largest white death toll in any Indian war in the history of the United States.

"A most frightful insurrection of Indians has broken out along our whole frontier," Minnesota's secretary of state wrote in a telegram to the War Department in Washington. "Men, women, and children are indiscriminately murdered." State and national newspapers carried stories of "shocking barbarities" committed by the Dakotas. Some were exaggerated, but many were horribly real.

The Dakota war demanded and won Lincoln's attention, and by early September he had made winning it a national priority. By the end of September, state and federal forces had crushed the uprising. Then the machinery of legalized white vengeance shifted into high gear.

"The Sioux Indians of Minnesota must be exterminated or driven forever beyond the borders of the state," Minnesota governor Alexander Ramsey told a special session of the state legislature. "The public safety imperatively requires it. Justice calls for it. Humanity itself, outraged by their unutterable atrocities, demands it. The blood of the murdered cries to heaven for vengeance."

Vengeance was quick and thorough, with the guidance of the U.S. government, whose agent for the Sioux in Minnesota listed proposed strategies for dealing with Indians that included "extermination, massacre, banishment, torture, huddling together, killing with small-pox, poison, and kindness."

A military commission took over the administration of justice, such as it was. In trials that sometimes lasted ten minutes or less, the commission convicted and sentenced as many as 40 Indians a day to death by hanging. In its final ten days of work, the commission judged 250 cases. Many Dakotas were "condemned on general principles" rather than evidence, according to Stephen Riggs, a missionary turned prosecutor. The military commission sentenced a total of 303 Dakotas to hang.

That number, though, would be reduced by Lincoln after he came to understand that mere Indian resistance to white encroachment had been deemed a crime worthy of death. In deciding who should and should not be hanged, Lincoln drew a distinction between those who took part in massacres or raped white women and those who merely fought in battles. He told the U.S. Senate he was "anxious not to act with so much clemency as to encourage another outbreak on one hand, nor with so much severity as to be real cruelty on the other."

Advised that these kinds of lawyerly distinctions would cost him dearly in the election of 1864, Lincoln replied, "I could not afford to hang men for votes."

On December 26, 1862, in Mankato, Minnesota, four thousand civilians gathered around a giant scaffold, awaiting a mass hanging. The event had had to be postponed until after Christmas because there was not enough rope for all the nooses. As fourteen hundred soldiers stood guard, Minnesotans jockeyed for the best sight lines, climbing buildings and sitting on roofs. Soon the trapdoors fell, and thirty-eight Dakota men were hanged. After his rope broke, one man had to be rehanged. It remains the largest mass execution in American history.

On the evening of the hanging, almost as soon as the thirty-eight corpses had been dumped into a mass grave, a team of doctors dug them up and hauled them away for use as medical cadavers. The lead doctor was William W. Mayo, famous for establishing a medical practice that would become the Mayo Clinic.

In the weeks and months after the mass hanging, Minnesotans and their politicians also demanded collective vengeance against all

Dakotas. About sixteen hundred of them, mostly the elderly, women, and children, were marched more than a hundred miles to an internment camp. En route and at the camp, about three hundred Indians died of hunger, disease, exposure, and vigilante attacks. The rest were banished to Dakota and Nebraska territories.

In the spring of 1863, a federal law—the Dakota Expulsion Act—abrogated all existing treaties with the tribe and made it illegal for any Dakotas to live in Minnesota. To make certain all Dakota men had vacated his state, Governor Ramsey put out a $25 bounty on their scalps.

The mass cleansing of Indians, together with the federal Homestead Act, remade Minnesota as peaceful, prosperous, churchgoing farm country. Between 1850 and 1870, the population of the state grew more than 7,000 percent, from 6,077 to 439,706.

The pattern repeated itself again and again across the West. Indians were provoked. They fought back. They were punished with extreme prejudice and expelled from their own lands. When asked to investigate Colorado's Sand Creek Massacre—the mass killing and mutilation in 1864 of Cheyenne and Arapaho women and children by the U.S. Army—a major general in Kansas told his boss in Washington that white vengeance was too strong to stop: "The popular cry of settlers and soldiers on the frontier favors an indiscriminate slaughter, which is very difficult to restrain."

When it came to hanging Indians, the popular cry could also become official U.S. Army policy. In Special Order No. 11, Colonel Thomas Moonlight ordered an "example" hanging of two Oglala Lakota Sioux chiefs at Fort Laramie, Wyoming.

In May 1865, the two chiefs—Two Face and Black Foot—had arrived at Fort Laramie with a captive white woman, for whom they hoped to collect a reward. About a year earlier, the woman, Lucinda Eubank, had been captured in a raid on her family's farm by a band of

Cheyennes. They had killed her husband, raped her repeatedly, and then sold her to the two Oglala chiefs. Now the chiefs had brought the woman to Colonel Moonlight, hoping to secure his good opinion and perhaps receive a rumored cash reward.

But the colonel concluded—despite considerable evidence to the contrary—that the two chiefs had been her kidnappers and tormentors. Moonlight ruled that they needed to be hanged in a way that would teach other Indians to behave. His special order spelled it out, saying they would be "an example to all Indians of like character, and in retaliation for the many wrongs and outrages they have committed on the white man."

Moonlight insisted that the Indians, once hanged, should remain on public display for several weeks. "The execution will be conducted in a sober soldierly manner and the bodies will be left hanging as a warning to them," his order said. Moonlight later served as the Kansas secretary of state and was appointed governor of the Wyoming Territory.

N ot being left for days at the end of a rope in Oregon City may have been the one mercy the five hanged Cayuses were shown. They were cut down after about forty-five minutes, placed in a wagon, and hauled to the edge of town, where they were buried in an unmarked grave.

Once hanged, Telokite and his compatriots became an afterthought to the white people of Oregon. The precise location of their remains was of no great interest to the territorial government or its officials— and it was never officially recorded.

Hoping to bring the remains back to Cayuse country, the tribe has made many inquiries over the years. But state and local officials have said they do not know where the graves are. Based on oral histories, old newspaper stories, and a 1929 aerial photograph, local historians say that the suspected burial site is a parcel of land that was once a peach orchard. It now belongs to the transportation department of Clackamas County, Oregon. The remains of the Cayuse Five—perhaps in the wooden coffins that Governor Lane sold to Marshall Meek at a profit—may lie underneath what is now a gravel and sand storage shed.

No one, so far, has seriously looked.

CHAPTER TEN

"SEEING THAT THEY
STOOD ALONE"

A fter the hanging in Oregon City, a different kind of noose
began to tighten around the necks of Indians in the Pacific
Northwest. White settlers rushed into the Oregon Territory, drawn west by the free land made available by the Donation
Land Claim Act, which Congress approved four months after the
Cayuses were cut down from the gallows. In just three years, nearly
twenty-four thousand settlers showed up, and Indians became a minority in their own land.

Pressure on small tribes like the Cayuses and the Walla Wallas,
with about six hundred total members, was particularly acute. Their
lands in the Blue Mountains and the Walla Walla Valley were extensive, fertile, and tantalizing to white ranchers and farmers, thousands
of whom were passing through Cayuse country on their way to the
Willamette Valley. Their property "contains more good tillable land
than there is in the four New England states—Connecticut, Vermont,

New Hampshire and Rhode Island," the superintendent of Indian affairs for Oregon wrote to his boss in Washington in 1851, who added that, as "these tribes have become so nearly extinct, I suggest the propriety of early provision being made by Congress for purchasing their lands." Three years later, as white settlers continued to roll in, another superintendent of Indian affairs said it was all but impossible to "restrain our enterprising citizens" from stealing Cayuse land.

Across the Northwest, conflict broke out between encroaching whites and nervous Indians. On the Oregon Trail in present-day Idaho, Shoshone Indians killed eighteen whites after one of the Indians was shot for trying to steal a horse. White settlers were killed by Indians near Seattle, which resulted in the lynching of an Indian who may or may not have been responsible. Meanwhile, gold discoveries lured whites into Yakama country, north of the Columbia River. Whites and Cayuses south of the river stole one another's livestock.

In the spring of 1854, Congress acted to solve the "Indian problem" in the territories of Oregon and Washington, which by then had been carved out of the northwest corner of the Oregon Country. Congress authorized the negotiation of "treaties of cession" with Northwest tribes. The word "treaty," though, was farcical. There was no equality between parties in these kinds of treaties, nor was there much negotiation. The federal government imposed its will upon reluctant, angry, and often confused Indians. Signatures or X marks on paper sanctified a treaty as a legally binding agreement between contracting parties—until the federal government decided to change the terms or abrogate the entire deal.

Soon after the Cayuse Five were hanged, the federal government decided to refine its methodology for taking Indian land. Instead of making treaties that forced Indians to march off to a faraway land— such as when Andrew Jackson compelled Cherokees to leave the Southeast in the 1830s, for what would become Oklahoma—the new approach made treaties that forced tribes to live on dramatically shrunken parcels of their existing land. They were called reservations. Indians were expected to retreat into them voluntarily after the conclusion of the compulsory treaty process. The reservations were supposed to be temporary holding stations that Indians would leave as soon as they learned how to live among whites.

Several of the first Indian reservations in the United States were created in the Pacific Northwest, where there was an urgent need to control Indian conflict with white newcomers who, in growing numbers, kept squatting on desirable Indian land. As federal and territorial officials rushed to respond, they very rarely enforced rules against white land theft. Instead they devised legal methods to get Indians off the land whites wanted most. Forced confiscation had a neutral-sounding legal name: "extinguishment." As the commissioner of Indian affairs explained to Congress, "With many of the tribes of Oregon and Washington territories, it appears to be absolutely necessary to speedily conclude treaties for the extinguishment of their claims to the lands now or recently occupied by them. . . . Yet the Indian tribes still claim title to the lands on which the whites have located, and which they are now cultivating . . . [which results in] the murder of white settlers, and in hindering the general growth and prosperity."

The great white extinguisher of the Pacific Northwest was Isaac Ingalls Stevens, the first governor of the Washington Territory. He was short, handsome, nattily dressed, ambitious, obsessive, impatient, and notably young—just thirty-five when President Franklin Pierce appointed him governor, an appointment that also made him superintendent of Indian affairs. For good measure, Stevens also sought out and won an appointment as chief of a War Department survey that was mapping the northern United States for a railroad right-of-way to the West Coast.

Stevens was a New England Puritan of good family and excellent political connections. He had a fine mind for mathematics, having

Isaac Stevens, the first governor of the Washington Territory, led treaty negotiations that forced many Indians of the Pacific Northwest to surrender their land and move to reservations. In 1855, he presided over a council in Walla Walla that took away about 90 percent of the land of the Cayuses, the Walla Wallas, and the Umatillas and sent them to live together on a reservation in northeast Oregon.

graduated first in his class at the U.S. Military Academy, where he was a standout in engineering. He distinguished himself in the Mexican War, during which he was badly injured. He limped from war wounds for the rest of his short life. At age forty-four, he would be killed in the Civil War battle of Chantilly.

When it came to doing business with Indians, Stevens had little personal experience or academic preparation. Instead, he was a cocksure embodiment of the paternalistic attitudes of his time and social class, according to Kent D. Richards, whose biography of Stevens is subtitled "Young Man in a Hurry."

"He assumed the superiority of European civilization and the necessity of removing the Indian from its path," Richards writes. "He hoped the removal could be accomplished peacefully and that, during a period of benevolent care, the Indians could be educated to cultivate the soil and become productive, valued members of white society."

Stevens's self-confidence and organizational skills allowed him to wrap up ten treaties in thirteen months. He started after Christmas in 1854 and by mid-February had pressured nine Indian tribes and bands around southern Puget Sound to surrender nearly all their land in exchange for three tiny reservations. In return, the Puyallups, Nisquallies, Squaxins, Steilacooms, and other Indian landowners were granted rights to hunt, fish, and gather food at their "usual and accustomed stations." They were also to receive modest cash payments for twenty years, at which time the government expected them to be acculturated enough to enter white society.

The extraordinary success of Stevens's first treaty council can be measured in the magnitude of the Indians' loss of land. In a little over a year, Stevens seized two and a half million acres for white people. He left less than four thousand acres for the Indians—which, the treaty said, the federal government could later take if it so desired. As Stevens's wife, Meg, explained in a letter to her mother, "Mr. Stevens has [the Puget Sound Indians] right under his thumb—they are afraid to death of him and do just as he tells them."

Up next for Stevens were tribes to the east of the Cascades— including the Nez Perces, Yakamas, Walla Wallas, Umatillas, and Cayuses. Those Indians, though, were not under his thumb. Unlike Indians on the coast, most of them had not been pushed to the brink of extinction by multiple epidemics of white men's diseases. They were much better armed. Horses gave them mobility. They were capable of engaging whites in a hit-and-run war. Since the hanging of the Cayuse Five and the accelerated invasion of white settlers, Indians on the Columbia Plateau had been anticipating a white attempt to take all their land. Some of them, including the Cayuses, the Walla Wallas, and the Yakamas, had made preparations for total war with the Americans. A letter from a Catholic priest living among the Yakamas said in 1853 that the "tempest is pent up ready to burst" as the tribes had "united themselves for war. . . . The cause of this war is that the Americans are going to seize their lands."

The Indians were also preparing to meet with Stevens. About a dozen chiefs came together and discussed how they should bargain with him, according to A. J. Splawn, a white settler who lived among the Yakamas for half a century and collected their accounts of that meeting. Nearly all the tribes, with the notable exception of the Nez Perces, agreed that there should be "no land for sale." If Stevens wanted to call their land a reservation, he was welcome to do so. But he would have to honor traditional tribal boundaries and seize none of it—or else he'd face an "uprising from every quarter."

Stevens dispatched his lieutenants to eastern Washington and Oregon in March 1855 to invite the chiefs to meet with him. Most of them accepted, and a grand council was set for May in the Walla Walla Valley. Before it began, Stevens's secretary, James Doty, warned his boss that negotiations could easily turn to chaos. "The general opinion is that neither the Cayuse or the Walla Walla will enter into a Treaty," Doty wrote, "and in case they are urged so to do, will create a disturbance and break up the Council."

If anything, Doty underestimated the risk. The Cayuse had suggested to other tribes that they use the council as a chance to surround Stevens and kill him.

Stevens did not seem worried, at least in public. Before traveling to the council, he announced, "I confidently expect to accomplish the whole business, extinguishing the Indian title to every acre of land in the territory."

Privately, he was less sure. Aware of threats to his life, he insisted that the U.S. Army provide protection. He rode into the Walla Walla Valley flanked by forty-seven soldiers.

On May 21, 1855, Stevens and his party arrived for the grand council in a driving rain. The Yakama tribe had chosen the site, a traditional Indian meeting ground on a verdant grassland near Mill Creek, a small tributary of the Walla Walla River. A young lieutenant with Stevens described it as "one of the most beautiful spots of the Walla Walla Valley, well wooded and with plenty of water." The Blue

Mountains rose in the southeast. The Columbia River, swollen with spring snowmelt, was thirty miles to the west. Just seven miles away, as Stevens and his men were well aware, a burned-out mission marked the site where the Cayuses had murdered Marcus and Narcissa Whitman seven and a half years earlier.

The precise location of the council is a matter of some scholarly dispute, but it was within what are now the city limits of Walla Walla. Many historians believe the talks were conducted on ground that would become the campus of Whitman College.

Over thirteen days, five thousand Indians—warriors, women, children—and many thousands of their horses gathered in camps that encircled Stevens and other white men from the government. It was one of the largest tribal gatherings in the history of federal treaty making, and it would forever change the lives of Indians on the Columbia Plateau.

Since the tribes came from the Washington and Oregon territories, Stevens was joined at the council by Joel Palmer, superintendent of Indian affairs for Oregon. He was not a favorite of the Cayuses. When Cayuse warriors killed the Whitmans, Palmer had been the first official to call for collective punishment of the entire tribe, insisting that its members forfeit all rights to their lands.

Stevens, Palmer, their attendants, and their guards pitched tents in a camp near a dining arbor. It had been built from poles and boughs as a place where Stevens, Palmer, and their entourage could eat and meet with chiefs. A larger arbor—a kind of stage for speeches—was built nearby as the central focus of the council. It faced the Blue Mountains, and there was ample space in that direction for Indians to assemble on the plain. In the shade of the big arbor, Stevens's men built a long table from rough pine logs. There, government secretaries would sit, taking minutes of the entire proceedings.

Despite the careful preparations, the tribes did not show up for the meeting for three long days. While Stevens and Palmer waited, they discussed how many Indian reservations should be created. The guidance Stevens had received from the Office of Indian Affairs in Washington, D.C., took a hard line: as quickly as possible, the Indians were to be "colonized in suitable locations" away from land that whites viewed as valuable and away from key transportation routes. Stevens was also instructed to pack the largest possible number of tribes into the smallest possible number of reservations.

The Nez Perces arrived first. Twenty-five hundred of them rode in on horseback, two abreast in a long, snaking column. Half of all the Indians who showed up at the council would be Nez Perces. The entrance seemed intended to demonstrate that they had the military muscle and the numbers to dominate decision-making among the Indians. Lawrence Kip, an army lieutenant assigned to the event, described the sensational show:

> They were almost entirely naked, gaudily painted and decorated with their wild trappings. Their plumes fluttered above them, while below, skins and trinkets and all kinds of fantastic embellishments flaunted in the sunshine. Trained from early childhood almost to live upon horseback, they sat upon their fine animals as if they were centaurs. . . . They would gallop up as if about to make a charge, then wheel round and round, sounding their whoops until they had apparently worked themselves up into an intense excitement. Then some score or two dismounted, and forming a ring, danced for about twenty minutes, while those surrounding them beat time on their drums.

After the theatrics ended, about twenty Nez Perce chiefs dismounted and shook hands with Stevens and Palmer. The headman

Arrival of the Nez Perce Indians at Walla Walla Treaty May 1855

The Nez Perces were the first Indians to show up at the Walla Walla Council, where they negotiated the most favorable deal with white men, keeping nearly all their traditional land. They arrived on horseback, twenty-five hundred strong, in a display of military strength that showed they would dominate decision-making among the Indians.

among them was called Lawyer. As his name suggested, he was a cautious, dignified, rule-following leader—the kind of chief Stevens needed to make the council a success for white people. Lawyer wrote and spoke English, as well as the Flathead and Spokane languages. He had been charming, impressing, and cooperating with white people since the 1830s, when he traveled to a rendezvous of American trappers in the Rockies. His father, Twisted Hair, had welcomed and helped the Lewis and Clark Expedition when it passed through Nez Perce country a half century earlier. In the 1840s, Lawyer had attended a Fourth of July banquet with white settlers in the Willamette Valley. But by far the most significant and sustained white influence

on Lawyer's thinking and behavior was the Reverend Henry Spal-
ding, whom Lawyer had welcomed and protected during the years
Spalding and his wife lived among the Nez Perces in their mission at
Lapwai.

Spalding was not present at the council. He was struggling during
the spring of 1855 to eke out a living in the Willamette Valley, a failed
missionary turned failed bureaucrat. He had won a well-paying appointment in 1850, the year of the Cayuse hanging, as an Indian agent
and had been considered for a posting east of the Cascades as agent in
charge of Cayuse country. He desperately wanted the position, as it
would have put him back on the Columbia Plateau, back in the neighborhood of his beloved Nez Perce converts. But when the Cayuses
heard of it, they vehemently objected; he never got the job.

Though Spalding was stuck that spring in the Willamette Valley, he
nevertheless had an indirect influence on the grand council through
his former pupil Lawyer. The Spaldings and the Whitmans, as we
have seen, came west not only to spread their Calvinist faith, but to
inculcate behavior they believed Indians must adopt to have a chance
of surviving the depredations of white people. The missionaries had
tried to persuade the Nez Perces and the Cayuses to abandon their
roaming ways and settle down—to farm, attend school, and accept
edicts from white governments. Among the Cayuses, the Whitmans
failed at all of this and paid for it with their lives. But Henry and Eliza
Spalding succeeded in ways that would reverberate for decades, helping to shape the destiny of the Nez Perces for good and for ill.

The missionary couple captured the hearts, minds, and long-term
loyalty of a number of Nez Perce elders—none more important than
Lawyer, a man of many talents. He would become a farmer, an interpreter, a teacher, a diplomat, a Christian, and a passively obedient en-
abler of white authority. He was also an accomplished buffalo hunter,
an unselfish leader, and a fearless combatant in a number of Indian

wars. A war injury had crippled him and given him status as a wise wounded warrior. Most important for his survival, Lawyer was a cagey politician who played the long game. With white support, he managed to win and wield power for nearly a quarter century as chief of the Nez Perces.

Lawyer
Hathal-Restiot
Head Chief of the Nez Perce Tribe

Chief Lawyer of the Nez Perces was a warrior, a linguist, a Christian, and a shrewd compromiser who avoided conflicts with whites. In return, he secured land and other concessions for his faction of the Nez Perces. His legacy, though, was stained among many members of his tribe, who accused him of betraying its non-Christian members.

This was a much more difficult achievement than it might have seemed. The Nez Perces were not the monolithic, statelike tribal unit that whites like Stevens assumed them to be. They were a loosely allied geographic cluster of Indian bands who happened to speak the same language—and many deeply resented the white presumption that Lawyer was their senior chief.

Even as Lawyer hung on to power, his legacy was challenged and tainted. But not by white people. For many decades after his death, he was a great favorite of settlers and historians. The first biographer of Isaac Stevens (his son Hazard Stevens) singled out Lawyer for his "unrivaled wisdom" at the Walla Walla Treaty Council, celebrating his effort to make Indians "adopt the customs and civilization of the whites, and [preserve] the unbroken friendship between the two races." As late as the 1970s, Lawyer's biographer, Clifford Drury, described him as "wiser than most of his contemporaries. Lawyer realized that the white man with his superior skills, material resources, and overwhelming numbers was destined to rule over all of the Indian tribes of the Northwest. For him, armed resistance was folly."

But many Nez Perces, then and now, viewed Lawyer as a "Red Judas" or "Uncle Tomahawk." When the federal government reneged on many of its treaty promises, he acquiesced. The decisions Lawyer made at Walla Walla would, within twenty years, lead to a disastrous war that defeated, divided, and relocated many of his people.

But at the grand council, Lawyer was perfectly positioned to secure for the Nez Perces the most generous deal on offer from the U.S. government. His tribe was powerful, and he was friendly—at a moment when Stevens desperately needed a powerful Indian friend, one who could be manipulated into persuading the rest of the tribes to give up most of their land.

After their eye-catching entrance on the morning of May 24, Lawyer and his chiefs joined Stevens at his tent, where they sat for a considerable time, smoking pipes together and talking. Everyone seemed to get along well. The next evening, Lawyer and his entourage dined with Stevens.

The Cayuses made a radically different—and more warlike—first impression when they thundered into the Walla Walla Valley on a Saturday evening, five days after the whites arrived and two days after the Nez Perces. Merging their mounted warriors with those of the Walla Wallas, apparently in an attempt to look more numerous and

Over thirteen days at the Walla Walla council, about five thousand Northwest Indians—one of the largest tribal gatherings in the history of federal treaty-making—negotiated treaties that would send them to reservations. The chiefs sometimes had meals with Governor Stevens and his men.

formidable, the Cayuses were the most intimidating among the four hundred or so Indians whose late arrival stirred up anxiety among the vastly outnumbered whites.

"They were in gala dress, all mounted and whooping and screaming like demons or rather like an Indian War Party," wrote Doty, the secretary to Stevens. They circled the encampment two or three times and then retreated about a mile to make their own camp. That evening, six Cayuse chiefs rode over to Stevens's tent. They shook hands, "but in no cordial manner." They refused an invitation to sit and smoke with Stevens. They declined any and all gifts of U.S. government food and provisions, which Stevens had brought to the council as sweeteners and which filled a nearby building. The Cayuses refused to converse, saying they would save their words for later. "It was not, as we had reason to believe afterwards, a friendly visit," wrote Kip, the army officer. Rather, it was "a reconnaissance to learn our numbers and estimate our powers of resistance."

The next day was Sunday, an occasion for Nez Perce elders to showcase the Protestant beliefs and rituals that Spalding had drilled into them. They prayed several times during the day and convened a church service that Stevens attended. Officiating was Timothy, an English-speaking acolyte of Spalding's who closely followed Presbyterian rituals of worship. Stevens, a Protestant, was impressed and comforted by what he witnessed, writing in his journal that "the Nez Perces have evidently profited much from the labor of Mr. Spalding, who was with them ten years, and their whole deportment throughout the service was devout."

That same day, several white army officers rode through the Cayuse camp, where they saw no evidence of Sunday piety. Young warriors cleaned their guns and groomed their horses. While the Nez Perces attended to their Christian rituals, the Cayuses projected menace. The mixed messages were not lost on Stevens, who wrote in his journal, "The haughty carriage of these [Cayuse] chiefs and their manly character have, for the first time in my Indian experience, realized the description of the writers of fiction."

I t took until the following day, Monday, May 28, seven days after the whites had arrived, for all the major tribes to show up. The proceedings began the next day. From a bench in front of the arbor, Stevens and Palmer addressed the assembled Indians, spread out in front of them in concentric semicircular rows in order of power and importance: chiefs up front, and warriors, women, and children toward the rear. The audience often exceeded two thousand.

The pace of the council was mind-numbingly slow. It was interrupted by rain, prolonged by translation, and paralyzed by long, rambling speeches. Periodically, the council was suspended for an entire day: by restless young Indians who wanted to race horses, by devout Indians who wanted to worship Jesus, or by seething Indians who wanted to discuss among themselves how to respond to proposals from Stevens and Palmer—or whether they should just kill them.

On Tuesday, Stevens addressed his opening speech to an audience of eighteen hundred Indians but had to abandon his remarks when rain came. Finally, on Wednesday the sun shone, and Stevens spoke at length to an audience he clearly did not understand. Throughout his hours of talking, he kept referring to "the Great Father," by which he meant the president of the United States.

"The Great Father has heard much of you, he first learned of you from Lewis and Clark. . . . I went back to the Great Father last year to say that you had been good, you had been kind, he must do something for you."

As Stevens explained it, the Great Father wanted Indians in the Northwest to own big farms, raise lots of livestock, learn to read and write, and become master tradesmen.

"Why did the Great Father answer in this way? Why did he send my brother [Joel Palmer] and myself here this day to say this to you? Because you are his children. His red children are as dear to him as his white children. His red children are men, they have hearts, they have sense. . . . The Great Father has been for many years caring for his red children across the mountains."

Stevens then praised the many treaties the Great Father had made over previous decades with Indians east of the Rockies. He falsely characterized them as benevolent compacts that sheltered the "red man with farms and with schools and with shops and with laws."

The assembled Northwest Indians were well aware that this was condescending nonsense. They were far from naive when it came to the treachery of white men. Older chiefs at the council owned vast

In long lectures at the Walla Walla council, Governor Stevens told the Northwest tribes that the "Great Father" in Washington, D.C., had for many years been "caring for his red children." His Indian listeners were by then well aware of the genocidal policies of the U.S. government, which for decades had been taking Indian land and destroying Indian lives.

herds of horses, cattle, and considerable acreage of cultivated land. For nearly four decades, they had been doing business with white trappers, traders, missionaries, horse dealers, small-town merchants, and government agents from Great Britain, Canada, France, and the United States. They had traveled extensively—east of the Rockies on buffalo hunts, south to California on slave raids, north to Canada for horse trading. Their ranks had been joined by mixed-race Indians from east of the Rockies who had reported in graphic detail about how the Great Father's treaties had sanctioned genocide—taking nearly all the Indian land and forcing tens of thousands of Indians into permanent exile that shredded their culture, stole their wealth, and broke their hearts.

The chiefs listened in gloomy silence as Stevens continued, in broad generalities, to explain the purpose of the Walla Walla council. He said the Great Father wanted "you and ourselves to agree upon tracts of land where you live." On these tracts, he said, Indians could be protected from "bad white men" while receiving payments of money, enjoying gifts of blankets and calico, and learning how to succeed in white society. "Then you the men will be farmers and mechanics, or you will be doctors and lawyers like white men," Stevens said.

Near the end of a speech that lasted for most of the afternoon, Stevens subtly and briefly announced the cost—for the assembled Indians—of making a deal: nothing less than the surrender of all Indian land not enclosed in a reservation. As Stevens put it, "Now we want you to agree with us to such a state of things; you to have your tract with all these things, the rest to be the Great Father's for his white children."

None of this went over well.

Stevens had patronized and insulted his audience—one that was desperately worried about its future. He was also maddeningly imprecise. He did not specify how many reservations there would be, where they would be located, how large they would be, or what tribes would be forced to move to which reservation.

All week, the whites continued their speeches in this vein. On Saturday, June 2, Palmer explained why the Indians had no choice but to accept the loss of most of their land.

"If there were no other whites coming into the country we might get along in peace," he said. "You may ask why do they come? Can you stop the waters of the Columbia River from flowing on its course? Can you prevent the wind from blowing? Can you prevent the whites from coming? You are answered no. . . . You cannot stop them, our chief cannot stop them, we cannot stop them. They say the land was not made for you alone."

Still, neither Palmer nor Stevens would be specific. The chiefs were irate. When they were finally asked for their thoughts, the elderly chief of the Walla Wallas, Peo-Peo-Mox-Mox, complained:

"We have not seen in a true light the object of your speeches, as if there was a post set between us, as if my heart cried from what you have said, as if the Almighty came down upon us here this day, as if He would say, 'What are you saying?' . . . You have spoken in a manner partly tending to Evil. Speak plain to us."

The only Indian leader not frustrated by the days of mealymouthed white speechifying was Lawyer. On June 4, when Stevens finally announced that there would be just two reservations, it became clear why the Nez Perce chief had been so agreeable: the largest reservation would be for the Nez Perces. It would encompass nearly all their traditional lands—7.7 million acres in present-day Oregon and Idaho. The other reservation was for the Yakamas and was considerably smaller, about 1.13 million acres. It would force the Yakamas to cede to the Great Father about 90 percent of their traditional territory, which was north of the Columbia River in south-central Washington.

It was a shrewd offer by Stevens, intended to secure the support of the two most populous and powerful tribes at the council while backing all the other Indians into a corner, none more so than the Cayuses, the Walla Wallas, and the Umatillas, who would have to abandon all of their traditional land and move to the Nez Perce or Yakama reservation.

The Cayuses seethed. One chief said the land was his mother and now white people were stealing her away from him. Another mocked Lawyer for embracing a deal that made no sense. Five Crows, the powerful Cayuse chief who had been converted to Christianity by Spalding, and who stood accused of raping Lorinda Bewley Chapman, stunned the assembled tribal leaders by announcing that the enduring alliance between the Cayuses and the Nez Perces could endure no more.

"Listen to me you chiefs," Five Crows said. "We have been as one people with the Nez Perces. This day we have been divided."

The Cayuses and other embittered tribes demanded another day of recess. That night, Lieutenant Kip and another officer rode among the Indian camps and noticed "a more hostile feeling towards the whites getting up among some of the tribes"—especially the Cayuses.

"The Cayuses we have known have never been friendly, but hitherto they have disguised their feelings. Tonight . . . they showed a decided opposition: we were motioned back, and the young warriors threw themselves in our way to obstruct our advance. . . . How long will it be before we have an actual outbreak?"

When the council gathered again on Thursday, June 7, the chiefs, with the predictable exception of Lawyer, rejected Stevens's proposal. The most agonized complaint came from the chief of the Umatilla tribe, Owhi. If he sold his land to white people, he said, his creator would punish him with everlasting damnation.

Five Crows, a Cayuse leader at the Walla Walla council, believed his tribe had been betrayed in treaty negotiations by a longtime ally, the Nez Perces. He startled the assembled Indians by announcing a split between the tribes. "Listen to me you chiefs," he said. "We have been as one people with the Nez Perces. This day we have been divided."

"The Great Spirit made our bodies from the earth, we are different from whites," he said. "Shall I give the land which is a part of my body and leave myself poor and destitute? Shall I say I will give you my land? I cannot say so. I am afraid of the Great Spirit. I love my life.

The reason why I do not give my land away is I am afraid I shall be sent to hell."

That evening Lieutenant Kip again rode through the Indian camps. The Nez Perces were happily gambling in their lodges. But aside from them, the "Cayuses and other tribes are very much incensed against the Nez Perces for agreeing to the terms of the treaty."

The anger—and the perception among army officers that the Cayuses might be on the brink of leading a murderous attack too powerful to defend against—was communicated to Stevens and Palmer. That evening they did something that was exceedingly rare in a negotiation between Indians and white agents of the U.S. government. They reconsidered. They compromised.

The next morning, Stevens and Palmer offered a third reservation. It was for the Cayuses, the Walla Wallas, and the Umatillas. Critically, from the Cayuse perspective, the reservation would be on a piece of their traditional land near the Blue Mountains and included long stretches of a river, the Umatilla, that was rich with salmon. The Cayuses, if they took the offer, would remain on at least some of their ancestral home. Unlike many peoples in the Northwest and all across the United States, they would not be exiled to the territory of another tribe.

Still, the government offer was exceedingly stingy. It would take away more than 90 percent of the combined territory of the three tribes. Cayuse chiefs resisted signing until the last possible moment. Their signature would signal a retreat, a swallowing of pride, and a repudiation of warrior traditions that for centuries had given them power beyond their numbers.

In the end, there was no alternative. They could not fight the white hordes without Indian allies. Cayuse leaders were proud, angry, and quick to violence, but they were not irrational.

On the final day of the council, June 11, 1855, Lawyer and more than thirty other chiefs and headmen came forward and wrote their names or scratched their mark on treaty paper. According to an official journal of the council, "Then the Cayuse, seeing that they stood alone, also came up and signed their Treaty."

ACT THREE

———— ·❦· ————

LIE

CHAPTER ELEVEN

AUTHENTIC ACCOUNT

As the Cayuses struggled for their very survival, Henry Spalding despaired of his new life among American settlers in the Willamette Valley. Despite having spent the first three decades of his life in the uniformly white small towns of upstate New York, he wrote that he "never felt at home among the whites." Short of money and with four young children to provide for, he jumped from job to job in the 1850s, working as a teacher, farmer, school commissioner, postmaster, roving minister, justice of the peace, Indian agent for the federal government, and pontificator in local and East Coast newspapers. All the while, he ached to return to Nez Perce country, where he wanted to resume the only thing he had ever been good at: missionary work among Indians whose language he had learned, whose leaders he had trained, and whose culture he felt he understood. If he could find a way to return to the Nez Perces, he believed, his Christian followers, especially Chief Lawyer and the devout headman Timothy, would welcome him back and allow him to rebuild his ministry.

Spalding's abrasive personality, though, stood in the way of his return, costing him federal appointments and forcing him out of jobs, which made him wild with resentment. When he pleaded with the American Board in the 1850s to send him back to the Nez Perces, several of his fellow missionaries strongly advised against it. They said Spalding was unstable. "I deem him wholly unfitted in body and mind," wrote the Reverend Elkanah Walker, who had known Spalding since 1838. The Reverend Cushing Eells, another longtime acquaintance, said that Spalding "does not possess very largely of a cooperative disposition. . . . He has not been a discreet, prudent missionary—is often precipitous. He appears to suffer from mental or moral obliquity, which has occasioned much reproach."

Deepening Spalding's darkness was the death of his wife. Eliza had been a loving and moderating presence in his life. She had also been crucial to his success among the Nez Perces. Her steady temperament won trust and devotion and helped rein in her hotheaded husband. With Eliza gone, Spalding told foolish lies. He recklessly created conflict. He even turned his wife's gravestone into anti-Catholic agitprop. "She always felt that the Jesuit Missionaries were the leading cause of the massacre," it read. In later years, Spalding repeatedly claimed that Eliza had been murdered in 1847 by the Cayuses at the Whitman mission and that Catholic priests were "the instigators of that heart sickening & bloody butchery." In fact, Eliza died in bed of natural causes, on January 7, 1851, four years after the massacre, surrounded by her husband and family at their home in the Willamette Valley.

As we know, when the American Board sent Spalding to Oregon, it told him, "Do nothing to irritate." As a middle-aged minister in the 1850s and '60s, he was, if anything, more irritating than ever. Whenever he could, Spalding published his anti-Catholic, paranoiac, and false fulminations in the newspapers. In so doing, he offended a number of very important people, in Oregon and in Washington, D.C. He falsely accused Dr. John McLoughlin, a former friend, of saying that "Doct. Whitman and Mrs. Whitman got just what they deserved" and that "Spalding ought to be hung." In 1851, after he was dismissed, for absenteeism, from a job as a federal Indian agent, Spalding wrote and published a series of letters that accused his former supervisor of being a crook, an incompetent, and a papist who discriminated against Protestants. One of these letters was published in a Christian newspaper on the East Coast, where it came to the attention of President Millard Fillmore. Fillmore wrote a letter in 1852 noting that Spalding's claims were "destitute of truth."

That assessment of nearly everything Spalding said and wrote was shared by some of the most prominent newspaper editors in the Pacific Northwest in the second half of the nineteenth century. "They all refused their columns to Mr. Spalding," according to a letter in the Portland *Morning Oregonian*. "He felt it keenly. It troubled him, and he often spoke about it to his friends, and blamed the papers considerably."

Asahel Bush, the influential editor of the *Oregon Statesman*, described Spalding in 1855 as "a lunatic upon the subject of Catholicism" and not "sane on any subject."

S palding, though, was never merely a crackpot. There was a cunning to his madness—and to the reckless accusations and fantastic claims that came out of it. He had a keen sense of the prevailing prejudices of Protestants in nineteenth-century America, writing that the "community are indignant at the conduct of the Catholics." He spent the final three decades of his life inciting that indignation—and feeding off the fires he helped set.

Marcus and Narcissa Whitman were not dead six months before

he found a way to wrap the factual particulars of their lives and murders around his most enduring fabrication: the Whitman Saved Oregon story.

It first surfaced, in bare-bones form, in the early summer of 1848, as part of an obituary printed in Protestant newspapers in Chicago and Boston. Although unsigned, "The Death of Dr. Marcus Whitman" bears Spalding's unmistakable literary fingerprints. It includes details, phrasing, and sectarian venom he would repeat and refine in sermons, letters, lectures, and essays over the coming decades.

> In the winter of 1842, Dr. Whitman made his last visit to the United States, clothed in skins. He then performed, almost alone, the perilous journey across the plains, traversing snows and swimming their icy streams, that he might communicate important intelligence to the American Board in regard to their stations, and prevail upon his countrymen to commence at once an emigration, in order to save Oregon from the grasp of Great Britain, as well as to preserve it from the power of the Jesuits, with whose schemes he had become acquainted.

After this tantalizing preview, the story slipped out of public sight—for eighteen years. The long dormancy of the incipient lie coincided with a depressing and often desperate time for Spalding, marred by job setbacks, personal loss, an increasingly acrimonious relationship with the American Board, and searing public condemnation from enemies he had made in the Catholic Church, the U.S. government, and local newspapers.

Amid it all, as the editor of the *Oregon Statesman* called his sanity into question, Spalding began to live a hidden life as the local leader of the secret Supreme Order of the Star-Spangled Banner. He became president of Preble Wigwam No. 38, the order's chapter in Linn County, Oregon. He hosted meetings in his home, where members vowed to vote only for American-born Protestant politicians who opposed immigration and committed themselves to doing everything in their power to vilify and undermine Catholics.

For Spalding, it was a shrewd—and stealthy—political play. To be appointed to a government job in Nez Perce country, he needed help from elected federal officials and their top regional appointees. And the Order of the Star-Spangled Banner—widely known as the "Know-Nothings" because members denied all knowledge of their society—was fast becoming a formidable political force, with secret cells across the United States and in nearly every community in Oregon. Leading newspapers in Oregon encouraged the group (also called the American Party), attacking Catholics and turning against "foreign influences," especially the Hudson's Bay Company, which continued to operate in Vancouver.

The Know-Nothings enjoyed exponential national growth and exercised extraordinary political influence in the mid-1850s. In little more than two years, membership soared from forty-three individuals in New York City to more than a million nationwide. In 1855, the year Spalding joined, the Know-Nothings elected eight governors and more than a hundred members of Congress, along with mayors in Boston, Philadelphia, and Chicago and thousands of lower-ranking politicians. Even Millard Fillmore, after leaving the White House in 1853, became a member. No nativist political organization in the United States had ever grown so fast and achieved so much so quickly.

Then, as now, nativists derived their power from stoking and exploiting fear of foreigners, and there was plenty of fuel for that fire between 1845 and 1854. The influx of immigrants had never been higher—"more than had come in the seven previous decades combined," according to historian Tyler Anbinder. This amounted to about

15 percent of the population, or about 2.8 million people. They came mostly from Ireland and southern Germany, and their religion was as alarming to many Protestants as their numbers: by the 1850s, most were Roman Catholics.

Spalding's anti-Catholicism had found formal academic support in the 1830s, when he was a student at Lane Theological Seminary, in Cincinnati. His primary intellectual influence there was the Reverend Lyman Beecher, a Yale-trained Presbyterian minister with a national reputation for attacking Catholics as agents of a plot against America. Just before Spalding traveled to Oregon, Beecher wrote *A Plea for the West,* a book that explained how Catholic immigrants, priests, and Catholic schools were attempting to steal away the western frontier. When Spalding later claimed that papists had instigated the killings of the Whitmans and schemed with the British to take Oregon, he was not being particularly inventive. Opinion makers like Lyman Beecher had trained Spalding—and Protestants throughout the United States—to perceive the world through the nativist lens of a papist conspiracy. As seen through that lens, Catholics were hell-bent on destroying the ethnic and religious homogeneity of the country—and it was a seemingly commonsense assumption that they were trying to steal the West for the pope.

In "The Paranoid Style in American Politics," historian Richard Hofstadter wrote, in 1964, that "heated exaggeration, suspiciousness, and conspiratorial fantasy" have always infected public life in the United States. He traced a facts-be-damned style of political discourse that for two hundred years obsessed over the menace posed by Freemasons, international bankers, and Communists hiding in the State Department. One of the most hysterical and sustained of these obsessions focused on Catholic immigrants in the middle of the nineteenth century, when, as Hofstadter wrote, Protestants "invented an immense lore about libertine priests" and their licentious misbehavior with nuns behind convent walls.

In 1836, the year Spalding traveled west with the Whitmans, the most successful book of this lurid genre appeared in print. Called *Awful Disclosures*, it was written by Maria Monk, a young woman who escaped a nunnery in Montreal, where she claimed she was taught to "obey the priests in all things." Babies fathered by priests, she wrote, were killed, but only after they were baptized, so they could go to heaven. Although Maria's mother later said that her daughter had been disturbed since childhood, when she stuck a pencil in her head, and although Maria died in prison after being arrested in a brothel for petty theft, the book was bought, and believed, all across America. It became, as Hofstadter wrote, "probably the most widely read contemporary book in the United States before 'Uncle Tom's Cabin.'"

Foreign-born Catholics were relatively slow to settle in the Pacific Northwest. But early white settlers—many of them farmers and small-town merchants from Missouri—had been steeped in the anti-Catholic hysteria that made *Awful Disclosures* a must-read. As Spalding intuited, Oregonians were primed and ready to believe in outrageous papal plots, notwithstanding that there were few local Catholics around to carry them out. Soon after the Whitman killings, a petition to expel Catholic clergy from Oregon was introduced in the territorial legislature. It failed, but seeds of anti-Catholicism found fertile soil, fertilized year after year by Spalding's sermons and by published claims that priests had played a role in the Whitman Massacre and that Catholics had conspired with the British to try to steal Oregon from Protestant America.

Nativism and bigotry in Oregon would endure well into the twentieth century. By majority vote, they were enshrined in the new state's constitution. A Black exclusion provision made Oregon the only free state admitted to the union with a constitutional clause banning African Americans from entering the state or owning property there. Although rarely enforced, the law effectively kept Blacks out. In 1860, a year after it became a state, there were just 128 African Americans in Oregon. The law wasn't removed until 1926. The state population is still just 2 percent Black, and Portland—for all its progressive bona fides—remains the whitest of America's big cities.

Nativist loathing of Catholics went hand in glove with racism, and both thrived in Oregon into the late 1920s. They helped create and energize the largest Ku Klux Klan chapter west of the Rockies, which became a formidable statewide political force after World War I. With the backing of the Klan and the winking approval of a Klan-friendly candidate for governor, voters in Oregon approved a law in 1922 that would have shut down all Catholic schools in the state—had the law not been declared unconstitutional in 1925 by the United States Supreme Court.

Spalding's anti-Catholic screeds, which found their way into religious newspapers, both in Oregon and in the East, kept his name on the minds of influential Protestant organizations. The Congregational Association of Oregon passed a resolution in 1859 recommending that the federal Office of Indian Affairs appoint Spalding to be "teacher of the Nez Perce." Three years later, he was appointed superintendent of instruction on the Nez Perce Reservation.

By then he was remarried—an arranged match to Rachel Smith, the sister of a friend's wife. Told that Spalding needed a helpmate, she had come out to Oregon from Boston in 1852. Rachel was not nearly as well educated as Eliza and had few of her linguistic or missionary gifts. But she was devoted to Spalding, was good to his children, and eagerly joined him on the reservation as a teacher.

The return of Reverend Spalding delighted many Nez Perces, especially those he had converted in the late 1830s and '40s. "They seemed most pleased at the prospect of having a school started amongst them & also of having a minister who could preach to them in their own language," said J. W. Anderson, the federal Indian agent at the reservation, which by this time was located in the Idaho Territory. "Every Sabbath the Indians in great numbers attended Mr. S's preaching. . . . Although Mr. S had been absent from the tribe many years yet they retained all the forms of worship that he had taught them."

The good feelings did not last.

The year after Spalding returned, the U.S. government announced that it wanted more Nez Perce land. Gold had been discovered on the reservation. Although white miners had no legal right to do so, they stormed onto the reservation with mules and mining equipment, and federal authorities made no serious effort to stop or remove them. Instead, the government demanded that the Nez Perces give up nearly seven million acres of land. This amounted to about 90 percent of what had been guaranteed to them just eight years earlier by Isaac Stevens at the grand council in Walla Walla.

This time around, a treaty council was held on Nez Perce land at Lapwai, where Spalding built his original mission, and the federal official in charge of the negotiations was Calvin H. Hale, superintendent of Indian affairs for the Washington Territory. There were many echoes, though, of what had happened in Walla Walla. Again, the key to the U.S. government's negotiating strategy was to convince Chief Lawyer to give them everything they wanted. The land seizure was once again crafted in a way that would do minimal harm to the property holdings and financial interests of Lawyer and his Christian followers, who, under the terms the government was offering, would be allowed to keep much of their land on the northern end of the reservation.

Spalding was enlisted as an interpreter for this council. But many

Nez Perces did not trust him. They demanded he be replaced. These were Indians whose families had never become Christian and who lived on lands that whites wanted to take. That carve-out included some of the most magnificent wildlands in the United States—mining areas in the Bitterroot Mountains, the Snake and Salmon river valleys, and the spectacular Wallowa country, a highland in the northeast corner of Oregon that is often compared to the Swiss Alps.

In the end, Chief Lawyer played the same role he had in Walla Walla, grumbling a bit before accepting virtually all the government's demands. The papers he signed came to be known as the "steal treaty." In doing so, Chief Lawyer tore the Nez Perce people apart.

On Lawyer's side were the "treaty Indians," the Christians who, under the 1863 treaty, retained nearly all their land. They amounted to just one-third of the tribe. Nearly all the other Nez Perces—the mostly non-Christian and "non-treaty Indians"—lost. They became landless in the eyes of the federal government, although they refused to move. One of their leaders, Joseph the Elder, had been converted by Spalding. But after the 1863 treaty, he destroyed the Bible Spalding had given him.

The division of the Nez Perces—a crippling and enduring schism that Spalding's missionary labors had helped create—would lead to one of America's last Indian wars. Fourteen years later, Chief Joseph, son of the chief who destroyed Spalding's Bible, would join with the leaders of two other non-treaty Nez Perce bands in a fight against the whites who kept moving onto their traditional territory. They waged a tactically brilliant three-month campaign. It ranged 1,500 miles from the Wallowa through Yellowstone country and north toward the Canadian border. About seven hundred Nez Perces, just two hundred of whom were warriors, engaged two thousand U.S. soldiers in four major battles and dozens of skirmishes. The military skill of the Nez Perces was "unequalled in the history of Indian warfare," said General

Nelson Miles, an experienced Indian fighter who marched across Montana to engage them. Another army commander, General John Gibbon, who was pinned down by Nez Perce snipers in the Battle of the Big Hole, would later describe the U.S. fight against the Nez Perces as "an unjustifiable outrage upon the red man, due to our aggressive and untruthful behavior."

The commanding general of the U.S. Army, William Tecumseh Sherman, of Civil War fame, said that the fight against the Nez Perces was "one of the most extraordinary wars of which there is any record." He said that the Indians "displayed a courage and skill that elicited universal praise. They abstained from scalping; let captive women go free; did not commit indiscriminate murder of peaceful families, which is usual, and fought with almost scientific skill, using advance and rear guards, skirmish lines, and field fortifications."

In the end, though, the Indians' courage, skill, and humanity did not bring victory. A few miles from the Canadian border, the exhausted and outnumbered Nez Perces were captured.

"I am tired of fighting," Joseph was reported to have said. "My people, some of them, have run away to the hills, and have no blankets, no food; no one knows where they are—perhaps freezing to death. I want to have time to look for my children and see how many of them I can find. Maybe I shall find them among the dead. Hear me my chiefs. I am tired; my heart is sick and sad. From where the sun now stands I will fight no more forever."

These eloquent words, reported in newspapers across the country, have endured in history. They are perhaps the most widely quoted remarks of any Native leader in America's Indian wars. But the evidence that Joseph actually spoke them is "highly questionable," according to historian Elliott West, a Nez Perce scholar. The "best guess," according to West, is that the highly polished speech was written by Charles Erskine Scott Wood, who graduated near the top of his class at West Point and was an aide to an army general at the time of the surrender. Wood probably based his version of Joseph's speech, West writes, on a message of surrender that the Nez Perce leader dispatched to army commanders.

After Joseph's defeat, General Sherman, for all his kind words about the Nez Perces as noble warriors, punished Joseph and his people with exile—to eastern Kansas; then to Oklahoma, where many died of disease; and finally to the Colville Reservation, in north-central Washington State. Joseph died there in 1904. His doctor, observing that Joseph was in deep despair in his final years, believed the cause of death was sorrow.

As for Spalding, he wanted only to spend the rest of his life on the northern part of the Nez Perce Reservation, where life went on much as it had before the 1863 treaty. The minister and his wife were well paid to be teachers there. Christian Nez Perces, some in their second and third generations, kept showing up to hear Spalding preach.

Inevitably, however, Spalding got in his own way. His superior, the senior Indian agent on the Nez Perce Reservation in 1864, was a Catholic named James O'Neil. By the fall of 1865, O'Neil had sacked Spalding and his wife. They were forced to leave the reservation. "I am starved out and crowded out . . . salary cut off and back salary not paid for two years," he wrote at the time. "It is a shameful disgrace."

H is disgrace would increase, as would his rage. For he would soon discover that Congress had published a bitingly personal attack on his character and truthfulness, by none other than his Catholic rescuer turned nemesis, Father Brouillet.

In the months after Brouillet had risked his life to preserve Spalding's, the priest's reward was to read crude innuendoes and vague accusations from Spalding in Oregon newspapers, blaming Catholic priests in general and Brouillet in particular for inciting mass murder. Brouillet quickly wrote a response: "Protestantism in Oregon: Authentic Account of the Murder of Dr. Whitman, and the Ungrateful Calumnies of H.H. Spalding, Protestant Missionary."

Brouillet, then thirty-four, was a highly educated and formidable adversary. Born near Montreal, he was just twelve when he entered Saint Hyacinthe seminary, in Quebec, where he quickly became an exceptional student. While studying for the priesthood, he mastered English, Latin, and Greek and served as a professor of grammar and literature. His academic training helped Brouillet become an exacting and analytical writer. Unlike Spalding, prone to embellishment and invective, Brouillet minimized passion and systematically marshaled evidence.

The priest had another crucial advantage over the minister: he had seen the crime scene at the Whitman mission with his own eyes. He knew that Spalding, for all his breathless, blood-splattered descriptions of what happened there, had not. Brouillet also knew, from his own personal dealings with the minister, that Spalding made things up. The priest said he had written his "Authentic Account" to counteract such "misguided men . . . who profess the purest principles of Christian charity [but] whose only aim seems to be the achievement of an enviable notoriety, through the fabrication of falsehoods and the circulations of 'facts,' founded upon fiction."

Although Brouillet wrote his critique of Spalding on the immediate heels of the Whitman killings, it was not published for five years. Like so many Oregonians, Brouillet had hurried to California during the forty-niner gold rush, at the request of his archbishop, who sent him to San Francisco to raise cash for the debt-ridden Oregon diocese. After returning to Oregon in 1850, it took him another three years to find a publisher. His essay appeared in 1853 in a Catholic periodical in New York. But outside of the priesthood, few readers saw it, especially in faraway Oregon.

Spalding probably never would have seen Brouillet's "Authentic Account" but for the labors of a confidential agent of the U.S. Treasury named J. Ross Browne. Browne was dispatched to the Northwest in the mid-1850s to investigate the slipshod operation of new Indian reservations in the Oregon and Washington territories. He also made inquiries into the causes of the brief wars that had broken out after Governor Stevens confined Indians to reservations. In the course of his research, he happened upon a copy of Brouillet's essay and sent it to Washington, thinking it would be of interest to the commissioner of Indian affairs.

Though he had not intended for it to be published, the U.S. Congress printed Browne's thirteen-page essay as an official document, and did the same with Brouillet's much more substantial, fifty-three-page attack on Spalding. House Executive Document No. 38 appeared in 1858, a Senate version a few months later. Since then, Brouillet's "Authentic Account" has been printed multiple times, most often in response to periodic eruptions of anti-Catholicism in Oregon.

Writing with the authority of an eyewitness and the felicity of a classically trained scholar, Brouillet savaged Spalding:

> A certain gentleman, moved on by religious fanaticism, and ashamed of owing his own life and that of family and friends to some priests, began to insinuate false suspicions about the true cause of the disaster—proceeded by degrees to make more open accusations, and finally declared publicly that the Bishop of Walla Walla and his clergy were the first cause and great movers of all the evil. The gentleman is the

Rev. H.H. Spalding, whose life had been saved from the
Indians by a priest at the peril of his own.

In the body of his essay, Brouillet enumerated Spalding's false claims
and rebutted them one by one. His analysis included this perceptive
and quietly damning observation: "Mr. Spalding's memory has given
way to his imagination." Brouillet added that Spalding could never
have accused Catholics of causing the Whitman Massacre "without being moved by blind, unjust, and too violent religious prejudices."

I t is not known exactly how or when Spalding became aware of
what he called the "hellish success" of Brouillet's "Authentic Account." It clearly wounded and may have shamed him. In any case, he
was not cowed.

To get even, Spalding would publish and popularize a story that
cast Catholics as treasonous murderers. At the same time, it would
exalt Marcus Whitman as a larger-than-life missionary patriot who
died so Oregon might live as part of the United States.

That would be *his* authentic account.

First, though, he had to finish making it up. So far, he had written
only the barest germ of this story, published in Whitman's 1848 obituary. He would also need to persuade the Protestant establishment—
those in Oregon who largely knew him to be an unreliable ranter and
those on the East Coast who didn't know who he was—to swallow his
story.

To sell his fable and to sell himself, he found a small circle of missionaries who encouraged him, helped him flesh out his fabrications,
and persuaded influential Protestants on the East Coast to believe him.

Before we delve into these labors, it is crucially important to remember that Spalding was knowingly telling a falsehood when he claimed that Whitman traveled to Washington on a patriot's quest to save Oregon. The evidence is in his own words, in the form of a letter he wrote on October 10, 1843, to a missionary colleague in Hawaii. The date of the letter, which was not discovered until eighty-nine years after it was written, is key. Spalding wrote it immediately after he spoke with Whitman and learned about the outcome of the doctor's just-completed journey to the East Coast.

It unambiguously confirms that Whitman traveled east to save his mission in Oregon. There is no mention in the letter that Whitman spoke with President Tyler or any officials in the federal government. There is no claim that Whitman had saved Oregon, that he had tried to save Oregon, or even that Oregon needed saving. There is nothing about a British plot to steal the territory from the United States or Catholic collusion in such a plot.

Instead, Spalding explains in the letter that Whitman traveled to Boston and "simply obtained the consent of the board" for "the rescinding of the vote to give up this part of the mission."

By the 1860s, however, that succinct, fact-based account had become null and void—in Spalding's mind. Once he began peddling the Whitman Saved Oregon tale, Spalding would never again acknowledge the real reason for Whitman's trip to Boston.

CHAPTER TWELVE

COLLABORATE

H enry Spalding was holding court on the horrors of the Whitman Massacre when the Reverend George H. Atkinson fell under his spell. It was June 29, 1848, a Thursday evening in early summer in the Willamette Valley. The Whitmans had been dead exactly seven months, and Atkinson, having journeyed to the Northwest by ship, via Hawaii, had just arrived in Oregon City to begin a new life as a Congregational missionary.

The seventh son of an eminent Puritan family, educated at elite New England schools, Atkinson was newly ordained and bursting with ambition. At age twenty-nine, he knew nothing of Indians or of the West, but he was brainy, imaginative, and desperate to learn more. He believed that Protestant missionaries should take the lead in advancing civilization on the frontier. From the moment he heard about the Whitman killings, Atkinson sensed that Spalding possessed a seminal story of the West. It had mythic power to captivate and inspire Protestants in a new continental nation. As important, it placed Protestant missionaries in heroic roles as nation-builders, while casting Catholics as villains.

"We listened to Mr. Spalding's narrative of his escape from the Indians and the actions of the Catholics in the matter," Atkinson noted in his diary. "It kept us up late."

Mesmerized by the story, Atkinson pulled Spalding aside after dinner the next night, peppered him with questions, and "urged him to write very full accounts" of all the intrigues surrounding the massacre.

Atkinson had been in prep school in Vermont when Marcus and Narcissa Whitman trekked to Oregon in 1836. He was a senior at Dartmouth when Marcus made his winter ride in 1842. But after his evening encounter with Spalding, the attentive young minister became a lifelong booster of Marcus Whitman.

The Reverend George H. Atkinson, a New Englander whose grandfather commanded troops at the Battle of Bunker Hill, became one of the most prominent missionaries in Oregon, where he helped Henry Spalding invent and popularize the myth that Marcus Whitman had saved the territory. Atkinson traveled back to the East Coast in the late 1850s, where he persuaded prominent Protestants to believe and publicize Spalding's lie.

In the coming years, Atkinson would help Spalding invent, revise, promote, and legitimize the story of how Whitman saved Oregon. In the process, he enabled Spalding to transcend his tainted reputation in Oregon and win over the Protestant power structure in Boston, New York, Philadelphia, and Washington.

To be fair, there was far more to Atkinson's long and successful life than being Spalding's shill. Atkinson became well known as the Father of Education in the Pacific Northwest and was arguably its most accomplished missionary in the second half of the nineteenth century. A blue blood whose family had arrived in New England in 1663 and whose grandfather commanded troops at the Battle of Bunker Hill, Atkinson had come off the boat in Portland, Oregon, with the first textbooks to be sold in quantity in the territory. That first year, he saw to it that many more textbooks arrived and that his master plan for public education and school taxes got passed into law by the territorial legislature. He trained the first teachers for Oregon schools and helped establish academies, seminaries, and universities, including Whitman College, where he was a longtime trustee. He became superintendent of public schools in two of Oregon's most populous counties. He led prison reform, served as Oregon's penitentiary commissioner, built dozens of churches, established a system for meteorological records, developed innovative methods of gardening, wrote extensively on politics and history in local newspapers, preached on Sundays, and at age forty-seven climbed snowcapped Mount Hood (elevation 11,250 feet). After his death, his name was inscribed on a wall in the Oregon State Senate chamber.

His life was that of an idealist who delighted in getting his hands dirty. His long relationship with Spalding, documented in letters, reveals a savvy image-maker who kept bending and rebending historical facts to make Protestant missionaries look influential and heroic.

"We ought to rejoice, Dear Bro., that God has placed us in this land in which we can do so much for the future intellectual and moral welfare of the people," Atkinson wrote to Spalding in the year after the two men met. "We are directing the course of the little rills and streams which shall by and by become mighty rivers. We are laying foundations upon which the superstructure of our future society is to be built."

Spalding, as we know, was rarely in a rejoicing mood, especially in the early 1850s. His wife was dead, his career in tatters. Newspapers would not print his rants; colleagues doubted his rationality. The American Board declined to help him find work. None of this, though, dampened Atkinson's devotion. "May these frequent sufferings," he wrote to Spalding, "be as the refiner's fire and as the burnishing of your armor for the conflict ahead."

Atkinson assured Spalding that he had "one of the fairest prospects for usefulness in the territory." When Spalding lost his job as a federal Indian agent, Atkinson offered to help secure his back pay. Atkinson later used the Oregon Congregational Association to assist Spalding in landing a teaching job on the Nez Perce Reservation. Atkinson wanted to help Spalding write a glorious history of missionaries in Oregon, with a focus on the Whitmans. Seven years after the two men met, Spalding accepted the offer. He added that he had come to trust Atkinson's judgment more than his own, suggesting Atkinson write the first draft.

"Your attachment to the cause of truth & especially to the cause of missions in Oregon will carry you through all difficulties," Spalding wrote, noting that any attempts on his own part would be blinkered by emotion, "dwelling upon the bloody wrongs inflicted upon our mission at its overthrow and upon my beloved [Eliza] dead now even while I am penning these lines."

A few weeks later, Spalding warned his younger friend that their collaboration could be harmful to Atkinson's reputation and would surely require a thick skin. "You will receive the most tremendous tirade of abuse," Spalding wrote, as soon as the public knew "that you have taken up in my behalf."

Atkinson ignored the warning. The two ministers began a decades-long exchange of ideas and letters that focused on what Atkinson later called the "great historical fact" that "Dr. Whitman had done so much to save Oregon."

Atkinson was the author of the first two extended versions of this story. Both omitted the real reason for Whitman's winter ride to the East, and, rather strangely, Atkinson's two tales contradicted each other in some key details. It is not known how much either of these stories relied on Atkinson's imagination or on Spalding's interpretation of history, as told to Atkinson over the years in person and in letters. The best guess is that they were mashups—informal and uncorrected collaborations between the two ministers. Many of Spalding's early letters to Atkinson were lost when "rats and mice got in and made their nests" in a storage box—or so Atkinson said. In any case, he wrote the first version on November 20, 1858, and mailed it to the American Board in Boston.

It claimed that in the spring of 1842 Whitman had realized that the U.S. government had a "tendency" to "give Oregon to the English." To reverse that tendency, Whitman raced to Missouri, Atkinson wrote, where he organized a large wagon train that brought hundreds of American settler families to the Northwest. In this version of the story, there was nothing about Whitman going to the White House and changing the mind of the president. It focused instead on Whitman's mobilization of the wagon train, which Atkinson described as "the one that saved Oregon to American interests."

In fact, Whitman did not travel east in the early spring of 1842; he did not leave Oregon until the fall of that year. As for the large convoy of wagons that left Missouri in 1843, the historical record is clear: though Whitman traveled with and at times guided it, he had nothing to do with pulling it together. There is also no historical evidence of a "tendency" by the U.S. government at that time (or any time) to give Oregon to the British.

Atkinson's second version, mailed to the American Board just ten months later, is longer, more imaginative, and considerably more entertaining, although equally bankrupt as history. It introduces what would become enduring fictional elements in the Whitman lie. Atkinson places Whitman in Washington, where, "clad in his buffalo robe," he saved Oregon "by dint of earnest pleading." He supposedly persuaded Secretary of State Daniel Webster and President Tyler not to sign a treaty that would have traded Oregon to the British for codfishing interests off the coast of Newfoundland. There was no such pending treaty, and no historical evidence that the Tyler administration seriously considered any such trade.

When Atkinson's letters arrived in Boston in 1858 and 1859, the American Board ignored them. In all likelihood, the Reverend Selah B. Treat, the board's corresponding secretary, did not believe these out-of-the-blue, fantastic claims about Marcus Whitman, arriving more than ten years after the missionary's death.

By then, Treat, a lawyer with a doctorate in divinity, had been managing Oregon's missionaries for more than a decade. He had taken up his position in 1847, shortly before the Whitmans were murdered, replacing the Reverend David Greene.

Like Greene, Treat came to regard Spalding as unreliable and somewhat embarrassing, having received many long, heated, and irrational letters from him over the years. (Besides their content, the form of his letters was maddening; Spalding's handwriting was terrible, often bordering on indecipherable.) Treat had corresponded in the 1850s with other missionaries in Oregon, who wrote that Spalding was unstable and unfit to return to work among Indians. Treat was also among the many clerics at the American Board who had never been impressed by the missionary work of Marcus Whitman.

In the first decade and a half after Whitman's murder, the American Board did virtually nothing to commemorate him. In fact, it equivocated about whether he had been competent in his role. Nine months after Whitman's death, a notably neutral obituary appeared in *The Missionary Herald*, the house newspaper of the American Board, a publication overseen by Treat.

"He was a diligent and self-denying laborer in the work to which he consecrated his time and energies," said the most complimentary sentence in the 162 words devoted to Whitman and his legacy.

As for his "famous ride" to Washington, to save Oregon from the British, the *Herald* reported nothing of the kind. Instead it wrote, "He made a visit to the Atlantic States in the spring of 1843, being called hither by the business of the mission."

The *Herald* did acknowledge that Whitman's tragic death had given him a measure of notoriety. But it did not place him in the pantheon of famous, history-making missionaries. When the American Board published a memorial volume in 1861 that celebrated its first fifty years of sponsoring missionaries around the globe, it made no mention of him.

Under Secretary Treat, this assessment of Whitman's significance persisted for nearly two decades. It probably would have persisted forever were it not for a series of audacious and coordinated maneuvers by Spalding and Atkinson.

S palding anticipated early in 1865 that he was going to lose his federal teaching job among the Nez Perces—and that he and his second wife would be forced to leave the reservation in Idaho. To salve his ego and resurrect his reputation as a founding father of old Oregon, he launched what would become a years-long campaign of lectures and publications that fleshed out the Whitman Saved Oregon story—and, of course, made himself the story's principal narrator. Using Atkinson's earlier letters as a kind of outline, Spalding expanded the story and heightened the melodrama.

It appeared first as an eleven-part, almost book-length series of articles published throughout 1865 in *The Pacific*, a San Francisco–based newspaper owned by the Congregational Church. Atkinson was the paper's Oregon editor.

The series concluded with an account of "Dr. Whitman's Winter Journey" that included several vividly drawn scenes, complete with fly-on-the-wall quotations that were not included in Atkinson's earlier letters. As before in Spalding's writing, there was plenty of anti-Catholic venom, but this third version of the saving-Oregon story shifted the missionary doctor's motivation. It focused on Whitman's patriotism and portrayed him as a fearless and farsighted champion of Manifest Destiny.

The most compelling new scene was written in the frothy style of a dime novel. It focused on a purported turning point in the history of the West that occurred in October 1842, when Whitman was urgently called away from his mission to treat a sick man at nearby Fort Walla Walla. While the doctor was at the fort, Hudson's Bay Company traders and Catholic priests invited him to dinner. Midway through the meal, news came by messenger that a large group of Catholic settlers from Manitoba, Canada, had arrived in the Oregon Country and would soon take up residence.

Spalding takes up the tale:

> An exclamation of joy burst forth from the whole table,
> at first unaccountable to Dr. Whitman, till a young priest,

perhaps not as discreet as the older, and not thinking that there was an American at the table, sprang to his feet, and swinging his hand exclaimed, "Hurrah for Columbia, Oregon; America is too late, we have got the country."

In an instant, as by instinct, Dr. Whitman saw through the whole plan clear to Washington. . . . He immediately rose from the table and asked to be excused, sprang upon his horse, and in a very short time stood with his noble "cayuse," white with foam, before his door, and without stopping to dismount he replied to our anxious inquiries with great decision and earnestness, "I am going to cross the Rocky Mountains and reach Washington this winter, God carrying me through, and bring out an emigration over the mountains next season, or this country is lost. . . . I am a missionary, it is true, but my country needs me now."

And taking leave of his missionary associates, his comfortable home and his weeping companion, with but little hope of seeing them again in this world, he entered upon his fearful journey . . . and reached the city of Washington last of March, 1843, with his face, nose, ears, hands, feet and legs badly frozen.

For all its gripping details and patriotic flair, Spalding's account of Whitman's 1842 dinner at Fort Walla Walla was historically impossible and wholly made up. According to Spalding's own diary and a letter written by Whitman, the Canadian settlers—twenty-three families and eighty children—arrived in Oregon a full year before Whitman was supposedly shocked to hear about them. Their arrival in the fall of 1841 had occasioned no alarm—from Whitman or from any American missionary—that Oregon was soon to be stolen away by the British.

Be that as it may, Spalding proceeded to explain how Whitman—five months after that fateful, albeit fictional, dinner in Walla Walla—changed the geographical destiny of the United States by confronting the president in the White House.

> The Doctor next sought an interview with President Tyler, who at once appreciated his solicitude and his timely representations of Oregon, and especially his disinterestedness through hazardous undertaking to cross the Rocky Mountains in the winter to take back a caravan of wagons. . . .
>
> [Tyler told Whitman that] his frozen limbs were sufficient proof of his sincerity, and his missionary's character was sufficient guarantee for his honesty, and he would therefore as President rest upon those and act accordingly . . . and no more action should be had towards trading off Oregon till he could hear the result of the expedition. If the Doctor could establish a wagon route through the mountains to the Columbia River . . . he would use his influence to hold on to Oregon.
>
> The great desire of the Doctor's American soul, and Christian withal, that is, the pledge of the President that the swapping of Oregon with England for a cod fishery, should stop for the present, was attained, although at the risk of life, and through great sufferings and unsolicited, and without the promise of expectation of a dollar's reward from any source. And now, God giving him life and strength, he would do the rest; that is, connect the Missouri and Columbia Rivers with a wagon track so deep and plain that neither national envy nor sectional fanaticism would ever blot it out.

In addition to publishing his story in the church-owned *Pacific* newspaper, Spalding sought a wider secular audience, so he sent it to the Portland-based historian Frances Fuller Victor, in the form of a thirty-four-page letter. Written while he was still on the Nez Perce Reservation, it is a near-verbatim version of what *The Pacific* published in the fall of that year. Victor incorporated some of it into her widely read biography of Joe Meek. She would later regret having given credence to Spalding's claims—and, as we shall see, began to investigate them. Spalding also published a similarly expansive, slightly gorier version of his Whitman Saved Oregon lectures as a nine-part series in the *Walla Walla Statesman* in February 1866.

A s Spalding successfully peddled his story in the West, Atkinson traveled to Boston to put a positive spin on it for the American Board.

"While East in 1865, I called upon Rev. S. B. Treat and made known the facts as stated to me by Mr. Spalding. He was much surprised that Dr. Whitman had done so much to save Oregon," Atkinson later wrote.

Treat was more than surprised. He did not trust Spalding and was inclined to doubt anything he said. As Atkinson diplomatically put it, Treat "intimated that Brother Spalding wrote and said extravagant things, sometimes, and they [the American Board and its newspaper, *The Missionary Herald*] must be careful of quoting and relying on him implicitly."

Treat, though, had a considerably higher opinion of Atkinson. The two ministers were cut from the same Calvinist cloth; both had received doctor of divinity degrees from Andover Theological Seminary. In addition, Atkinson had credentials that mattered in Boston: a proper New England bloodline, a Dartmouth degree, and a remarkably long and impressive record of getting things done in Oregon.

Atkinson used his credentials and credibility to improve Treat's opinion of Spalding, while being careful not to overpraise his friend back in Oregon.

"I replied that I knew Brother Spalding's rather erratic way of leaping to conclusions, but on more acquaintance I usually found him very correct in the statement of facts, though strong in prejudice against the Jesuits."

As Spalding's advocate, Atkinson had traveled to Boston with an ace up his sleeve. He told Treat that, in addition to him, there was another highly credible missionary who could attest to the truth of Spalding's story about Whitman saving Oregon.

"Mr. Treat, I wish you to know these facts as they are for the honor of God in your missions in Oregon, and for the encouragement of the churches. I refer you to Rev. Cushing Eells to confirm what I say. He is very careful in all his statements. You can all rely upon him."

Like Treat and Atkinson, Eells—born in Massachusetts, educated at Williams College, and trained in theology at East Windsor Theological Seminary, in Hartford, Connecticut—was a properly credentialed New England Calvinist. The American Board had sent him to Oregon in 1838 as part of the party of missionary reinforcements that went out to help the Whitmans and Spaldings.

Eells worked for nearly nine years at a mission near modern-day Spokane, Washington, where he and his wife failed to convert a single Indian. The Whitman killings forced him to flee to the west side of the Cascades, where he became an educator. He founded a school in the Willamette Valley that, with Atkinson's help, became Pacific University. In 1862, Eells returned to the site of the Whitman killings, where, again with assistance from Atkinson, he founded Whitman Seminary, which later became Whitman College.

Over the years, Eells had won a reputation with the American Board for probity and for candor in his assessments of Spalding. In the mid-1850s, Treat had asked Eells if he believed Spalding was qualified to resume work as a missionary on the Nez Perce Reservation. Eells responded with a scorching letter that described Spalding as indiscreet, imprudent, and dishonest. It concluded, "Mr. Spalding is especially wanting in those qualities which it is very desirable should be possessed in a high degree by a person going to labor as a missionary among the N.P. Indians."

For all these reasons, Treat respected Eells and trusted his judgment, as Atkinson shrewdly guessed. Treat wrote Eells, asking him if claims about Whitman saving Oregon should be regarded as "perfectly reliable."

Treat's question reached Eells at a critical moment in his new job as principal of Whitman Seminary, which he had founded in honor of his murdered friend. Eells was living in Walla Walla in the spring of 1866, supervising construction of the school's first building. When it opened that fall, Whitman Seminary would be in debt. Eells urgently needed to raise the school's profile, find paying students, and attract donors from around the United States. What could be more useful in addressing those needs than for Marcus Whitman to be recognized in influential and well-to-do Protestant circles on the East Coast as a martyr who saved the Pacific Northwest from the grasping hand of the British?

Though he knew the actual reasons for Whitman's winter journey to the East, he chose to vouch for Spalding's lie. "The single object of Dr. Whitman in attempting to cross the continent in the winter of 1842–43, amid mighty peril and suffering, was to make a desperate attempt to save this [Oregon] country to the United States," he wrote.

That Eells was lying—or unconsciously choosing to remember the past in a way that benefited him and his new school—is clear from his own contemporaneous writings. Those documents—a letter and a joint missionary resolution he signed—show that in the fall of 1842 Eells knew that Whitman had rushed to Boston "in regard to the interests of his mission."

Yet in his letter to Treat, Eells claimed that all his personal experience as a missionary in Oregon supported Spalding's fiction: "I have been an eye and ear witness since August 1838 [and] I am prepared to say, that to my mind there is not a shadow of a doubt that Dr. Whitman by his efforts with President Tyler and Secretary Webster in 1843, and his agency during the same year in conducting an immigrant wagon train from the western frontier to the Columbia River was instrumental in saving a valuable portion of this northwest to the United States."

That letter was all the encouragement Treat needed to re-remember Marcus Whitman, elevating him from murdered mediocrity to martyred hero.

Treat printed Eells's "Letter from Walla Walla" as the lead article in the December 1866 edition of *The Missionary Herald*, deeming it "entirely trustworthy." In its approving comments about the letter, the newspaper chose to ignore its own files, which had said in the 1840s that Whitman came east on missionary business. At the direction of Treat, the *Herald*'s coverage of Whitman's newly discovered heroism explained that he probably would not have come east "had it not been for his desire to save the disputed [Oregon] territory to the United States."

The American Board could now claim—and it did, in *The Missionary Herald*, when it published the letter from Eells—that the work of its missionaries in Oregon had been far more valuable than was previously understood. Besides serving God, Whitman and his colleagues had helped knit together the United States as a continental nation, while defending it from the dark designs of foreigners and Catholics.

The paper credited Whitman with heroism that was both religious and secular.

"It was not simply an American question," the *Herald* said. "It was at the same time a Protestant question. He was fully alive to the efforts which the Roman Catholics were making to gain the mastery on the Pacific coast; and he was firmly persuaded that they were working in the interest of the HBC with a view to this very end. The danger from this quarter made a profound impression upon his mind."

Further cementing Spalding and Atkinson's new and heroic version of Marcus Whitman, Treat decided to celebrate the late missionary during the American Board's annual meeting in Pittsfield, Massachusetts, in the fall of 1866. Treat wrote Eells to thank him for his letter and to inform him how thrilled everyone at the meeting had been to learn about Whitman. "The topic excited a great deal of interest in Pittsfield," Treat wrote. "It has been noticed by the papers, extensively, secular as well as religious."

Whitman was well on his way to becoming a religious icon. His story could be used to raise donations for Protestant churches, the American Board, and church-sponsored schools like Whitman Seminary. Atkinson—an entrepreneurial minister who always looked to the future—was the first to recognize and exploit Whitman's money-raising potential.

Treat invited him to speak about the "Fruits of the Oregon Mission" at an American Board meeting in Norwich, Connecticut, in 1868. Editors of the *Herald* wrote that those who attended "will not soon forget the thrilling interest excited" by Atkinson as he lectured on "facts that were within his knowledge."

Those "facts" were an inspirational distillation of the story he had helped Spalding fabricate, sweetened with memorable quotations that Atkinson had newly made up. He quoted President Tyler as saying, "Dr. Whitman, since you are a missionary, I will believe you." Since

John Tyler had died in 1862, it seems that Atkinson and Spalding felt entirely comfortable making up quotes and attributing them to the former president.

In Norwich, Atkinson tugged at heartstrings. He said Whitman had risked his life to save a precious corner of America—only to be slaughtered by Indians, along with his lovely and devoted wife. Then he challenged the assembled Protestants to put their money where Marcus Whitman had lost his blood:

"Our missionary brother fulfilled duty to God and to his country. He sleeps in the mound near the spot on which he fell. His surviving friends near, have established 'Whitman Seminary,' which ought to be a college, endowed by the *voluntary* gifts of a grateful people."

At the end of his speech, Atkinson noted that "the Rev. C. Eells, one of the surviving missionary brethren of Dr. Whitman, and Principal of the Whitman Seminary, with other trustees, will gratefully receive and apply any aid which the benevolent may wish to bestow."

I n the late 1860s, as the Whitman lie found favor among Protestants in New England, where it began to fill church offering plates, the Cayuses were beginning to feel the effects of another kind of lie.

The reservation they shared with the Walla Wallas and the Umatillas had supposedly been set aside "for their exclusive use," according to the treaty they had reluctantly signed in 1855. But in the decade since they had surrendered 90 percent of their traditional territory, the reservation had been encircled by white farmers who openly connived to take its best farm and grazing land with direct access to water. As one federal Indian agent described the Indians' predicament in 1868, they "are being constantly annoyed, harassed, and impoverished by their too close proximity to white people who want their land."

Just as terrifying to the Indians, the reservation—where treaty law forbade "any white person" from residing without permission—had become a heavily traveled crossroads for ill-behaved and often drunken white men rushing back and forth to nearby gold fields. A "great thoroughfare from all Oregon, Washington Territory and San Francisco to the mining regions of Idaho and Montana passes through" the reservation, wrote J. W. Perit Huntington, the superintendent of Indian affairs for Oregon.

An endless parade of white travelers and extensive freight transportation, Huntington added, was forcing the Cayuses, Walla Wallas, and Umatillas into "contact with many of the lowest and most corrupting sort of whites. . . . Immense quantities of ardent spirits are daily hauled through the Indian settlements, and there are always men who will furnish it to the Indians. . . . Some thoughtless whites have talked quite freely about driving the Indians off [their reservation] and taking possession by force. . . . The Indians are hence very uneasy and very much alarmed."

Part of the Indians' problem was their highly visible success—in the eyes of white neighbors and passersby—as horse breeders and farmers. The 384 Cayuses on the reservation had five thousand horses, worth $80,000, which amounted to thirteen horses, valued at $208, per tribal member. In addition, as federal Indian agents pointed out in their annual reports to Washington, some Cayuse families were successfully raising wheat and vegetables on small but well-watered plots near the Umatilla River. White neighbors grumbled that if the Indians could be forced off the reservation, more land could be put under the plow and farm production could explode.

When the Cayuses journeyed away from the reservation to hunt, fish, or gather roots, they frequently ran afoul of white farmers, ranchers, and miners. Fences blocked their access to traditional places for hunting and gathering. Roving groups of miners decimated local deer and other game. Farmers' hogs sniffed out and ate camas root, an important Cayuse food.

To prevent clashes between white settlers and the Cayuses, federal Indian agents were ordered to restrict off-reservation travel, enforcing a "pass system" created by the Office of Indian Affairs. The system, policed in Oregon by the U.S. Army, contravened explicit guarantees written into the treaty that Cayuse leaders and U.S. officials had signed a decade earlier at the Walla Walla council. It said their rights to hunt, fish, and gather in traditional off-reservation locations were "secured to them." The treaty had been ratified by the U.S. Congress, giving it the power of law. But the message the Cayuses were getting from their white neighbors—as well as local, state, and federal officials—was that the law did not mean what it said.

A third collaborator with Spalding in the Whitman Saved Oregon lie conducted his operations exclusively on the home front—in Oregon.

He was William H. Gray, the carpenter and mechanic who in 1836 joined the Whitmans on their way west. As mentioned earlier, it was Gray's accounts of the jealousy and backbiting between Spalding and Whitman that had played a pivotal role in the board's decision in 1842 to close Whitman's mission and fire Spalding. As Gray learned, to his shock, in the autumn of 1842, the board had also decided to fire him.

That humiliating chapter of his personal history, however, never appeared in any of Gray's extensive writings about Whitman. Gray denied that he had ever learned about the board's decision to close Whitman's mission, and he never acknowledged that Whitman rode east in a panicked attempt to reverse it.

Like Spalding, Gray was a virulent anti-Catholic. He also nursed lifelong grudges against the Hudson's Bay Company and the British. He had been slighted by Dr. John McLoughlin, who once denied Gray a seat at the HBC's dinner table in Vancouver. After settling in the Willamette Valley in the 1840s, Gray became a respected citizen, eminent pioneer, and opinion leader. He was a journalist, a territorial legislator, and a historian who founded the Oregon Pioneer Society, an influential group that for several decades defined the history of Oregon.

In 1865, when the Whitman Saved Oregon tale was about to go public, Spalding invited Gray to help spread the word. In a letter, Spalding told Gray that he was "welcome to use" the story and to peruse all the documents and depositions that he had collected in support of it.

By the fall of that year, Gray was on board. He regurgitated parts of the story in the *Marine Gazette,* published in Astoria, Oregon. He then rolled the entire story into seven chapters of a book that he published in 1870: *A History of Oregon, 1792–1849, Drawn from Personal Observation and Authentic Information.*

Gray's book did not have much influence outside of Oregon. Contemporaneous journalists and historians judged it to be grievance-driven bunk. The nineteenth-century American historian Hubert Howe Bancroft called Gray "the most mendacious missionary." In addition to his lies, Gray struggled mightily with basic facts. He testified, during an 1865 lawsuit involving the HBC, that Whitman had traveled to Washington in 1842 for an interview with President Millard Fillmore—who occupied the White House from 1850 to 1853.

Leading Protestants in Oregon, however, admired Gray's book. It lionized Protestant missionaries and demonized priests. It helped legitimize anti-Catholicism in Oregon as late as the 1930s, stoking grassroots support for nativist organizations like the Ku Klux Klan.

The *Pacific Christian Advocate*, the voice of mainstream Protestantism in Oregon, praised Gray for "his utter abhorrence of the Roman Catholic priests and Jesuits as the instigators of the Whitman massacre."

Gray would stand by the Whitman Saved Oregon story all his life. Although he had quit missionary work five years before the Whitmans were killed, he and his wife arranged to have their remains reburied at the massacre site. There, they would share the posthumous glory of Marcus and Narcissa Whitman.

Gray's gravestone, which remains on display at what is now the Whitman Mission National Historic Site, falsely identifies him as "a leading spirit in securing the Oregon of 1843 to the United States."

CHAPTER THIRTEEN

BROTHER SPALDING GOES TO WASHINGTON

As a missionary turned propagandist, Spalding was off to a splendid start. Five years after he and his collaborators created it, various iterations of his Whitman story had appeared in newspapers in Oregon, Washington, California, Ohio, Michigan, New York, and Massachusetts. It was at the heart of William Gray's purportedly authentic published history of Oregon. In New England, Presbyterian and Congregational ministers were preaching about it. It was helping to raise money for the debt-ridden Whitman Seminary.

Spalding, though, was far from content. Indeed, he was angrier than ever. The cause of his public fury and private humiliation was Brouillet, the vexing priest who had saved his life in 1847 and then accused him—quite accurately—of being an ingrate and a liar, in what were now official publications of the U.S. House of Representatives and the U.S. Senate.

Spalding had become obsessed with what he called the "fearful power of this Romish Congressional Document." He convinced himself, rather hysterically, that it was being "furnished abundantly to the ten times ten thousand Romish priests who throng the Indian country."

Soon after the Whitman Massacre, Spalding had claimed that Brouillet was a principal conspirator in the killings. His early accusations, though, were couched in rumor and wrapped in innuendo. When he learned that Congress had published Brouillet, Spalding stopped equivocating. Brouillet was a "monster," Spalding wrote, "the murdering priest who caused the butchery of Doc Whitman."

When he wrote those words, Spalding was sixty-seven years old. His thirty-four years in Oregon had been marked by physical hardship: Nez Perce warriors beat him up and pushed him into a fire; he had run desperately for days from Cayuses intent on killing him. In Indian country and among whites in the Willamette Valley, he had often been seriously ill, sometimes in bed for weeks. As he aged, his illnesses lingered.

Yet Spalding caught a second wind in his late sixties. He was invigorated by Brouillet's published attacks. They made him crazy angry in a way that emboldened his ambition, fired his imagination, and sharpened his focus. His life suddenly had purpose. With new spring in his step, Spalding embarked in 1870 on an extraordinarily ambitious crusade to sell Whitman's heroics to the Oregon Legislative Assembly, to churches, to newspapers across the country, and to Congress. He intended to travel to Washington, D.C., and publish his "manifesto" at federal expense. It would introduce all Americans to his story about Marcus Whitman, demolish Brouillet, and maybe even give him another shot at returning to Nez Perce country as a federal Indian agent.

"He may be insane," wrote the editors of the Albany (Oregon) *State Rights Democrat*, which published many of Spalding's writings, "but it is the same kind of insanity with which Columbus, and Fulton, and Morse, and Field, were afflicted when trying to impress their earnest convictions upon the public."

A staged studio photograph from the 1860s captures the messianic mindset that seized Spalding in this final chapter of his life. It depicts him as a kind of living national monument—a prophet of Manifest Destiny and a Merlin of the missionary arts who was perched on the far western edge of the American experience.

Tools of the preacher's trade, as he practiced it among the Nez Perces, surround him: a Bible, cradled in his right hand; a wood-handled steel hoe firmly gripped in his left; a large woodman's ax standing beside his left leg; a draft animal's yoke resting at his feet. Behind him, hanging from the wall, is a painting of Jesus. Bristly cuttings of Ponderosa pine, the evergreen tree common in the high country of eastern Oregon and Idaho's Clearwater lands, are scattered at his feet.

The Reverend Henry Harmon Spalding posed for this peculiar photograph in Oregon in the 1860s, when he was feverishly publicizing the Whitman myth. Spalding persuaded several newspapers in the West to print—at astonishing length—his claims. But some of the region's leading editors viewed him as a fanatical liar; one called him "a lunatic on the subject of Catholicism" and not "sane on any subject."

Wearing a dark waistcoat, a white shirt, and a black cravat, he sits stiffly on a four-legged stool. Care has been taken to comb his hair up and over his bald pate. Snarls in his chaotic black beard have been combed out. His whiskers are gray, but only around the edges. He looks younger than his years, his dark eyes cold with purpose.

M ore than a year before he left for Washington, Spalding had begun collecting testimonials and resolutions that damned Brouillet's "depraved heart" for producing "foul and libelous slanders" and celebrated Spalding for collecting "authentic documents for a truthful history of the whole matter." They demanded redress by act of Congress.

> *Resolved* . . . That in our judgment a grievous wrong has been done Dr. Whitman and his martyred associates [by congressional publication of Brouillet's writings] . . . and that, in common with our patriotic fellow-citizens of the Pacific coast, we unite in asking Congress to rectify this wrong, in part, at least, by adopting and publishing a document [written by Spalding] which shall contain an answer to the above-named document; and we feel the utmost assurance that the sacred regard for the truth of history ever entertained by your honorable body, and the high name ever placed by you upon unselfish patriotism, will lead you once to see both the justice and patriotism of our request.

The signatories of these resolutions were mid-nineteenth-century Protestant worthies in the Pacific Northwest. They included Joel Palmer, the former superintendent of Indian affairs who had helped hammer out the Indian treaty at Walla Walla; George Abernathy, a former provisional governor of Oregon; D. W. Ballard, governor of Idaho; and, of course, the Reverend George Atkinson, whose landmark work in advancing public education in the Northwest had made him a highly respected public figure.

Only one of the signatories had any firsthand knowledge of what Whitman did on his famous trip east. He was Asa Lovejoy, the pioneer who accompanied the missionary on part of his journey but dropped off before he reached St. Louis. Like everyone else who claimed that Whitman saved Oregon, Lovejoy had no direct knowledge of what the doctor did or did not achieve in Washington, D.C. But like everyone else who signed the document, he agreed to tell Spalding what the author of the myth wanted to hear: "I have no doubt," he wrote, "the doctor's interviews with the President and others resulted greatly to the benefit of Oregon and the entire coast."

Spalding also set up meetings or attended annual conferences of all the mainstream Protestant denominations in Oregon—Presbyterians, Methodists, Congregationalists (led by Atkinson), Baptists, and the Christian Church. Those churches, as Spalding explained, represented thirty thousand of "the best inhabitants" of Oregon. They all signed on to the demand that Congress replace Brouillet's "brand of infamy" with Spalding's "sacred regard for unselfish patriotism." The resolutions all sounded the same because Spalding either wrote them or had a heavy hand in determining what they should say. When he pulled it all together, Spalding had more than eighty pages to present to Congress.

Before he departed from Oregon, Spalding got in touch by mail with family, friends, ministers, businessmen, and politicians from Boston to Washington. They were told to expect him and urged to support his crusade for Marcus Whitman.

His final preparatory step before heading east was to travel to Salem, Oregon, to win the endorsement of the state legislature. He also wanted to have his manifesto printed at state expense. He had arranged for R. H. Crawford, a friend and state senator from Linn

County, where Spalding lived, to introduce Senate Joint Memorial No. 5 on October 12, 1870. The wording of the proposed resolution was relatively benign. It said nothing about murderous priests. Instead it endorsed Spalding's manifesto as a way of honoring Whitman and correcting historical errors about Oregon, which it claimed Congress had inadvertently allowed into the official record when it published Brouillet's writings.

After quick approval in a friendly senate committee, the resolution endorsing Spalding's manifesto was brought up for a vote on the floor of the state senate. It was there that Spalding's national ambitions collided with his lingering local reputation as a "lunatic," as Asahel Bush, the newspaper editor in the state capital, had once called him.

Senators toyed with Spalding and made fun of his precious manifesto. In response to a committee request that eight hundred copies of it be printed, one state senator offered an amendment that called for printing eight hundred copies of the New Testament. Another said the state should print eight hundred copies of William Gray's *Authentic History of Oregon,* which had come out earlier in the year and been panned in some Oregon newspapers. A third called on the state to print eight hundred copies of Spalding's lectures, which had already appeared at colossal length in various local newspapers over the past five years. In the end, nothing was printed. On a vote of 13–7, the senate voted to "indefinitely postpone" any endorsement of Spalding and his documents.

When Spalding's daughter Amelia learned what had happened, she wrote an alarmed letter to her stepmother. Amelia knew that her father was soon to leave for the East Coast, where he planned to present his manifesto to Congress. She believed he was setting himself up for more mockery and deeper humiliation that might occasion the onset of severe mental illness.

"I think it worse than useless for Father to go East with the hope of getting anything done," she wrote. "I know how it will hurt him to be treated as he was at Salem. He is so easily excited that to be so disappointed in what has been his heart's work for so long I know that it will take his mind from him and I know that he would be in no fit state to travel so far alone."

Amelia underestimated her father's stamina. She also failed to appreciate a maxim of the mythmaker's art: gullibility grows with distance. The more miles her father put between himself and the Willamette Valley, the more his audiences savored his frontier "authenticity" and the more they believed his thrilling story. He may have been seen as a false prophet in the Oregon legislature, and a lunatic by Oregon editors, but in Chicago, New York, Boston, Philadelphia, and Washington he would be perceived as a wise and seasoned missionary with a fresh take on Christian patriotism.

Spalding had not been east since the wagon train era. During his time on the frontier, America had been transformed by technology, war, and population growth. Telegraph lines, railroads, and efficient mail service had sewn together the continent. The Civil War had ended slavery. Ulysses S. Grant, the general who won the war, had also won the White House. There were 38.5 million Americans in 1870, more than twice as many as when Spalding rolled west with the Whitmans three decades before.

Spalding caught a steamer south to Sacramento, then boarded a transcontinental train, the tracks of which had been completed just the year before. Stopping in Chicago in late November 1870, he got his first hint of how easy it was going to be—compared with the mockery he had endured in the Oregon State Senate—to sell himself and his fable about Marcus Whitman.

"One day last week a man of humble appearance, about seventy years of age, called at our office. . . . For four hours of the rarest interest we listened to the wonderful story," wrote the Reverend S. L. Humphrey, editor of a Congregational weekly in Chicago called *The Advance* and chief of the Chicago branch of the American Board of Commissioners for Foreign Missions.

Under the headline "An Evening with an Old Missionary," the Protestant newspaper printed and celebrated nearly everything Spalding had to say. Spalding liked the article so much he made it a prominent part of the manifesto he planned to present to Congress.

In upstate New York, relatives and old friends welcomed Spalding like a returning war hero. They gave him new clothes, packed a Presbyterian church to hear him preach, and listened, spellbound, to his claims about Whitman. Local newspapers celebrated his homecoming and spread his story as western gospel. "I am amazed at the unbounded sympathy & tender care bestowed upon me," Spalding wrote to his wife in early December.

His amazement increased in New York City, where he was welcomed and fed by a wealthy businessman, William E. Dodge, who "took me in his arms with the tenderness of a son . . . and then assured me of his warmest support in Washington." Besides owning a major trading company, Dodge was both a former vice president of the American Board and a former congressman with powerful friends on Capitol Hill. Eager to help Spalding elevate the national profile of Protestant missionaries and build the Whitman legend, Dodge wrote a letter of introduction to a number of powerful men in Washington, including Vice President Schuyler Colfax, House Speaker James G. Blaine, three other House members, and four members of the Senate.

The venerable Oregon missionary was coming to Washington to correct a "great wrong" done by Congress, the letter said. It asked lawmakers to consult "with other friends of Protestant religion, to see if we cannot wipe out this stain." As part of his pre-trip planning,

Spalding had already been in touch with Oregon's most influential members of Congress, Senator Henry Winslow Corbett and Representative Joseph S. Smith. The two Protestant men had agreed to present his documents to Senate and House committees on Indian affairs.

Dodge purchased passage for Spalding on a steamer to Boston. There, he visited the head office of the American Board, which had been laceratingly critical of him for nearly three decades.

Part of his rehabilitation in the board's eyes had been engineered, as we have seen, by the adroit advance work of Atkinson, with the assistance of Reverend Eells. But it was the fundraising value of the Whitman Saved Oregon story that suddenly made Spalding a very valuable missionary. His story excited churchgoers, and the more widely it was disseminated, the easier it was for the board to collect the cash it needed to support missionaries around the world. The once hostile board secretary, the Reverend S. B. Treat, greeted Spalding warmly and promised his full cooperation.

Spalding, who never gave up his desire to live among the Nez Perces, had picked the perfect moment to come east, renew his ties to the American Board, and seek favor in Washington. After the Civil War, Protestant missionaries—most of them Methodists, Presbyterians, and Baptists—had turned their attention from abolishing slavery to tackling what they regarded as America's second great moral abomination: cruel and corrupt treatment of Indians. With authority granted by Congress and President Grant, they were taking command of the educational, economic, and cultural lives of nearly a quarter million Indians in the West.

Congress had created a Board of Indian Commissioners, which Grant filled with zealous and well-heeled Protestant philanthropists. Backed by federal money and enforced by federal law, it was an unprecedented attempt to do what Spalding and Whitman had tried and mostly failed to do with the Nez Perces and the Cayuses in the 1830s

and '40s. In their first report on how to rescue Indians, they emphasized "the religion of our blessed Saviour" as "the most effective agent
for the civilization of any people."

Spalding arrived in Washington on January 5, 1871, as this religious takeover of reservation life was accelerating across the West.
Members of Congress, who funded the reservations, and federal bureaucrats, who managed them, were eager to hear from a minister
with Spalding's long experience. He was introduced in the capital as
"the oldest living Protestant missionary in Oregon."

In Washington, Spalding's energies did not seem like those of an
aging man. He moved quickly and deftly, using his religious connections and manipulating the federal bureaucracy in a way that soon
won official standing for his manifesto. He gave a copy of it to a Methodist minister, Alfred B. Meacham, who had been appointed by Grant
as superintendent of Indian affairs for Oregon. Meacham forwarded
the document, which became known as "Early Labors of Missionaries
in Oregon," to his senior boss, Secretary of the Interior Columbus
Delano. Inside Delano's department, Spalding's bundle of misinfor-
mation, anti-Catholic hysteria, and questionable testimonials was
treated as an honest account of Oregon's missionary history.

In less than three weeks, Spalding met with a sympathetic group of
senators, including Corbett from Oregon and Samuel Pomeroy of
Kansas. They agreed to help him. A week later, Senator Pomeroy won
unanimous consent in the Senate for a resolution that required the Interior Department "to furnish to the Senate any information" in its
files about the early labors of missionaries in Oregon. The deceptive
documents Spalding had just planted at Interior were promptly forwarded to the Senate.

While he was lobbying Congress and manipulating the bureaucracy, Spalding also tended to his image.

He had his portrait taken (without a hoe, ax, or Bible this time) at the studio of famed Civil War photographer Mathew Brady. He encouraged the Reverend Dr. John C. Smith, at whose Washington home Spalding was receiving free lodging, to write a long letter to *The New York Evangelist,* a Presbyterian weekly. The letter praised Spalding "for his meek and quiet spirit, his great industry and constant labor in the duty which called him to this capital."

The climax of Spalding's journey to Washington—indeed, the climactic scene of his life— occurred on February 9, 1871. The Senate was slogging through the routine business of its Thursday-morning calendar. It referred a House public lands bill to a finance committee. It ordered the printing of extra copies of a report on Canadian trade. Then, as Spalding anxiously watched from the Senate gallery, Vice President Colfax took the floor. He "laid before the Senate" the entire manifesto that Spalding had brought from

Spalding posed for this portrait in the studio of Mathew Brady during his highly successful 1871 trip to Washington, D.C., where he persuaded the U.S. Senate to print his manifesto claiming that Whitman had saved Oregon. Federal publication of the story gave it credibility, and it soon appeared throughout America as historical fact in textbooks, encyclopedias, and major newspapers like *The New York Times.*

Oregon, asking that it be referred to the Committee on Indian Affairs and printed.

In all likelihood, none of the senators had read or would ever read the turgid document. If they had, they would have discovered what one historian later called a "ridiculous collection of fabrications, exaggerations and flat-footed contradictions."

Certainly, the Senate had no idea that it was about to give its official stamp of approval to a falsehood that for decades would be taught in Sunday schools and public schools all across America as the official history of the Pacific Northwest.

Instead, on the morning it came up for consideration, Spalding's manifesto was nothing more than the usual legislative back-scratching among senators. It was a minor regional matter to be dealt with and forgotten. The national press showed no interest. After considering Spalding's manifesto, the Senate moved quickly to consider a tax relief petition from dealers of snuff and cigars in Logansport, Indiana.

But for Spalding, it felt as though the Lord had finally answered his prayers. From his seat in the gallery, he scribbled a letter of exultation:

> *Dearest Wife: Glory to God & bless his holy name. Victory complete. The Senate has just ordered by unanimous vote my manifesto printed. . . . I can hardly believe my eyes & ears. . . . Every Senator seemed my friend.*

Near the end of his two-page letter to his wife, Spalding's joy began to ebb; he shifted his focus to a more characteristic concern: vengeance. He believed the Senate's decision to publish his manifesto meant that he would now be able to get even—with Roman Catholics in general, with Brouillet in particular, and with all the other doubters, haters, and backstabbers in Oregon who had impugned his character and questioned his rationality.

"Tell my friends and enemies," he wrote, "that my visit to Washington to vindicate our faithful dead & Protestantism has been a complete success."

Four days later, when Spalding was reading and correcting proofs of his manifesto at the congressional printing office, he again wrote to his wife. He said he was still struggling to contain his happiness or believe his senses.

In addition to the Senate's order to print fifteen hundred copies of his manifesto, now called Executive Document No. 37, the Grant administration had offered him a job on the Nez Perce Reservation. He was to be superintendent of instruction, with an annual salary of $1,200 (about $25,000 now). He also landed an unpaid position as missionary to the Nez Perces for the Presbyterian Board of Foreign Missions.

Spalding's triumph in Washington was complete.

"Dear wife," he wrote, "Glory to God for his victory given to truth over calumnies."

In October 1871, Spalding returned yet again to his old mission at Lapwai, on the Nez Perce Reservation. He also returned to form as his maddeningly paradoxical self. A charismatic evangelist. An insufferable irritant.

He complained about books used in reservation schools, calling them "works of the Devil." He demanded that Indian children study his Nez Perce translation of the New Testament. He complained about the reservation's interpreter, Perrin Whitman, a nephew of Marcus Whitman and a fluent speaker of the Nez Perce language. Spalding claimed, with no evidence, that Whitman was pro-Catholic and guilty of serious moral turpitude.

Most damaging for Spalding's job security, he complained about his immediate boss, Presbyterian Indian agent John Monteith, accusing him of nepotism and mismanagement. Spalding was also outraged that Monteith refused to allow him to decide what was taught in schools on the reservation.

As he had done many times before, Spalding irritated himself out of a job. Monteith reported to his superiors that the minister was acting like a "dictator," making demands that were "wild and childish." Eight months after he returned in triumph to Lapwai, Spalding was fired and told to leave. It was his third involuntary departure.

But his short return to his old mission was also an astonishing success, if measured by the hundreds of Indians he baptized. His presence helped spark a major religious awakening among the "treaty Nez Perces," many of whom had drifted away from Christianity during Spalding's periodic and extended absences, which began in 1847.

To jump-start the resurgence, Spalding baptized his longtime friend Lawyer, the much-maligned head chief. By this point Lawyer was recognized as chief by only a third of the Nez Perces. He had betrayed the rest of the tribe when he signed the 1863 treaty that protected only his landholdings and those of his followers.

When Spalding reappeared on the reservation, large crowds gathered to hear him preach. His presence helped bring more than six hundred Indians back into the church. "His work in Christianizing the treaty or reservation Nez Perces had finally succeeded," historian Josephy wrote in his definitive history of the tribe, which credits Spalding's return for making churches, congregations, and Native preachers enduring features of life on the reservation.

Although he was exiled from Lapwai in 1872, Spalding continued his work as a Presbyterian missionary in the Washington Territory, preaching to and converting sizable numbers of Spokane Indians. While celebrating his seventieth birthday in 1873, Spalding added up his lifetime tally of Indian baptisms. They totaled 1,207. The number is a useful gauge of his profound impact as a missionary on the lives of the Columbia Plateau Indians. By comparison, records show that Marcus and Narcissa Whitman converted two Cayuses.

Five months before his seventieth birthday, Spalding received a letter from Atkinson, inquiring as to whether he was absolutely sure about two key claims in the Whitman melodrama: Did the U.S. government really intend to swap Oregon for a cod fishery off the coast of Newfoundland? And did President Tyler really change U.S. government policy toward the Oregon Country because of Marcus Whitman's winter ride to Washington?

Atkinson had been challenged about the story by a widely respected student of Pacific Northwest history, Elwood Evans. A lawyer and historian in the Washington Territory, Evans was among the first residents of the Northwest to use documentary evidence to assess the veracity of the Whitman myth.

Evans had not always been a doubter. Indeed, he was an early supporter of the Whitman Saved Oregon story, and had even contributed a testimonial to Spalding's manifesto. But since then, Evans had been sifting through his large collection of historical documents and was beginning to suspect that the Whitman story was phony. He eventually concluded that it was a "systematic deception by ministers."

"What was Dr. Whitman's statement to you when [he] returned in 1843?" Atkinson asked, referring to Spalding's first conversation with Whitman after the doctor came back from his trip to the East Coast.

The letter must have come as a shock to Spalding. But apparently he never replied. While cutting wood in November 1873, he fell, broke a rib, and suffered internal injuries.

Though bedridden and feeble, he continued to baptize Indians.

Among the last to receive the sacrament from Spalding was Umha-walish, a leader of the Umatilla tribe, and his wife. When they came to him on his deathbed, he baptized them and renamed them Marcus and Narcissa Whitman.

He died on August 3, 1874, at age seventy-one, having achieved the principal goals of his life. At the end, he had been vindicated by Congress and was surrounded by Indians he had converted to Christianity.

S palding's vindication continued beyond the grave. A decade after his death, textbooks used in public and private schools throughout America began repeating his story as bona fide history. Whitman's winter ride to Washington became the most important "fact" in explaining how the Pacific Northwest had come to be a vital part of the continental nation.

Horace E. Scudder's 1884 *History of the United States of America*, one of the country's earliest and most widely used standard textbook histories for high schools, devoted most of its five-page chapter on Oregon to the reasons for and consequences of Whitman's "terrible ride" to Washington, D.C. The text featured a dramatic painting of "Whitman starting for Washington."

"Dr. Whitman's errand was to make clear to the administration at Washington the value of Oregon, and then to organize companies of emigrants," wrote Scudder, who also adapted the Whitman story into a widely used book for young children. "Dr. Whitman was on the watch, and determined to save Oregon for the United States," it read.

Based in Boston most of his life, Scudder was an eminent nineteenth-century man of letters. He served as a literary adviser for the textbook publisher Houghton, Mifflin, and was the editor of *The Atlantic Monthly* for nearly a decade. Within a year of its publication, his *History of the United States of America* had been adopted by New York City public schools, elite private schools across the Northeast, and public and church-affiliated schools throughout the country. It influenced the entire textbook industry, persuading authors of many other standard history texts to include the Whitman story.

The martyred hero of Oregon was also a regular fixture in Sunday schools, thanks to books such as *The Story of Marcus Whitman,* made available by the Presbyterian Board of Publication.

Library reference books also jumped on the Whitman bandwagon. The story even appeared in the 1884 American edition of the *Encyclopaedia Britannica,* published by Scribner's in New York. The author of the *Britannica* article was none other than the Reverend George Atkinson, who apparently had overcome his doubts about Spalding's commitment to historical truth, even if his concerns were never answered.

I n the late 1880s, as Spalding's spurious tale of white missionary heroism swept across the United States, true stories of white greed and lawlessness were quietly unfolding in Oregon. Hungry for fertile land, white farmers and ranchers demanded that their elected officials give them legal access to the Umatilla Reservation, to which the Cayuses were now confined.

"In consequence of the large immigration of persons to this country from the Eastern States, which is increasing every year, almost every piece of land of any value in Umatilla County has been located on, and lots of people are awaiting the time when those Indians here will have their lands" taken away from them by Congress, Indian agent E. J. Sommerville wrote in 1884. "And indeed it is very natural that this should be so, as the arable land [on the reservation] is amongst the finest in Oregon, or indeed in any other state of the Union."

To acquire hundreds of square miles of agricultural land that whites judged as excess to Indian needs, a bill was passed in Congress in 1885 to divvy up the Umatilla Reservation. It allotted land, some valuable, some not, to every Indian male—and made most of the rest of the reservation's farm and grazing land available to whites. Federal officials pressed the Indians in the summer of 1885 to come to a meeting and agree to abide by the new law. But the Indians kept delaying, explaining that they were too busy tending their crops and herds to give a final answer on the matter.

The Indians knew, of course, that their rights under federal and state law were all but certain to bend to the will of white people. A grisly reminder of that maxim had just occurred on the reservation.

On May 13, 1884, two young white men, Henry N. Barnhart and Francis M. Anderson, used a revolver to shoot and kill an Indian named William, who served as a policeman with the reservation's newly established police force. The white men were indicted by a grand jury and tried for first-degree murder in nearby Pendleton, Oregon. Evidence at trial showed that the murdered man, referred to as Indian William in legal documents, was "well known to the merchants and other persons in Pendleton for his integrity, sobriety, and other good qualities." It also showed that he was killed "without cause."

But in Oregon in the mid-1880s, white juries had never viewed it as a crime for a white man to kill an Indian. That precedent carried the day in the case of Indian William. A white jury acquitted Barnhart and Anderson.

S palding's trip to Washington would have enduring and poisonous consequences for the Cayuse people. After Congress endorsed the lie that a missionary had saved Oregon and after it became a staple of history textbooks, the killing of Marcus Whitman grew in national significance. It was no longer the frontier crime that the Cayuse Five had been tried and hanged for—one that grew out of a measles epidemic and Indian fear of white domination. Instead, after Spalding succeeded in marketing Whitman as a Christ-like patriot, his murder took on the trappings of an American tragedy. It was an affront to good Christian people and a heinous test of Manifest Destiny. And the Cayuses—deep into the twentieth century—were branded as the bad Indians who did it.

CHAPTER FOURTEEN

THE OLD COLLEGE LIE

As the Umatilla Reservation came under ever-increasing pressure from acquisitive whites, Spalding's lie about Marcus Whitman found its most ardent institutional champion: Whitman College. Twenty years after Spalding's death, and nearly three decades after Cushing Eells corroborated Spalding's fraud to help preserve his private school in Walla Walla, the college was again in dire trouble and in urgent need of a fundraising miracle.

It was the summer of 1894. The faculty had not been paid for several months. Enrollment had sputtered, with only forty students registered for the fall term. To pay operating expenses, the college had been burning through its endowment—in violation of the school's charter. That endowment, never large, was all but gone. The scruffy campus of six and a half acres in Walla Walla had three wooden buildings with mortgages the college could not afford.

It could not appeal to its neighbors for rescue. The wheat-growing country around the college was mired in a depression made worse by a rail strike and an early-summer flood on the Columbia River. The cost of planting and harvesting a bushel of wheat was far higher than the price it could sell for.

The college president, James F. Eaton, a New York–born, Phi Beta Kappa graduate of Williams College, had lost the support of faculty, staff, students, and trustees. Accused of elitism and blamed for wrecking the school, he resigned under pressure in September and left town.

"Except for a faithful few," said a history of the college, "no one seemed to believe in its future or to care much whether it lived or died."

Searching for a savior, college trustees played a long shot. They hired a thirty-year-old Congregational minister, the Reverend Stephen B. L. Penrose. When he accepted the job, he was thought to be the youngest college president in the United States. He was shockingly green, with no experience as an academic administrator and no track record of doing what successful college presidents must do—raise money.

Like his failed predecessor,

Whitman College president Stephen B. L. Penrose seized on the Whitman myth in the 1890s to rescue his nearly bankrupt school. Calling it "an inspiring story of pioneer devotion," he promoted it in Chicago and on the East Coast, raising donations that secured the future of the college. Even after the story was exposed as a lie, Penrose continued for decades to teach and promote it.

Penrose was an upper-crust easterner with an elite education—Phi Beta Kappa at Williams, doctor of divinity from Yale. His wealthy and politically powerful family had lived in Philadelphia for six generations.

He grew up in a big house where Irish servants picked up his dirty clothes and called him "Little Sunbeam." At Williams he played baseball, bicycled, and mastered Greek and Latin, which he later taught.

After divinity school at Yale, he made an odd choice for a classically trained Penrose of Philadelphia: he became a home missionary for the Congregational Church, accepting an assignment that in 1890 deposited him in an all but empty corner of southeastern Washington State. It was not quite the Russian steppes, but it was arid, windswept, and very lonesome. His Congregational church in the tiny farm town of Dayton had six resident members, all over sixty, three of them invalids. Penrose taught Sunday school, cleaned the grounds, and somehow attracted new members who revived the church. Hungry for more challenges and more human contact, he joined the board of trustees of Whitman College—thirty miles from Dayton.

Whitman College took a chance on Penrose because he had near-perfect credentials for a liberal arts school with elite aspirations and no money. The college envisioned itself as the Williams of the West, and Penrose had excelled at Williams. Whitman College was almost broke, and Penrose's services were almost free. He cut his salary from $2,000 a year to $1,500, while insisting that he would pay his own travel costs and purchase his own stamps.

Penrose was ambitious, even a bit messianic. He believed a good life was impossible without a good college education. Still, his résumé was laughably thin, and he had no firm idea how he was going to steer Whitman out of bankruptcy.

He said he trusted in "Divine guidance," and that may have been what directed him to the Whitman College library, where he stumbled upon a handsomely printed book about Marcus Whitman. It claimed that the missionary had been murdered as part of a British conspiracy. Penrose was thunderstruck. He "realized at once" that he had found an "amazing story" that could be used to save the college. Americans would find the story thrilling and irresistible, he believed, and they would be bound by their love of God and country to give money to Whitman College.

Penrose knew nothing about the life and times of Marcus Whitman when he picked up *Oregon: The Struggle for Possession*, by the Reverend William Barrows. The book looked authoritative. It had all the trappings of serious scholarship. Complete with maps, index, and a list of authorities, its 363 pages had been published in 1883 in Boston as part of Houghton, Mifflin and Company's prestigious "American Commonwealths" series, which assigned noted scholars to write state histories. The editor of the series was none other than *History of the United States of America* author Horace E. Scudder, another fellow Williams man.

What Penrose did not know—or did not care to know and would never be interested in learning—was that the book he had fallen in love with was an error-riddled recapitulation of Spalding's fabrications about Whitman. Furthermore, its author was not a noted scholar. Before writing the book, Barrows, a Congregational minister, had worked as a secretary for the Massachusetts Home Missionary Society. After *Oregon: The Struggle for Possession* was published, he had become the East Coast fundraiser for Whitman College, a job that he had failed at, never raising more than a few hundred dollars a year.

It is not clear how Barrows managed to persuade Houghton, Mifflin to publish his shoddy scholarship as part of its American Commonwealths series. Scudder later regretted his role in editing the book, saying that he was "sorry that it ever appeared." In years to come, debunkers of the Whitman legend would bemoan the extraordinary influence of the book, while subjecting Barrows to scorching ridicule. One of them, Edward G. Bourne, a professor of history at Yale, called it "one of the most remarkable perversions of history ever published," in a letter to *The New York Times*. He estimated it to be "the source from which millions of readers have learned a story of Oregon which is a grotesque distortion of the real facts."

Stephen Penrose knew none of this. He was desperate to revive a dying college, and he chose to believe Barrows's book, which struck him as an "inspiring story of pioneer devotion."

In a pamphlet called "The Romance of a College," Penrose boiled the Whitman story down to its essence: "But why does that vast [Pacific Northwest] country belong now to the United States, and not to Great Britain? *Because Marcus Whitman was prophet enough to foresee its value, and hero enough to risk his life to save it.*"

The cover of the eleven-page pamphlet displayed an American flag. Inside, the text boldly—and, of course, falsely—declared that Dr. Whitman single-handedly prevented foreign schemers from stealing the wonderful part of America that would become Oregon, Washington, and Idaho. Part passion play, part dime novel, it edited out complexities in the Whitman fable. It did not demonize Catholics (a prejudice that was by then fading among many American academics and some American Protestants). Instead it amplified Whitman's supposedly patriotic acts, turning fabricated history into melodrama for the masses.

As Penrose summarized the story: Whitman was alarmed to learn that leaders in Washington, D.C., were "about to abandon" Oregon. He also knew that Great Britain was "planning to seize it." As a patriotic man of God, he rushed east in the winter to save the Northwest, obliged along the way "to subsist on mule-meat and dog-meat." In the White House, he made a strong impression on President Tyler with his frostbitten limbs and missionary sincerity. He then led back to Oregon a wagon train "that decided the destiny of a great empire, by reason of one man's prophetic heroism."

Marcus Whitman, not unlike Jesus Christ, had paid the ultimate price, Penrose wrote. Repeating claims made up by Spalding and echoed by Barrows (though leaving out the role of the Catholics), Penrose wrote that the British Hudson's Bay Company had incited Indians to kill the missionary doctor and his wife. His pamphlet emphasized the savagery of Indians, claiming that "every vestige of civilization was destroyed" at the Whitman mission.

After describing the Whitmans' murder, Penrose shifted to another heartrending, but more contemporary, melodrama: the plight of "a little, struggling college . . . the only memorial of a national hero," which was in urgent need of money, at least $100,000.

"If this endowment is not secured," Penrose wrote, "the college must die."

The climax of Penrose's pitch came in a final reference to the three stars in the flag on the cover of his pamphlet. Mixing the gore of Christian imagery with the glory of American conquest, he wrote, "Why are those three stars marked in red? They stand for the three states which Marcus Whitman saved, baptizing them with his blood."

For the next year and a half, Penrose took his pitch back east, where the money was.

His first stop was Chicago, home to more than fifty Congregational churches. More important, as it turned out, Chicago was also home to two elderly men—a millionaire philanthropist and a scrappy newspaper editor—who came to believe the Whitman Saved Oregon story with the same unshakable intensity as Penrose.

The millionaire was Dr. Daniel "D. K." Pearsons, a tall, bright-eyed financier with mutton-chop whiskers and strong opinions. When Penrose first met him in early 1895, Pearsons behaved like a cartoonist's caricature of a plutocrat. Wearing a silk hat on the back of his head and sitting in a swivel chair at a rolltop desk in his office in the

Chicago Tribune building, Pearsons commandeered his initial conversation with the young president of Whitman College.

"Dr. Pearsons poured out a vigorous stream of talk, a tirade upon the financial ignorance of colleges, upon college football which he detested, and upon the inadequacies of college presidents whom he had

D. K. Pearsons, a Chicago millionaire and small-college philanthropist, was a fervent believer in the Whitman myth. He gave it credibility in Chicago and donated large amounts of money to Whitman College when it was teetering on the edge of bankruptcy.

known," Penrose recalled. Then, like the White Rabbit in *Alice in Wonderland*, Pearsons peeked at his watch, realized he was late, and ran off to catch a train.

Just before he vanished, however, he said, "Come tomorrow at the same time, and then you do the talking."

Born and raised in Vermont, Pearsons was a medical doctor who in the 1850s moved to Illinois, where, at his wife's urging, he gave up the practice of medicine for more lucrative endeavors. He specialized, at first, in selling farmland on commission. Soon the Illinois Central Railroad Company asked him to sell its vast landholdings. He became rich, important, and respected in Chicago after investing his profits in the city's real estate, banks, and rail transit companies.

By the time he met with Penrose, Pearsons was seventy-four years old, retired, worth more than $5 million (about $153 million now), and a major donor to small Christian colleges, mostly in the West. Typically, he would offer a school $100,000 for its endowment if it could raise a matching amount. The schools he helped—and in some cases rescued—include Pomona College, in Claremont, California;

Pacific University, in Forest Grove, Oregon; and Beloit College, in Beloit, Wisconsin. When trustees of Whitman College heard in the early 1890s that Pearsons was making these large gifts, they wrote to him and asked for one. He offered $50,000, if the college could raise another $150,000.

For Penrose—whose college could not pay its faculty or its mortgages—the millionaire's conditional offer "seemed absurd under the circumstances." But no one else was offering Whitman College large sums of money under any conditions. So Penrose had hurried to Chicago and humbly presented himself to Pearsons in the faint hope that he could sweet-talk him into a more generous offer.

When Penrose showed up on the second day at Pearsons's office, the old man again did all the talking, and the college president again listened dutifully. Finally Pearsons began to ask questions, and Penrose explained his desperate need for cash. The chemistry between the two men changed.

"After that all ice disappeared," Penrose recalled, "acquaintance rapidly ripened into friendship, and the interest of the Doctor in Whitman College steadily grew. It became one of his favorite colleges and he took thenceforth a fatherly interest in [me]."

Pearsons also became a fervent believer in and influential advocate of the Whitman Saved Oregon story. The millionaire's enthusiasm for all things Whitman would soon erase one of Penrose's most urgent worries: the college's $12,500 in mortgages, which were accruing interest at 8 percent a year and which the college could not keep up with.

At their second meeting in Chicago, Penrose nervously broached the subject with Pearsons, explaining that he hoped to find a private individual in the East who would lend that amount at 6 percent. With brusqueness that shocked Penrose, the old man shouted, "Nonsense. It's not a business proposition. Nobody would lend you the money."

Hearing this, Penrose was embarrassed and felt hopeless—and looked it. Pearsons saw the effect of his outburst and reversed course.

"I'll lend you the money," he said. "Sit down and make me out a note."

A few months later, Penrose mailed Pearsons a check with the first year's interest payment on the loan. Without explanation, the Chicago financier mailed it back, uncashed. When Penrose got married the following year, Pearsons forgave the entire debt as a wedding present. In total, Pearsons would give more than $213,000 in matching and unmatched contributions to Whitman College. The money helped save the college from collapse and paid for its first permanent buildings.

Pearsons also took command of a campaign to mobilize Congregational churches throughout Chicago and its suburbs for a "Whitman Day." On Sunday, June 30, 1895, ministers took to the pulpit in at least forty-one churches (by a count in the *Chicago Tribune*), where they explained how Whitman saved Oregon and ranked his greatness alongside that of Lincoln, Grant, and Homer.

For its evening service celebrating the "Hero of Oregon," South Congregational Church, in Chicago, was festooned with American flags. To kick off the patriotic program, two choirs and the congregation joined soloist Myrtis C. Chandler in singing "The Star-Spangled Banner." The Reverend Willard Scott then began to speak:

> The story of the United States for the first fifty years of this century is that of a rising tide of national feeling which did not stop until it had reached the Pacific and firmly planted its flag on all the land between the two seas, and it is the purpose of our service this evening to recall the brilliant part of Marcus Whitman in that westward movement for a wider and more glorious America. No greater story belongs

to any people, and to none more than to him and to his
heroic wife are the praises due for its consummation.

At each of the churches that devoted their Sunday services to
Whitman, sermons ended with a stem-winding, soul-stirring, guilt-
inducing pitch for money. The message, in a nutshell, was that if Whitman College went broke, the grisly murder of its namesake and his
amiable wife would have been for naught.

The most over-the-top version of this closing argument came from
the Reverend D. F. Fox at the California Avenue Congregational
Church:

> It is a sure proof of decline when a nation forgets the hero-
> ism and self-sacrifice of her saviors. . . . With Lincoln's and
> Garfield's, let our children remember the date of Whitman's
> martyrdom as one of the sacred days in the calendar. We
> need not peer into the gloom of antiquity for a hero. Here
> stands Marcus Whitman.
>
> Greece had her bards, Rome her orators, France has her
> Pantheon, and England her Westminster by which they eu-
> logize in speech and enshrine in mausoleum the great name
> and fair fame of those to whom a nation's tribute is due.
> Marcus Whitman saved Oregon once. In the endowment
> and perpetuation of Whitman College, our Dr. Pearsons
> has made it possible to save her again. Rather than any
> monument of marble, our hero shall pass on into our na-
> tional life and greatness through the gates of learning. . . .
> Let our Homer sing his name. Tell it unto thy children; and
> children's children, and when Whitman College shall have
> been endowed . . . let a great college hall be erected from a

patriotic fund, to which each shall contribute; and above its entrance let all who behold, read: "Sacred to the memory of Dr. Marcus Whitman and Narcissa Whitman; while lifting up the banner of the cross in one hand to redeem and save savage souls, they thought it no wrong to carry the flag of the country they loved in the other."

The largest newspapers in Chicago joined with the churches in urging readers to give to Whitman College, which they described as a monument to a dead hero. The *Chicago Tribune* approvingly noted that local philanthropist Pearsons had taken the college "under his helpful and practical wings." The *Tribune, Inter Ocean, Evening Post, Daily News,* and *Advance* all printed news stories that drew on Penrose's pamphlet; some of them excerpted it. None of the newspapers doubted that Whitman was a national hero or questioned the claim that he had saved the Pacific Northwest for the union.

Oliver W. Nixon, a Chicago newspaper editor, became Whitman's hagiographer and publicist. His 1895 book, *How Marcus Whitman Saved Oregon,* "was like a giant virus" that spread the Whitman lie across America, helping to raise money for Whitman College. When the lie was debunked, Nixon refused to concede error. "Let us die with armor on," he wrote.

Working alongside Pearsons to burnish Whitman's legacy and save the college was Dr. Oliver W. Nixon, a nearly deaf, white-bearded journalist who had become Marcus Whitman's self-appointed publicist, biographer, and trumpet blower.

Nixon was a close friend and philanthropic adviser to D. K.

Pearsons. It was at Nixon's suggestion that his rich friend first offered $50,000 to the college, and Nixon had convinced Pearsons of Marcus Whitman's rightful place in the pantheon of American heroes. "Pearsons had a score of colleges to be interested in; Nixon had but one," said the student newspaper at Whitman College. With his narrow and obsessive focus, Nixon "did the college a great service" by making sure that the old philanthropist's friendship with Whitman College remained "warm."

Like Pearsons, Nixon was a septuagenarian former medical doctor, a profession he was forced to give up during the Civil War. While he was serving as chief surgeon for the 39th Ohio Volunteer Infantry at the Battle of New Madrid in Missouri, artillery explosions had ruptured Nixon's eardrums. After the war, he could not hear the complaints of his patients well enough to treat them.

Before his medical training and before the Civil War, Nixon had traveled extensively across the West, spending about a year in the Oregon Territory as a teacher. Marcus and Narcissa Whitman were murdered just three years before he arrived.

"It was a time when history was being made," he later wrote. "The Great Tragedy at Waiilatpu was fresh in the minds of the people. With such surroundings one comes in touch with the spirit of history."

Nixon, though, would never come in touch with the actual history of Oregon. Instead, he convinced himself that Spalding's fable about Whitman—widely published in the early 1880s in history books, public school texts, Protestant newspapers, and the *Encyclopaedia Britannica*—was the one true account of how the territory became part of the United States. Like many amateur historians who have unshakably strong opinions, Nixon seems to have conflated what he read with what he believed he had seen and heard. He always insisted that "he did not have to depend on what was in the books to know what Whitman did and how he died." He believed that contemporaneous written records of individuals with firsthand knowledge of Whitman's death and of his ride east were less authoritative than the information he claimed to remember from his brief sojourn in the West.

"In my historical facts I have tried to be correct and to give credit to authorities where I could," he wrote. "I expect some of my critics will ask, as they have in the past: 'Who is your authority for this fact and that?' I only answer, I don't know unless I am authority."

Nixon's true expertise was in weaving together Spalding's lies with genuine historical materials—such as the diaries of Narcissa Whitman and the letters of Dr. Whitman—in a way that supported a highly readable narrative. At the same time, Nixon downplayed or ignored historical materials that raised doubts about Spalding's story.

In 1878, Nixon became the literary editor and part owner (with his brother) of the *Inter Ocean*, a major daily newspaper in Chicago. From this powerful editorial perch he attempted to raise awareness in the late 1880s and '90s of what he believed to be the overlooked greatness of Marcus Whitman. His efforts included an annual editorial in the *Inter Ocean* on the anniversary of Whitman's murder. Under the headline "Neglected Hero," it began, "The history of the race furnishes multiplied proof that many of the wisest and most deserving have grown into their honors in the estimation of their fellows years after they have rested in their graves."

Whitman's reputation rose from his grave as never before in 1895. Nixon made it happen with a late-in-life literary eruption. In April of that year, to help Penrose prevent Whitman College from going under, Nixon took off four weeks from his editing duties at the *Inter Ocean* and pounded out a 333-page paean to his hero.

How Marcus Whitman Saved Oregon included faux-realistic paintings of Whitman's famous ride, of his conversation in the White House with President Tyler, and of his murder. It was an infectiously readable—and totally credulous—version of Spalding's fabrications. In the early 1880s, William Barrows's *Oregon*, with its similarly triumphal account of Whitman's exploits, had hit a sweet spot among scholars and Protestant ministers, circulating in most of the country's big-city and university libraries. Nixon's fin de siècle book was aimed at the Protestant masses and proved an even greater success.

"It ran through five editions and became the most widely distributed and most popular book on Whitman of that generation," Clifford Drury, a historian who specialized in Whitman, wrote in 1973. "Since Nixon's book got into so many public and church school libraries, it is still being quoted as authoritative by uncritical readers." More than four decades after Drury wrote those words, the book was still available in hardback, paperback, and Kindle format on Amazon.

"It was like a giant virus," said Michael Paulus, who for many years was chief archivist at Penrose Library, on the campus of Whitman College. "Nixon flooded the market and his story was accessible."

As *The Boston Globe* noted on the occasion of the book's fifth printing, Nixon's "graphic picture of life on the plains and mountains in pioneer days and his description of the thrilling adventures of the patriotic hero . . . are fascinating, and hold the reader's attention as surely as could the most exciting of borderland romances."

The popularity of Nixon's book owed much to the timing of its release. It was published at a singular moment in America's understanding of itself as a nation of heroes. That moment had been manufactured in Chicago at the Columbian Exposition—the greatest of all world fairs. More than twenty-seven million spectators—about 43 percent of the population of the United States at the time—swarmed in 1893 to a fairgrounds that became known as the "White City." There, as historian Joy S. Kasson wrote, they witnessed "a triumph of show business, economic boosterism, and national self-congratulations."

One of the most popular and profitable parts of the extravaganza, staged just outside the fairgrounds, was Buffalo Bill's Wild West show, which earned the largest profits in its history with a performance of "The Battle of the Little Big Horn; or, Custer's Last Charge."

Like Spalding's fable about Whitman, the Little Bighorn show was a calculated mix of fact, invention, and patriotic razzle-dazzle. It reimagined the battlefield slaughter of General George Armstrong Custer—whose death, like Whitman's, was largely his own fault—as an epochal American tragedy. The show then used Custer's demise as an excuse and justification for American expansionism. The program had the requisite happy ending, with a crowd-pleasing appearance by Buffalo Bill, who galloped onstage after Custer's death to continue the Christian work of Manifest Destiny.

The arts pages of the *Inter Ocean*, which Nixon edited and helped write, urged all Chicagoans to see Buffalo Bill's artful showcase of "great realism and thrilling effect."

In crafting his bestselling Whitman book, Nixon clearly parroted Buffalo Bill's money-making formula—from the pulp fiction sentiments to the well-made depictions of fake events to the book's Wild West subtitle: "A True Romance of Patriotic Heroism, Christian Devotion and Final Martyrdom." In the process, he succeeded in turning a dead missionary into a pop culture phenomenon and making his legend part of America's song of itself.

After his book came out in the spring of 1895, Nixon celebrated his success by taking eastern journalists out west in a private railroad car for a tour of Whitman world—old and new. They saw the mission where he was killed, the sad hump of ground where he and his wife were buried, and the Walla Walla campus of the up-and-coming college he inspired. There, Nixon advised college students to "talk Whitman, preach Whitman, and sing Whitman songs. Show to the world the grand character of the man that pettifogging historians have endeavored to hide."

I n years to come, the credibility of Nixon's book would be demolished by those pettifogging historians. They would single it out, along with Barrows's *Oregon*, as one of the most deceptively influential histories ever written about the West.

"If it is within the bounds of possibility to produce a more worthless and misleading book than Barrows' *Oregon*, Dr. Nixon has furnished it to us," William I. Marshall wrote in 1906.

In 1901, Yale history professor Edward Bourne wrote that he was impressed with Nixon's storytelling skills, but not with his honesty: Nixon "has made his book as interesting as a narrative as it is utterly untrustworthy as history."

Nevertheless, Whitman College, under President Penrose, awarded Nixon an honorary doctor of laws and invited him to give the dedication speech for the college's first brick building, which was built with D. K. Pearsons's money. *The Whitman College Quarterly* described Nixon as "the gentle-hearted, noble-minded man to whom the rescue of Whitman's name from oblivion is largely due."

Nixon and Pearsons became strategic advisers to Penrose. After guiding his efforts to gobble up donations in Chicago, they helped him plan, execute, and staff a multiyear fundraising campaign along the East Coast, with a focus on New England.

As the campaign began, the burden of selling the college fell primarily on Penrose. He traveled, by his own estimate, forty thousand miles, scurrying among New York, Philadelphia, Boston, Cleveland, Andover, Worcester, Pittsfield, Springfield, Hartford, and New Haven, and many smaller towns in between. In churches, clubs, prominent business firms, summer hotels, and rich people's houses, he handed out his pamphlet and endeavored "to raise money by telling everywhere the Whitman story."

Using Spalding, Barrows, and Nixon as his gospels, Penrose sanctified his Whitman sermons with invocations of God's will and America's greatness.

"The story of the saving of the Northwest for God and the United States is the story of the acts of one of God's disciples," said Penrose as he began an address to the Congregational Club in Worcester, Massachusetts, on April 20, 1896. By then, he had been on the road for more than a year, and in that time his sermons had become highly polished crowd-pleasers with long pauses built in for applause. The *Worcester Daily Spy* reported that "the young man's earnestness, power and enthusiasm carried the audience by storm."

In addition to his standard recitation of the Whitman myth, his speech in Worcester had a fiery—and factually wrong—finale. At a time when there were at least nine other colleges in the Northwest, Penrose claimed that Whitman was "the only college in a region that is as big as all New England and Pennsylvania." Then, with a rhetorical flourish that mixed vagueness with grandiosity, he declared that his college was "saving Oregon for God and the United States."

When the applause faded, Penrose said he did not like to beg, but his college had practically no money. He mentioned D. K. Pearsons's conditional gift of $50,000, which would be forthcoming if the school could collect $150,000 more. Two-thirds of that money had been pledged, Penrose said, but where the rest would come from, he did not know. He said he would be staying on in Worcester for a limited time, during which he would be glad to accept contributions.

ACT FOUR

EXPOSE

CHAPTER FIFTEEN

SKULLS, BONES, MONEY

I n late October of 1897, fifty years after Marcus and Narcissa
Whitman were killed, Stephen Penrose organized the unearthing of their bones. For the president of Whitman College, the dig
was a continuation of the feverish fundraising campaign he had begun in Chicago two years earlier by tapping into the fortune of D. K.
Pearsons.

Joined by a newspaper reporter, two college students, a contractor,
and several workmen, Penrose journeyed seven miles from his Walla
Walla campus to the burial mound at the Whitman mission. There,
while digging in shallow soil, they found four well-preserved, nearly
intact human skulls, including those of the Whitmans. They packed
the skulls, along with a few scattered bones, into a box and hauled it
back to the college. There, the bones were analyzed by local physi-
cians and placed in a glass case for public viewing. For a time, Penrose
showed off the skulls at his house.

When Matilda Sager Delaney, an elderly survivor of the Whitman killings, came to the house to inspect them, she wanted a closer look at the skull believed to be that of Marcus Whitman. She asked Penrose to take it from a glass case and hold it up—a task requiring some delicacy. Two tomahawk blows had punctured the back of the skull, and the top of it had been sliced in half longitudinally using one of Dr. Whitman's surgical saws.

As he held up the skull, while carefully holding it together, Mrs. Delaney revisited her childhood at the mission: "As I went back in memory and imagined the skull clothed with flesh, I felt it was Dr. Whitman."

Accounts of the disinterred bones soon found their way into newspapers, large and small, all across the United States. The national coverage was part of an elaborate, year-long, multi-platform publicity campaign to mark the fiftieth anniversary of the massacre. With the campaign, Penrose was aiming for nothing less than nationwide acceptance of the claim that Whitman was a national hero who saved three states for the Union. As this perception grew, he hoped, so would donations to Whitman College.

Fifty years after the Whitman killings, Whitman College president Penrose led an excavation party out to the mission site, where the remains of Marcus and Narcissa were buried in a mass grave. The skull of Dr. Whitman was unearthed, along with three other skulls and a number of scattered bones. For a time, Penrose displayed the bones at his house in Walla Walla.

In addition to skulls and bones, Penrose collected hair from among the remains, which he displayed in the college chapel and publicized in *The Whitman College Quarterly*. It included locks of golden hair that supposedly came from Narcissa, as well as darker hairs said to have been shorn from Dr. Whitman's head while he was alive. "The hair is brown in color, showing no trace of gray," Penrose wrote admiringly in the *Quarterly*, a publication he created, wrote, and edited beginning in 1897 as part of his all-out fundraising push.

With Penrose as impresario of relics, chief of publicity, and master of ceremonies, the main event of the golden anniversary of the killings was spread out over two press-friendly days in Walla Walla, November 29 and 30. Special trains hauled in spectators from all across the Pacific Northwest, including newspaper reporters, ministers from Congregational churches, and eight aging survivors of the massacre.

Not invited were the Cayuse Indians, about four hundred of whom were then living on the Umatilla Reservation, thirty-five miles south of Whitman College. Their absence surprised no one. To whites, they remained notorious as the savages who had killed the Whitmans. More than any other regional tribe, they were demonized by whites all across Oregon, Washington, and Idaho. An essay published a few days before the anniversary made plain the enduring virulence of white hatred of the Cayuses. The author was Edmond Stephen Meany, a highly respected professor of history at the University of Washington in Seattle. "I never read the details of that awful scene," Meany wrote, "but my blood fairly boils with indignation over the treachery and ingratitude of those miserable Cayuse fiends."

The gala opening event of the massacre anniversary was on Monday, November 29, fifty years to the day after the killings. Small's Opera House in Walla Walla was packed. Massacre survivors were seated in special boxes to the right of the stage. The sixty-voice-strong Whitman memorial chorus sang "Send Out Thy Light."

For the keynote address, the Reverend Leavitt H. Hallock, a Whitman trustee, a fundraiser for the college, and a riveting speaker, delivered a long and ornately worded speech about Whitman saving Oregon.

"Half a century ago tonight lifeless bodies lay unburied at the close of a day of terror and irreparable disaster," Hallock said. "Today, springing as the seed, the spirits of these slain come again, looming into the sky as great souls, modest in themselves, but epoch-making in our country's history."

Hallock vowed to "put the emphasis where truth demands" and tell the tale of how "this Northwest empire swung into the lap of the United States." Then he repeated the entire Whitman lie, falsely accusing Jesuits of tricking Indians into killing Marcus Whitman and spuriously comparing Whitman to George Washington and Abraham Lincoln:

"As truly as the fate of freedom turned upon the work of Washington, or fetters fell from the Black man by the stroke of Lincoln's pen, so surely was Oregon saved to the union by timely tidings, carried by Whitman to the White House at peril of his life."

The next morning at nine, "vast throngs" gathered in stormy weather on Main Street in Walla Walla, which was festooned with flags and bunting. The crowd included the visiting massacre survivors, white veterans of local Indian wars, local schoolchildren, a band, a drum corps, the mayor of Walla Walla, the city council, Whitman College students, faculty, staff, and trustees, and, of course, Penrose. Shops, businesses, and schools in Walla Walla were closed for the day, to maximize the number of people who could attend.

The crowd marched across town to the Oregon Railroad and Navigation Company train depot, where special cars had been hired to transport people out to the site of the Whitman mission. Those who took the free train ride to the mission were greeted by the 4th U.S. Cavalry, which escorted visitors to the old mission grounds.

Whitman boosters from all over the Pacific Northwest—led by missionary turned fabulist historian William H. Gray—had raised money to buy a marble-topped mausoleum for the recently disinterred bones and skulls. Boosters had also purchased an eighteen-foot marble shaft to be erected on a hill near the grave. But neither the shaft nor the tomb, both ordered from Vermont, had arrived in time for the anniversary. As a result, the bones and skulls were still back at the college in glass cases when the ceremony took place. "It was a matter of deep regret to all," Penrose later wrote.

Penrose spoke first at the mission grounds, then left it to Catherine Sager Pringle, a survivor of the massacre, to make brief remarks:

"Fifty years ago today we went as prisoners of a savage band of Indians—no hope of escape—all dark and despair. But Providence made a way of escape and we stand here today.

Catherine Sager Pringle, a witness, at age twelve, to the Whitman killings, returned to the mission grounds for the gala fiftieth anniversary of the event and delivered a speech, thanking the people of Walla Walla for "burying our dead, and for their royal entertainment."

"We desire to thank the people of Walla Walla and the Northwest for their presence here, for their kindness in burying our dead, and for their royal entertainment."

E ven with bones unburied and marble in transit, the anniversary of the massacre was a public relations triumph.

As Penrose had intended, the anniversary brought about a phoenixlike rebirth in the financial fortunes of Whitman College. Just two years after its near collapse, the school had become what Penrose called "a going institution." Enrollment was up, the faculty was growing, paychecks were arriving on time, new buildings were being erected. Local contributions to the endowment had jumped by $53,000. Total fundraising would reach $150,000 in 1898, triggering the promised $50,000 from D. K. Pearsons, with more donations rolling in every month. Robert L. Whiting, a professor of history at Whitman, acknowledged decades later that without the sudden influx of money raised by the Whitman Saved Oregon story, the college "would surely have perished."

The rise of Whitman College was suddenly big news—in Walla Walla, across the Northwest, and around the country. In a church service in Washington, D.C., U.S. Supreme Court justice David Josiah Brewer compared Marcus Whitman's service to his nation favorably to that of Secretary of State William H. Seward, who had negotiated the purchase of Alaska. In Philadelphia, a statue of Whitman was placed in front of the iconic Witherspoon Building, which housed the Presbyterian Board of Publication and Sabbath-School Work. In Congregational churches throughout the United States, ministers told worshippers that Whitman was the first to discover a Hudson's Bay Company plot to steal the Oregon Territory and the first to report it to federal officials in Washington. The missionary doctor, the ministers said, deserved full credit for saving three states for our country. The *Seattle Post-Intelligencer* wrote that the "fiftieth anniversary of the Whitman massacre finds a sudden luster beginning to glow around the name of Marcus Whitman."

Whitman's story popped up in prestigious newspapers and popular magazines. It also won over eminent intellectuals all across the United States, especially on the East Coast.

On the fiftieth anniversary of the massacre, *The New York Times*, in a story headlined "How Oregon Was Saved," repeated major elements of the Whitman fiction. The first sentence of the story refers to "the brave and patriotic Dr. Marcus Whitman and his noble wife, by whose agency largely the Territory of Oregon was saved to the United States."

The story printed fabricated quotations, recounted incidents that did not occur, and falsely accused the Hudson's Bay Company of having done "work on the minds of the Indians, with the result" that Whitman and his wife were murdered. The story closely followed the false narrative that Penrose had so crisply written up in his fundraising pamphlet. To Penrose's delight, the *Times* also noted that "Whitman College has since been founded" as a tribute to the missionary's memory.

The article in the *Times* was written as straight-ahead news. By unambiguously declaring that Whitman had saved Oregon, it ignored published information that had been widely available for a decade. In particular, the *Times* ignored a two-volume work of history by Hubert Howe Bancroft that had been published in San Francisco in 1886, was sold across the country, and was mentioned in the book pages of the *Times* itself. The book, *History of Oregon*, carefully explained the actual reason for Whitman's winter journey to the East Coast in 1842–43: he rode to save his job, not his country.

In Oregon, the largest newspaper had for years dismissed the Whitman story as a false and self-serving invention of Protestant clerics. In "Whitman Once More," an editorial published in *The Oregonian* a few months before the fiftieth anniversary of the massacre, the newspaper said, "The Presbyterian-Congregational missionary societies wanted a hero for the Northwest, where they had done a good deal of work, and the untimely and pathetic fate of Dr. Whitman gave them the man."

None of this, though, seemed to penetrate editorial offices on the East Coast. *The Ladies' Home Journal*, the country's most influential women's magazine, marked the anniversary of the massacre by publishing a lavishly illustrated story that echoed nearly every false claim in the pamphlet Penrose had written when he became president of Whitman College. The article included artist illustrations of events that never occurred, such as Whitman kneeling in a snowstorm as he prayed for Narcissa and for the Oregon Territory that the British were supposedly scheming to take. The article, entitled "When Dr. Whitman Added Three Stars to Our Flag," concluded with a solicitation for donations to Whitman College:

"The fitting title of [the school's] history is 'The Romance of a College.' But Whitman College is not a romance. It is a reality worthy of the confidence and aid of all American citizens in remembrance of the hero and heroine, the patriotic martyrs of Oregon—Marcus and Narcissa Whitman."

The Whitman myth—which by that point had been circulated in congressional documents, books, newspapers, magazines, sermons, and lectures—now gained solid purchase in the minds of America's intellectual elite. Before the turn of the twentieth century, New York University asked a select group of establishment thinkers—college presidents, history professors, senior judges, authors, and editors—to name the most deservedly famous Americans. In the category for missionaries and explorers, Marcus Whitman ranked fourth—behind Daniel Boone but ahead of Meriwether Lewis and Sam Houston.

The rising notoriety of Whitman—and the pecuniary advantages of recounting his adventures before paying audiences—was beginning to attract new and unwelcome grifters. They began to infest the church lecture circuit, particularly in New England. Prominent among the opportunists was a man who called himself the Honorable John Wilder Fairbank. From Boise to Boston, between 1895 and 1907, he delivered an illustrated lecture entitled "The Ride That Saved an Empire." Fairbank, a traveling man of "seedy appearance" who sometimes said he was from Boston and other times claimed to be from Seattle, charged twenty-five cents for adults, sixteen cents for scholars, and twelve cents for children under twelve. He falsely led his audiences to believe that some of the money he raised would be forwarded to Whitman College.

In his lecture, Fairbank seemed less constrained by historical facts than perhaps any other Whitman apostle:

"Two names I purpose linking together before the youth of our land—Abraham Lincoln and Marcus Whitman. Two patriots, two martyrs, these two men, lineal cousins, with the blood from their Whitman sire in their veins, no wonder they did such noble deeds, stood at their posts, died for their country. All honor to such heroes of the past. Let us keep in touch with them through the onward march of the twentieth century. In the interest of truth, justice, and American honor."

Back in Walla Walla, Penrose became alarmed that Fairbank and others of his ilk were profiting off the story—in his view, bleeding "large sums of money from Whitman College." In a letter, he warned church pastors in New England to pay close attention "when they allow Whitman collections and gifts to be taken from their churches." Penrose emphasized that New York and New England churches should open their fundraising doors to only one person.

"Miss Virginia Dox," he declared, "is our only authorized Eastern agent."

Virginia Dox, a missionary in the West in her youth, was a singularly successful fundraiser for Whitman College at the turn of the twentieth century. An enthralling booster of the Whitman myth, she raised money all across New England, where she knocked on the doors of wealthy widows and widowers, imploring them to help a small but worthy college out west.

I n the last five years of the nineteenth century, Virginia Dox collected more cash for Whitman College than Penrose. The donations she corralled in the Midwest, New York, and New England were second only to the monies the college collected from D. K. Pearsons, who had helped recruit Dox as a fundraiser and later called her "the greatest woman in America." Oliver Nixon said that in New England, she increased the number of "interested hearers and listeners of the Whitman story" from ten to ten thousand in less than five years.

Miss Virginia Dox, as she was known, befriended Pearsons and Nixon while she was living in Chicago in the early 1890s. She was a redhaired, well-spoken, serious-minded woman. Then in her forties, she had polished her lecture skills in churches while delivering talks about her adventures as a young missionary in the West.

When Penrose was visiting Chicago in 1895, Pearsons and Nixon had suggested to him that Dox become financial agent for the school. Penrose hired her immediately, and his decision paid off in spades.

"It is faint praise to say that but for the labors of this gifted, eccentric, indomitable woman the first financial campaign of Whitman College would have ended in failure or been long delayed," he later wrote.

Dox was born in New York in 1851, four years after the Whitman Massacre. Never married, she finished college in Illinois and attended medical school for two years at the University of Michigan. She chose not to become a doctor, signing up instead as a missionary for the Congregational Church. In that capacity, she taught school, preached Protestant Christianity, and tried to slow the spread of Mormonism in Idaho. She also worked at a federal boarding school for the Osage Indians in Oklahoma, where she replaced a white teacher who had beaten an Indian child to death. A chief of the Osage people adopted her as his daughter to protect her from vengeance-seeking adults in the tribe and to help her win acceptance as a teacher. In the late 1880s, the Congregational Church paid Dox to go on national speaking tours and raise money for other missionaries.

Dox never visited the mission where the Whitmans lived and died. She never visited Whitman College. But her years in the West had given her a visceral feel for the hardships of missionary life. When she shifted her fundraising focus to Whitman College in 1896, she devoured Nixon's book and became a zealous convert to the Whitman cause. "Whitman College is bound to become the greatest Christian institution in the country," she wrote Penrose. "No other college has such a history back of it."

Dox adapted the Whitman legend into a pulse-quickening, heart-rending one-hour lecture and began delivering it as many as five times a day—with passion, conviction, and wit. Ministers who hosted her in their churches were humbled by her gifts for enrapturing a congregation and persuading its members to reach for their wallets. One of the ministers, the Reverend D. M. Fisk of Toledo, Ohio, said Dox told the Whitman story "with a power, a self-restraint, a sustained interest that hold her hearers' absolute attention from start to finish. . . . No pastor in the land need hesitate as to the wisdom of inviting this royal woman to his pulpit, and no congregation should be small when she is announced to speak."

During her six years on the road raising money for Whitman College, Dox exchanged scores of letters with Penrose. In the process, they became close and trusted friends. Her letters were unguarded, revealing, and, at times, downright wicked. She referred to her vast epistolary output as "Doxology."

After talking people out of their money in churches and lecture halls, Dox extracted larger donations by hanging around in towns and villages and insinuating herself into the drawing rooms of the wealthy—especially widows and widowers. She perfected her craft after 1897, when she shifted her hunting grounds from the Midwest to wealthier, more compact New England.

"This week a rich old widower who doesn't go to church anymore and who is very close-fisted gave me $15 and invited me to stay to dinner," she wrote Penrose from Worcester, Massachusetts. "Then he wanted to give us something from his wife's things, and had me help him look over trunks and boxes. . . . I hope to get a lot of money out of him for you. They say no one else could have gotten a cent out of him but me. It was funny, my poking around in his wife's trunks, and I hardly kept my face straight. He thinks I am a very wonderful woman, and I believe he would have given me everything in the house had I wanted it for the college."

Dox's letters complained bitterly about fundraising competitors from other colleges. She called Pomona College president Franklin

Ferguson "a vile man" who "ought to be behind bars." She accused him of having "hypnotized" D. K. Pearsons to win the old millionaire's money—and trick him into giving more of it to Pomona than to Whitman. She closed her complaints by instructing Penrose to "please burn this letter."

Dox warned Penrose not to work too hard, saying, "You don't want to be a nervous, fidgety, broken-down College President." At the same time, she was determined that Penrose know how hard she worked: "I go from house to house and from shop to shop. I climb fences over into the fields; take long walks in the country; visit wagon shops, blacksmith shops, stables, even cigar shops, to get the little money I raise."

In her letters to Penrose, she called Whitman "our old hero" and said his name "is fast-becoming a household word." When people declined to give her money or in the rare cases when they challenged the truth of the Whitman story, she did not let it upset her—with one notable exception.

In Canandaigua, New York, during the massacre anniversary year of 1897, she met with a nephew of Marcus Whitman's named Franklin Henry Wiswell, whose late mother, Alice, was Dr. Whitman's only sister.

"He poured a tirade of abuse on my head; said both you and I were in this work for personal greed," she reported to Penrose. "Said Marcus Whitman was no more a hero than he was. [He said that Dr. Whitman] only did his duty, as every man should do; that it was folderol to say that Oregon would not have been saved to our Union but for him. Many other bitter and cruel things he said."

Dox continued to raise money for Whitman College until the spring of 1901, when she resigned as field agent. She had exhausted herself. Her doctor told her she had "overtaxed nerves."

The confidence Dox had in the Whitman myth was as strong as her faith in God. But it absorbed a terrible shock in the first week of that year, when she picked up a newspaper and read what she said was "a dreadful article."

It described a prominent scholar's attack on the truthfulness of the stories being told about Marcus Whitman. The scholar had made his attack "before some great education association." Dox dashed off a letter to Penrose, warning him to beware of trouble.

CHAPTER SIXTEEN

"A DEFENSELESS LITTLE WESTERN INSTITUTION"

Stephen Penrose was already doing damage control. Several weeks before he received Dox's letter, he had sensed that serious trouble was afoot. That's when the American Historical Association, a congressionally chartered group of the country's leading historians, had released the official program for its sixteenth annual convention. It announced that Edward Gaylord Bourne, professor of history at Yale, would be delivering a paper in Ann Arbor, Michigan, on December 28. His subject: "The Legend of Marcus Whitman."

When Penrose learned of the paper and saw the word "legend," he wrote to Bourne at once, telling the professor that "your distance from the scene" made it difficult to understand the subtleties and complexities of the Whitman story. Describing himself as someone who had made "a careful study of the early history" of Oregon, Penrose offered to help Bourne learn more. "I hope that you will do justice to the facts in the case," Penrose wrote. "In investigating the story of the early days one is obliged to depend more on the testimony of surviving witnesses than on books or written matter."

It was a weak and labored argument, and Penrose, a graduate of Williams and Yale, surely knew it. Bourne was at the forefront of a new breed of "scientific" historians who were taking control of history departments at major universities across the country and challenging the veracity of long-accepted stories—from antiquity, from European history, and from the recent American past. They were skeptical of the after-the-fact memories of informants who may or may not have witnessed events they described. They were digging up contemporaneous written records and comparing them with all available documentary evidence. In the process, they were unraveling and discrediting beloved national myths, such as the story of George Washington, his little hatchet, and the "I cannot tell a lie" cherry tree. Taken seriously for years—and taught to generations of schoolchildren—that story had been examined by historians and utterly debunked.

At the turn of the twentieth century, the Whitman story was ripe for the same kind of treatment. Nearly everyone in America had heard of Marcus Whitman by then. Teachers and textbooks in public, private, and Sunday schools had informed them that he had saved Oregon; the story had been validated by the most authoritative publications, from the *Encyclopaedia Britannica* to *The New York Times*.

At the same time, original written records that contradicted the claim were absurdly easy to find. About four thousand pages of them—more than a million words' worth of letters from Marcus and Narcissa Whitman, Henry Spalding, Cushing Eells, William Gray, and all the other missionaries sent to Oregon by the American Board—were on file in one building: Congregational House, at 14 Beacon Street in downtown Boston. In addition, government records on the diplomatic history of how the Oregon Country became part of the United States—which make no mention of a missionary doctor on horseback—were readily available in major university libraries.

Those missionary letters and official documents told an explosive story. It obliterated the one Spalding had persuaded Congress to print in 1871, the one American children were reading in school, the one Penrose, Nixon, and Dox were still peddling—to the financial benefit of Whitman College.

By the autumn of 1900, Bourne had pulled together an original, accessible, and carefully footnoted exposé sure to command the attention of the mainstream press. Just five years earlier, the president of the American Historical Association had enthusiastically endorsed the Whitman Saved Oregon story. Now Bourne was ready to rip it to shreds. In the process, he believed, he would fundamentally alter the public's perception of how the United States had come together.

As he explained to the editor of *The American Historical Review* in the weeks before he spoke in Ann Arbor:

"The case is very clear, I think. Spalding is one of the most indefatigable old frauds I have ever come across. . . . I expect the article will raise some dust in the religious papers, but you will see that I have refrained from any accusations except when the case is too plain to be denied. The whole thing is one of the most curious things I have ever studied."

The next day, Bourne wrote in his diary, "I feel very well satisfied with it on the whole and think it will excite considerable comment." In another message to his editor, he explained how the Whitman legend was ludicrous and his paper was "impregnable."

"More inaccurate invention of history will rarely be found and I think the publication will help as well as amuse the readers," he wrote.

He also threw a punch at Oliver Nixon, comparing the Chicago editor's arguments for Whitman saving Oregon to "the performance of a medicine man. He [Nixon] must have been a fraud."

———

Bourne loved a fight. "He was a born controversialist and he liked to argue," a longtime friend wrote in a eulogy. He nearly died of a tubercular infection of the hip when he was ten years old. The disease forced him onto crutches for three years, stunted the growth of his right leg, and lamed him for life. He compensated by developing immense physical strength, endurance, and daredevil dexterity. He relished the notoriety that came with controversy and was unmoved by harsh personal criticism, even seeming to enjoy it.

Bourne was an elite New Englander whose family lineage could be traced to the *Mayflower*. His father was a well-known Congregational minister. Like his father, Bourne attended Yale, where he earned his undergraduate and doctorate degrees in history, and where he returned, at thirty-five, to take a job as a professor of history.

By then he was an academic highflier, having published *Spain in America, 1450–1580*, a four-volume landmark work of scientific history. It explained the rise and spread of Spanish colonialism with painstaking attention to primary sources, but without the racial and cultural condescension that stained the scholarship of many other white Protestant academics. Bourne's scholarship won frequent acclaim, and he was often a headliner at meetings of the American Historical Association.

In 1899 one of his Yale students, Arthur H. Hutchinson, told him about the Whitman fiction, which the younger man had investigated while at the University of Washington in Seattle. Hutchinson believed the Whitman legend was little more than a "publicity stunt" to raise money for Whitman College. He brought his research notes and his conclusions to Bourne, asking for help in finding a publisher, and the professor tried to interest *The American Historical Review* in the student's paper.

Unfortunately for Hutchinson, the *Review*'s editor, J. Franklin Jameson, did not trust the student's research and found his writing style to be immature. But Jameson hinted that he would eagerly publish a paper that exposed the Whitman myth—if Bourne were to write it.

Over the next year, the professor spent long days poring over missionary letters and other files in the American Board library at the Congregational House, in Boston. He got considerable help, too, from Frances Victor, the prolific Oregon-based historian best known for her biography of Joe Meek.

Victor, then seventy-four and living in Portland, was at first a reluctant collaborator. She had been trying for many years to find a national audience for her own investigations of the Whitman fiction. Although her work had been mostly ignored in the East, it was thorough, honest, and groundbreaking. She was the principal researcher and ghostwriter of Hubert Howe Bancroft's *History of Oregon*, which had correctly characterized Whitman's winter ride to the East as an effort to save his mission, not his country. Victor had also published an article in a California magazine in 1880 that called the Whitman story a "well-invented romance." Her skepticism, persistence, and evidence-based writing had for many years infuriated Protestant ministers in Washington and Oregon. Many of them dismissed her scholarship out of hand because she was a woman; they accused her of being pro-Catholic. But Victor, like Bourne, did not back away from controversy. She was also quite willing to blow her own horn. "It's a question if the truth of the Whitman myth would ever have been raised but for me," she told Bourne.

In the 1890s, Victor had tried to sell her own exposé of the Whitman fable to *The American Historical Review*. But the journal wanted Bourne—a Yale man, a frequent contributor, and a scholar known well by the prominent male historians who would attend the annual conference in Michigan. Victor was miffed, but in a remarkable display of collegiality and character, she helped Bourne. She sent him long, gossipy letters about the history of pioneers and Protestant missionaries in Oregon. She noted in one of her letters that "I discovered so much falsehood in the narratives of pioneers—especially of religious pioneers."

B ourne was not, as we shall see, the preeminent expert on the myths surrounding Marcus Whitman. But he possessed the requisite credentials—panoramic historical perspective, impeccable reputation, and establishment prestige—to call out the obvious falsehoods in Spalding's stories about the missionary doctor.

"Familiar as the student of history is with the growth of legend," Bourne began, "it is frequently assumed that these products of fancy develop only in the absence of documents and contemporary records. . . .

"For examples of the complete legendary reconstruction of history we naturally turn to the Middle Ages," he said, citing the fifteenth-century tale of William Tell, who was said to have shot an apple off his son's head, an act that supposedly started a revolution in Switzerland. "That such a reconstruction of history should take place in the latter half of the nineteenth century in the United States and should involve an event of such immense importance and world-wide publicity as the acquisition of Oregon will seem little short of incredible," Bourne wrote.

The professor went on to demolish Spalding's claims as "not only fictitious but impossible." Oregon was never in danger of being lost to Great Britain. President Tyler and Secretary of State Webster never considered trading Oregon for a Canadian cod fishery. Any honest history, Bourne said, must acknowledge that "the true Marcus Whitman" never saved Oregon, nor was he murdered as part of a Catholic-British plot.

Bourne waited until the end of his talk to mention the money that was being raised on the back of the Whitman legend. When he did, he chose not to impugn the motives or integrity of those who were raising it. Academic scruples perhaps prevented him from making assumptions; in any case, he did not mention Stephen Penrose by name.

"The results of this investigation will come to many as a shock," he said. "Extraordinary efforts have been made in good faith to disseminate the story of Marcus Whitman in order to raise money for a suitable memorial and especially for Whitman College, and to many interested in these enterprises this criticism of the Whitman legend will doubtless seem most unfortunate."

The press, having helped popularize the Whitman myth, now delighted in tearing it down. Newspapers celebrated Bourne's critique and amplified its shock. The day after he presented his paper, the *Los Angeles Times* reported from Ann Arbor: "It looks as though many pages printed in American histories concerning the exploits of Marcus Whitman . . . will have to be torn out."

Though Bourne had been careful not to call the Whitman story a fraud intended to raise money, the press was less delicate. The *New York Tribune* observed that "almost from the start [the Whitman legend] was widely disseminated for the purpose of enlisting interest in and contributing for Whitman Seminary, now Whitman College."

The New York Times, which had reported the Whitman legend as fact in 1897, reversed course a week after Bourne's speech, although the newspaper did not issue a correction to its previous coverage of Whitman.

The most gleeful reaction to Bourne's investigation, not surprisingly, came from the Catholic press, which for decades had scorned the Whitman story as a vengeful invention of Henry Spalding. Under the headline "'The Legend of Marcus Whitman,' Founded on Anti-Catholic Hatred," *The American Catholic Historical Researches* described Bourne's investigation as "very critical and most exact."

In Chicago, Oliver Nixon had known in advance that the Bourne "shock" was coming. Since early December, he and Penrose had been exchanging letters, proposing strategies of response and counterattack. Nixon had consulted with Pearsons, too. The two elderly men instructed Penrose not to be alarmed. As Pearsons put it, "Let them fire away. They can't hurt us." Nixon agreed that the professor's attack would come to nothing. "The Good Father has so helped us during the past five years that nothing they can do can turn aside the work," he assured Penrose.

Nixon's confidence—and his calm—disappeared after he learned the stinging details of Bourne's attack. In his paper's first footnote, Bourne had impugned Nixon by name, saying he "is either ignorant of or suppresses essential facts."

Deeply offended, Nixon counterpunched in every medium available to him—writing essays in the pages of the *Inter Ocean* and western and religious newspapers and sending ferocious personal letters to Bourne. Before going public with his anger, Nixon sought scholarly ammunition from the Reverend Myron Eells, son of the founder of Whitman College and a bookish champion of the Whitman legend.

"If you . . . will furnish me with material facts not in my reach, I will use them unmercifully upon the calumniators. . . . Up and at them is my motto. Let us die with our armor on," Nixon wrote to Eells.

In the weeks and months that followed, Nixon was unable to find much ammunition. He could not challenge Bourne on substance.

Instead, Nixon's counterattacks became increasingly emotional, ad hominem, and unhinged.

"Without an effort of the imagination one can see the learned professor in his velvet-cushioned chair pondering his problem and sharpening his blade and seeking his opportunity," Nixon wrote in an editorial. "Whatever explanation he may make, his whole effort is calculated to destroy not only the fame of Marcus Whitman but also the struggling little college at Walla Walla, erected to his memory."

His letters to Bourne became vaguely threatening. "You and your coworkers have undertaken a task which you will live to regret, and your children after you."

A week later, Nixon ended a six-page typewritten letter to Bourne with this anguished accusation: "Every single name you denounce except my own is the name of a dead man, and has nothing on earth except a memory. I am an old man ready to depart at the sound of taps, but I shall hope to keep my mental and physical strength to the last hour and die fighting the enemies of these the grandest heroes who have lived in our century."

In Walla Walla, Penrose initially told newspapers that the professor from Yale, "without personal knowledge or facts," was merely recycling old and discredited claims by Whitman's enemies.

"I am glad he has done so," Penrose said. "It will only result in bringing the truth of the old story once more before the American people."

His feigned optimism soon collided with reality. In a letter from Boston, Virginia Dox told Penrose that the professor from Yale "has done much to hurt your work here in the East." Wealthy donors had begun to distrust stories about Whitman's heroism and were refusing to follow through on pledges of money for the college.

Penrose assured Dox that time was on their side. "Though Prof. Bourne has shown a mean spirit in some things, he has simply had the effect of giving the story and Whitman College a vast amount of free advertising. There is never any need of hurry in answering falsehood. The truth will in the end prevail."

In letters to Bourne, however, Penrose sounded a note of panic and struggled to control his rage:

> You have been prejudiced at the start, and certainly your
> public reference to Whitman College and your insinuation
> that this story had been promulgated from the very beginning
> in the selfish interests of Whitman College was utterly out of
> place in an historical address and was unworthy of you. It was
> understood by the reporters as a slur on the College. It has
> been so understood by almost everyone who has read your
> address and whether you intended it or not it was most
> unfitting that a Professor in Yale University should go out
> of his way to attack a defenseless little western institution
> from his high position as Professor of History.

To mount a public defense of Whitman and the college, Penrose turned to Myron Eells, who took a proudly unscientific approach to history. Within a few weeks, Eells published a long and dizzyingly detailed rebuttal of Bourne for *The Whitman College Quarterly*. Thousands of copies were reprinted as a pamphlet, and Penrose mailed them off to wavering donors around the country.

In the pamphlet, Eells argued that contemporaneous documents, which Bourne valued above other evidence, were often unavailable in the rough-and-tumble of the American West. So historical truth had to be cobbled together, he said, from the memories of witnesses. "Sometimes in order to obtain the truth it is necessary to go outside of scientific history," Eells wrote.

Bourne's paper on Whitman had upset not just the college's most ardent supporters but also Protestant book critics, religious scholars, and church officials. They perceived a spiritual threat from Bourne— to biblical history and to Christianity itself. They also detected a "moral incapacity" in Bourne, by which they meant he gave more weight to primary sources than to the memories and deeply felt beliefs of Christian patriots.

"A ghoul, in Oriental faith, is an evil spirit who digs up graves in order to rob the dead of their jewels," wrote the journalist and critic William Livingston Alden in the *Chicago Tribune*. "Once in a while there appears a bit of so-called 'historical criticism' which, in its animus, is of that sort. . . . It is the deep misfortune of certain historical writers to labor under a moral incapacity to understand the higher forms of unselfish devotion. Not being able to appreciate it, they turn to denying and maligning it."

The uproar was good for Bourne's career. He expanded his Whitman paper and made it the centerpiece of a book, *Essays in Historical Criticism*. Scribner's rushed it into print in the fall of 1901 and bought display advertising for it in the book section of *The New York Times*, describing it as "the only complete account in print of one of the most extraordinary pieces of fictitious history that has ever gained acceptance in modern times."

In his book, as in the paper he presented in Ann Arbor, Bourne was careful not to criticize the character or achievements of Marcus Whitman himself, focusing instead on the falsehoods invented after his murder.

"That Marcus Whitman was a devoted and heroic missionary who braved every hardship and imperiled his life for the cause of Christian missions and Christian civilization in the far Northwest and finally died at his post, a sacrifice to the cause, will not be gainsaid," Bourne wrote. "That he deserves commemoration in Oregon and Washington is beyond dispute."

As upset as they were by his criticism of the Whitman legend, many of Bourne's adversaries appreciated the professor's generous words about Whitman. They thanked Bourne for his graciousness and called him a gentleman. Unfortunately for them, another debunker of the Whitman legend surfaced at the turn of the twentieth century—one who was far better informed and much less polite.

CHAPTER SEVENTEEN

MEPHISTOPHELES AND THE ORIGINAL SOURCES

William I. Marshall was the principal of a public elementary school in Chicago and the secretary-treasurer of his neighborhood Unitarian church. But he was nobody's gentleman when it came to trumpeting the manifest mediocrity of Marcus Whitman. He was not "in any sense of the term a great man," Marshall wrote. "Though he was undoubtedly a very zealous missionary, he was far from being a wise, or a far-seeing, or a magnanimous, or a prudent, or a successful one." Indeed, Marshall believed it was historically accurate to describe Whitman's character as "third or fourth rate."

Marshall seemed to take pleasure in airing the dirty laundry of the "small-souled and narrow-minded" missionaries in Oregon who squabbled in the 1830s and '40s over inconsequential things, disgraced their Christian values, and betrayed the Indians they failed to convert.

He hounded Whitman's latter-day disciples, accusing them of

"gross and inexcusable" errors and threatening to "utterly annihilate" their reputations. He accused the Congregational and Presbyterian churches, along with their missionary societies and Whitman College, of using the Whitman story as a scheme to "extract pennies from Sunday school children."

Among the dead, his favorite target by far was Henry Spalding, who he said was "a constitutional & persistent liar from his youth & lied quite as constantly before he was crazy as afterwards." His favorite living target was Oliver Nixon, a fellow Chicagoan, whom he called the "most wildly hysterical of all the advocates of the Whitman legend."

Nixon, in turn, dreaded and loathed Marshall, calling him "pestiferous," a "monomaniac," "a literary leach," and "Mephistopheles."

A s an irritating personality, as a man who was energized by insulting his enemies, William Marshall was not unlike Henry Spalding.

Like Spalding, Marshall grew up in hardscrabble circumstances and came of age without a father. His father, a masonry contractor in Fitchburg, Massachusetts, died when William was seventeen. The boy dropped out of high school to help support his family and two years later headed west, moving to Ohio, where he taught school for $10 a month and boarded with his students' parents. A careful reader and energetic teacher, he impressed an alcoholic turned teetotaler named Platt Rogers Spencer, the creator of the Spencerian penmanship system. As Spencer's disciple, Marshall became a traveling salesman in Ohio, expostulating on the life-changing magic of fine cursive handwriting. He also taught young men and women how to keep proper business records. Working with Spencer, Marshall helped set up—and run—a business school in Columbus.

Marshall busted out of the world of inkpots and ledgers after a school friend in Virginia City, Montana, invited him to check out Montana's Alder Gulch mine, where ten thousand men were mucking for fortunes in the richest streambed gold mine ever discovered. Marshall raced west and stayed in Montana for ten years, but he never struck it rich. Instead he moved out of the mines into public schools, becoming a principal in Virginia City and later superintendent of schools in surrounding Madison County. He also studied law and won admittance to the Montana bar. Skilled in the excavation and analysis of historical documents, he became an expert on mining in the Rocky Mountains and a champion of the splendors of Yellowstone National Park. He moved back home to Fitchburg in 1876 to turn his western expertise into a successful living as a lecturer.

Although it did not square with his understanding of western history, Marshall believed the Whitman Saved Oregon story was "substantially true" when he first heard it. Not only was Marshall a churchgoing Protestant—and so inclined to believe the Protestant missionaries who were the sources and champions of the Whitman story—he also saw in it an opportunity for personal enrichment.

The year was 1877. Marshall was thirty-seven years old and supporting his wife and young daughter by giving illustrated lectures about the wonders of the West. He traveled to major East Coast cities, talking about Yellowstone National Park and Montana gold mining, Yosemite and the big trees of California, the growing influence of Mormons, and urbanization of the West Coast. When he heard the amazing story that a courageous missionary doctor had thwarted a British-Catholic scheme to steal the Pacific Northwest, he snapped to attention. Marshall recognized the story as a potentially moneymaking injection of energy into his somewhat tired stockpile of Far West spiels.

"I saw in it the material for a VERY POPULAR lecture on Oregon, especially for the church lecture courses," he wrote. "I could have made a good liberal income of ten or fifteen, and probably, twenty or twenty-five thousand dollars, for as many years as I should continue to lecture."

Eager for cash but wary of telling a tall tale, Marshall traveled from Massachusetts to Oregon in 1882. By then he had pulled together a lecture on Whitman's ride and had begun booking venues in which to deliver it. In Oregon, he began looking for evidence that the story was at least "reasonably probable."

He failed to find it.

William I. Marshall, a school principal in Chicago, became obsessed in the late 1800s with exposing the Whitman story as a fraud that funded Whitman College and Protestant missionaries. He described Spalding as a minister who "lied quite as constantly before he was crazy as afterwards." After decades of being ignored by academics, Marshall's careful research helped demolish the Whitman myth.

Marshall made a pilgrimage to Whitman's grave, where a man living on the mission grounds told him that there was "very great doubt" about the story. Disappointed but hardly defeated, he went to Portland and met with Matthew P. Deady, a federal judge in Oregon, a builder of libraries, and a respected local historian.

"There is no truth in the story," Deady told Marshall. Real evidence to support it, the judge said, had not turned up.

Hoping to salvage something for a Whitman lecture, Marshall wrote to Elwood Evans, the Washington State historian and librarian. Evans said the story had originated in "systematic deception by ministers" who took it for granted that their lies would be "unexamined, unchallenged." Marshall also wrote to Frances Victor, the Oregon historian. She, too, said the story was untrue and cautioned Marshall not to waste his time trying to chase it down.

Marshall hated to be told what to do, and he still believed there was money to be made off Whitman. For the next two years, he continued to search for hard evidence that Whitman's ride had changed American history. Guessing that there might be confirmation in the letters that Oregon missionaries had written to the American Board in Boston, he asked Charles Hutchins, business manager of *The Missionary Herald*, to make inquiries to see if any were kept on file.

Marshall regarded Hutchins as a friend. They often sat together on trains traveling the fifty miles between Boston and Marshall's home in Fitchburg. When Hutchins told Marshall there were no missionary letters, Marshall believed him. (He would later criticize himself for assuming too much—and for not independently verifying that Hutchins had told him the truth.)

Unable to find any evidence that Whitman saved Oregon, Marshall felt he had no choice but to discard the lecture he had written. On November 13, 1884, at the Peabody Institute, in Baltimore, at the end of a revised lecture on Oregon, Marshall said that Whitman's ride had done nothing to save the Northwest.

"It was undertaken solely on missionary business, and had no political result," he said. "If Whitman had never been born," Marshall concluded, the Pacific Northwest states would never have been lost and the border of the United States and Canada would be "precisely as it is today."

With that, Marshall began to set a course that would sabotage his career as a paid public speaker. For Americans, especially Protestants, wanted to believe that Whitman saved Oregon from the British. Telling them a complex truth about Whitman's failure as a

missionary—and an uncomfortable truth about Spalding's lying—
was not a crowd-pleaser.

In fact, it soon poisoned Marshall's lecture bookings. He was
no longer welcome on the East Coast church circuit, where demand
grew in the 1890s for polished talkers who could rhapsodize about
Whitman's winter ride—Stephen Penrose, Virginia Dox, and the Honorable John W. Fairbank among them.

"Stating the FACTS about that ride—its purpose and its results—
will make a lecture for which there will never be a particle of call by
churches," Marshall grumbled in a letter written in 1888. "I mention
this that you may understand . . . how VERY reluctantly I came to the
conclusion that the whole story is a pure fabrication no more like HIS-
TORY than the story of Jack the Giant Killer."

The year before he wrote this aggrieved letter, Marshall discovered
that his supposed friend Charles Hutchins had deceived him. Marshall, an obsessive and relentless researcher, had by then gained personal access to the American Board archives in Boston, where he
discovered many hundreds of original letters from the Whitmans, the
Spaldings, and other missionaries. The more he read, the more certain
he became that the Whitman story was a fraud masterminded by
Spalding—with a large circle of missionaries, church officials, American Board officers, hack historians, avaricious lecturers, and credulous newspaper editors all too willing to join the con.

Having collected irrefutable evidence of widespread intellectual
skullduggery, Marshall offered in 1888 to present his findings in a paper to the American Historical Association, the same outfit of high-
minded, high-status university academics that Professor Bourne would
address twelve years later.

Nothing came of the offer.

Marshall was an amateur. He lacked class, pedigree, polish. He had
no academic credentials, no institutional backing, and no publisher in

New York or Boston. He had anger issues. As one reviewer would say, "He shows not enough of the even tenor of the true historian."

After his debunking of Whitman's story soured his lecture bookings, Marshall moved to Chicago to join his brother in the insurance business. Insurance would be his living until he returned to public education and became a principal in the schools of Chicago.

His Whitman obsession, though, never abated. Indeed, it took over his life and drained his bank account. Whenever he could escape work, Marshall searched for more documents, conducted more interviews, and took more research trips. He traveled to Washington, D.C., six times to look at documents in the state, war, and navy departments, as well as in the Library of Congress. He journeyed four times to California, Oregon, and Washington State, where he copied diaries, uncovered letters, and conducted interviews with surviving pioneers of the Oregon Trail. He read every book and every magazine article printed in the United States and Britain on the acquisition of Oregon. He read all the floor debates and all the committee reports from the seventeen sessions of Congress that mentioned Oregon prior to Whitman's ride in 1842. He studied the Louisiana Purchase, the Treaty of Ghent, and all other international treaties bearing on Oregon. He scoured the vast archives, letters, and journals of the Hudson's Bay Company. And, of course, he read, copied, and reread all the relevant and available letters and diaries of all the missionaries sent by the American Board to Oregon.

As his expertise grew, so did his peevishness. He sought out conflict with other Oregon scholars, eagerly turning molehills into mountains. In letters to academic rivals, he was a stranger to prudence, restraint, or common courtesy.

His frustration is understandable. His maniacal crusade paid him nothing and for nearly two decades accomplished next to nothing. That he had documented truth on his side was cold comfort. The harder and longer Marshall worked to find contemporaneous sources that revealed the lies of Spalding and his disciples, the more those lies were believed by the American public.

Bile had begun to rise in Marshall's throat when William Barrows's error-ridden and grossly misleading *Oregon* was published in 1883— by which time Marshall had already spent years looking for hard evidence of the myth, to no avail. Leading East Coast publishers of high school and college textbooks then accepted and amplified the Whitman story, which forced millions of American students to memorize the tale Marshall knew to be a hoax. Marshall, meanwhile, researched and wrote the manuscript of a book (finished in 1888) that exposed the hoax. It relied on primary sources that no one else had examined or analyzed. It was solid scientific history, well ahead of the curve. But no publisher would print it.

Living in Chicago made everything worse for Marshall, especially in the mid-1890s, when the *Inter Ocean*, the large-circulation daily newspaper owned by Oliver Nixon and his brother, began to celebrate and lionize Whitman several times a year. With Nixon and D. K. Pearsons leading the charge, saving Whitman College had become a Protestant cause célèbre in Chicago. Then came the glowing reviews, runaway popularity, and multiple printings of the Whitman book that Marshall regarded as the most fraudulent and inane of them all: Nixon's *How Marcus Whitman Saved Oregon*.

Unwilling to suffer in silence, Marshall attempted an insurgent counterattack. He mailed his research to leading American historians, imploring them to examine the sources he had discovered and urging them not to repeat the Whitman myth in their books and lectures. He warned that if they did, "they would soon have the mortification of having its total falsity exposed and be compelled to revise it out."

Almost every historian ignored Marshall and discarded his letters. Few replied. "I was sneered at and abused as an ignoramus who didn't know what he was talking about," he wrote.

In late November of 1897, there was a distant flash of light in the West. It shone in Walla Walla, of all places, not far from the campus of Whitman College. At St. Patrick Church, a Catholic priest named Michael Flohr delivered a provocative speech entitled "The Other Side; or Oregon Saved Without Whitman." The priest based it entirely on Marshall's research and timed its delivery to coincide with the gala fiftieth-anniversary celebrations of the Whitman Massacre.

It was a smart publicity play on the part of the priest. Thanks to the tireless efforts of Penrose, Walla Walla was crawling with out-of-town visitors, including reporters from newspapers all over the Pacific Northwest. Hungry for controversy, they packed into St. Patrick Church, and Father Flohr did not disappoint. He cited documentary evidence (unearthed by Marshall) showing that Spalding was an anti-Catholic liar and that Whitman traveled east to save his mission, not his country. Had Whitman never been born, the priest said, echoing Marshall, Oregon would still be part of the United States.

Although Flohr did not mention Marshall by name, he said he was indebted "to an eminent, scholarly, Protestant gentleman for all these documents, and this argument." Flohr's speech helped create an enduring schism among newspaper editors in the Northwest. Those in Spokane, Seattle, and Walla Walla tended to stick with Whitman as the savior of Oregon, while many in Portland and Salem were convinced of Spalding's fraud and Whitman's insignificance.

F inally, after twenty years of thankless and unremunerative research, Marshall's analysis of Northwest history began to find a bit of traction in Chicago. He was invited to address the city's Education Institute and the Chicago Historical Society on the subject of the Whitman myth. Gaining confidence, he decided to try to drive the Whitman myth out of America's schoolbooks. In 1898, he wrote to all the authors of widely circulated American history textbooks that endorsed the Whitman Saved Oregon story. He included documentary evidence that it was a fraud and warned them that unless they corrected their books in all future editions, they would expose themselves to academic disgrace.

By the summer of 1899, Marshall had won his first converts. Wilbur Fisk Gordy, author of *A History of the United States for Schools*, published by Scribner's, wrote Marshall: "I am entirely satisfied of the correctness of your position, and that you are doing a great work for the truth of history. . . . The next edition of my school history will not contain the name of Marcus Whitman."

By the next summer Marshall had received similar commitments from the authors and editors of more than half a dozen nationally circulated schoolbooks. They were now planning to correct the Whitman story or excise it altogether. One of them was Horace Scudder, the editor of Barrows's *Oregon* and author of one of the first high school history books to spread the Whitman fable.

Marshall also changed the mind of an important and influential Ivy League historian. He convinced Harvard Professor John Fiske, who had been instrumental in bringing Darwin's ideas about evolution to America, that he had been misled and mistaken when he lectured about Whitman's heroic achievements.

Even as Fiske congratulated Marshall on demolishing what he called "the Whitman delusion," he counseled him to cool off.

"You will pardon me for saying that I think the force of your arguments would be enhanced if your style of expression were now and then a little less vehement," Fiske wrote. "I quite sympathize with your feeling toward the humbug which you are exposing, but it seems to me that there is great value in a quiet form of statement, even approaching to understatement, for it gives the reader a chance to do a little swearing at the enemy on his own account."

As Marshall became less of an outcast, his presence in Chicago became more of an annoyance to Oliver Nixon. Bad blood between the two men had first surfaced in the mid-1890s, when Nixon's book became popular and Marshall began contacting and haranguing reviewers, scholars, and other notables who praised it.

When the American Historical Association announced in the fall of 1900 that Edward Bourne would deliver a paper challenging the Whitman legend, Nixon suspected Marshall's involvement. "Our man Marshall has been on his high horse," Nixon wrote to Penrose. "He has been very active in sending around his typewritten chapters, in which he denounces Whitman and claims to annihilate the myth."

Nixon's suspicions were confirmed—in his mind, at least—when Marshall showed up at the historians' meeting in Ann Arbor. After Bourne read his paper, Marshall took the podium to praise it as "very admirable" and to elaborate on the "phenomenal and totally conscienceless" lies of Spalding and other creators of the Whitman fable.

"The sensationalism of all this is apparent," Nixon wrote in the *Inter Ocean,* characterizing the events as a kind of conspiracy. "Marshall was not there by accident. . . . [He and Bourne] intended to deceive and stampede the public with absolute indifference to the honor and good name of the American Historical Society."

I n fact, Marshall and Bourne had never met until the night before they both spoke in Ann Arbor. It was then that Marshall read the professor's paper for the first time. Neither of them had been aware of the other's existence or that anyone was out there doing similar research on the same subject.

Though the American Historical Association had refused to allow Marshall to speak at its conferences in the late 1880s, his success in the late 1890s in warning textbook authors to be on their guard against the "Whitman delusion" had won the approval of eminent historians. This time, they decided to overlook Marshall's amateurism, lack of credentials, and dyspeptic excesses, and they invited him to the conference.

When Marshall rose to speak in Ann Arbor, he was neither thankful nor gracious. He chided the historians for snubbing him back in 1888 and scolded them, too, for turning up their elite noses for so long at his well-sourced revelations about the Whitman fraud:

"Had it been taken up by the association [twelve years ago], it would never have been in a single school history, nor in any other book having any extensive circulation, and such a totally worthless book as Barrows's *Oregon* would long since have been withdrawn from sale, instead of being pushed into every library to befog and mislead the American people about the true history of the acquisition of nearly one-twelfth of all our national domain on this continent."

After Bourne and Marshall delivered their respective papers, they quickly came to like and admire each other. They became collaborators and supportive friends. When Bourne expanded his paper into a book for Scribner's, he thanked Marshall "for the most painstaking examination of the [Whitman legend] that has ever been made." Bourne also incorporated into that book many of Marshall's discoveries, repeatedly saying in footnotes that he was "indebted" to the school principal from Chicago.

Although Marshall had worked on the Whitman investigation at least ten times longer than Bourne and was vastly more knowledgeable on the subject, he did not begrudge the Yale professor's success or the fact that Bourne had become the face of the anti-Whitman campaign.

"It is very amusing," he wrote to Bourne, "that so far, I, though the original sinner in this matter, have gone entirely 'unwhipped of justice' and all the scourging has fallen on your poor back. Still, I fancy it does not make you writhe very much."

The two men exchanged letters of mutual congratulation. They reveled in the anger their research had triggered, especially the many tirades that issued forth from Oliver Nixon. Marshall said that he enjoyed "harrowing up the old gentleman's soul."

After decades of scorn and obscurity, Marshall felt vindicated. His letters to Bourne were giddy. He joked that if Nixon, Penrose, Virginia Dox, and other aggrieved champions of the Whitman legend could have their way, Bourne would be stripped of his professorial robes, crowned with a fool's cap, and forced to sit in a dunce's corner. With Bourne as their captive, Marshall wrote, the Whitmanites would be "gleefully chuckling" to one another, saying:

> "Now at last are we avenged of those pestiferous and
> presumptuous mortals who, for these many years, have been
> insisting that the business of historians is not to write down
> any kind of a story that is likely to be popular, but is to tell
> the truth, and that they may know the truth, to go to
> contemporaneous documents to establish the facts of history."

Outside of Marshall's mockery, the Whitmanites did, indeed, seek vengeance. Throughout the first decade of the twentieth century, their denunciations of Bourne and Marshall appeared in newspapers, magazines, and religious publications all around the country. Pro-Whitman scholars, including Myron Eells in Washington State and William Mowry in Massachusetts, published scholarly-looking books with complicated arguments and countless footnotes.

But they were swimming against the tide, especially on the East

Coast. Nine months after Bourne and Marshall spoke in Ann Arbor, *The New York Times* book section published a prominent and brutally critical review of Mowry's *Marcus Whitman and the Early Days of Oregon*. It said, in effect, that the book was ahistorical gibberish, that Whitman most assuredly had not saved Oregon, and that all honest students of history must give honor where honor is due:

> No one who was present at the last meeting of the American Historical Association will forget the impression caused by Prof. Bourne's judicial and convincing demonstration, which was followed by a crushing weight of testimony collected by Principal W. I. Marshall of Chicago in exposing the true character of the Whitman myth.

The myth soon started to appear on lists of tales debunked by science. Academic historians compared it to Washington and the cherry tree, the myth of the Southern Cavalier, and the claim that Rome was founded by Romulus and Remus. The editor of *The American Historical Review*, J. Franklin Jameson, wrote in 1902 that the "Whitman legend is fatally damaged, so far as any use of it by trained historians is concerned"—though Jameson added that "the passionate revilings to which we have seen [Bourne] subjected in many newspapers make it plain that the legend will die hard."

In Chicago, Marshall did everything he could to accelerate the legend's demise. Having managed to save some money from his job as a principal, he embarked on a final trip to the Pacific Northwest to find and copy documents that had escaped his earlier investigations. He hoped to tie up all loose ends and publish his *summa historica* on Marcus Whitman the following year.

With his eyes on that goal, Marshall showed up in July of 1902 at the home of Myron Eells, who lived on the Kitsap Peninsula, in western Washington State.

In print, Eells had been more sharply critical of Marshall than of Bourne, suggesting that Marshall was immature, ungentlemanly, and gratuitously cruel.

Not to be outdone, Marshall had written two harshly critical essays about Eells. The first one, which Eells had read, called him a "fool."

Marshall, though, did not allow personal animus, however bitter or unresolved, to come between him and an original source. He needed to examine certain sections of Henry Spalding's diary that were then in the sole possession of Eells. Marshall knocked on his enemy's front door and asked if he could stay for a few days to study the document.

In his diary, Eells wrote about the visit and marveled at Marshall's effrontery:

July 28, 1902. Mon.

Prof. W. I. Marshall of Chicago left this morning after being with us two days. He is a noted anti-Whitmanite, & very cranky. Did not think of it at first, & perhaps it was as well, but think I would have been justified in refusing to allow him to come into the house, after he had published a pamphlet that [said] my father (as well as myself others) was a fool friend of Dr. Whitman, & sent it to all the members of the Am. Historical Soc., unless he had first apologized.

As it was, when he was hungry, I fed him, thirsty, gave him drink, tired, furnished him a bed, & treated him as gentlemanly as I could. He came to look at & make extracts fr. Mr Spalding's Journal. That he should come at all & make such a request, & then accept all our hospitalities, in my opinion shows that he has more cheek than most any man I ever saw.

CHAPTER EIGHTEEN

LOST CAUSE

A t the rate of one Whitman scholar per year, Oliver Nixon, William Marshall, Myron Eells, and Edward Bourne all died in the first decade of the new century. The curious cluster of mortality—four combative historians gone in four consecutive years, orphaning four books and countless arguments about one arcane subject—all but silenced the national debate about the heroic status of Marcus Whitman.

Nixon was first. He died in 1905, at age seventy-nine, while on holiday with D. K. Pearsons.

Marshall was next. He died in 1906, at age sixty-six, shortly after finishing his life's work, which he entitled *Acquisition of Oregon and the Long Suppressed Evidence About Marcus Whitman*. The manuscript gathered dust in Chicago for five years until friends in Seattle published it. The book was staggeringly long—two volumes, 818 pages.

It was also self-righteous, mind-numbingly detailed, and repetitive. Sales were close to nil, as Marshall had gloomily predicted. But scholars saw it as an important contribution. *The American Historical Review* said it presented "more fully and emphatically than any previous work" the evidence against Whitman saving Oregon.

Then it was Eells in 1907, at age sixty-three. His posthumously published book, *Marcus Whitman: Pathfinder and Patriot*, insisted that Whitman really did save Oregon. Scholars ignored it, as did the public.

The last and youngest to go was Bourne, who died in 1908 at age forty-seven, of a resurgence of the tuberculosis that had crippled him as a boy. The Yale professor's attack on the Whitman legend, a mere bagatelle in his illustrious résumé as a scholar, was mentioned prominently in obituaries.

With all these voices silenced, Marcus Whitman faded from America's collective memory as the twentieth century gathered pace. His name largely disappeared from national newspapers and magazines. Encyclopedia editors and most school history book authors heeded Marshall's warning and removed all references to the thrilling horseback ride that saved Oregon.

There was, however, a region of the country where the Whitman enchantment grew stronger and more resistant to historical evidence: the Pacific Northwest, especially the region east of the Cascades, where the last combatant in the Whitman wars still had many good years ahead of him.

Stephen Penrose was in his early forties when Marshall and Bourne passed away. Having revived Whitman College by going all in on the Whitman fabrication, he had no intention of bending his beliefs to the arguments of so-called scientific historians.

But sensing that the Whitman legend had become a lost cause on the national stage, Penrose and his followers narrowed their focus. They launched a multipronged, multidecade pro-Whitman marketing campaign targeted at residents of the Pacific Northwest. It helped raise money and increased name recognition for Whitman College—and boosted pioneer pride across much of the region.

In the American South, many whites took the sting out of their famous lost cause by reimagining the "real" reason for the Civil War. It was not a greed-driven fight to preserve their right to enslave human beings, they falsely claimed; it was a principled defense of states' rights. And it only made sense to memorialize the champions of that noble fight—Confederate officers—by casting them in bronze and standing them up on pedestals in hundreds of town squares. More than seven hundred Confederate monuments were built in the first half of the twentieth century.

In those same decades, the regional marketing of the Marcus Whitman legend used a similar sleight of hand. By selling Whitman as a pioneer hero and framing the settlement of Oregon as a glorious Christian melodrama, the propaganda campaign tapped into a deep well of denial about what white settlers had done—and were still doing—to Indians like the Cayuses, the Walla Wallas, the Umatillas, and the Nez Perces.

At Whitman College, the campaign kicked off in 1916 with a scathing ad hominem attack on two dead anti-Whitmanites from out of state. It appeared in an essay entitled "Some Observations upon the Negative Testimony and the General Spirit and Methods of Bourne and Marshall in Dealing with the Whitman Question."

William D. Lyman, a close friend of Penrose, a son of early Oregon immigrants, and the only Whitman College professor to have a campus building named after him, wrote the essay for the University of Washington's historical quarterly. Lyman was a popular professor whom some students called "Daddy" and whom Penrose praised for "his unparalleled knowledge of Northwest history."

In his essay, Lyman was more hit man than scholar. He described Bourne as a "supercilious and academic" opportunist who went "gunning" after the reputation of Marcus Whitman as part of a diverting exercise in Ivy League condescension toward yokels in the West. To a modern reader, Lyman's critique of academic expertise feels familiar: a harbinger of Trump-era culture wars, when many viewed the findings of science as affronts to patriotic values.

Lyman's essay was also an appeal to regional pride. He defended Marcus Whitman and the honor of the Northwest by impugning the eastern elitism of Bourne.

> What can Professor Bourne of Yale and his major students find to expose? They must find something in order to maintain their reputation as "scientific historians." Well, here is that Whitman story which some missionaries and college builders in a distant state seem to take much comfort in as an example of heroism and patriotism! How would it do to punch the eyes out of that by way of a little class practice? Such seems to me largely the attitude of Professor Bourne.

As for Marshall, he was not to be trusted, Lyman wrote, because of his "habitual anger, vilification, and general bad temper [which is] inexcusable in a historian."

Lyman also complained that Marshall said bad things about local heroes. "His stock in trade is the imputation of dishonesty and falsification to men who the Pacific Northwest honored in their time as models of Christian devotion and honesty."

When Lyman published his essay, veneration of Whitman was a fundamental part of the Whitman College experience. President

Penrose himself taught a history class that presented the Whitman legend as established historical fact. In 1919, when the college celebrated Penrose's twenty-fifth year as president, students wrote and performed a play—*The Masque of Marcus Whitman*—that credulously depicted how Whitman saved Oregon. It also suggested that the blood of slaughtered missionaries had consecrated the soil of the Pacific Northwest, which helped turn the wilderness into farms and towns—and brought forth a small liberal arts college founded "in faith and love for Whitman's fame."

It was as if Bourne's and Marshall's work had never existed.

Even after the Whitman myth was debunked, it endured as historical fact in the Pacific Northwest, thanks in large measure to outdoor theatrical extravaganzas staged in Walla Walla and written by Whitman College president Penrose. The pageants used thousands of local actors and hundreds of head of livestock to dramatize how "Doctor Whitman . . . saved this land of ours."

To spread Whitman's fictional glory beyond the campus and across the Northwest, Penrose began to think big in the 1920s. He wrote the script for an outdoor extravaganza—"How the West Was Won"—to be performed on the seventy-fifth anniversary of the Whitman Massacre. An unidentified Indian chief appeared on the cover of the show's program, but Indians were bit players in the pioneer-centric production. It celebrated four civilizing forces: explorers, fur traders, settlers, and, of course, missionaries.

The script singled out "Doctor Whitman . . . who saved this land of ours."

Penrose persuaded the town of Walla Walla to fund and stage his play on a Cecil B. DeMille scale. The pageant recruited 2,506 actors, dancers, and singers, who performed on a stage wider than a football field. Many of the actors were descendants of Oregon pioneers. Stage props included fifty-foot-high painted foothills that seemed to rise into the actual foothills of the nearby Blue Mountains. A tributary of the Walla Walla River was diverted to flow alongside the stage. In addition to the vast cast, the stage was intermittently populated with five hundred head of cattle, horses, and mules. A pageant producer was imported from Boston to keep the cast, the beasts, the choir, and the orchestra from running amok.

The production was a hit. About thirty thousand spectators paid to attend the two-day event in June 1923, many of them driving to Walla Walla from Seattle and Portland. By popular demand, the pageant was produced again in 1924, drawing similarly huge crowds.

Both years, the script of the show, as written by Penrose, included claims that had been shown in the published work of Bourne and Marshall to be false and fabricated:

> A rumor reaches the good Doctor's ears,
> The rumor of a treaty to be signed
> Which shall abandon Oregon to England,
> And, like a swift hawk launching on its flight,
> He speeds him east and rides to Washington
> Through winter snows to let the truth be known.
> Oh there was dauntless courage, and the stuff
> Of heroes! Was there ever ride so great
> To save an empire being thrown away?
> The President is won. The Doctor turns,

Defiant of his Boston Mission Board,

And guides a caravan across the plains.

Gladly he rides towards home—and wife beloved.

With the prestige of his college behind him and with the resources of business-minded boosters in Walla Walla, Penrose had successfully repackaged and recycled the Whitman fable—bringing it to a new generation that included thousands of local performers and tens of thousands of audience members from across the region. Regional newspapers applauded the pageants and rarely, if ever, bothered with historical corrections. As in the American South in the first decades of the twentieth century, where locals blandly welcomed statues of Confederate generals, the renaissance of the Whitman lie in the Northwest was celebratory, patriotic, and fuzzy on facts.

A decade after the first outdoor extravaganzas, Penrose and the city of Walla Walla did it all again. To mark the centennial of Whitman's arrival in Oregon in 1836, Penrose wrote and the city staged another spectacle, called "Wagons West!" The four-day event included three thousand performers, hundreds of head of livestock, and, of course, the claim that Whitman saved Oregon.

New this time around was an ingenious plan to recruit the U.S. government as a player in the Whitman propaganda campaign. The "Wagons West!" pageant was staged, in part, to make money—more than $10,000, which was enough to buy thirty-five acres of land at the old Whitman mission, outside Walla Walla. The pageant operators then gave the mission grounds to the federal government as a gift. But the gift came with strings: federal tax dollars must be used to memorialize the Whitmans—forever.

A 1936 law passed by Congress and signed by President Franklin Roosevelt authorized the transaction, which had been negotiated by leaders in Walla Walla working with members of Congress representing Washington and Oregon. The law turned the mission grounds into a national monument (later the Whitman Mission National Historic Site) managed by the National Park Service.

The law specified that the property "shall be a public national memorial to Marcus Whitman and his wife, Narcissa Prentiss Whitman, who here established their Indian mission and school, and ministered to the physical and spiritual needs of the Indians until massacred."

While the legislation memorialized the Whitmans as martyred pioneer missionaries, it did not mention the Cayuse tribe by name, nor did it bother to explain that they killed the missionaries in response to a catastrophic measles epidemic—in line with their own laws and customs—and fear of white land theft. At the urging of local tribes, the National Park Service would later make a series of adjustments in its exhibits at the mission to include and emphasize this history and hire local descendants of the Cayuse, Nez Perce, and Walla Walla tribes.

Penrose, though, failed to get his version of the Whitman story into the legislation that created the historic site. The law made no mention of Whitman's ride. It did not affirm that the missionary doctor had saved Oregon from the British. For all of Penrose's lectures, newspaper essays, and outdoor extravaganzas, when it came to long-term federal stewardship of the Whitman mission site, he failed to overcome Bourne, Marshall, and the indisputable evidence they had found of Spalding's lies.

P enrose's tenure as president of Whitman College would last until 1934, a remarkable forty years—as would his muleheaded promulgation of the Whitman lie.

In fairness, there was much more to Penrose than his stubbornness. Under his leadership, Whitman College secured a lasting and well-deserved reputation as one of the better liberal arts colleges in the United States, and perhaps the best in the Northwest. Following the lead of Yale and Harvard, Penrose quietly and gradually severed the college's ties to the Congregational Church, transforming the school into a rigorous, secular, and selective college—the closest he could come to creating a Far West replica of his alma mater, Williams College.

Penrose was seventy-two when the Whitman mission site was handed off to the federal government. By then he was blind and had been pushed out as president, having stayed in office far too long. He had burdened the college with crippling debt when the Great Depression sank the economy of the Pacific Northwest. Chester C. Maxey, a professor at the college and later its president, described Penrose's final years as president as "tragic and pathetic."

Penrose died in 1947 at age eighty-two, having outlived his major rivals in the Whitman wars by more than three decades. No one would ever again be so relentless—or effective—in tending the embers of the Whitman legend. But in the mid-twentieth century, an exceptionally influential alumnus of Whitman College took up the cause.

William O. Douglas—who costarred in the 1919 Whitman College production of *The Masque of Marcus Whitman*—would become the longest-serving U.S. Supreme Court justice in history. From this exalted perch, he managed to keep the legend alive.

President Franklin Roosevelt had appointed Douglas to the Supreme Court in 1939. A social friend of the president's, he moved in an elite circle of Roosevelt's New Deal advisers. Douglas possessed all the necessary credentials for easy confirmation in the Senate (the vote was 62–4): he had graduated second in his class from Columbia Law School, worked at an elite Wall Street law firm, taught financial law as a professor at Yale Law School, and was appointed by Roosevelt in 1934 to the Securities and Exchange Commission, which he later chaired.

With an Ivy League pedigree, a world-class legal mind, and a gift for lyrical writing, Douglas served on the high court for 36 years, 211 days—longer than anyone else to date. But he was always an ornery iconoclast who never quite fit in.

Douglas grew up without a father—and with little money—in Yakima, a fruit-growing town in eastern Washington, about 140 miles west of where Marcus Whitman was murdered. To help his mother with money, Douglas picked cherries in high school, where he graduated as the valedictorian. While on scholarship at Whitman College, he worked

Supreme Court justice William O. Douglas, an alumnus of Whitman College, served longer on the high court than anyone else. From that perch, he used his influence and contacts to place a story in *Life* magazine in 1943 that credulously repeated the debunked Whitman myth and celebrated the "epic journey which helped save the Oregon Territory for the U.S."

as a janitor and waiter. His upbringing, particularly his summers among migrant farmworkers, shaped his politics and his jurisprudence. He was attuned to the vulnerabilities of the poor, of African Americans, and of alienated young people. He read the First Amendment as a near-absolute ban on government restrictions of speech, the press, and political association. As a Supreme Court justice, he was a crusading liberal and a singularly insistent opponent of the Vietnam War. In 1973, he ordered the military to stop bombing Cambodia.

The military ignored his order and it was quickly overturned by eight other justices.

In his life outside the court, Douglas refused to narrow his interests or trim his appetites. He tried to become Roosevelt's vice presidential running mate in 1944. He rode (and often fell off) horses, occasionally drank to excess, wrote more than thirty books, kept mistresses, cursed at his court colleagues, and married four times, twice to women who were at least three decades younger than him. His judicial opinions were usually short, elegantly written, and sometimes factually sloppy. His politics and his personal life outraged many Republicans in Congress. They loathed Douglas and periodically tried to impeach him.

One constant in his life was what he called his "deep sentiment and affection" for Whitman College, where he graduated Phi Beta Kappa in 1920 and served as student body president. When the hundredth anniversary of Whitman's ride to the East rolled around in 1943, Justice Douglas did not hesitate to use his position and his social contacts to spread the false story of what the ride accomplished.

In the spring of that year, he contacted a New York friend, Henry R. Luce, editor in chief of *Time* and *Life* magazines. In that pre-television era, Luce's publications were the gatekeepers of popular culture in America, interpreting news, sports, history, and the arts for tens of millions. More than any other picture magazine, *Life* shaped the country's understanding of itself.

In September 1943, *Life* published "Marcus Whitman and His Famous Ride," a five-page, eleven-photograph spread that celebrated the "epic journey which helped save the Oregon Territory for the U.S." It was by far the biggest splash of national publicity for Whitman since the 1890s—and one of the most credulous.

Letters between Justice Douglas and Winslow Anderson, then

president of Whitman College, show that *Life* received its research materials for the article from Douglas, who received them from Whitman College. The *Life* article included a flattering photograph of the college, calling it "a lasting memorial" to the martyred missionaries.

"I think that Mr. Luce and his associates did a particularly splendid job," Anderson wrote Douglas a few days after a copy of *Life* arrived at Whitman College. "I am indebted to you for your good offices in convincing Mr. Luce that this story should be told in *Life*. I am certain that Whitman will receive dividends from this excellent publicity."

T en years later, in 1953, an eight-foot statue of Marcus Whitman was unveiled and dedicated in Washington, D.C. The legislature in the State of Washington—where public schools still lionized Whitman and where the influence of Penrose's outdoor productions still lingered—had decided that Whitman was "a deceased resident worthy of national renown" and that he would be the first person from the state to be honored in the National Statuary Hall of the U.S. Capitol.

The decision had detractors back home. When the bill to select Whitman as the state's most distinguished son was being considered, anonymous opponents sent a scolding postcard to state legislators. Its authors appear to have consulted the writings of Bourne and Marshall.

"Did Whitman's trip save Oregon? It DID NOT!" the postcard said. "The Whitman legend is 90% fictitious. . . . DON'T VOTE A MEMORIAL WHICH WILL MAKE WASHINGTON STATE THE LAUGHINGSTOCK OF THE NATION."

The postcard made some lawmakers wary. They voted for a Whitman statue but refused to pay for it, calling instead for private donations. It took three years before schoolchildren, churches, clubs, and private individuals could scrape together $30,000 for the statue and for hauling it across the country. A disproportionate share of the money came from sparsely populated towns near Whitman College.

By the time Douglas delivered the speech that dedicated the statue, he had become somewhat wary of the Whitman legend. He (or perhaps his law clerks) had done serious homework. His speech owed more to Bourne and Marshall than to the fevered fictions of Henry Spalding, or the evidence-blind boosterism that abounded at Whitman College.

That day in the U.S. Capitol, Douglas dialed back Whitman's historical importance, saying it was "probably too extravagant" to think that he saved Oregon. Douglas explained to an audience of three hundred in Statuary Hall that Whitman's ride "was not inspired by the threat of British claims."

Cautiously, truthfully, and with what seemed to be deliberate blandness, Douglas concluded that the Pacific Northwest became part of the United States through a combination of treaties and westward migration. "This extension of empire was a complex of many forces," he said. "Whitman played an important role in showing the average family that this new frontier was within their reach."

Douglas had been steeped in the Whitman Saved Oregon story. But time, distance, and the inexorable weight of evidence had made it too ludicrous to be repeated by a justice of the Supreme Court—even if he was a proud native son.

D ouglas's tepid dedication speech marked a turning point: it signaled the beginning of the end of the Whitman enchantment in the Pacific Northwest and at Whitman College.

The college began to tiptoe away from the propaganda surrounding its namesake in the second half of the twentieth century. All references to Whitman saving Oregon had been cut from the college catalog by 1965. Also excised was a mention of "the gallant attempt of Dr. and Mrs. Whitman to bring the Christian religion to the western wilderness." By the start of the twenty-first century, the catalog had whittled down its Whitman reference to one sentence.

In the most recent online version of the college's history, there are two sentences about the Whitmans, one of which is misleading. It says Marcus and Narcissa came west "to teach the Cayuse Indians to read and write their native language" and that they ended up providing "assistance to Oregon Trail travelers." In fact, they came west to convert the Cayuses to a strict version of Calvinism—and utterly failed. It does not mention that they were killed by Indians.

In the 1960s, campus opposition to the Vietnam War and the civil rights movement helped raise student awareness of the mistreatment of American Indians in the Northwest and across the country. As a result, the college halted an orientation program that for decades had transported all freshmen out to the Whitman Massacre site for a hagiographic history lesson about the missionary martyrs.

Since then, most students at the college "know little or nothing about [the Whitmans] and care even less," according to a National Park Service history of the federal site. It notes that "apathy is felt not just among students, but among college officials as well."

Apathy, in fact, became university policy, and it came from the top. Robert Skotheim, who took over in 1975 as the second-longest-serving president of the college, after Penrose, recalled that by then "Marcus Whitman was gone as a presence at the college."

Skotheim said he did everything he could *not* to revive it during his thirteen years as president.

"I had so little interest in Whitman the historical figure," said Skotheim, who carefully ignored anything and everything related to the question of whether Whitman saved Oregon. Skotheim said he never once heard the name of William Marshall. "The story of Whitman College in the twentieth century is an increasing lack of interest in how it all came to be. The college has been professionalized. World and national history are far more important than local history."

Skotheim raised money for the college by ignoring Marcus Whitman and celebrating the achievements of Stephen Penrose, who turned the school into "the Williams of the West," as well as the most secular private college in the region. "Penrose ended up blind, with a detached retina," Skotheim said. "He became in his way a martyr like Whitman."

Skotheim doubted that Penrose went to his grave believing that Whitman had saved Oregon. "In the end, Penrose didn't care," Skotheim said. "He had saved Whitman College."

Strategic forgetting of the legend of Marcus Whitman allowed the college to quietly glide away from discomfiting questions about how it had used the much-disputed story.

"Whitman College has never apologized for founding itself on the Whitman lie," said Skotheim. "It was irrelevant. The college that Stephen Penrose made was not interested in looking back. The erosion of interest continued until it became positive repudiation."

Nothing crystalizes the college's repudiation of Whitman more than its treatment, in the early 1990s, of a newly cast bronze statue of the missionary doctor. It is a replica of statues that still stand in the U.S. Capitol and in the Washington State Capitol, in Olympia. A foundry in Walla Walla had donated the replica to the college, and many members of the faculty despised it. They did not want it to occupy a place of honor at the college.

"We all agreed that it should be placed as far away from the campus as possible," said Dennis Crockett, an associate professor of art history and a member of the committee that recommended where the statue should be placed.

By the 1990s, the Whitman College faculty had come to abhor this large bronze statue of Marcus Whitman and did not want it on campus. It was exiled to a far corner of the college property, near a railroad track, so that, as one professor explained, "in the case of a derailment, it would be destroyed."

The committee unanimously decided to locate the statue on a scruffy triangle of college property on the eastern edge of campus, a few feet from a little-used railroad track.

"My recommendation was to place it as close to the railroad tracks as possible, so that, in the case of a derailment, it would be destroyed," Crockett said. "It has been an embarrassment for me and everyone I know since it was erected. There is some solace in the fact that most visitors to Walla Walla are unaware that it is attached to the college."

I n the twenty-first century, the connection between Whitman College and its namesake has grown ever more remote. Most students have little or no idea who the Whitmans were, what they did, or why they were murdered. Students are also largely oblivious to the patriotic lie that Spalding and other ministers concocted about Whitman; they are not aware that it hoodwinked most of the United States in the late 1800s and well into the 1900s. Nor are they aware that the college's long-serving president Stephen Penrose peddled it up and down the East Coast in order to save their school from bankruptcy.

"The strangest part to me is not what Penrose did but how it is not mentioned at all today at Whitman College," said Kate Kunkel-Patterson, who studied history at Whitman College and graduated in 2013. She works as an interpretive guide at the Whitman Mission National Historic Site, which now offers visitors a nuanced and historically accurate account of the murders at the mission. "There is very little knowledge at the college about what happened out there at the mission."

Periodically, a few Whitman students focus on the Whitman story—and become upset. The college mascot was changed in 2016 from the Missionaries to the Blues, a reference to the nearby mountains. The name of the student newspaper was changed from *The Pioneer* to the *Wire*. The next year, on October 9, 2017, vandals sprayed red paint on the Whitman statue near the railroad tracks. They also used black paint to deface an idealized portrait of Narcissa Whitman that had hung for years in Prentiss Hall, a dormitory on campus.

The college responded to the vandalism by creating an exhibit called "A Proper Monument?" It asked students to think carefully about the appropriateness of any memorial to the Whitmans—including the college itself.

"Whitman College is the most important monument to the Whit-

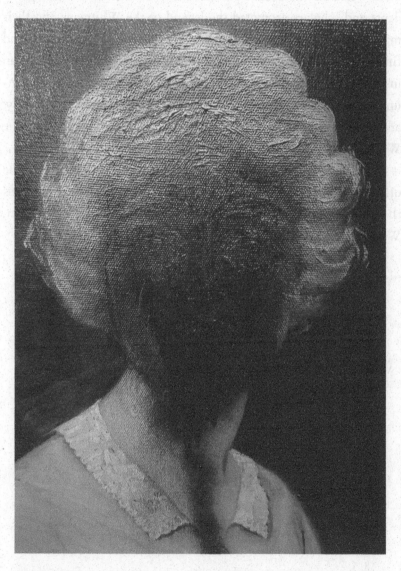

In 2017, on-campus vandals used black paint to deface an idealized painting of Narcissa Whitman that had hung for years in Prentiss Hall, a dormitory at Whitman College. The college administration responded by asking students to think critically about the value of any memorial to the Whitmans, including the college itself.

mans," said an interpretive placard in the exhibit. "Successive presidents and scholars promoted the legend of the Whitmans and their martyrdom, and that legacy in turn gave the College the prestige and financial clout it needed to thrive. No matter what course we, as an institution, choose to take in addressing the presence of colonial monuments on our campus, we cannot escape the fact that this community, and our presence in this part of the world, is a living monument to the Whitmans. It is up to us to decide what that means."

Not everything at Whitman, though, is up for discussion. The official college seal—created during Penrose's time—still includes the three stars representing Whitman's supposed rescue of Oregon, Washington, and Idaho from the grasping hands of the British.

ACT FIVE

REVIVE

CHAPTER NINETEEN

PREDATORS

For more than a century, it was never quite clear to the Cayuses whether they were citizens of a sovereign nation, wards of the federal government, or prey in a lawless holding pen surrounded by white people who viewed them as subhuman.

Their unease was well grounded. When the Cayuses, along with the Walla Wallas and the Umatillas, moved to the reservation in 1859, agents from the U.S. Office of Indian Affairs said that it would be impossible to protect them from "unprincipled white men." The peril was threefold.

First, the reservation was near the Oregon Trail, which kept serving up wagonloads of white people in desperate need of good, cheap land. The reservation was also near mines that were a magnet for unscrupulous white men on the make.

Second, land on the reservation was clearly worth stealing. In 1860, an agent from the U.S. Office of Indian Affairs described the seductiveness of the reservation's farm- and rangeland, as seen through the eyes of white people:

> At the western base of the Blue Mountains a belt of land of varying width, extending from ten to fifteen miles, and well watered by mountain springs, contains much fertile land, which would, I have no doubt, under proper culture, well repay the labors of husbandry. As a natural pasture it can scarcely be excelled for beauty and productiveness.
>
> The bottoms on the Umatilla [River] are, to about half their extent, covered with a thick growth of cottonwood, alder, and birch.
>
> The remaining half is open prairie, much of it very fertile . . . [which] can be readily irrigated, and are well-suited to gardens.
>
> On the north side of the Umatilla the country is an elevated table land. . . . Covered with luxuriant bunch grass, it affords a pasture ample for thousands of cattle and sheep. The winters are said to be mild, the snow never falling to a great depth or lying long. . . .
>
> Having explored this reservation twice, first in February and afterwards in July last, I feel confident that in regard to soil, climate, and the extent of the hunting and root grounds, it has peculiar facilities for becoming self-sustaining at an early day.

Third, the treaty that created the reservation guaranteed everything and nothing to the Indian tribes ordered to live on it.

In theory, the treaty assured the Indians that they would have a protected existence on land that was to be theirs in perpetuity. In reality, as a federal Indian agent on the reservation wrote in 1866, the treaty compelled Indians to live "in constant fear that the reservation will be taken from them and thrown open to settlement by the whites." Another federal Indian agent said, "It is hardly to be expected that the Indians can retain this reservation much longer unless the strong arm of the Government protects them."

The U.S. Senate ratified 376 Indian treaties between 1778 and 1868. Then Congress halted treaty making in 1871, reasoning that defeated and impoverished Indians were hardly sovereign nations. In what could have put an immediate end to all the Indian reservations created by those treaties, the Supreme Court ruled in 1903 that Congress had unilateral power, should it choose to use it, to break treaties with Indian tribes.

Congress, though, never mustered the clarity of purpose either to abrogate the treaties or honor them. It let them twist in the prairie wind. John Marshall, chief justice of the Supreme Court in the early nineteenth century, acknowledged the strange ambiguity of the treaties that governed Indian Country. He described the treaty relationship between Indians and the U.S. government as "anomalous," "complex," and "unlike that of any other people in existence."

For reservation Indians, government policies flip-flopped every few decades. American presidents, Congress, and Indian affairs bureaucrats in Washington alternated between seasons of paternalistic concern and racist neglect, between efforts to protect reservations and crusades to "terminate" them. Perhaps the only consistent federal policy was a chronic failure to fund the promises and enforce the protections that had been spelled out in treaties. Other than the occasional tug of a guilty conscience or the rare exposé in the press, nothing restrained or sanctioned politicians whose policies betrayed Indians. American Indians were not granted full citizenship until 1924. It took another forty years before all fifty states allowed them to vote.

Most of the treaties, including the one that created what became known as the Confederated Tribes of the Umatilla Indian Reservation, were hurriedly concocted writs of dispossession. The main ingredients: coercion, condescension, and land theft. They often included special gifts of land and loot to agreeable chiefs, harsh punishments for Indians who drank alcohol, and assorted inducements for Indians to plow up land, build fences, send children to school, and be "civilized."

U.S. agents who negotiated the treaties expected that reservations would be temporary. They were to exist during the twenty years that treaties obligated the federal government to make cash payments to the tribes—and then fade away as Indians mastered the art of behaving like whites.

Yet the actual words in the treaty that created the Umatilla Reservation define it as a homeland that "shall be set apart" for the tribes.

The words established inherent rights and nothing in the treaty says those rights should one day fade away. Indeed, the treaty language—when parsed by federal judges—would eventually give Indians a chance to play offense against whites.

"The treaty was not what we wanted," said Antone Minthorn, a Cayuse–Nez Perce elder who served for many years as the top elected

Antone Minthorn, a Cayuse elder and longtime elected leader of the Umatilla Reservation, helped revive the reservation and restore its principal river by using patience, smart lawyers, sound science, and comprehensive land-use planning.

leader of the Umatilla Reservation. "But it gave us a chance to have a future."

That future, though, was a long, long time in coming. Powers and protections implicit in the treaty did not kick in until the final third of the twentieth century. Until then, violations of treaty rights took on a unique twist on the Umatilla Reservation. In addition to white self-dealing and land grabbing, there was an enduring appetite in white society for collective vilification of the Cayuses, still infamous as the killers of Marcus and Narcissa Whitman.

Just before the turn of the nineteenth century, when whites were commemorating the fiftieth anniversary of the Whitman Massacre, a circuit court judge in eastern Oregon had examined how the Cayuses were faring on the reservation. Judge Stephen H. Lowell's assessment, published in *The Whitman College Quarterly*, predicted that the Cayuses would not survive and made it clear that this would not be a bad thing.

> Theoretically, under the law, the Indian is residing upon his allotment, sowing the seed, reaping the harvest, and practicing all the arts of the peaceful tiller of the soil, while his children are in attendance upon school, preparing for a part in the civilization which a bountiful, but somewhat neglectful government, is assuring them. Actually he has no use for his land, except to lease it to the whites, while he, clad in blanket of vivid hue, loafs in his tepee beside some stream, content in the thought that his squaw will do what work must be done, and that the rental from his land will buy the little he needs to eat and wear. Nor is he anxious that his children should be educated, and they rarely attend school at his suggestion or compulsion. The burden of interesting the young and impressing them with the need of education he leaves to school

authorities. The average Indian will not work nor is he ambitious to change either his own or his children's condition. . . .

They appear doomed to early practical extinction. Year by year they are decreasing in numbers. . . . Measuring the effect of another fifty years by the half century about to close, when the one-hundredth anniversary of the Whitman tragedy shall be observed, the race which committed the terrible crime will have passed forever.

The ancestral territory of the Cayuse, Walla Walla, and Umatilla tribes covered 6.4 million acres—a temperate rangeland nearly the size of Massachusetts—in what is now northeast Oregon and southeast Washington State. It straddled the Columbia River, from which the tribes once took and consumed an astounding 2.3 pounds of salmon per person per day.

Treaty negotiations at the Walla Walla council of 1855 pushed the tribes south. It moved them about twenty-five miles away from the Columbia River and the chinook, coho, and sockeye salmon that had nourished their families, structured their lives, and figured strongly in their spiritual beliefs. The treaty also took away 96 percent of their territory, leaving them with 245,699 acres, a reservation a bit larger than New York City.

In the process of taking nearly all their land, white agents of the federal government did acknowledge that the tribes were losing territory to which they had a valid "right, title and claim." They also acknowledged the permanence of their legal claim to the reservation land they were being sent to live on. That land "shall be set apart," the treaty said, "for their exclusive use, nor shall any white person be permitted to reside upon the same without permission."

The clarity of this language, though, did little to restrain the

behavior of nineteenth-century white farmers, ranchers, and speculators. They believed Indians did not need and were incapable of using
good farm and cattle land—and they acted accordingly.

W. H. Barnhart, the federal Indian agent who lived on the Umatilla
Reservation in 1866, wrote that whites were constantly cooking up
"various pretexts to locate" themselves on Indian land. These included, he said, "occasional attempts to exasperate the Indians in the
commission of some overt act which will . . . give an excuse for plung-
ing the country into another Indian war, the end of which, they well
know, would be the expulsion of the Indians from the coveted tract."

Local politicians and newspaper editors were just as acquisitive
and insistent. They wanted to round up all the Indians on the Umatilla Reservation and send them off to other reservations, to the Pacific coast, or to parts unknown. A front-page editorial in the *Oregon
Statesman* described the Cayuses, Walla Wallas, and Umatillas as
"savage vagabonds who are making no progress, whatever, in civilization." It suggested that "all these useless and unproductive people"
should, at a very minimum, be "restricted to less than one-third of the
territory they now occupy." The editor of the *East Oregonian*, a newspaper published in Pendleton, a small farm town near the reservation,
wanted the Indians to be sent elsewhere: "We favor their removal as it
is a burning shame to keep this fine body of land for a few worthless
Indians."

At public meetings all across eastern Oregon, white farmers echoed
these arguments and demanded action from state lawmakers and members of Congress. The Oregon legislature, which did not have the authority to scuttle a federal Indian treaty on its own, formally requested
that Congress "extinguish" the reservation. The legislature's request
was itself deceptive. It grossly exaggerated the size of the reservation,
saying it was "about five hundred thousand acres," which was twice its
surveyed size. State lawmakers also misrepresented the number of

Indians who lived there, claiming it was 500, about a third fewer than the 682 inhabitants counted by the Office of Indian Affairs.

"The Indians go off to hunt, fish, and graze, while they give little or no attention to the cultivation of the soil, although a large proportion of the tract is admirably adapted to agriculture," said the request that the Oregon legislature sent to Congress in 1875. "It is therefore a matter of great inconvenience to the present settlers to have so large a tract of land in their midst held as a reservation, which, while it is of little value to the Indians, would be settled and made productive of great agricultural wealth."

Both houses of Congress agreed, in a joint resolution, that it was an injustice for so few Indians to inconvenience so many white farmers in Oregon. In the early 1870s, Congress appointed commissioners to negotiate with Umatilla Reservation chiefs and persuade them to get off the reservation. When the Indians refused in those talks to abandon land that was guaranteed to them under a Senate-ratified treaty, Congress found ways to make it happen anyhow.

As part of a pattern that became increasingly prevalent across Indian Country, Congress passed several laws in the 1880s that slashed the acreage of the Umatilla Reservation by more than a third. Inside what was left, new federal allotment laws rejiggered how the land was owned. Much of it was taken out of tribal collective ownership and allotted to individual Indian households. Lacking farming experience and without farm equipment, nearly all of them struggled to raise crops on their assigned land, although many profitably raised livestock. Soon, nearly all of the Indians had little alternative but to lease their farmland to whites, most of whom already owned large farms or ranches on the periphery of the reservation.

White leases and white ownership created a checkerboard of non-Indian landholdings across the reservation, which by 1979 had shrunk by nearly two-thirds, to 85,311 acres. The checkerboard pattern remains, with about half the best farmland inside the reservation owned by whites. Surrounded by white neighbors, tribal members found it difficult to eke out a living from small and scattered land parcels. White trespassers, meanwhile, squatted on land that was held in trust for the reservation, "denuding these lands of the timber in a most reckless manner," according to a federal Indian agent. In addition to squatters, there was a conspiracy in 1908 among two former Oregon legislators, five ranchers, and a local banker to illegally take possession of 30,000 acres of land inside the reservation.

White predation on the Umatilla Reservation was hardly unique. Around 1900, the federal government backed away from enforcing treaty provisions all across Indian Country. "Most federal officials considered the treaty system nearly if not totally defunct," according to historian Francis Paul Prucha. "The early twentieth century was marked by strong-minded commissioners of Indian affairs [who] had a common goal of assimilating the individual Indian into white society, with little regard for tribal holdovers and the treaties once made with the tribes."

While taking the Umatilla Reservation's best agricultural land, white farmers also dewatered its only river. With help and money from the federal government, irrigators sucked so much water from the lower Umatilla River that it went dry every summer. As a result, all the salmon that spawned on the reservation and migrated to and from the Pacific Ocean—via the Umatilla and Columbia rivers—were wiped out for most of the twentieth century.

Water diversion started modestly in 1870. Downstream from the reservation, a ditch funneled water from the Umatilla River to Pendleton, the nearby white community. Pendleton's petition for water—to be used in a mill and for irrigation—claimed that the withdrawal could be done "without any injury or detriment to the Indians." It was quickly approved by the Office of Indian Affairs, on the "express condition that no permanent [water] rights shall attach or become vested."

The 1855 treaty that created the reservation should have stopped the Office of Indian Affairs from giving away the water. It contained clear and unambiguous language that protected Indian fishing, saying that "the exclusive right of taking fish in the streams running through and bordering [the] reservation is hereby secured to said Indians." The treaty also said that the Indians had the right to go off their reservation to fish "at all their usual and accustomed stations."

The end of the nineteenth century, though, was a time when federal bureaucrats ignored the senior water rights that treaties guaranteed. Without lawyers, without self-rule, and without the help of federal Indian agents, reservation Indians were in no position to restrain their white neighbors. Small and supposedly temporary irrigation withdrawals from the Umatilla River kept getting larger—and turned into a permanent water right under Oregon law.

Then the federal government stepped in to help irrigators help themselves to the entire summertime flow of the river. As *The Oregonian* would later put it, "the United States promised the river twice"— first to the tribes, and then to farmers.

The Umatilla Project, as the 1904 irrigation scheme was called, was run by the Bureau of Reclamation, a federal agency created by Congress as part of the National Reclamation Act of 1902. The goal was to make the semideserts of the West bloom, transforming arid but fertile land into productive farms. It was a massive engineering effort, one that turned western rivers into plumbing systems while ignoring the consequences for fish, wildlife, riverine ecology, and, of course, Indians. The official slogan of the Bureau of Reclamation was "Our Rivers: Total Use for Greater Wealth." For more than half a century, neither the bureau nor its funders in Congress viewed Indian treaty rights, salmon extinction, or ecosystem ruin as reasons to shy away from maximum use of any western river.

When the bureau built Grand Coulee Dam, on the Columbia River, in the late 1930s and early '40s, it was by far the biggest concrete dam on earth, and it would forever alter the flow and character of the largest river in the West. Bureau engineers, however, made no provision in dam design for salmon passage. They put a sudden and permanent end to one of the world's longest and healthiest runs of chinook salmon, the largest of which migrated all the way up the river into British Columbia, a distance of more than a thousand miles. Nor was the bureau worried about the dam's effect on upstream Indians, who went into a decades-long tailspin of alcoholism, traffic deaths, house fires, domestic violence, and nutritional problems. In its annual report in 1937 on construction progress at Grand Coulee, there were two brief mentions of Indians; both were in a paragraph that also discussed "rules governing ownership of dogs."

Western writer Wallace Stegner monitored the bureau as it maimed rivers throughout the West: "From the beginning, its aim has been not the preservation but the remaking—in effect the mining—of the West. . . . It discovered where power was, and allied itself with it: the growers and landowners, private and corporate, whose interest it served."

Near the end of the twentieth century, a historian for the Bureau of Reclamation looked back at its nine decades of involvement in the Umatilla Project. There is not a single word in this official history about the Indian treaty that was ignored or the wild salmon runs that disappeared. The paper focused exclusively on drainage problems solved, crops grown, and irrigators served.

Antone Minthorn, the tribal leader, attended countless meetings with white farmers and federal bureaucrats who vacuumed up the summer flows of the Umatilla River and extirpated its salmon. "The irrigators have taken it all," he said. "And their attitude is that so far as we're concerned, the fish can walk."

B y the 1940s, when Minthorn was a boy, salmon were already long gone from the Umatilla River and all of its tributary creeks.

Gone, too, were about half the twelve hundred Indians who were enrolled members of the reservation. Many of them, as children during the first three decades of the twentieth century, had been required to leave home and attend government-run Indian boarding schools, where they were dressed in military uniforms and marched to meals. "The schools were created by the Office of Indian Affairs (BIA)—since 1947, called the Bureau of Indian Affairs. They assumed that "the way to 'civilize' the Indian was to take Indian children, even very young children, as completely as possible away from home and family life."

Antone Minthorn's father attended the Chemawa Indian School, in Salem, Oregon, and the Haskell Indian School, in Lawrence, Kansas. Those schools often succeeded in teaching literacy and trade skills that turned into lifetime occupations. The schools also allowed young people to find spouses and form lasting friendships. But long-term separation of Indian children from their families often caused confusion and depression. The schools alienated children from tribal values without giving them the tools necessary to succeed among whites. Congress allocated eleven cents a day to feed them, which left many children malnourished and living in overcrowded dormitories where tuberculosis and infectious eye disease were epidemic. To keep the underfunded schools solvent, students were forced to work in dairies, orchards, and cornfields. Their mail was opened, discipline was brutal, and sexual abuse was common. There "was a constant violation of the children's personalities."

Government-run Indian schools enabled and encouraged a steady exodus from reservations. They convinced young Indians that they were more likely to find good jobs and better housing elsewhere. By the mid-1940s, only about six hundred tribal members remained on the Umatilla Reservation, where unemployment hovered at around 50 percent. Almost all Indian-owned farmland was leased to white ranchers at scandalously low rents—about $6 an acre per year, which was one-sixth what a white farmer would pay to rent land of equal quality from a white landowner.

Over the decades, tribal identity weakened on the reservation, partly because young people sent to boarding schools married into faraway tribes with different languages. Although words and place-names survive, the last fluent native speakers of the Cayuse language died in the 1930s. Among the Indians who still identified as Cayuse, many were unwilling to do so in public. They believed that their people remained known as killers of the Whitmans and were still hated by white people.

Herds of the Cayuse ponies that had helped define the tribe's culture were mostly gone. They had begun to disappear at the end of the nineteenth century, a trend that accelerated sharply when the U.S. Army arrived in trains during World War I and rounded them up while promising to pay $1.60 a head. Some of those payments did not reach Indian owners until after World War II. Other horses were taken east in trains to pull streetcars in Chicago. During the Great Depression, most of the remaining herds ended up in Portland, where they became glue, fertilizer, and dog food. A text panel at the reservation's tribal museum, called "Horseless," accompanies a display of stacked mock cans of Kalo Dog Food, made in Oregon, in part from reservation ponies.

In the 1940s, most housing for Indians was dilapidated, without electricity or indoor plumbing, and widely scattered across the reservation.

Indians survived by combining land rental fees with sporadic government assistance—and by hunting, fishing, and gathering. Alcoholism was rampant as young men and women returned from World War II and Korea.

The reservation was governed, in theory, by the General Council, a body that included all enrolled tribal members. But the council was a sparsely attended assembly, meeting infrequently in a barnlike building. Actual governance was in the hands of the superintendent of the reservation, a BIA appointee. He had de facto control over leases of tribal land and was "assiduously courted by white ranchers, who were prominent citizens of Pendleton," according to a tribal history. One of those citizens was the white sheriff of Umatilla County, who leased six hundred acres of reservation farmland owned in common with the tribes. When his below-market-rate lease came up for renewal, he sent deputies out to round up reliable Indians who would renew it at favorable terms during public votes of the General Council. The BIA's superintendent kept a careful watch over the tribal voters, making sure that the interests of white ranchers were taken care of.

The shady reign of outsiders on the reservation collided in the mid-1940s with a generation of young Indians who were coming home from fighting in World War II. More than a third of the adult Indian male population in the United States went off to that war, where their training and experience in integrated units raised their aspirations and increased their awareness of inequity and injustice on the reservation. Not unlike their ancestors who traveled and fought all over the West during the early nineteenth century, many of the veterans who returned to the Umatilla Reservation were battle-hardened and unwilling to be pushed around.

Among them was William Minthorn, Antone's father, a staff sergeant in a battalion of combat engineers who fought the Japanese in the Pacific during the disease-plagued New Guinea campaign. He came home from the war with jungle rot and was hospitalized for several months before being discharged in 1946, at age forty-three. When he recovered, he attended Gonzaga University, in nearby Spokane, and graduated with a degree in civil engineering.

Returned Indian veterans, including William Minthorn, began to wrest control of the Umatilla Reservation away from the Bureau of Indian Affairs—and the white farmers whose interests it usually served. The veterans helped create the Eastern Oregon Electric Cooperative, which strung the first power lines to many Indian homes. Over bitter objections from the BIA superintendent on the reservation, they also hired the reservation's first tribal lawyer.

Charles F. Luce, a former U.S. Supreme Court law clerk with a struggling law practice in Walla Walla, became the first tribal lawyer for the Umatilla Reservation in 1946. He drafted a new constitution for self-rule and won multimillion-dollar settlements for the tribes from the federal government.

He was Charles F. Luce, a twenty-nine-year-old polio survivor who walked with a limp and had a fledgling law practice in Walla Walla. Luce grew up in Racine, Wisconsin, and was a newcomer to the Pacific Northwest, scrambling to make a living. He was a New Deal Democrat, an oddity in the farm country of eastern Washington. Even more unusual in Walla Walla at the time were his lawyering credentials. He had a law degree from the University of Wisconsin and a master's in law from Yale and had worked in Washington as a law clerk to Supreme Court justice Hugo Black. Luce would go on to an extraordinary career: President John F. Kennedy picked him to lead the Bonneville Power Administration, which sells electricity from federal dams on the Columbia to the entire West. He was appointed undersecretary of the interior and later became chairman and chief executive of Consolidated Edison, the giant New York utility.

But in 1946, Luce was an attorney for a small electric cooperative in eastern Oregon, a job that put him on the road in rural areas to explain how federal loans could pay for power lines. Leaders from the Umatilla Reservation attended one of those meetings and were impressed. They soon asked Luce to be their tribal attorney. Eager to make a difference in the world, he went to work for the tribes, charging $5 an hour plus travel expenses. Together they sought to blow up the status quo on the Umatilla Reservation, create a new system of self-rule, and assert the land, water, and fishing rights that were guaranteed in the language of the treaty of 1855.

The timing was finally right. Under Roosevelt's New Deal, the pendulum of federal policy toward Indians had swung in the 1930s from BIA control to democratic empowerment. Congress passed the Indian Reorganization Act in 1934, which halted the loss of reservation land to whites through allotment and created mechanisms for taking some of it back. With a majority vote of enrolled members, a reservation could, under the new law, adopt a constitution and bylaws for a sovereign tribal government.

But the first time that members of the Umatilla Reservation had a chance to grant themselves self-rule, they rejected it. In a vote in 1935, they chose to stick with the system they knew—a traditional form of governance led by headmen who worked with a paternalistic bureaucracy dominated by the BIA.

A decade later, returning veterans of the Second World War forced a second vote. They asked Luce, their newly hired lawyer, to draft a new constitution. By then, hundreds of other tribes all across the

United States had road-tested various forms of self-government, which allowed Luce to pick and choose the elements that might work best. Under the constitution that Luce wrote, power resided in a nine-member board of trustees elected by secret ballot from among tribal candidates.

Although the vote on the new constitution was advertised far in advance, fewer than one in five enrolled members of the reservation chose to cast a ballot. Native people, then as now, sometimes express disapproval through silence or nonparticipation. Among those who did show up at the polls on November 4, 1949, it was a contest between those who feared the future and those who hated the past. More precisely, it was between those who favored keeping a system of headmen who worked with domineering federal bureaucrats and those who wanted to turn the reservation into a self-governing entity that operated more like a business. The new constitution won by just 9 votes— 113 to 104. With that weak and wobbly mandate, the era of self-rule began.

CHAPTER TWENTY

BROKE

Self-rule worked no miracles. It failed for decades to bring about widespread improvements in living standards. And the pace of young Indians leaving the reservation accelerated.

Antone Minthorn left when he was eighteen and would stay gone for most of the next two decades. He was off to become an urban Indian, joining hundreds of thousands of young American Indians who left reservations for cities in the mid-twentieth century.

Minthorn moved first to Spokane, where, like his father, he attended Gonzaga University. But he was restless at the Jesuit college, with its heavy doses of theology and philosophy, and dropped out halfway through his senior year. He joined the Marines in 1957 and stayed in the Corps for six years, three in active service. He never considered moving back home. "On the rez, there were no jobs, there was no economy, and a lot of our people went off to San Francisco," he said. "So I followed them."

San Francisco was a job training center under the Urban Indian Relocation Act, a law passed by Congress in 1956 to lure young people away from reservations and assimilate them into urban America. For Indians between the ages of eighteen and thirty-five, the government paid for vocational education and health insurance. Relocation funds also helped some of them pay rent and buy furniture and household goods. The program—together with the mobility caused by World War II—triggered historic change in how and where Indians lived. Chicago, Denver, Los Angeles, and Minneapolis, as well as Portland and Seattle, also became relocation hubs. It was the largest and most sustained geographic shuffling of American Indians since the reservation system was established in the nineteenth century. Fewer than 10,000 Indians lived in cities in 1930; forty years later, there were more than 340,000. About half of the country's 1.4 million American Indians lived in cities by 1980.

Like all federal efforts to engineer the lives of Indians, the Relocation Act had unintended consequences, some of them appalling. For those who did not move, poverty and unemployment worsened as reservations hollowed out. For those who did, culture shock was common, which sometimes resulted in homelessness, ill health, and suicide.

Yet cities were also laboratories for reinvention. As Tommy Orange, a member of the Cheyenne and Arapaho tribes of Oklahoma, wrote in *There There*, his novel about urban Indians, "We did not move to cities to die. The sidewalks and streets, the concrete, absorbed our heaviness. The glass, metal, rubber, and wires, the speed, the hurtling masses—the city took us in. . . . Getting us to cities was supposed to be the final, necessary step in our assimilation, absorption, erasure, the completion of a five-hundred-year-old genocidal campaign. But the city made us new, and we made it ours."

Antone Minthorn landed smoothly in San Francisco. After nearly

four years at a Jesuit college and six years in the Marines, he was accustomed to living and working among white people. His arrival was
also perfectly timed. President Lyndon B. Johnson's War on Poverty
was raining federal dollars on the Bay Area in the form of legal services, preschool education, and job training. San Francisco was a hot-
bed of progressive ideas and idealistic young people, many thousands
of whom were newly arrived, smart, striving young Indians. Minthorn
got married, and three of his eight children were born in San Francisco. He found a job as a community organizer and became convinced
that he was living at the epicenter of change in America.

"Everything was going on when I was in San Francisco," he said.
"The [Robert F.] Kennedy assassination, the civil rights battles, the
war on poverty, and all the community action."

With talented young Indians like Minthorn away in San Francisco and other West Coast cities, the Umatilla Reservation
fell into decline, as did hundreds of others. The federal government
had again reversed direction on Indian policy, turning away from its
New Deal–era commitment to tribal self-rule. Throughout the 1950s
and well into the '60s, Washington undermined support for tribal institutions of any kind.

Under Presidents Truman and Eisenhower, Congress passed laws
intended to slash the cost and complexity of solving the "Indian problem." Relocation of Indians to cities was only one component of what
became known as the "era of termination." Congress moved to cancel
Indian treaties, get rid of tribal sovereignty, and end the legal relationship that had existed between tribes and the federal government.

"It is the policy of Congress, as rapidly as possible, to make the
Indians within the territorial limits of the United States subject to the
same laws and entitled to the same privileges and responsibilities as

are applicable to other citizens of the Unites States, to end their status as wards of the United States," said a House resolution passed in 1953.

Termination legislation would strip more than thirteen thousand Indians in 109 tribes of their tribal affiliation, remove about 1.4 million acres of land from tribal trust status, and launch decades of court challenges. "It became federal policy to try to absorb Indians into the mainstream, whether they wanted to be absorbed or not," David Treuer wrote in *The Heartbeat of Wounded Knee*, his history of American Indians since 1890.

Congress selected Oregon as one of six early states where Indians faced a forced divorce from federal support. It ended federal law enforcement on Oregon reservations in 1953; state authorities soon took over criminal and civil cases. A much tougher termination law was approved the following year, which halted federal services and sold off the tribal lands of Indians in western Oregon. The Umatilla Reservation, on the east side of the state, was not included in that order, but it was placed on a termination "hit list" for the coming decade.

Panicked elders on the Umatilla Reservation begged Congress to reconsider, arguing that it would be a cruel betrayal for the federal government to walk away from the promises it had made (and recorded in a treaty) while taking nearly all the Indians' ancestral land. Termination, the elders said, would lead to more white predation.

"The tendencies of the white man to cheat and defraud the Indian have not changed over these last hundred years since the signing of the treaty," wrote chiefs of the Cayuse, Walla Walla, and Umatilla tribes. "If this is so, then how can it be argued with any sincerity that the ability of the Indian to defend himself against these white man tendencies has changed?"

As a result of the 1953 legislation, the Umatilla Reservation lost federal funding for tribal education. Most Indian children were bused to public schools in nearby Pendleton. Now charged with criminal law enforcement, Oregon authorities angered the tribes by dispatching state wardens to enforce fish and game laws inside the reservation.

Thankfully, the most devastating effects of termination—forced sale of land and unilateral abrogation of treaty promises—were delayed. They eventually fizzled out in the late 1960s, when Congress, never an institution consistent in its attentions to American Indians, lost interest in tearing apart reservations. The Umatilla Reservation, like many others in the Pacific Northwest and all across the West, was battered, depopulated, and impoverished, but it survived.

When the pendulum of federal Indian policy swung back in the direction of tribal rights, Congress restored several reservations in western Oregon and elsewhere in the West (although some land by then had been sold into private hands and could not be returned). There would be no quick legislative fix for a separate—and far more damaging—federal assault on reservation land, water, and fish. From the 1950s through the 1980s, the Bureau of Reclamation, the Army Corps of Engineers, and the military-industrial complex joined forces to unleash a frenzied and reckless era of environmental overreach in the Columbia River Basin.

It began with an urgent and noble cause: winning World War II.

By sheer luck, Grand Coulee Dam, built as part of Roosevelt's New Deal, was completed just in time for the power from its hydro-electric turbines to be channeled into weapons fabrication. Electricity from Grand Coulee produced about one-third of the country's aluminum and half of its warplanes. Bombers rolled off Boeing's assembly lines in Seattle at the rate of sixteen a day. Three shipyards in Portland used power from Grand Coulee to build about 750 warships.

Perhaps more important, a "mystery load" (55,000 kilowatts, more electricity than all the civilians in the Northwest used in 1945) found its way from Grand Coulee to a secret downstream bomb factory that became the Hanford Nuclear Site. Grand Coulee Dam powered the production of the plutonium that armed the atomic bomb dropped on Nagasaki, Japan, on August 9, 1945, killing about thirty-nine thousand people, some immediately and others over time. Together with the bomb dropped on Hiroshima three days earlier, the bombs convinced the Japanese to surrender.

Without Grand Coulee, Truman later said, "it would have been almost impossible to win this war."

Intoxicated by victory, the builders of dams concluded that if one gargantuan concrete plug in the Columbia River Basin was good for America, then 274 hydroelectric dams would be even better. In addition to generating vast amounts of cheap electricity, dams smoothed out dangerous rapids and flooded the impassable falls that had made the Columbia–Snake river system unsuitable for industrial water transport. Federal money outfitted many of the big dams with shipping locks, which turned the two rivers into a series of long, skinny, slow-moving lakes suitable for moving farm and industrial goods from Idaho to the Pacific and then off to the Far East. The barges that moved wheat and alfalfa down the dredged-out Snake and Columbia were twice as heavy as those on the Mississippi—and considerably cheaper to operate.

The engineered rivers of the Pacific Northwest began transporting a quarter of America's feed grain and more than a third of its wheat to foreign markets. The federal dams that turned the Columbia and Snake rivers into an electricity, transportation, and irrigation machine primed the economy of the Pacific Northwest for explosive high-tech growth. They helped transform Seattle and Portland into "smart cities" and greased the way for the emergence of the trillion-dollar companies—Microsoft and Amazon—that are headquartered in the Seattle area.

Big Tech has built vast "server farms" near dams on the Columbia, taking advantage of cheap electricity.

From the beginning, though, dams were an economic, cultural, and religious affront to Indians—and a lasting torment. As soon as the dams were finished, rising water drowned the best places to fish for salmon, especially on the mid-Columbia. The most infamous drowning occurred in 1957, when the Army Corps of Engineers completed work on The Dalles Dam. Its reservoir quickly submerged Celilo Falls, where Indian tribes from the Umatilla and several other reservations had fished for a millennium.

After the drownings of the "usual and accustomed" fishing stations that were supposedly protected by Indian treaties, the dams caused a slow-motion tragedy. Wild Pacific salmon evolved over thousands of years to migrate in cold, swift rivers. But as the Columbia–Snake river system was reengineered to become a series of slow-moving, sun-heated puddles separated by lumps of concrete, it killed millions of migrating juvenile salmon trying to make their way to the Pacific from spawning streams of the interior. At the other end of the salmon life cycle, adult fish returning from the Pacific were plenty strong enough to make their way up dammed rivers if there were fish ladders. Grand Coulee Dam had none, but downstream nearly all the other dams on the Columbia and Snake rivers did. The navigability of the river system for adult salmon, however, became a moot point as the engineered river killed off so many juvenile fish before they could reach the sea. Since the last big dams were completed in the 1970s, several of the Columbia's salmon runs have been wiped out, and about two-thirds of those that remain are at high risk of extirpation.

After World War II, the more-is-better federal philosophy that dammed Northwest rivers was also applied to the plutonium factory at Hanford, Washington. In secret, and with a near-total absence of environmental restraint, the government accelerated production, churning out fifty-three tons of plutonium, the currency of the Cold War. It amounted to 60 percent of the U.S. nuclear arsenal. In the process, 61 million gallons of high-level radioactive waste were pumped into 177 underground tanks, about 40 percent of which began to leak. Another 400 billion gallons of contaminated liquid were dumped on Hanford's sandy soil. There it began drifting sideways toward the Columbia, and some of it leached into the river. The sum total of Hanford's mess created what the U.S. Department of Energy called "the single largest environmental and health risk in the nation." Luckily for people in downstream cities like Portland and Vancouver, the Columbia was big and swift enough to dilute and sweep away most of the contamination, averting a downstream public health disaster.

The most susceptible victims of the radioactive and chemical waste that found its way into the river were the same people who were most harmed by dams on the Columbia—Indians who ate a lot of fish, including those who lived on the Umatilla Reservation. Hanford biologists secretly discussed the "advisability of closing" downstream stretches of the river to fishing. They never did.

Besides being sloppy and reckless, the military technocrats at Hanford were deceptive. While guaranteeing that the air around the plutonium factory was safe, they secretly released radioactive iodine (which accumulates in the thyroid and can cause disease) from smokestacks at Hanford in 1949. The purpose of the "green run," as the experiment became known, was to study how radiation would disperse downwind over the farms and rangelands of eastern Washington and northeastern Oregon, including the Umatilla Reservation. The amount of radiation released in the experiment—which remained secret for thirty-seven years—was more than seven hundred times greater than what was released during the partial meltdown at the Three Mile

Island nuclear plant, which caused panic across much of the East Coast in 1979.

Independent medical studies of Hanford "downwinders" found that their rates of thyroid disease (and other radiation-related illnesses) were no higher than in the rest of the United States. But decades of secrecy and lies at Hanford did infect downwinders—on white farms and on Indian reservations—with paranoia about the federal government.

Paranoia increased in the 1960s when the army began stockpiling chemical warfare agents, including nerve gas, at the Umatilla Chemical Depot, a few miles west of the Umatilla Reservation. The federal government later built a factory at the depot to incinerate much of the country's stockpile of chemical and nerve agents. There were no official reports of major leaks at the depot, although sirens periodically went off due to operator error.

The chemical weapons site—and the nuclear waste mess at Hanford—ended up in the vicinity of the Umatilla Reservation for a reason that was obvious and humiliating to the Indians. Although the Whitman Mission National Historic Site was nearby, federal authorities viewed the region as mostly empty and relatively expendable, if anything were to go wrong.

I n the mid-twentieth century, as Congress tried to "terminate" the Umatilla Reservation and federal agencies seeded its surroundings with salmon-killing dams, aging containers of nerve gas, and plumes of radioactive waste, the U.S. government threw the besieged Indians a bone.

It was wrapped inside the Indian Claims Commission Act, which Congress passed in 1946 in the hope that the law would put an end to complaints from Indians about being wronged and cheated. The act offered Indians cash for proven and legitimate grievances, but it required that all their claims be filed within five years. (The deadline was later extended another five years.)

As tribal attorney Charles Luce studied the law, he saw opportunity for the Umatilla Reservation. So did its elected leaders, who wanted to use their new authority under the constitution to create jobs and social services that would lure tribal members back to the reservation. To begin to build an economy, they needed cash.

The most promising cash-generating legal grievance was The Dalles Dam, which had drowned the Indian fishery at Celilo Falls. The falls were a spectacular site. Huge slabs of rock girdled the Columbia, squeezing it into a riotous stretch of rapids and cataracts. At its narrowest point, the big river was just seventy-five feet wide. Through this gap, fur trader Alexander Ross had written in the early 1800s, the river "rushes with great impetuosity; the foaming surges dash through the rocks with terrific violence; no craft, either large or small, can venture there safely."

As it tumbled, frothed, and fell eighty feet in a half mile, the river disoriented adult salmon swimming upstream to spawn. This made the big fish easier to catch. Indians built wooden platforms out over the river and fished with nets at the ends of long poles. Celilo was by far the best place in the mid-Columbia to harvest large numbers of the best-tasting and most valuable of all Pacific salmon: the chinook, some of which weighed as much as a hundred pounds. Those salmon were called "June hogs," for the month they were most easily caught.

The Corps of Engineers, which had been widely criticized for submerging Celilo Falls, knew that The Dalles Dam was ripe for litigation under the Indian Claims Commission Act. Years before the dam was completed, the corps decided to avoid protracted and embarrassing court battles and began to settle with the affected tribes. Luce soon made the Umatilla Reservation part of those settlement negotiations and presented documentary evidence that two of its three tribes—the Walla Wallas and the Umatillas—had for centuries depended on salmon they caught at the falls.

For the loss of the fishery, Luce in 1953 negotiated a payment of $4.6 million, worth about $44 million today. It was a potentially game-changing windfall for a depopulated reservation where the annual income for the tribe as a whole was less than $30,000. If used properly, the settlement, paid when the elected tribal government was only four years old, could have provided plenty of capital to fund a broad range of economic ventures and social programs.

Disagreements about how to use the compensatory cash, though, caused nearly as much heartbreak as the flooding of Celilo Falls. Even celebrating the settlement was humiliating for the Indians. Luce, who lived in Walla Walla, invited members of the reservation's board of trustees and their wives to a party in a private room at the Elks club, which often hosted local business groups. After he made the booking, Luce received a telephone call from the club's grand exalted ruler, who did not want any Indians at his club. "The Elks Club is a white man's club," he told Luce. Stunned and embarrassed, the lawyer moved the party to his house. Many local restaurants at the time refused to serve Indians. In Oregon, restaurants were forbidden by law from selling liquor to Indians.

More vexing was deciding how to spend the settlement money. The tribal board of trustees wanted, at the very least, to set some of it aside for economic development and social needs, including improved housing and clean water on the reservation. But in 1953, half the twelve hundred enrolled members lived off the reservation. They wanted a 100 percent per capita payout, a demand that also suited many Indians on the reservation. The vote was overwhelming in support of the payout: every enrolled member of the reservation received $3,494.61.

The tribal government got nothing, and nothing was done to improve the economy or social conditions on the reservation.

In the 1960s, however, there was a second chance. With the help of an anthropologist from the University of Washington, Luce worked for more than seven years to pull together another grievance under the Indian Claims Commission Act. It said that the Cayuse, Walla Walla, and Umatilla tribes had not been adequately paid for 4.3 million acres of land they lost after signing the Walla Walla treaty of 1855. Luce took the claim to trial in Washington, D.C., and won another settlement. It was $2.45 million ($17 million in 2020 dollars).

Again, the board of trustees wanted to set aside at least some of the money for the future. It had a plan for an industrial park, job training, and a recreational complex next to the interstate highway that cuts through the reservation.

William Minthorn, Antone's father and an elected member of the board, was part of a delegation that went to Washington in 1969 to try to persuade Congress to back the tribes' development plans and to prevent the "dissipation" of the money in cash payments to non-reservation Indians.

"We need this," Minthorn told a Senate subcommittee on Indian affairs. "If young people want to do anything, they have to leave the tribal area. They have to go to the city or to other areas." His own son, Antone, was by this time part of that diaspora, raising his young family in San Francisco and showing no signs of coming home.

"Our people are divided on the disposition of the judgment funds," the elder Minthorn told the committee. "If they decide on a full per capita distribution, they can go cut their own necks off. If they decide the other, they will do the future generation some good."

In the end, William Minthorn's trip to Washington accomplished little, but the little proved to be important. Congress did not require that any of the settlement money be held in reserve for economic development. Back on the Umatilla Reservation, tribal members took a vote and, once again, the majority chose full per capita payouts, which after settlement costs amounted to $1,800 per tribal member. At the time, a majority of members lived off the reservation. For those on the reservation, the cash did little or nothing to improve living conditions, according to a tribal history. The trip to Washington, however, did result in a set-aside of $200,000 for a scholarship fund that has helped generations of tribal members. Luce also used his share of attorney fees to establish a scholarship fund in memory of his young daughter, who was killed in a sledding accident. Both funds exist today.

For good measure, the tribal majority voted in December of 1969 to remove from office every member of the board of trustees who had wanted to use some of the money for tribal development. William Minthorn was among those sacked.

T wo decades of self-rule under a new constitution had done little to improve life on the reservation. At the same time, federal efforts to terminate the reservation had done substantial damage. Children were still being sent off to Indian boarding schools. Young adults continued to move away. Those who remained, according to a tribal history, were "swamped with alcoholism." For more than a year, the tribal General Council could not make any decisions, for lack of a quorum at meetings. And the Umatilla River continued to turn to dust every summer as white farmers took all of its water to irrigate their fields.

The reservation was infected with "negativity, despair, doubt, and jealousy" in the early 1970s, according to a history published by the Umatilla tribes. "Our own people proved to be adversarial," the history said, adding that "we had no reasonable expectation to believe" that anything would change for the better.

In the summer of 1970, a reporter for the Associated Press, Allen L. Nacheman, showed up on the Umatilla Reservation and wrote an arrestingly dismal story that found its way into newspapers all across the United States, under the headline "This Oregon Indian Reservation Is a Slum with Land."

The story cited government statistics showing that the Cayuses, the Walla Wallas, and the Umatillas were, "by almost any definition of the word," living in a slum. They were very poor (annual household income was $1,018). They were ill-housed (30 percent without indoor toilets). They were in chronic need of government help (a third on some form of assistance and another third not organized enough to ask for it).

"There are men in these shacks who pass the odd months looking at soap operas on daytime television because the occasional work available in town seems rarely to go to an Indian," wrote Nacheman.

"And in each of these cold-water shacks with outhouses and thin walls and daylight coming through a thousand tiny openings, there are the daily back slips and degradations that come with being very poor and grudgingly dependent. And for a people who consider themselves the first Americans, the only true Americans, the dignity of the centuries begins to slip away."

The story was painful to read, and it appeared at a time when the depopulated reservation had hit rock bottom. An official history of the reservation said that in 1970 the tribal government was "broke and completely disorganized."

CHAPTER TWENTY-ONE

WHITE PEOPLE'S MONEY

Prospects for a better life on the reservation began to change just three days after publication of the Associated Press story. Tribal leaders who had been working for years to gain traction for self-rule discovered that they had a powerful—and unlikely—champion in the White House.

In a special address to Congress on July 8, 1970, President Richard Nixon pledged to "create the conditions for a new era in which the Indian future is determined by Indian acts and Indian decisions." He said the federal government would "break decisively" with a past that had been poisoned by white "aggression, broken agreements, intermittent remorse and prolonged failure."

Nixon would resign from office in disgrace in 1974, leaving behind a legacy of lies and paranoia, corruption and obstruction of justice. But he had been raised a Quaker, a Christian denomination that treats Indians as spiritual equals and supports tribal lands. One of his biographers, John Aloysius Farrell, points to Nixon's forward-thinking policies on Indians, on affirmative action in federal contracts, and on protection of the environment—and assesses him as "the last progressive Republican" president. In any case, there is broad scholarly agreement that the policies Nixon put in place before he was forced out of office established him as the most effective champion of American Indians ever to serve in the White House. "He was the Abraham Lincoln of the Indian people," according to Peter MacDonald, a longtime leader of the Navajo Nation.

Forced termination of Indian reservations, Nixon said, was wrongheaded and cruel. He replaced termination with policies that gave tribes control over federal aid programs on reservations. And he followed through with substantial amounts of federal money for Indian Country. His administration more than doubled the budget of the Bureau of Indian Affairs, created loan programs for economic development, and dedicated new funds for healthcare and clean water. Nixon's speech in the summer of 1970 was sweeping and eloquent, and it marked a turning point in Indian well-being:

> This, then, must be the goal of any new national policy toward the Indian people: to strengthen the Indian's sense of autonomy without threatening the sense of community. We must assure the Indian that he can assume control of his own life without being separated involuntarily from the tribal group. And we must make it clear that Indians can become independent of Federal control without being cut off from Federal concern and Federal support.

In the summer that Nixon made his astonishing overture to Indians, Antone Minthorn decided that he and his family had been in San Francisco long enough. He came home to a reservation that was ripe for change. He became part of a self-rule revolution that would be as seismic in its impact as it was deliberate in its execution.

Minthorn and his fellow Indian returnees (some of them veterans coming home from war in Vietnam) revived the reservation with patience, negotiations, smart lawyers, sound science, and large doses of comprehensive land-use planning.

While he was deliberate and careful in all his dealings with white people, Minthorn was also angry. Indeed, he remembers being furious when he came back to the reservation in 1970—and he was still furious nearly five decades later when he granted an interview for this book. What especially outraged him was the claim in white history books that Marcus and Narcissa Whitman were "massacred" by the Cayuses. Like many Cayuse elders I interviewed, Minthorn talked about the Whitman killings with an emotional immediacy that was astonishing—as though the Whitmans had just been killed in the past week. That emotional immediacy is widely felt on the reservation when it comes to the Whitmans and the hanging of the Cayuse Five— and it is not just elders.

"That word 'massacre' implies there was something arbitrary about what the Cayuses did," Minthorn said. "It was not at all arbitrary. Cayuse leaders repeatedly told Marcus to stop bringing in white people who were taking their land and giving them disease. They repeatedly warned Marcus and his wife to leave Cayuse land. Marcus did not listen. The white people kept coming. The Cayuses retaliated. They killed the Whitmans."

Minthorn said two centuries of white predation—his tribe's loss of ancestral land, the mass death of Indians from European diseases, the theft of water from the Umatilla River, the lingering canard that the Cayuses were murderers without conscience—will always make him angry and resentful.

"It ain't over," he told me. "It's not over at all."

Anger and resentment, though, were not productive emotions in 1970. The smart way to wrest back control of the reservation from federal bureaucrats and white interlopers was to be coolheaded and technocratic and use the white man's processes for Indian justice.

As a returnee, Antone Minthorn was a part-time reservation Indian in his mid-thirties. He worked as an intern at the Tribal Development Office while attending Eastern Oregon State College, then Portland State, and finally the University of Oregon, where he took master's degree courses in comprehensive urban planning.

Thanks to Lyndon Johnson's War on Poverty and Nixon's "New Deal for Indians," a "federal gravy train was running right through the reservation," as a tribal history put it. There was money for many tribal members to go to college and technical schools, as well as for the tribal staff to expand in a single year from seven members to more than a hundred.

In a stroke of good luck, the tribal government was also empowered by first-in-the-nation changes in state land-use laws. The Oregon legislature required all local governments to zone all the land within their jurisdiction. It also required every city and county in the state to prepare a comprehensive development plan. Oregon's aggressive planning laws were part of a remarkable shift in its politics in the second half of the twentieth century. Renouncing whites-only frontier traditions, it became one of the country's more reliably progressive and left-leaning states, even as it remained overwhelmingly white.

The Umatilla Reservation was neither a city nor a county under Oregon's planning laws, but the Board of Commissioners for Umatilla County (which itself had become more progressive on Indian issues in the 1970s) decided that it would honor planning and zoning decisions made by the tribal government.

The upshot of the changes in Oregon law was a sudden surge in the real-world influence of tribal planners like Antone Minthorn and his coworkers.

"When we started making our plans, we didn't have the kind of economy where we got the benefit of our work," he said. "We were still working for whites. It was their economy. But when we adopted comprehensive land-use planning and zoning, we really started to manage our own affairs. We were the boss."

One patch of real estate on the reservation that had can't-miss potential for commercial development surrounded exit 216 along Interstate 84. That federal highway is the major east–west road across Oregon, and exit 216 is the only interchange within the borders of the reservation that offers any services to travelers.

When the Tribal Development Office began working up a reservation-wide land-use plan for the tribes in the mid-1970s, Minthorn went to the Umatilla County Department of Land Use Planning. There, he was alarmed to find documents showing that white businessmen had beaten Indians to exit 216. "Every quadrant around the interchange," he said, "was already proposed for development by non-Indians."

After his fateful discovery, the tribal government marshaled its limited resources and began to acquire all available land around the interchange, much of which was owned individually by tribal members. The tribes then used zoning and planning laws to write rules for land use near the highway exit, making certain that most future commercial development could occur only on land owned or controlled by the tribes.

The tribal government was slow to decide how that development could proceed. It avoided outside consultants, using its own staff accountants, planners, and lawyers to examine and manage projects.

It took fifteen years, until 1985, for the first significantly profitable business—a tribal grain elevator for regional farmers, both white and Indian—to open on the reservation. The tribe flatly refused "joint venture" offers that reserved management for off-reservation whites.

"If anybody wanted to do anything on the reservation, they had to come to us," said Minthorn.

W hite irrigators, though, continued to do what they wanted with the lower Umatilla River. As they had done since the early 1920s, farmers and ranchers commandeered all of the river's summertime water for their fields, pastures, and orchards. It was an annual environmental calamity that dried up lower stretches of the river, infuriating everyone on the reservation. The tribal government, though, could not fix it with zoning, planning, or the levers of self-rule that Richard Nixon had given them. The expropriation of the river—and the disappearance of its salmon—epitomized the enduring dominance of the white people who encircled the reservation.

The long-festering problem fell into Antone Minthorn's lap in 1981, when he moved out of the planning office and was elected chairman of the general council, making him spokesman for the tribal voting population.

It was as good a time as any to confront the irrigators. Americans were waking up by then to the damage that big federal dams had done. Congress decided in 1980 that stopped-up rivers like the Columbia and the Snake could no longer be managed solely by federal technocrats focused on maximizing electricity production and speeding freight barges to global markets. As part of the Northwest Power Act, it demanded that other stakeholders—including Indian tribes—become part of the decision-making process. The new law forced the Bonneville Power Administration, the agency that sells electricity from federal dams, to spend a sizable chunk of its revenue on river restoration and salmon recovery.

Congress had already passed the Endangered Species Act and the Clean Water Act, both of which took some power away from dam builders and farmers, giving it to biologists from state fish-and-wildlife agencies, regulators from the Environmental Protection Agency, federal judges, and tribal governments. The U.S. Supreme Court, in a landmark ruling on a lawsuit brought by Indians in Washington State, had recently upheld the right of Northwest Indians to catch half the salmon that passed by their "usual and accustomed" fishing stations. The court also ruled that the Northwest tribes must be allowed to co-manage fishing resources with state and federal agencies.

All these pro-Indian federal decisions provoked a sustained, emotional, and racist backlash among many white residents of the Pacific Northwest. They had grown accustomed to deciding what rivers should be dammed and what fish should be caught. In 1984, voters in Washington State approved an initiative that declared Indian treaties "unconstitutional" and called on Congress to rescind special fishing rights for Indians. The judge who famously ruled that Indians have a right to half the Northwest's fishing harvest, George H. Boldt, was hung in effigy. "All we want is to be treated equally," grumbled the leader of a protest by white fishermen.

The irrigation farmers whose livelihoods depended on damming and dewatering the Umatilla River were suddenly nervous. Sure, they had legal claim, under Oregon law, to water they removed from the river. Now, though, the irrigators were being forced to play defense. Congress, federal agencies, federal courts, and national public opinion were all pressing to undo the excesses of the dam-building era.

And nothing looked more excessive, when it appeared in newspapers, than a photograph of the lower Umatilla River in summer. It was a stinking mudhole. As the Portland *Oregonian* described it, those stretches of the Umatilla were "a polluted sink of sewage and farm wastes, a perennial violator of the federal Clean Water Act."

In the early 1980s, irrigators had no choice but to start talking with the Confederated Tribes about their competing rights to the water in the Umatilla River. Both sides could rightly claim that the federal government had promised the river to them. Oregon senator Mark Hatfield presided over one of those heated and inconclusive meetings—and returned to Washington, D.C., believing that the water dispute was hopelessly deadlocked and would end in a long and expensive court battle.

Tribal leadership saw it differently. Although Minthorn was as angry with the irrigators as any Indian on the reservation, he and others decided it would be expensive, risky, and slow to sue them to win control of the river.

"We had both been promised the same thing, the same water," he later said. "We could fight each other, or we could join together and find a solution to our common problem. We would spend the money to restore the water, not pay lawyers to fight with our neighbors."

Sidestepping a century of mutual resentment, the Indians and the irrigators devised a plan that would keep water in the river. It would also allow irrigation farming to continue—with help from the nearby Columbia River.

The plan was this: every bucket of water that stayed in the Umatilla River for salmon migration—and was not diverted for irrigation—was replaced by a bucket of water pumped out of the Columbia and delivered to the irrigators for their crops.

The tribal team, including Minthorn, and the irrigators traveled together to Washington to sell their compromise. They even stayed in the same hotel. Ultimately, they persuaded Congress to pay for the $100 million project, which included new pumping stations and feeder canals. The Bonneville Power Administration was ordered to pay for a fish hatchery on the reservation and for restoration of the watershed. It was also required to provide electricity to pump water from the Columbia.

The Umatilla Basin Project, as it became known, began to show significant results in 1994. After an absence of more than seventy years, salmon began swimming up the Umatilla River to spawn. By 2004, there were twenty thousand adult salmon migrating up the river during the summer. At the same time, many hundreds of thousands of hatchery-bred juvenile salmon were leaving the reservation, swimming downstream to the Columbia and out to the Pacific, where (tribal fish biologists hoped) some of them would grow into adulthood and after three or four years return to spawn in the Umatilla and its tributaries. Senator Hatfield called the agreement between the Indians and the irrigators "a compromise the likes of which I have seen few times in my public life."

Antone Minthorn, who was born in 1935, recalls that he personally had never seen a salmon in the Umatilla River until the 1990s, after he and the tribal leadership brokered the deal that brought them back. Since then, people on the reservation have been able to catch and eat fresh salmon from their local river.

Minthorn is now in his mid-eighties and no longer an elected tribal leader. He agreed to an interview in a conference room in the reservation's Nixyáawii Governance Center. With ninety thousand square feet of space, the $22 million glass-and-steel building is a potent symbol of what Indians like Minthorn have accomplished and of their ambitions for the future.

It all started, Minthorn explained, with calculated Cayuse belligerence back in 1855 at the Walla Walla Treaty Council.

"These were tough guys just taking care of their people," he said.

There are an inordinate number of Indians named Minthorn on the Umatilla Reservation and across Oregon. Many of them are not related to one another. The surname was taken by some tribal children and teenagers who attended the Chemawa Indian School in the Willamette Valley during the late nineteenth century, when its superintendent was Dr. Henry J. Minthorn.

One Cayuse who inherited the name is Les Minthorn. He spoke to me on the reservation when he was eighty-five. Like Antone Minthorn (no relation), Les fled the reservation during the 1950s. He joined the army, accepted federal relocation assistance in California, and worked in Portland making torpedo gyroscopes for the navy. He moved back home in the early 1970s, after Nixon raised

Les Minthorn, a longtime tribal leader and descendant of Cayuses who took part in the Whitman killings, helped bring casino gambling to the Umatilla Reservation. Profits from the casino, Minthorn said, have given the tribes "leverage we never had before."

the curtain on a better Indian life. Since then, Les, like Antone, has spent most of the past half century as a senior leader of the tribal government, including chairman and treasurer of the board of trustees.

According to the oral tradition he learned from his mother, Les descends from a Cayuse family that took part in the killings at the Whitman mission. His ancestral uncle was Telokite, the chief who initially welcomed the Whitmans but later turned against them for refusing to pay rent for the Cayuse land they occupied and for welcoming thousands of white newcomers to the region. For his role in the Whitman killings, Telokite was convicted of murder and hanged in Oregon City.

Tomahas, the Cayuse who was accused of initiating the Whitman killings by using his tomahawk to split open Dr. Whitman's skull, is also an ancestral uncle. He, too, was found guilty of murder and hanged in Oregon City. Les carries the Indian name of his ancestor, Kiamasumkin, who was also among those hanged in 1850 and who was the only one who asserted his innocence from the time of his arrest to the day of his death.

But Les didn't learn these stories as a boy:

> I didn't know anything about this until I came home from the army. My mother took me in the bedroom and she told me that our ancestors were hanged by white people. I was flabbergasted. I had just spent three years serving the country that hanged them.
>
> My mother said our people never speak about this because of what it would imply: that we were just savages who could not separate right from wrong.
>
> You had a dominant white society on our land, invading us. They were very vocal about saying, "You can only speak English, and this is no longer your land, your fish, your wildlife." There was no validation from the whites that anything we said or did was right. And then our people started dying of white-man diseases and Marcus Whitman could not do anything to stop it.

When I heard my elders talk about all these things, I felt like we had been used. I felt resentment for whites making fun of us because we did not have a concept of private land ownership. We were told that our land now belonged to whites. It all just kind of put a chip on my shoulder.

When I got elected, I wanted to get us back on the track of making sure that we mattered, but we needed good people, good minds to go on offense. So I put together a team. The first dozen or so years was doing nothing but building capacity—it was like assembling Lego blocks, staff, staff, staff.

He recruited accountants, biologists, water experts, and, of course, lawyers. In 1976 he flew to Washington, D.C., to fetch home a young lawyer named Bill Johnson, who was the first member of the Umatilla Reservation to graduate from law school and pass the Oregon bar.

"Les Minthorn showed up in D.C. and said, 'We need you back at our rez,'" said Johnson, who is of Cayuse and Walla Walla descent. "He told me that he wanted to build a tribal court and that he wanted me to help run it. I was thinking, *Oh my God, I don't know how to do that*. But Les was insistent."

Johnson became chief judge of the Umatilla Tribal Court and persuaded the tribal leadership to make the judiciary an independent branch of the reservation government. Congress, in its desire to terminate tribal sovereignty, had given criminal jurisdiction over the reservation to the State of Oregon in the mid-1950s. Johnson helped claw it back. Under his management, the judiciary has become "one of only a few tribal courts in all of Indian Country" with sentencing authority in most criminal cases, according to a profile of Johnson in *The Federal Lawyer* magazine. Johnson's court was also among the first to prosecute non-Indians for domestic violence against Indians on the reservation.

The first member of the Umatilla Reservation to graduate from law school, Bill Johnson is chief judge of the Umatilla Tribal Court, which is one of only a few such courts in the country with sentencing authority over most criminal cases. "We wanted to do it ourselves, and we have done it," he said.

The reservation also created its own police force. The State of Oregon no longer regulates hunting and fishing on the reservation. "We wanted to do it ourselves, and we have done it," Johnson said.

Self-rule had allowed the Umatilla Reservation to take control of courts, protect natural resources, hire technocrats, and enforce development plans. But as Les Minthorn put it, "We didn't have any money."

Though federal aid for Indians had risen sharply in the 1970s, it stalled out in the '80s and then declined steadily into the new millennium. By 2003, per capita federal expenditures on Indian healthcare were half what the government was spending on healthcare for inmates in federal prison. Federal spending had become "not sufficient to address the basic and very urgent needs" of Indians, according to the U.S. Commission on Civil Rights.

A handful of reservations made ends meet by selling off their natural resources. The Crows in Montana had coal. The Salish and Kootenai tribes in Idaho had hydropower. The Confederated Tribes of Warm Springs, in Oregon, had old-growth timber. But the Umatilla Reservation offered nothing that was especially valuable. Geographically small, its natural resources consisted of farmland, some timber, and lots of gravel.

It did, however, have once-a-week bingo in the tribal gymnasium, which attracted non-Indian players who drove out to the reservation— sometimes from as far away as Portland, a four-hour trek. So in 1988, when Congress passed the Indian Gaming Regulatory Act, which required tribes to negotiate gambling agreements with states, Les Minthorn guessed that it might offer the reservation a way to make serious money.

"It seemed like something that would give us leverage we never had before," he said.

Moving deliberately, as always, the tribal government established a gaming task force and took seven years to debate, plan, finance, build, and open a casino near exit 216, where it had successfully wrested development rights back from white businessmen in the 1970s. The tribal leadership surveyed reservation residents, both Indian and white, as well as whites in nearby Pendleton, and two-thirds of those contacted supported a casino and the jobs that it would create. Tribal leaders negotiated a gaming compact with the State of Oregon. They found a casino company from Atlantic City to finance construction and manage the gaming operation under a five-year contract.

After all the due diligence, it became clear almost overnight that gambling would generate more cash than the reservation had ever seen. Five months before the Wildhorse Casino was ready for customers, the tribal government opened a makeshift gaming room with a hundred video slot machines packed into a trailer outside the construction site. Six hundred gamblers a day streamed in on the interstate and jammed the place.

When the $7.5 million casino opened in the early spring of 1995, with three hundred video slot machines, card games, and a bingo hall, profits overwhelmed projections. The tribal government had expected to make $1.5 million in the first year; it raked in $5 million.

After three and a half years, with profits growing rapidly, the tribal government discovered that white bankers suddenly liked and trusted Indian leaders from the Umatilla Reservation—and were willing to make loans at favorable rates. The reservation borrowed money to pay off the casino management company, and tribal members took over about 90 percent of senior management jobs. Most of the casino workforce was from the reservation or members of other tribes. With more jobs, tribal membership began to grow. There are now more than 3,100 members.

"We exercised our first real sovereignty without the feds or the states interfering," said Les, who became chairman of the tribal gaming commission in the mid-1990s. "It was revenue that came from the gaming floor—tribal dollars."

The Umatilla tribal voters, as Les and other tribal leaders knew, had twice paid financial windfalls to individuals, without reserving money for business investment or reservation infrastructure. When gambling profits surged in the 1990s, about half of the profits were pumped back into the casino operation and its related businesses—a hotel, a golf course, a cineplex, an RV park, and restaurants. The tribal government began buying back reservation land. It opened a business park, accelerated commercial farming, and purchased a local country club golf course. In downtown Pendleton, where Indians were once denied seats in restaurants, the Wildhorse Casino bought Hamley's, an iconic steak house and western store that takes up half a city block. For more than a century, Hamley's had been a symbol of white cowboy culture.

Of the remaining half of the gambling profits, about 80 percent paid for tribal salaries and social programs like housing, scholarships, and healthcare. The rest of the money was distributed in modest annual cash payments to tribal members, about $400 four times a year.

The Umatilla Reservation is not an outlier. Gambling operations have been massively beneficial to much of Indian Country, injecting more than $30 billion a year in gross revenues into reservations across the country. An independent study of more than 450 tribal gaming businesses in thirty-one states found that they are responsible for "a far-reaching and transformative" improvement in income, employment, education, and housing and in reductions of smoking, heavy drinking, and obesity. Unlike federal development money, which has never been consistent or reliable, gambling operations have produced sustained incomes for many reservations. "Indian gaming is simply the most successful economic venture ever to occur consistently across a wide range of American Indian reservations," said Kevin Washburn, an assistant secretary of Indian affairs at the Interior Department.

What makes gaming work for Indians is that most of the money lost in slot machines, blackjack tables, and roulette wheels stays on the reservation. It is recycled there as salaries, new infrastructure, expanded social services, housing development, and seed capital for new businesses. The Indian gaming act requires that gambling halls be located on reservation land and that profits be invested in the general welfare of the tribes. The result, according to economists, is "an intense and particularly local concentration of tribal gaming's benefits."

From his perch on the reservation's gaming commission, Les Minthorn has been carefully monitoring the benefits of gambling for his people.

"The most important thing that happened was freedom," he said. "We did not have to sell our land, our water, our children. Are we a communist state in the way we use the profits? I think so, and it has been good for all of us. There are no millionaires on this reservation from gaming."

With self-rule firmly in place and gambling money flowing, the Umatilla Reservation moved at the end of the twentieth century to take back its history.

Just down the road from the casino, the tribal government used grants, loans, and gambling money to build the $18.3 million Tamástslikt Cultural Institute. The word "tamástslikt" means "interpret, turn over, or turn around." The 45,000-square-foot museum—featuring basalt and big windows that allow the surrounding landscape to be part of the exhibit—tells the story of white settlement on the Columbia Plateau from the perspective of those who were settled upon, dispossessed, and demonized.

"As we look at it, the settling of the West was the unsettling of the West," Bobbie Conner, the institute's director, told me. "It's our country, not their country, that these immigrants were coming to. They were unsettling our homeland. And so they were the heathens, not us."

A placard inside the museum tells visitors why the Cayuses decided that Marcus Whitman needed to die: "The headmen met in a council and made an agreement that the Doctor should be killed because two hundred of the people had died after taking his medicine."

Bobbie Conner returned to the reservation in 1997 to work in the tribes' economic and community development department. As director of the institute, it became her job to make sure the tribal government was prepared to present its side of history in 2003–2006, when the United States commemorated the bicentennial of the Lewis and Clark Expedition.

Conner is of Cayuse, Umatilla, and Nez Perce ancestry. Before she went off to college and graduate school, before her degrees in business and public administration, before she directed the Sacramento district office of the U.S. Small Business Administration, she grew up riding

Bobbie Conner, director of the Tamástslikt Cultural Institute, on the Umatilla Reservation, said that from the tribes' point of view, "the settling of the West was the unsettling of the West.... And so they were the heathens, not us."

horses and picking berries about a mile and a half from where the museum now stands. As a high school student, she rode as an "Indian princess" for a nearby rodeo, started the high school Indian club, and worked at the Hamley's western store the tribal casino now owns.

"In my wildest dreams as a kid growing up here, I could not have imagined a multimillion-dollar tribal cultural facility that told our story to the rest of the world," she told me.

More fundamentally, she said, self-government and economic recovery have changed the way Indians on the reservation think about their future.

"It's not just people being able to afford childcare or a new car," she said. "We have people who want to own homes. They think about building equity. We have more people going to college because expectations have risen." There is also an abundant scholarship fund, which had reached nearly $8 million in 2016.

Similarly, she said, the return of salmon to the Umatilla River has "enormously benefited" the reservation's ecosystem, leading to a rebound in the number of cougars, bears, beavers, and ospreys.

I asked Conner if the revival of the reservation has made it possible for the Cayuse people to forgive and forget the many decades of being demonized by whites as savages who massacred Marcus and Narcissa Whitman.

"No," she said emphatically. "That heartbreak is still there."

She explained that no matter how thoroughly the tribe has tried to explain the context of the killings—that their land was being overrun, that their children were dying of measles, that the Whitmans had refused to leave Cayuse land—the historical "murderer" label has not faded.

"There is a shared grievance that we were dealt with unjustly," she said. "We were hated not only by whites, but by other Indians who blamed us for their troubles with whites. There was also self-loathing because of what we wrought on our own people, the wars and all the lost land. By virtue of blood, we share in what's now perceived as a criminal act."

After the Cayuses were hanged in Oregon City, she said, there was "a kind of shared code of silence" among members of the tribe, a silence that is part of "our historical trauma." Elders tell the story to each new generation, Conner said, but the inculcation of this oral history is conducted within families and not typically shared with outsiders.

To move forward, Conner said, the tribal elders want to find and repatriate the remains of the Cayuse Five—a process that she said is quietly being pursued. "We also would love to see them exonerated for doing what they did, which they thought was protecting their own people."

At lunchtime on weekdays, Les Minthorn occasionally drives across the reservation to the Wildhorse Casino. He goes there for a sandwich and to watch the crowds play the slot machines. He savors

After the Wildhorse Casino opened in 1995, its profits overwhelmed predictions, and white bankers—who had shunned the reservation for years—were suddenly willing to loan money to tribal businesses at competitive rates.

the irony of Indians building a prosperous future off the greediness of white people. He enjoys watching them lose.

"It couldn't happen to a better person," he told me with a sly smile.

Antone Minthorn, too, sometimes has lunch in the casino. He told me about one particularly satisfying reverie that came to him while waiting for his lunch.

"Seeing all those white people playing those slot machines, I said to myself, *Holy cow, look at what the hell we did.* We had a vision. We got the job done. We got our water back and got our fish back. We made an economy. All these Indian people are getting salaries, they're getting benefits. We are going to be okay."

EPILOGUE

In the spring of 2021, the Washington State legislature voted overwhelmingly to remove the statue of Marcus Whitman from National Statuary Hall in the U.S. Capitol, where it had stood for nearly sixty-eight years. The Associated Press characterized the vote as part of a year of reappraisal of Whitman, whose "actions have increasingly been viewed as imperialistic and destructive." The publication of this book (first edition in April 2021) heightened the scrutiny, the Associated Press said, by documenting how the well-known story about Whitman saving the Pacific Northwest from British rule was "fabricated."

The decision to strip Whitman's likeness from the Capitol also came amid a national reckoning over race and racism, and which historical figures ought to be immortalized in bronze. A few months before the state of Washington passed its law, Virginia removed a statue of Confederate general Robert E. Lee from National Statuary Hall, replacing it with a statue of civil rights icon Barbara Rose Johns. North Carolina voted to exchange a statue of its race-baiting former governor, Charles Aycock, for a statue of evangelist Billy Graham.

For its part, Washington State decided to swap out Whitman for a statue of Billy Frank Jr., a leader of the Nisqually tribe who was arrested more than fifty times for demanding the enforcement of tribal fishing rights and federal treaty law. "We expect to send our best from the state of Washington to be memorialized in the United States Capitol," Governor Jay Inslee said at a bill signing ceremony where he praised Frank for his "thirst for justice."

The governor left it to others to characterize Whitman, whose legacy was on increasingly shaky ground—at the college in Walla Walla that bears his name, at U.S. National Park Service sites in eastern Washington and northern Idaho, and on the west side of the Cascades in Oregon City, where the justice of the 1850 hanging of five Cayuse men for killing Whitman was newly called into question.

A few days after the governor signed the bill to replace Whitman's statue, students at Whitman College renewed their demand that an identical statue be evicted from its low-rent perch near railroad tracks on the edge of campus, where it has periodically been tagged with red paint. "This guy is a colonizer," sophomore Gillian Brown told the campus newspaper, "he's not someone to be celebrated." She was photographed using chalk to write on a campus sidewalk: "Statues are for heroes."

A team of art researchers in Walla Walla, with support from the college administration and an Indigenous students' club, concluded that the statue is a symbol of "frontier mythology" that has no place at the college. The statue, though, is owned by the city of Walla Walla, and the college said it had to respect the city's process of weighing community opinion before removing public art. Some Walla Walla residents wanted the statue to stay put, complaining about what they perceived as the politically correct bad mouthing of Whitman.

No public input was sought—and no public announcement was made—when the college removed from campus a 90-year-old monument to Narcissa Whitman. The large stone marker disappeared in December of 2020. For many years, it had stood outside of a residence hall that bears Narcissa's maiden name of Prentiss. Provost and dean of faculty Alzada J. Tipton told the campus newspaper that removal became a priority after the college concluded that the monument "did not contribute to a welcoming campus environment for all of our students."

All this raised the question of whether the college might decide to disavow all things Whitman, including its name. The historic link is tainted: the school escaped bankruptcy and prospered for decades by touting falsehoods about Whitman's heroism. Its campus is located on land taken from the Cayuses, Walla Wallas, and Umatillas. Some faculty members believe the college is stuck in a postcolonial rut. As Stan Thayne, professor of anthropology and religion at Whitman, told the campus newspaper, "Even if we remove the monuments and change the name of the college, the foundational violence of dispossession that they represent is still what enables our presence here."

Whitman College has never seriously considered changing its name, said Gina Ohnstad, interim vice president for communications. The school does not plan to make a formal apology for raising money off fictions about Whitman, Ohnstad said, nor does it plan to stop using its traditional coat of arms, which references one of the false claims about Whitman's accomplishments. The coat of arms includes three stars representing Oregon, Washington, and Idaho, which, as the discredited story goes, Whitman saved with his winter journey to the White House.

The college, though, has begun to work intensively with its tribal neighbors. Faculty and members of the administration have reached out in recent years to leaders and young people on the Umatilla Reservation, making them part of classes, freshman orientation, and field trips that explain how whites have dispossessed and demonized Indigenous people on the Columbia Plateau. The college has also worked with the tribes to develop a program for Whitman students to become tutors for reservation children.

In 2021, after Washington State ordered Whitman's statue out of the U.S. Capitol and during a wave of unflattering press that included this book, the college decided to make a significant gesture to the Umatilla Reservation, offering full scholarships to five tribal students.

The National Park Service, at the same time, increased its collaboration with tribes from the Umatilla Reservation in the management of the Whitman Mission National Historic Site, where the Whitmans lived and died. New exhibits and signs were jointly designed by experts from the tribes and the Park Service, along with a new curriculum for students visiting the site. "We are very much open to increased involvement with our tribal partners," said Steve Thede, superintendent of the site.

The increased willingness of the federal government to give the tribes a more influential voice was also coming from Washington, D.C., where President Joe Biden appointed and the Senate confirmed Deb Haaland, a member of New Mexico's Laguna Pueblo, as secretary of the Department of Interior. She became the first Native American to run the department, which for much of its history oppressed the country's Indigenous people.

Perhaps more important, Biden appointed, and the Senate confirmed, a leader of the Umatilla Reservation, Chuck Sams, to be director of the National Park Service. Sams, who is of Cayuse and Nez Perce ancestry, was a key source for the research of this book, putting me in contact with tribal leaders. And it was Sams, the first Native American to head the Park Service, who suggested to Whitman College that it offer five scholarships to students from the Umatilla Reservation.

In Oregon City, where remains of five hanged Cayuses are buried in graves lost to history, the city commission moved to make amends for what a city staff report said was likely a miscarriage of justice. "Scholarly research raised important questions about the trial and cast serious doubt on the guilt of the Cayuse Five," the report said. The city commission approved a plan in 2021 to work with the Umatilla Reservation to design and build a monument called the "Cayuse Five Tribute." It would be located on a promenade that overlooks Willamette Falls, not far from where the trial and hanging took place.

As for locating the remains of the Cayuse Five and returning them to Cayuse land for reburial, progress has been slow. Bobbie Conner, the Umatilla Reservation leader, said the tribal government hopes that publicity generated by a monument will raise awareness among non-Native residents of Oregon City, possibly persuading property owners and former property owners to assist in the search.

In northern Idaho, monuments that honor the legacy of the Reverend Spalding have largely escaped scrutiny—until now.

In a wooded and well-tended stretch of grassland at the confluence of Lapwai Creek and the Clearwater River, the Nez Perce National Historic Park includes the sparse remains of Spalding's old mission, his marble gravestone, and a church built after his death to honor his memory. Near the stone hearth from his original house, an interpretive sign placed by the National Park Service explained that Henry and Eliza Spalding "came here in 1836 to convert the Nez Perce not just to Christianity but to a new culture."

The Spaldings are buried side by side, not far from the fenced-in ruins of their mission. (Eliza's remains were moved to Idaho in 1913 from a cemetery in the Willamette Valley.) Their lichen-stained head-stone, placed in 1924 by the Presbyterian Church, is the most promi-nent grave marker in Spalding Cemetery, which is owned by the Nez Perces and remains an active burial ground for the tribe. An inscrip-tion on the headstone invokes the racist paternalism of the missionary era. It says the Spaldings, in their long ministry to the Nez Perces, "dispelled the darkness of this one benighted race and gave them THE LIGHT OF LIFE."

When I visited the site in the fall of 2020, nothing at the Nez Perce National Historic Park explained—or even mentioned in passing—the story of how Henry Spalding invented and popularized a fairy tale version of Northwest history that was endorsed by Congress, taught in public schools across the United States, and believed by tens of mil-lions of Americans.

That interpretive vacuum will soon be filled, the National Park Service said in the fall of 2021.

While there is no plan to remove headstones or change monuments, "we are going to change the way we talk about them," said Steve Thede, the Park Service superintendent in charge of the Nez Perce park and the Whitman site. Citing the publication of *Murder at the Mission*, he told me that documentation of Spalding's falsehoods "is pretty hard to argue with . . . We are moving into a much more holistic look at this."

The Presbyterian Church, too, is changing the story it tells.

In the summer of 2021, the Presbytery of the Inland Northwest formally apologized to the Nez Perce "for the actions of our mission-ary, the Rev. Henry Spalding." That apology was narrowly focused on Spalding's shadowy acquisition of Nez Perce traditional clothing and horse gear, which he shipped off to a friend in Ohio in the 1840s. The collection was not returned to Nez Perce ownership until the 1990s, when the tribe raised more than $600,000 to buy it back.

In its apology for the purloined artifacts, the church said "we are deeply troubled by how our predecessors attempted to eradicate the Nez Perce culture when sharing the love of the Creator, and how these actions reflected the evils of our colonialism . . ."

As for Spalding's long-playing lie about Whitman heroically saving the Northwest, the Presbyterian Church is "not yet" ready to issue an apology. "We have begun our reconciliation work," said the Reverend Sheryl Kinder-Pyle, executive presbyter of the inland Northwest region, "and recognize that the journey will be long."

ACKNOWLEDGMENTS

To research a story that began in the 1830s and continues into the present day, I needed lots of help—from the dead and the living.

Early missionaries in Oregon and their handlers back in Boston were spectacularly forthcoming—in the thousands of letters they wrote and saved. Two persistent historians—the late Clifford M. Drury (whose voluminous writings are often cited in these pages) and the late William I. Marshall (a pivotal character in this book)—devoted their lives, respectively, to finding truths and unraveling falsehoods in those letters. Without their obsessive work, it would have been all but impossible to understand the life and afterlife of Dr. Whitman or the machinations of the Reverend Henry Spalding.

I am also indebted to historian Sarah Koenig, an assistant professor of history at Ramapo College of New Jersey, a native of Oregon, and an expert on religion and race in the West. Her recent research discoveries and astute writing on the legend of Marcus Whitman informed

and inspired my inquiries into how a church-supported lie can perco-
late for so long in America.

To gain access to the letters themselves, I was helped by archivists
and libraries across the country, especially at the Whitman College
and Northwest Archives in Walla Walla, Washington. There, Ben
Murphy, archivist and head of digital services, helped me locate hundreds of documents and photographs. He suggested I look through
two boxes containing the delightful correspondence of Virginia Dox,
who perfected the art of raising money off the claim that Whitman
saved Oregon. Murphy also provided me with access to an unpub-
lished digital transcript of Oregon missionary letters that was
computer-searchable and saved me weeks of time. Archivist Eva R.
Guggemos at Pacific University in Forest Grove, Oregon, led me to
nineteenth-century documents that Drury and Marshall apparently
missed. The documents revealed Spalding as the local president of a
secret nativist society in Oregon that was anti-immigrant and anti-
Catholic. Guggemos also suggested that I carefully examine an ar-
resting photograph in the Pacific University archive. As reproduced
in this book, it shows Spalding—armed with a Bible and a hoe—in
the process of transforming himself from an angry missionary to a
triumphant propagandist.

The Oregon Historical Society in Portland was an essential resource for this book, and a skilled archivist there, Elerina Aldamar,
answered scores of inquiries over two years. I also received archival
help from the Beinecke Library at Yale, the Library of Congress, the
Pacific Northwest Collection at the University of Washington in Seattle, Washington State University in Pullman, the Washington State
Historical Society in Tacoma, the Tacoma Public Library, the Portland Public Library, the University of Puget Sound Library, and the
University of Oregon's online archive of newspapers.

The trial of the Cayuse Five in Oregon City has been somewhat neglected in histories of the Whitman Massacre and its legacy. The outstanding exception to this is *Juggernaut: The Whitman Massacre Trial 1850* by Ronald B. Lansing, a professor emeritus at Lewis & Clark Law School in Portland. Published in 1993 by the Ninth Judicial Circuit Historical Society, Lansing's book remains the best account of what went amiss in the first full-dress murder trial in the Oregon Territory. The book, together with its citations of trial documents and contemporary newspaper coverage of the trial, was invaluable. In a phone conversation, Lansing was patient and helpful. To visualize Oregon City at the time of the trial and the hanging—and for insight into what may have happened to the bodies of the Cayuse Five after they were executed—I was helped by another smart lawyer and Oregon historian, James Nicita. He drove me around his hometown of Oregon City and generously shared his research.

The early dependence of Whitman College on the claim that Marcus Whitman saved Oregon is a complex and controversial subject. To understand it, I was helped by the rigorous scholarship of two longtime and now-deceased professors of history at the college, Robert L. Whitner and G. Thomas Edwards. In a founder's day speech on campus in 1992, Whitner explained how Whitman College raised money for nearly a quarter century by publicizing falsehoods about Whitman as bona fide history—and would have gone bankrupt had it not done so. Edwards, in his two-volume official history of Whitman College that was published in 1992 and 2001, detailed how Whitman president Stephen B. L. Penrose marketed the Whitman Saved Oregon story well into the twentieth century while stubbornly rejecting the national consensus that it was fake history. (Mysteriously, at least to me, the candor of Whitner's speech and Edwards's books did not occasion much notice or comment outside the college campus.)

Former Whitman College president Robert A. Skotheim, in a long and generous interview at his home, helped me understand how he led the college in the 1970s and '80s as it quietly but definitively turned away from the Whitman myth. I also received information and guidance from several Whitman professors and former students, especially Christopher Leise, an associate professor of English; Dennis Crockett, an associate professor of art history; David F. Schmitz, the Robert Allen Skotheim Chair of History; Michael Paulus, a former archivist at Whitman College who is now dean of the library at Seattle Pacific University; and Kate Kunkel-Patterson, a former student who works at the Whitman Mission National Historic Site.

The Whitman Massacre generated an astonishing number of books, especially in the first six decades after the killings. A 1908 bibliography of volumes related to the Whitmans runs sixty pages. But few books—before then or since—have tracked the racist bullying, insults, land theft, water diversions, economic hardship, and emotional trauma that have rattled down the decades to the present day in the lives of the Cayuse people. In writing about those years and explaining the recent rise of the Cayuses, the Walla Wallas, and the Umatillas, I received invaluable help from Chuck Sams, communications director of the Confederated Tribes of the Umatilla Indian Reservation; Antone Minthorn, the longtime reservation leader; Les Minthorn, the leader who helped bring gambling to the reservation; Bobbie Conner, director of the Tamástslikt Cultural Institute; and William Johnson, chief judge of the Umatilla Tribal Court.

Bobbie Conner and Chuck Sams took time to read and offer valuable corrections and comments on the manuscript of this book. Laurie Arnold, director of Native American Studies at Gonzaga University and a member of the Sinixt Band of the Colville Confederated Tribes, also read the manuscript and provided useful comments. Their help and expertise have been invaluable, but any mistakes of fact or judgment in this book are, of course, my responsibility.

I thank my editor at Viking, Lindsey Schwoeri, who helped me refine these pages; also, Allie Merola, who helped pull all the pieces together. I must also thank Kathryn Court, a kind, wise, and recently retired editor who made it possible for me to write four books for Viking. As he has done for six books over four decades, literary agent Raphael Sagalyn supported this project from proposal to publication. And a nod of gratitude to my friend Tom Kizzia for exceptionally useful edits and suggestions about this book. Finally, thanks to my kids, Lucinda and Arno, and my wife and champion, Jessica Kowal.

NOTES

EPIGRAPH

xiii "What mattered was not": Julian Barnes, *The Noise of Time* (New York: Knopf, 2016), 202.

INTRODUCTION: The Good Doctor

xxiii **class play about the good doctor:** The one-act play was probably "Answering the Call," by Della Gould Emmons, a writer and historian in Washington State. Her book *Northwest History in Action: A Collection of Twelve Plays Illustrating the Epochs of Northwest History* (Minneapolis: T. S. Denison, 1960) included the Whitman play and was a state-approved textbook for public schools across Washington State in the 1960s. Emmons wrote several different versions of the Whitman play for schools, colleges, and civic groups. Throughout the first half of the twentieth century, plays about the Whitmans were performed in public schools in the Pacific Northwest. A typical title: "How Marcus Whitman Saved Oregon for the United States," which was performed in 1929 by sixth graders at Washington School, in Salem, Oregon. "Pioneers to View Pupils' Program," *Statesman Journal* (Salem, OR), April 5, 1929, 1–2.

xxiii **he had appeared in an opera:** The long list of Whitman-inspired entertainment includes Mary Carr Moore's four-act opera *The Cost of Empire, or Narcissa* (Seattle: Stuff Printing, 1912); Alice W. Rollins's poem "Whitman's Ride," *New York Independent,* November 25, 1897; Minnie Roof Dee's song "Whitman's Ride" (Portland, OR: Daniel H. Wilson, 1923); Ann West Williams's children's book *Narcissa and Marcus Whitman: Martyrs on the Oregon Trail* (New York: American Book-Stratford Press, 1954); the CBS radio play

"Roses and Drums: Dr. Marcus Whitman, Missionary and Surgeon," 1932; and the Christian educational DVD "No Turning Back" (Lewisville, TX: Accelerated Christian Education, 2009).

xxiv **excellent liberal arts college:** Whitman ranks forty-sixth in the nation among liberal arts colleges, according to the *U.S. News & World Report* "Best Colleges" rankings, accessed June 27, 2020, https://www.usnews.com/best-colleges/whitman-college-3803.

xxiv **Douglas condemned the "treachery":** *Acceptance of the Statue of Marcus Whitman Presented by the State of Washington* (Washington, D.C.: Government Printing Office, 1955), 57–63.

xxiv **called "thick darkness of heathenism":** Narcissa Whitman to her mother, Clarissa Prentiss, January 2, 1837, in Clifford M. Drury, ed., *Where Wagons Could Go: Narcissa Whitman and Eliza Spalding* (Lincoln: University of Nebraska Press, 1997), 123.

xxv **Before the revival took off:** Jill Lepore, *These Truths: A History of the United States* (New York: W. W. Norton, 2018), 190.

xxv **The result was Manifest Destiny:** Lepore, *These Truths*, 199; Elliott West, *The Last Indian War* (New York: Oxford University Press, 2009), xx.

xxv **"to overspread and to possess":** John O'Sullivan, quoted in an editorial in the *New York Morning News,* December 27, 1845.

xxv **to convert the "benighted Indians":** Narcissa Whitman to Jerusha Parker, July 25, 1842, in Archer B. Hulbert and Dorothy P. Hulbert, *Marcus Whitman, Crusader, Part Two, 1839 to 1843* (Denver: Steward Commission of Colorado College and Denver Library, 1941), 267; Marcus Whitman to Rev. David Greene, secretary of American Board of Commissioners for Foreign Missions (ABCFM), March 12, 1838, ABCFM photostats, 114–33, in Rick Laughlin, Missionary Correspondence Transcripts, Whitman College and Northwest Archives, Walla Walla, WA.

xxvi **often acted out in high school:** One of those student plays was "Marcus Whitman," also by Della Gould Emmons. It was first performed in 1951 by students at Pacific Lutheran University, in Tacoma, Washington, to help raise money to place a statue of Whitman in the U.S. Capitol's Hall of Statuary, in Washington, D.C. The play was later performed in high schools in Washington State.

xxvii **"We'll win that country":** Della Gould Emmons, "Marcus Whitman," 1951, partial script at Pacific Lutheran University Archives; complete script in Della Gould Emmons papers, unsorted boxes, Tacoma Public Library.

xxviii **couples often shared the same tent:** Narcissa Whitman to her sister Jane, March 31, 1836; Drury, *Where Wagons Could Go,* 47.

xxviii **"wicked jealousy" tainted their lives:** Narcissa Whitman to her father, Stephen Prentiss, October 10, 1840, Whitman family papers, 1838–1847, WA MSS 502, Beinecke Library, Yale University.

xxix **"has a disease in the head":** Rev. Asa Bowen Smith to Greene, October 21, 1840, in Clifford M. Drury, ed., *The Diaries and Letters of Henry H. Spalding and Asa Bowen Smith* (Glendale, CA: Arthur H. Clark, 1958), 203.

xxix **Roosevelt recognized his achievements:** Roosevelt sent a message from the White House to a centennial Whitman-Spalding Oregon Trail celebration. "Pioneer Missionaries Are Honored at Fete," *New York Times,* June 5, 1936, 4.

xxix "heroic patriotic Christian work": "Honor a Dead Hero: Services in Many Churches in Memory of Marcus Whitman," *Chicago Tribune,* June 29, 1895, 3.

xxix "most famous ride in American history!": "Marcus Whitman's Ride," *Detroit Free Press,* October 11, 1891, 2.

xxix more patriotically magnificent: L. B. Skeffington, "Where Rolls the Oregon," *Democrat and Chronicle* (Rochester, NY), November 21, 1938, 27.

xxx "exaggerated, uninformed, unrealistic": Wallace Stegner, *Where the Bluebird Sings to the Lemonade Springs* (New York: Penguin Books, 1992), xvi.

xxxi too dry for conventional farming: Stegner described "a dry core" of eight western states, including Arizona, Colorado, Idaho, Montana, Nevada, New Mexico, Utah, and Wyoming. To that list he added the western parts of the Dakotas, Nebraska, Kansas, Oklahoma, Texas—and the extensive arid lands of California, eastern Washington, and eastern Oregon. Two-thirds to three-quarters of both Washington and Oregon are semi-arid and not suited to rain-fed farming. Stegner, *Where the Bluebird Sings to the Lemonade Spring,* 60–61.

xxxi "sober national reflection": Patricia Limerick, *The Legacy of Conquest* (New York: W. W. Norton, 1987), 19.

xxxii "more frank about our failures": Ken Burns and Stephen Ives, "New Perspectives on 'The West,'" filmmakers' notes on documentary *The West,* PBS, https://www.pbs.org/weta/thewest/index_cont.htm.

xxxiii "preferred fable to fact": Larry McMurtry, *Sacagawea's Nickname: Essay on the West* (New York: New York Review Books, 2001), 3–4, 103–4.

xxxiii Buffalo Bill's Wild West Show: Joy S. Kasson, *Buffalo Bill's Wild West* (New York: Hill and Wang, 2000), 170–82.

xxxiv Kit Carson decided to cash in: See McMurtry, *Sacagawea's Nickname,* 20–21; Richard White, *It's Your Misfortune and None of My Own* (Norman: University of Oklahoma Press, 1991), 616–17.

xxxiv "If it isn't true": "Harding Takes Part in Pioneer Pageant of the Oregon Trail," *New York Times,* July 4, 1923, 1.

CHAPTER ONE: "Do Nothing to Irritate"

5 extinguished his animosity toward her: This is based on letters and diaries of Henry Spalding, as well as letters of Narcissa and Marcus Whitman. It is also drawn from biographies of the three missionaries by Clifford M. Drury, including *Marcus and Narcissa Whitman and the Opening of Old Oregon* (Seattle: Pacific Northwest National Parks and Forests Association, 1986), 1:148–61, and from Julie Roy Jeffrey, *Converting the West* (Norman: University of Oklahoma Press, 1991), 1–59.

5 "Act your pleasure": Spalding to Rev. David Greene, December 28, 1835, in Rick Laughlin, Missionary Correspondence Transcripts, Whitman College and Northwest Archives (hereafter Whitman College Archives). Unless otherwise noted, all missionary letters cited below were found in the Laughlin transcripts at Whitman College.

5 he would not travel with her: After going west, Spalding wrote about this in his diary of July 9, 1840: "That the root of all the difficulties in the Mission lay between us [he and Marcus Whitman], viz: in an expression I made while in the states respecting his wife

before she was married to Dr. Whitman, Viz.: that I would not go into the same Mission with her, questioning her judgment." Clifford M. Drury, ed., *The Diaries and Letters of Henry H. Spalding and Asa Bowen Smith* (Glendale, CA: Arthur H. Clark, 1958), 294; also Drury, *Marcus Whitman, M.D., Pioneer and Martyr* (Caldwell, ID: Caxton Printers, 1937), 119. His fellow missionaries wrote in letters that they had heard about this from Spalding and Whitman.

5   "I felt it my duty to consent": Spalding to Greene, February 17, 1836.

5   "I am willing to accompany Mr. Spauldin": Marcus Whitman to Greene, February 15, 1836.

6   "the same bitter feeling exists": Narcissa Whitman to her father, Stephen Prentiss, October 10, 1840, Whitman family papers, 1838–1847, WA MSS 502, Beinecke Library, Yale University.

6   towns were bursting with young people: Jill Lepore, *These Truths: A History of the United States* (New York: W. W. Norton, 2018), 190–91; Mary P. Ryan, *Cradle of the Middle Class: The Family in Oneida County, New York, 1790–1865* (Cambridge: Cambridge University Press, 1981), 12–13.

7   "desired to go to the heathen": Narcissa Whitman to the American Board, February 23, 1835.

8   imposing their values on others: For a detailed analysis, see Ryan, *Cradle of the Middle Class*, 9–12.

8   investigated sinful behavior: Jeffrey, *Converting the West*, 23–24.

9   "constant religious instruction": Marcus Whitman to American Board Secretary Dr. B. B. Wisnew, June 3, 1834.

10   "soon to have a definite course": Marcus Whitman to the American Board, June 3, 1834.

10   Parker had lifted most of his story: *The Christian Advocate and Journal and Zion's Herald*, March 1, 1833, Folio MMim10 C318, Beinecke Library, Yale University.

10   setting off a chain reaction: Drury, *Marcus and Narcissa Whitman*, 1:49.

11   "four of their chiefs": *The Christian Advocate and Journal and Zion's Herald*, March 1, 1833.

14   "Is there a place for an unmarried female": Drury, *Marcus and Narcissa Whitman*, 109.

14   "She will offer herself if needed": Drury, *Marcus and Narcissa Whitman*, 110.

14   Parker connected their needs: This is according to Parker's son, Samuel J. Parker Jr. See Drury, *Marcus and Narcissa Whitman*, 110, citing a Parker manuscript at Cornell University.

14   Whitman had previously met members: Marcus Whitman to Jane Prentiss, May 17, 1842.

15   "robed as the bride of death": Bernard DeVoto, *Across the Wide Missouri* (Boston: Houghton Mifflin, 1947), 247–48.

16   "Far in heathen lands to dwell": Drury, biographer of the Whitmans, mentions the solo in *Marcus and Narcissa Whitman*, 162. Drury said that in summer of 1935 he interviewed an "old lady whose grandparents were present at the wedding."

16   "secular concerns be limited": Greene to Marcus Whitman, March 4, 1836.

16   "not remarkable for judgment": Rev. Artemus Bullard to the American Board, 1835, in Archer B. Hulbert and Dorothy P. Hulbert, *Marcus Whitman, Crusader, Part One,*

1802 to 1839 (Denver: Steward Commission of Colorado College and Denver Library, 1941), 30.

17   "wicked life among wicked men": Spalding to the American Board, August 7, 1835.

17   "a cast off bastard": Spalding to Rachel Spalding, May 3, 1871, Mss 1201, Oregon Historical Society, Portland.

18   read with difficulty: Drury, *Diaries and Letters*, 245.

18   "wicked feeling he cherished toward them both": Harriet Prentiss (Mrs. J. W. Jackson) to Mrs. Eva Emery Dye, January 11, 1893, in Clifford M. Drury, *Marcus Whitman, M.D., Pioneer and Martyr* (Caldwell, ID: Caxton Printers, 1937), 84.

20   "the loveliness of the Gospel": Greene to Spalding, February 25, 1836.

20   "Do nothing to irritate": Greene to Spalding, February 25, 1836.

CHAPTER TWO: "What a Delightful Place"

21   "more comfort than we antisipated": Marcus Whitman to Rev. David Greene, September 5, 1836. Whitman was by far the worst speller among Protestant missionaries in the Northwest.

22   "I never was so contented": Narcissa Whitman to her sister Harriet and brother Edward, June 3, 1836.

22   object of a "gazing throng": Narcissa Whitman to Augustus and Julia Whitman, July 16, 1836, in Clifford M. Drury, ed., *Where Wagons Could Go: Narcissa Whitman and Eliza Spalding* (Lincoln: University of Nebraska Press, 1997), 58.

22   to have sex with young Indian women: These details about rendezvous behavior come from Bernard DeVoto, *Across the Wide Missouri* (Boston: Houghton Mifflin, 1947), 97–100.

22   Meek was made dizzy: Frances Fuller Victor, *The River West: A Classic Account of the Life and Adventures in the Northwest of Joseph L. Meek, Fur Trapper and Mountain Man* (Hartford, CT: R. W. Bliss, 1870), 203–8.

23   "Poor little trunk": Journal entry, August 13, 1836, in Narcissa Whitman, *My Journal, 1836* (Fairfield, WA: Ye Galleon Press, 1985), 27.

23   "Thus has vanished the great obstacle": Sen. Lewis Linn, Report on S. 206, S. Doc. No. 25-470 (1838).

24   squabbled in front of witnesses: This is according to a letter that William H. Gray, a member of the missionary party, sent to Greene, October 1840, cited in Clifford M. Drury, *Marcus and Narcissa Whitman and the Opening of Old Oregon* (Seattle: Pacific Northwest National Parks and Forests Association, 1986), 1:218–19.

24   "if I could have lived with him": Letter from Gray, cited in Drury, *Marcus and Narcissa Whitman*, 1:218–19.

26   "remarkably well & rested": Journal entry, September 2, 1836, in Narcissa Whitman, *My Journal*.

28   he recognized it as an "extraordinary event": Spalding to Greene, September 20, 1836.

28   "Laudable Endeavours to do Good": McLoughlin to Governor and Committee, Hudson's Bay Company, London, November 16, 1836, in Dorothy Nafus Morrison, *Outpost: John McLoughlin and the Far Northwest* (Portland: Oregon Historical Society, 1999), 249n538.

29 "What a delightful place": Journal entry, September 12, 1836, in Narcissa Whitman, *My Journal.*

30 known to white settlers as Waiilatpu: The Cayuse spelling and definition are from Bobbie Conner, director of the Tamástslikt Cultural Institute, which is located in Oregon and is part of the Confederated Tribes of the Umatilla Indian Reservation. The name "Waiilatpu" has commonly been translated as "place of rye grass."

30 planning a substantial farm operation: Marcus Whitman to Parker, October 8, 1836, in Archer B. Hulbert and Dorothy P. Hulbert, *Marcus Whitman, Crusader, Part One, 1802 to 1839* (Denver: Steward Commission of Colorado College and Denver Library, 1941), 233.

31 Spalding was astonished by their hospitality: Spalding to Greene, February 16, 1837.

31 "we will see the difference": Marcus Whitman to Parker, October 8, 1836.

31 "They are fond of domineering": Chief trader Samuel Black, report to the Hudson's Bay Company, Walla Walla, March 25, 1829, B 146/3/2, Hudson's Bay Company Archives.

32 "conk you on the head": Chuck Sams, communications director at the Umatilla Reservation, Oregon, interview with the author, July 6, 2018.

32 breeding horses around 1730: See Eugene S. Hunn, *Nch'i-Wana, "The Big River": Mid-Columbia Indians and Their Land* (Seattle: University of Washington Press, 1990), 22–23.

32 Horses made it possible: Thomas R. Garth, "Early Nineteenth Century Tribal Relations in the Columbia Plateau," *Southwestern Journal of Anthropology* 20, no. 1 (Spring 1964); 47.

33 Cayuses helped introduce horses: See Robert H. Ruby and John A. Brown, *The Cayuse Indians: Imperial Tribesmen of Old Oregon* (Norman: University of Oklahoma Press, 1972), 7–8.

33 even as their numbers dwindled: The Cayuse people have always had strict rules against marriage among relatives, according to Conner. She said the rules forbid marriage closer than a fourth or fifth cousin. As the tribe's population declined from disease and other causes in the eighteenth and nineteenth centuries, Cayuse men and women married outside the tribe, often to Nez Perce and Walla Walla people, and sometimes to slaves taken in raids.

33 expand their geographic range: Even before horses arrived on the Columbia Plateau, the Cayuses were long-distance travelers and traders, crossing the South Pass of the Rockies on foot into what is now Wyoming and using small watercraft to travel and trade on the western side of the Cascades.

34 "repeating many words of English": Meriwether Lewis, journal entry, January 9, 1806, Journals of the Lewis & Clark Expedition Online, ed. Gary E. Moulton, https://lewisandclarkjournals.unl.edu/item/lc.jrn.1806-01-09.

34 "knew far more about Europeans": Larry Cebula, *Plateau Indians and the Quest for Spiritual Powers, 1700–1850* (Lincoln: University of Nebraska Press, 2003), 44. Cebula's book is an excellent synthesis of research that shows how the Plateau Indians were caught up in a storm of technological and religious change before white people appeared in any numbers in the region.

35 "be seen of men no more": John K. Townsend, *Narrative of a Journey Across the Rocky Mountains to the Columbia River* (Philadelphia: Henry Perkins, 1839), 232.

35 "unremitting across-the-board decline": Robert T. Boyd, *The Coming of the Spirit of Pestilence* (Seattle: University of Washington Press, 1999), 262, 272. This book is the single best analysis of the catastrophic effect of white disease on Pacific Northwest Indians.

35 "a source of thanksgiving": Leslie M. Scott, "Indian Diseases as Aids to Pacific Northwest Settlement," *Oregon Historical Quarterly* 29, no. 2 (June 1926): 161.

36 "so good for the whites": Scott, "Indian Diseases," 146.

37 sign of the cross: See Hulbert and Hulbert, *Marcus Whitman, Crusader,* 87; Drury, *Marcus and Narcissa Whitman,* 42–43; and, for a lucid synthesis of scholarship on the meaning of the Indian visit to St. Louis, see Elliott West, *The Last Indian War* (New York: Oxford University Press, 2009), 35–38.

37 "if Mother could see me now": Narcissa Whitman, letter, in Drury, *Where Wagons Could Go,* 109.

38 Whitmans would almost always have domestic servants: See Julie Roy Jeffrey, *Converting the West* (Norman: University of Oklahoma Press, 1991), 106–7.

38 "My heart truly leaped with joy": Narcissa Whitman to her mother, December 5, 1836. This long letter, begun on December 5, covers events into the spring of 1837. Drury, *Where Wagons Could Go,* 122.

CHAPTER THREE: Cayuses in the Kitchen

40 "strong desire is manifest": Narcissa Whitman to her mother, December 5, 1836, Clifford M. Drury, ed., *Where Wagons Could Go: Narcissa Whitman and Eliza Spalding* (Lincoln: University of Nebraska Press, 1997), 125.

40 "little addicted to steal": Marcus Whitman to Rev. David Greene, May 5, 1837.

41 "a mortal beggar as all Indians are": Narcissa Whitman to her mother, January 2, 1837, Drury, *Where Wagons Could Go,* 123.

41 "they will not be allowed": Narcissa Whitman to her mother, February 18, 1837, Drury, *Where Wagons Could Go,* 125. For more on Narcissa's ambivalence toward the Cayuses, see Julie Roy Jeffrey, *Converting the West* (Norman: University of Oklahoma Press, 1991), 107–83.

42 "a Cayuse Girl": Narcissa Whitman to her mother, March 30, 1837.

42 His name was Telokite: There are many spellings for the name of the Cayuse leader Telokite, including the more traditional Tiloukaikt. For the sake of clarity, I am using the simplest I could find for his name and for other Cayuse individuals involved in the Whitman killings. These spellings are used in Ronald Lansing, *Juggernaut: The Whitman Massacre Trial, 1850* (San Francisco: Ninth Judicial Court Historical Society, 1993).

43 "I am astonished": Spalding to Greene, February 16, 1837.

44 "remnant of our earthly": These quotes are taken from Spalding's letters to the American Board in 1837.

45 "blooming in health": Narcissa Whitman to Elvira Perkins, June 25, 1839.

46 "so long as she looked natural": Narcissa Whitman to her mother, October 9, 1839, in *Transactions of the Nineteenth Annual Reunion of the Oregon Pioneer Association for 1891,* 126. Scanned PDF file at ScholarsArchive@OSU, Oregon State Univeristy, Gerald W. Williams Collection, Corvallis, OR, https://ir.library.oregonstate.edu/concern/defaults/0c483k697.

46 not available to the unconverted: For an insightful analysis of Narcissa Whitman's theological struggles, see Jeffrey, *Converting the West,* 144.

47 "proud, haughty, and insolent": Narcissa Whitman to her mother, May 2, 1840.

47   **accidents and illness on the Oregon Trail:** Death was common, with about one out of every ten travelers dying before reaching the West Coast. In a twenty-five-year period, more than sixty-five thousand deaths occurred along the trails to Oregon and California. The deadliest disease, by far, was cholera. Accidental shootings, drownings, and wagon injuries also killed many. Indian attacks, however, were quite rare, although they increased in the 1860s, after the start of the Civil War. In the Whitmans' time, Indians were far more likely to trade with traveling whites or work for them as scouts and guides. According to historian William L. Lang, Indians killed about four hundred whites before 1860 (out of about four hundred thousand travelers); white travelers killed more Indians, and no Indians or whites died from violence until 1845. See "Life and Death on the Oregon Trail," Oregon–California Trails Association, http://octa-trails.org/articles/life-and-death-on-the-oregon-trail/; see also William L. Lang, "Oregon Trail" (essay), *The Oregon Encyclopedia*, Oregon Historical Society, https://www.oregonencyclopedia.org/articles/oregon_trail/.

47   **"to do so little or nothing":** Narcissa Whitman to Elvira Perkins, January 1, 1840, *Transactions of the 21st Annual Reunion of the Oregon Pioneer Association for 1893*, 127. Scanned text at HathiTrust Digital Library, https://hdl.handle.net/2027/hvd.hx5pgg?urlappend=%3Bseq=915.

48   **"I am entirely unfitted":** Narcissa Whitman to her parents, October 6, 1841.

48   **hard to understand, harder to teach:** For a detailed examination of the missionaries' faith, see Genevieve McCoy, "Sanctifying the Self and Saving the Savage: The Failure of the ABCFM Oregon Mission and the Conflicted Language of Calvinism" (doctoral dissertation, University of Washington, 1991).

49   **"lost ruined + condemned":** Marcus Whitman to Greene, October 15, 1840.

49   **two Cayuses were admitted:** This is according to Bobbie Conner, director of the Tamástslikt Cultural Institute, part of the Confederated Tribes of the Umatilla Indian Reservation.

49   **"copies of their white neighbors":** Francis Paul Prucha, "Two Roads to Conversion: Protestant and Catholic Missionaries in the Pacific Northwest," *Pacific Northwest Quarterly* 79, no. 4 (October 1988): 130–32. Prucha explains at length that the Protestant missionary "approach was overwhelmingly ethnocentric."

50   **all while obeying the Ten Commandments:** Prucha, "Two Roads to Conversion," 130–32.

50   **"good Indian is a dead Indian":** The origin of this oft-repeated slur is explained by Caroline Fraser in *Prairie Fires: The American Dreams of Laura Ingalls Wilder* (New York: Metropolitan Books, 2017), 356 and 574n374. Fraser cites a printed record of the slur in a transcript of remarks made in the U.S. House of Representatives by Congressman James M. Cavanaugh. On May 28, 1865, he said, "I will say that I like an Indian better dead than living. I have never in my life seen a good Indian (and I have seen thousands) except when I have seen a dead Indian. . . . I believe in the policy that exterminates the Indians, drives them outside the boundaries of civilization, because you cannot civilize them."

50   **"What we most fear":** Greene to Marcus Whitman, October 17, 1838.

51   **"might as well hold back the sun":** Spalding to Greene, February 16, 1837.

52   **"crabby jealousies":** See Alvin M. Josephy Jr., *The Nez Perce Indians and the Opening of the Northwest* (New Haven, CT: Yale University Press, 1965), 173; Bernard DeVoto, *Across the Wide Missouri* (Boston: Houghton Mifflin, 1947), 19; and Elliott West, *The Last Indian War* (New York: Oxford University Press, 2009), 46.

52   **mountainous paper trail:** Clifford M. Drury, the preeminent Whitman scholar of the twentieth century, said in a speech at Washington State University on April 4, 1969, that

the letters of thirteen Oregon missionaries in the files of the American Board contain about one million words. "I shall never cease to be amazed," he said, "at the amount of original source material bearing upon the Oregon Mission that have survived the vicissitudes of time, the ravages of fire, and the carelessness of man."

52   "Scarcely one who is not intolerable": Diary entry, May 27, 1838, in Clifford Drury, ed., *On to Oregon: The Diaries of Mary Walker & Myra Eells* (Lincoln: University of Nebraska Press, 1998), 87.

52   "small, prudish soul": Josephy, *The Nez Perce Indians*, 173.

52   the "weeping one": Clifford M. Drury, ed., *The Diaries and Letters of Henry H. Spalding and Asa Bowen Smith* (Glendale, CA: Arthur H. Clark, 1958), 17.

53   "Not a child can be found": Drury, *Diaries and Letters*, 106.

53   damned to eternal fire: Drury, *Diaries and Letters*, 108.

53   "encourage their selfish desires": Drury, *Diaries and Letters*, 100.

53   "woman to be whipped": Drury, *Diaries and Letters*, 172.

54   "disease in his head": Asa Bowen Smith to Greene, October 21, 1840, in Drury, *Diaries and Letters*, 203–4.

55   "Duplicity is a trait in his character": William Gray to Greene, October 14, 1840.

CHAPTER FOUR: "Want of Christian Feeling"

57   "hope for permanent peace": Cushing Eells, Elkanah Walker, and Henry Spalding to Greene, June 8, 1842, in William I. Marshall, *Acquisition of Oregon* (Seattle: Lowman and Hanford, 1911), ii, 112.

57   "minds of all were relieved": Mary Walker's diary, June 4, 1842, in Clifford M. Drury, *On to Oregon: The Diaries of Mary Walker & Myra Eells* (Lincoln, Nebraska: University of Nebraska Press, 1963), 231.

57   "the want of harmony": Rev. David Greene to Spalding, February 26, 1842.

58   "extremely painful and humiliating": Greene to Marcus Whitman, February 25, 1842.

59   "He could never stop to parley": H. K. W. Perkins to Jane Prentiss, October 19, 1849, in Clifford M. Drury, *Marcus and Narcissa Whitman and the Opening of Old Oregon* (Seattle: Pacific Northwest National Parks and Forests Association, 1986), 2: Appendix 6, 393.

59   "in regard to interest of this mission": Resolution quoted in Drury, *Marcus and Narcissa Whitman*, 1:465.

60   "catastrophe" among Christians: Greene to members of the Oregon Mission, February 25, 1842.

60   "his great pique toward me": Narcissa Whitman to her father, October 10, 1840.

60   a pet of his daughter: Drury, *Marcus and Narcissa Whitman*, 1:476.

62   "Arrival from Oregon": Horace Greeley, "Arrival from Oregon," *New York Daily Tribune*, March 29, 1843, accessed at Chronicling America, Historical American Newspapers, Library of Congress.

63   Clearly unhappy to see Whitman: Marcus Whitman to Greene, April 1, 1847. In this letter, Whitman wrote, "You told me you were sorry I came."

64 "difficulties between Mr. Spalding": Minutes of the Prudential Committee of the American Board, April 4, 1843, in Drury, *Marcus and Narcissa Whitman*, 2, 57.

65 "nothing can save the Conjurer": Marcus Whitman to Greene, April 7, 1843.

CHAPTER FIVE: "A Thousand Little Harassing Events"

66 "saucy Indian got into the house": Narcissa Whitman to Mary Walker, November 5, 1842, in Clifford M. Drury, ed., *On to Oregon, The Diaries of Mary Walker & Myra Eells* (Lincoln: University of Nebraska Press, 1963), 238n43.

66 "Had the ruffian persisted": Narcissa Whitman to Marcus Whitman, October 7, 1842.

67 "a thousand little harassing events": Spalding to Greene, January 24, 1846, in Clifford M. Drury, ed., *The Diaries and Letters of Henry H. Spalding and Asa Bowen Smith* (Glendale, CA: Arthur H. Clark, 1958), 337.

67 "I have had a gun cocked": Spalding to Greene, January 24, 1846, in Drury, *Diaries and Letters*, 337.

68 "our heads severed from our bodies": Spalding to Elijah White, April 1, 1843, in A. J. Allen, *Ten Years in Oregon* (Ithaca, NY: Press of Andrus Gauntlett, 1850), 208.

68 taking church money: Alvin M. Josephy Jr., *The Nez Perce Indians and the Opening of the Northwest* (New Haven, CT: Yale University Press), 220–21.

69 "joyful countenance and glad hearts": Allen, *Ten Years in Oregon*, 182.

69 "If an Indian break these laws": Allen, *Ten Years in Oregon*, 189–90.

69 "were greatly pleased": Allen, *Ten Years in Oregon*, 186.

70 "whites liberty to exploit": Josephy, *The Nez Perce Indians*, 230.

70 "do not wish to be forced": Narcissa Whitman to Marcus Whitman, March 29, 1843.

70 "willfully takes life": Allen, *Ten Years in Oregon*, 189.

71 "Let yr single aim": Greene to Whitman, March 4, 1836.

71 "it will be strange": Marcus Whitman to his mother, May 27, 1843.

72 "An equivalent for Bostonians": Elliott West, *The Last Indian War* (New York: Oxford University Press, 2009), 46–47.

72 "land of pure delight": Quoted in Clifford M. Drury, *Marcus and Narcissa Whitman and the Opening of Old Oregon* (Seattle: Pacific Northwest National Parks and Forests Association, 1986), 2:61.

73 "no other individual": Jess Applegate, "A Day with the Cow Column," *Quarterly of the Oregon Historical Society* 1, no. 4 (December 1900): 361.

73 "If I never do more": Marcus Whitman to Greene, November 1, 1843.

73 "we have so eminantly": Marcus Whitman to Greene, April 18, 1844.

73 "settlement of this country by Americans": Marcus Whitman to his wife's parents, May 16, 1844.

75 "I did not fear to die": Marcus Whitman to Greene, November 11, 1841. Details of his confrontations are in this letter.

75 "they are agitated": Marcus Whitman to Greene, April 8, 1844.

75 "hope of permanent quiet": Marcus Whitman to Greene, October 26, 1845.

75 "I might be killed": Marcus Whitman to Walker and Eells, November 25, 1845.

76 "the air we breathe": Spalding to Greene, February 3, 1847.

76 priest had imprisoned a nun: Tyler Anbinder, *Nativism and Slavery: The Northern Know Nothings and the Politics of the 1850s* (New York: Oxford University Press, 1992), 9.

77 "selfish professors of false doctrines": *Notice and Voyages of the Famed Quebec Mission to the Pacific Northwest: Being the Correspondences, Notices, etc., of Father Blanchet and Demers* (Portland: Oregon Historical Society, 1956), 56 and 108.

77 "very bitter against the Protestant religion": Spalding to Greene, February 3, 1847.

78 "zealous advocate for Papacy": Marcus Whitman to Greene, August 3, 1847.

78 ignored McLoughlin's repeated warnings: See Theodore Stern, *Chiefs and Change in the Oregon Country* (Corvallis: Oregon State University Press, 1996), 2:77.

78 "All is known": This conversation and the scene that follows are from Clarence B. Bagley, ed., *Early Catholic Missions in Old Oregon* (Seattle: Lowman and Hanford, 1932), 188.

79 "nothing now but blood!": J. B. A. Brouillet, *Authentic Account of the Murder of Dr. Whitman and Other Missionaries by the Cayuse Indians of Oregon in 1847* (Portland: S. J. McCormick, 1869), 62.

80 "Were I to select": Spalding to Joel Palmer, April 7, 1846, in Joel Palmer, *Journal of Travels over the Oregon Trail in 1845* (Portland: Oregon Historical Society, 1993), 292.

80 at least two to one: A count of the number of settlers in the wagon trains of the 1840s and various white estimates of the Cayuse population in the 1840s–50s are compiled in Stern, *Chiefs and Change in the Oregon Country*, 2:365, 381. Estimates of Cayuse numbers were often unreliable guesses and varied widely from a low of 126 in 1851 to a high of 2,000 in 1848. Many historians put the tribe's numbers during these years as between 300 and 500.

81 "The poor Indians are amazed": Narcissa Whitman to her mother, August 23, 1847.

CHAPTER SIX: "Beastly & Savage Brutalities"

82 "Beastly & Savage Brutalities": Spalding to Greene, January 24, 1848. This language is in the second sentence of Spalding's letter, which details the "horrible massacre of our dear Br & Sist Doct & Mrs Whitman."

82 most contagious of all: Mandy Oaklander, "Why Measles Is the Most Contagious Virus," *Time*, February 3, 2015, http://time.com/3693618/measles-contagious/.

82 winter had been unusually long: Alvin M. Josephy Jr., *The Nez Perce and the Opening of the Northwest* (New Haven, CT: Yale University Press, 1965), 250.

83 brought the virus back: Robert Boyd, *The Coming of the Spirit of Pestilence* (Seattle: University of Washington Press, 1999), 146–48. Boyd, a research anthropologist at Portland State University, writes that there was a measles epidemic across North America at the time and that it generally diffused from east to west. But he points out that there were no reports in the diaries of Oregon Trail migrants in 1847 of deaths or illness from measles and says it is "unlikely" that they carried the disease overland to Whitman mission. Measles, however, was widespread in Northern California near present-day Sacramento in the summer of 1847, when Cayuses traveled there in search of cattle, and Boyd concludes that they were the most likely vectors "for this early appearance of the disease on the

Columbia Plateau." In many other outbreaks across the West, white settlers often did spread measles to Indians. Some tribal scholars challenge Boyd's argument, saying there is not enough evidence from 1847 to prove that measles was brought back to Oregon by Cayuse horsemen.

83   **It came from Joe Lewis:** Several survivors of the Whitman killings singled out Joe Lewis for spinning a conspiracy theory.

83   **the genocidal reality:** For a shockingly detailed and carefully documented account of mass "Indian removal" in the American Southeast in the 1830s, see Claudio Saunt, *Unworthy Republic: The Dispossession of Native Americans and the Road to Indian Territory* (New York: W. W. Norton, 2020).

84   **five Cayuses were dying every day:** Robert Boyd, "The Pacific Northwest Measles Epidemic of 1847–48," *Oregon Historical Quarterly* 95, no. 1 (Spring 1994): 17.

84   **"the evil would be removed":** Joseph L. Meek to Jonas Galusha Prentiss (older brother of Narcissa), July 8, 1848. Meek went to the mission after the killing. The letter is in Clifford M. Drury, "Joe Meek Comments on Reasons for the Whitman Massacre," *Oregon Historical Quarterly* 75, no. 1 (March 1974): 74.

84   **the back of Whitman's head:** The only white eyewitness to survive the attack on Marcus Whitman was eleven-year-old Mary Ann Bridger, a daughter of mountain man Jim Bridger. She was in the kitchen, sitting beside the doctor, when the attack began. The girl died four months later and never gave a formal deposition about what she saw, but she described the attack to several people. They included thirteen-year-old Catherine Sager, who was at the mission during the attack and wrote what is regarded as the clearest account of the killings. Catherine wrote that she spoke to Indians at the mission, and they were a second source for her account of how Whitman was killed. Mary Ann Bridger also spoke to two other younger Sager sisters, Matilda and Elizabeth, and to Eliza Spalding, the twelve-year-old daughter of Henry Spalding. They all later wrote about the killings, apparently relying on what Mary Ann had told them. Henry Spalding, too, talked to Mary Ann soon after the killing and used her account in his many published accounts of the attack on Dr. Whitman.

84   **splitting the top of his skull:** An examination of Whitman's skull in 1897 found fractures consistent with this description. "Description of the Remains Found in the Whitman Mound," October 21, 1896, Mss 105, Whitman College Archives.

85   **The attack was on:** There are at least twenty-five accounts of the killings from white people, some from eyewitnesses and others from individuals who spoke to eyewitnesses soon after the event. Many of the witnesses were young children, and many of the accounts were not written until decades after the event. Still, there are multiple similar accounts of how Marcus and Narcissa Whitman were killed. By far the most detailed and balanced synthesis of these accounts is in Clifford M. Drury, *Marcus and Narcissa Whitman and the Opening of Old Oregon* (Seattle: Pacific Northwest National Parks and Forests Association, 1986), 2:224–55. An examination of the relative reliability of the first-person accounts can be found in Tamara J. Luce, "Excavating First-Person Accounts of the Whitman Massacre," *Nebraska Anthropologist* 27 (2012): 112–36. A contemporary investigation of the killings by William McBean of the Hudson's Bay Company also supported accusations against Chief Telokite and Tomahas. McBean based his conclusion on interviews with three Cayuse chiefs.

86   **"save the little ones":** Catherine, Elizabeth, and Matilda Sager, *The Whitman Massacre of 1847* (Fairfield, WA: Ye Galleon Press, 1981), 60.

86   **"This will kill my poor mother":** S. A. Clarke, *Pioneer Days of Oregon History* (Portland, OR: J. K. Gill, 1905), 2:532.

86 **mutilated his face:** Catherine, Elizabeth, and Matilda Sager, *Whitman Massacre,* 62.

87 **Indians were determined:** The most authoritative source for this is Rev. Jean-Baptiste Brouillet, the Catholic priest who was at the Whitman mission the day after the killings. See J. B. A. Brouillet, *Authentic Account of the Murder of Dr. Whitman and Other Missionaries by the Cayuse Indians of Oregon in 1847* (Portland, OR: S. J. McCormick, 1869), 53. A slightly different account is in the priest's "Account of the Massacre," *Walla Walla Statesman,* April 13, 1866. A similar account is given by Spalding in several letters he wrote in the first five months after the encounter.

88 **"You have no time to spare":** Brouillet, *Authentic Account,* 53.

CHAPTER SEVEN: "Priests Wet with the Blood"

91 **"wonderfully miraculous":** Spalding to Frances Fuller Victor, June 29, 1865, WC Mss103, Spalding Collection, Box 4 (1857–1869), Spalding Family Collection, Whitman College Archives.

92 **the Cayuses missed him:** Spalding to Greene, January 24, 1848.

93 **"waft me over this river":** Spalding, "The Massacre of Dct. Whitman's Family and Escape of Rev. Mr. Spalding and Family," *Christian Observer,* October 28, 1848, 1. Image of newspaper in archives at Spalding Collection, Washington State University Library.

93 **"Anxiety prevailed over reason":** Spalding, "Massacre of Dct. Whitman's Family."

93 **"the horrible massacre":** Provisional Oregon Territory Governor George Abernathy to the Legislative Assembly, December 7, 1847, in Frances Fuller Victor, *The Cayuse War* (Corvallis, OR: Taxus Baccata, 2006), 97. This is a reprint of a multipart history written by Victor for the State of Oregon and first published in 1894.

94 **"hostages of peace":** Spalding to Blanchet, December 10, 1847, quoted in Victor, *The Cayuse War,* 83–84.

94 **"furnished me with provisions":** Spalding to Blanchet, December 10, 1847, quoted in Victor, *The Cayuse War,* 83–84.

95 **"Romish priests, who have lately":** Spalding, *Christian Observer,* October 28, 1848.

95 **speculated that Spalding lost his health:** Most prominent among them is Clifford Drury, whose lifetime of document research and many books are the fundamental building blocks of scholarship about the Whitmans and the Spaldings. Drury writes that the "most charitable explanation of this unreasonable and unchristian attitude of Spalding is that the terrible experiences through which he passed when trying to escape unsettled his mind." *Marcus and Narcissa Whitman and the Opening of Old Oregon* (Seattle: Pacific Northwest National Parks and Forests Association, 1986), 2:377

95 **"wrecked in health":** Frances Fuller Victor, *All Over Oregon and Washington* (Portland, OR: J. H. Carmany, 1872), 121.

97 **the provisional government was broke:** Victor, *The Cayuse War,* 98.

97 **"punishing the Indians":** Victor, *The Cayuse War,* 99.

98 **rather petulant instructions:** Victor, *The Cayuse War,* 106.

98 **her "golden hair":** Trevor Bond, "Hair and History," *Washington State Magazine,* October 24, 2014.

99 **"prevent further aggression":** Victor, *The Cayuse War,* 102.

99 "always a great evil": Clarence Bagley, ed., *Early Catholic Missions in Old Oregon* (Seattle: Lowman and Hanford, 1932), 201.

99 systematically poisoning them: The Cayuse concern about poisoning was not exclusively about measles. There is eyewitness testimony from John Young, a settler who worked at the mission in 1846, saying that Whitman ordered meat to be laced with arsenic and placed around the perimeter of the mission to kill wolves. Young said that "some Indians who happened to pass there took the meat and ate it; three of them were very sick, and were near dying." Whitman also ordered that a few large melons in his garden be treated with a "little poison" to make Indians slightly sick if they stole them, according to Young and Augustin Raymond, another settler who was at the mission. Cayuse leaders were aware of Whitman's actions and angry about them—before the measles epidemic of 1847. See J. B. A. Brouillet, *Authentic Account of the Murder of Dr. Whitman and Other Missionaries by the Cayuse Indians of Oregon in 1847* (Portland, OR: S. J. McCormick, 1869), 29–31.

100 The Indians, in fact, wondered: See Alvin M. Josephy, *The Nez Perce Indians and the Opening of the Northwest* (New Haven, CT: Yale University Press, 1965), 261.

101 "I will pay you a ransom": Victor, *The Cayuse War*, 87–88.

101 chiefs did not want to anger: Josephy, *The Nez Perce Indians*, 261.

101 accepted the ransom: William McBean, Hudson's Bay Company officer in Fort Walla Walla, to the governor of Oregon Territory, December 20, 1847, in "Memorial of the Legislative Assembly of Oregon Territory," H.R. Misc. Doc. No. 30-98, at 25 (1848).

102 "natural depravity of barbarians": Victor, *The Cayuse War*, 93.

102 "our mind recoils with horror": *Oregon Spectator*, January 20, 1848, Historic Oregon Newspapers, University of Oregon Library, https://oregonnews.uoregon.edu/lccn /sn84022662/1848-01-20/ed-1/seq-1/.

103 "Five Crows seized me": William H. Gray, *A History of Oregon, 1792–1849, Drawn from Personal Observation and Authentic Information* (Portland, OR: H. H. Bancroft, 1870), 498.

104 "Christian efforts in our behalf": Spalding to Greene, January 8, 1848.

104 "the hands of their parents": Spalding to Greene, January 8, 1848.

105 "ravens hovering over dead bodies": Spalding to Cornelius Gilliam, February 3, 1848.

105 "bloody savages who": Spalding to Greene, February 22, 1848.

105 "helpless young woman": Spalding, S. Exec. Doc. No. 41-37, at 39 (1871).

105 "few of the Cayuse are innocent": Spalding to Gilliam, February 3, 1848.

106 "require them to leave the country": Spalding to Gilliam, February 3, 1848.

106 "Bishop's foot was on my neck": Spalding to the editor of the *Oregon Spectator*, February 8, 1848. The *Spectator* had previously published the embarrassing letter Spalding wrote to Bishop Blanchet. So Spalding wrote this letter to explain himself. The *Spectator* refused to publish it, but it appeared in June 1848 in the *Oregon American and Evangelical Unionist*.

106 "priests wet with the blood": Spalding to the *Oregon Spectator*, February 8, 1848.

107 "clouds are gathering fast": Spalding to Greene, January 24, 1848.

107 "defend the murderers": *Oregon Spectator*, "Speech of Camash-pelloo," April 20, 1848, 1.

107 Cayuses had "bad hearts": *Oregon Spectator*, "Remarks of J. Palmer in Council with the Nez Perces, Walla Wallas, and Friendly Cayuses," April 6, 1848, 3

108 **"forfeited by them"**: *Oregon Spectator,* Statement "For the Specator" from H. A. G. Lee, Superintendent of Indian Affairs Territory of Oregon, July 13, 1848, 1.

CHAPTER EIGHT: A Proper Trial

110 **"we are justly proud"**: Spalding to Greene, January 24, 1848.

110 **tomahawk in its skull**: The account of Meek's visit to Washington is in Frances Fuller Victor, *The River of the West* (Oakland, CA: Brooks-Sterling Company), 1974 (reprint of original published 1870), 447–62.

111 **a mesmerizing talker**: Victor, *The River of the West,* 452.

111 **"perilous and distressed situation"**: James K. Polk, "Message Regarding the Oregon Territory," message to Congress, May 29, 1848, online at Miller Center, University of Virginia, https://millercenter.org/the-presidency/presidential-speeches/may-29-1848-message -regarding-oregon-territory.

112 **"a charnel-house"**: Joseph L. Meek, "To the Senate and House of Representatives of the United States," *Washington Union,* June 15, 1848, 1.

112 **more than quadrupling**: U.S Census Bureau, "Resident Population and Apportionment of the U.S. House of Representatives, Oregon," https://bit.ly/2P2ifVE.

112 **a race war in the early 1850s**: William G. Robbins, "Oregon Donational Land Act," The Oregon Encyclopedia, https://oregonencyclopedia.org/articles/oregon_donation_land _act/#.Xx7s1R17m50.

113 **Newspapers could not be printed**: Malcolm Clark Jr., *The Eden Seekers* (Boston: Houghton Mifflin, 1981), 219.

113 **about half the tribe**: Francis Norbert Blanchet, *Historical Sketches of the Catholic Church in Oregon During the Past Forty Years* (Portland: Oregon Catholic Church, 1878), 165.

114 **"melancholy and horrible affair"**: Priscilla Knuth and Charles M. Gates, eds., "Oregon Territory in 1849–1850," *Pacific Northwest Quarterly* 40, no. 1 (January 1949): 11–12.

114 **"license for the most atrocious outrages"**: Lane to secretary of war, October 22, 1849, Oregon Historical Society, Mss 1146, Box 5, 21.

115 **"explain all about the murderers"**: Blanchet, *Historical Sketches,* 180–81.

115 **"guilty barbarous murderers"**: Joseph Lane, "The Waiilatpu Massacre: The True Story of the Execution of the Whitman Murderers," *The Oregonian,* December 3, 1879, 1.

115 **Just five Cayuses**: Clifford M. Drury, *Marcus and Narcissa Whitman and the Opening of Old Oregon* (Seattle: Pacific Northwest National Parks and Forests Association, 1986), 2:391.

115 **tribe's best ponies**: H. O. Lang, ed., *History of the Willamette Valley* (Portland, OR: George H. Himes, 1885), 317–18.

116 **"So die we"**: Victor, *The River of the West,* 494.

116 **go indoors to make conversation**: "Cultural Landscape Report, Oregon City, Oregon, Public Draft," Willamette Falls Legacy Project, partnership of Oregon City, Clackamas County, and State of Oregon, October, 2017, 59–62, https://bit.ly/2CLdUUl.

116 **five sawmills and two gristmills**: Willamette Falls Legacy Project, 59–62.

118 **launching pad for getting rich**: E. Kimbark MacColl, *Merchants, Money, and Power: The Portland Establishment, 1843–1913* (Portland, OR: Georgian Press, 1988), 86.

118 their "abounding drunkenness": "Intemperance Again," *Oregon Spectator*, November 1, 1849, 2.

118 he secretly co-owned: *Oregon Spectator*, August 24, 1848, 1; Clark, *Eden Seekers*, 216.

119 he was wrong to claim: William I. Marshall, *Acquisition of Oregon* (Seattle: Lowman and Hanford, 1911), 2:240.

119 "public demanded an explanation": Diary of Rev. George H. Atkinson, 1847–1858, *Oregon Historical Quarterly* 30, no. 4 (December 1939): 345–46.

119 the one-acre island: Lane, "Waiilatpu Massacre."

119 collected a payment: Receipt for payment to the Oregon Milling Company, June 12, 1850, Mss 926, Joseph Meek Papers, Oregon Historical Society. I am indebted to James Nicita, a lawyer and historian in Oregon City, for unearthing this record.

120 slow filter of two interpreters: Among the five defendants, only Telokite, as mentioned earlier, is believed to have been somewhat fluent in English. He may have understood some of the trial proceedings without any translation, but it is also probable that he had never before heard courtroom jargon and was mystified by what was going on during the trial.

121 "rubbed up a little": Quoted in Harvey Elmer Tobie, *No Man Like Joe: The Life and Times of Joseph L. Meek* (Portland, OR: Binfords and Mort, 1949), 203–4.

121 Pratt was alert: Sidney Teaser, "First Associate Justice of Oregon Territory: O. C. Pratt," *Oregon Historical Quarterly* 49, no. 3 (September 1948): 171–91.

122 the judge looked elsewhere: For a superb book-length account of the legal and political issues raised in the Cayuse trial, see Ronald B. Lansing, *Juggernaut: The Whitman Massacre Trial, 1850* (San Francisco: Ninth Judicial Circuit Historical Society, 1993). My account of the trial draws on Lansing's analysis and the unusually extensive official court records, contemporary newspaper coverage, and the memories of Joe Meek, as collected by his biographer, Frances Fuller Victor.

122 "Claiborne led off": Victor, *The River of the West*, 495.

123 "language at once severe": *Oregon Spectator*, May 30, 1850, 2.

123 "Our beginning is small": Spalding to Rev. A. F. Walker, July 25, 1848, Mss 1210, Oregon Historical Society.

124 "heart like an ox!": H. S. Lyman, "Reminiscences. Anson Sterling Cone, et al.," *Quarterly of the Oregon Historical Society* 4, no. 3 (September 1903): 251–54.

125 "labored and very lucid": *Oregon Spectator*, May 30, 1850, 2. Also see Lansing's account of the legal questions, *Juggernaut*, 34–37.

125 "decency and respect": Lansing, *Juggernaut*, 66–67.

127 "different medicines from those": Bill of Exceptions from the Whitman Trial. This handwritten document, in the files of the Oregon State Archives, is a summary of motions, testimony, and rulings in the four-day trial, which ended May 24, 1850. The documents have been transcribed and reprinted in Lansing, *Juggernaut*, 100–104.

127 white demands for culprits: Tobie, *No Man Like Joe*, 200.

127 "killed their medicine men": Bill of Exceptions, in Lansing, *Juggernaut*, 103.

128 "bad medicine men": Bill of Exceptions, in Lansing, *Juggernaut*, 103.

128 "I do so swear": Lansing, *Juggernaut*, 74.

128   "Cayuse people know best": Court Amendments to Bill of Exceptions, May 24, 1850 (Judge O. C. Pratt's amendments to the defense counsels' account of the trial), Oregon State Archives, in Lansing, *Juggernaut*, 105.

CHAPTER NINE: Five at Once

130   "until you are dead": "Trial of Cayuse Murderers," *Oregon Spectator*, May 30, 1850, 3.

130   "were filled with horror": Frances Fuller Victor, *The River of the West* (Oakland, CA: Brooks-Sterling Company), 1974 (reprint of original published 1870), 495.

131   "die as a dog": "The First Woman Born in the West," *Ladies' Home Journal*, August 1913, 40.

131   "None of them expressed any sorrow": Victor, *The River of the West*, 494.

132   white Protestant missionary: Clifford M. Drury, *Marcus Whitman, M.D., Pioneer and Martyr* (Caldwell, ID: Caxton Printers, 1937), 458. Drury found a transcription of the October 1849 letter in the Whitman College Archives in the 1930s. It has since been misplaced or lost.

132   "self-denial that took her away": Drury, *Marcus Whitman*, 459.

133   "safe as anywhere in Christendom": Drury, *Marcus Whitman*, 459.

133   told him to go away: Francis Norbert Blanchet, *Historical Sketches of the Catholic Church in Oregon During the Past Forty Years* (Portland: Oregon Catholic Church, 1878), 181.

134   blame papists for Indian trouble: Samuel L. Campbell, *Autobiography* (Mannford, OK: Rowena Campbell Grant, 1986), 242–43.

134   "fruits of the eleven years": Blanchet, *Historical Sketches*, 181.

134   under a cloudless sky: E. Ruth Rockford, ed., "Diary of Reverend G. H. Atkinson 1847–1858; Part V, 1848–1851," *Oregon Historical Quarterly* 41, no. 1 (March 1940): 26.

134   men from the countryside: Hubert Howe Bancroft, *History of Oregon* (San Francisco: History Co., 1886), 1:90.

134   riding a white horse: Harvey Elmer Tobie, *No Man Like Joe: The Life and Times of Joseph L. Meek* (Portland, OR: Binfords and Mort, 1949), 303n37. Tobie cites the memory of Clella Glanville, a granddaughter of Meek, who said he rode a white horse and carried a sword. Meek said he had a tomahawk. Victor, *The River of the West*, 496.

135   walked across the bridge: Blanchet, *Historical Sketches*, 182.

135   alarmed by the death sentences: See Ronald B. Lansing, *Juggernaut: The Whitman Massacre Trial, 1850* (San Francisco: Ninth Judicial Circuit Historical Society, 1993), 96; Clifford M. Drury, *Marcus and Narcissa Whitman and the Opening of Old Oregon* (Seattle: Pacific Northwest National Parks and Forests Association, 1986), 2:331; *Sunday Oregonian*, September 24, 1933, 3.

135   only one defendant claimed innocence: This is according to Meek. See Victor, *The River of the West*.

135   No witness identified him: See Drury, *Marcus and Narcissa Whitman*, 2:329.

135   "it hurts me to talk about dying": Declaration by the five Cayuse Indians, June 2 and 3, 1850, Oregon City, Oregon State Archives.

135   white people should not hang them: Catherine, Elizabeth, and Matilda Sager, *The Whitman Massacre of 1847* (Fairfield, WA: Ye Galleon Press, 1981), 89.

135 archbishop held up a crucifix: Blanchet, *Historical Sketches*, 182.

136 "Now friends, now friends": Campbell, *Autobiography*, 243. Campbell was a frontiersman and pioneer who wrote that he knew all the executed Cayuses and visited them in jail before the hanging. The spelling of these words in the Nez Perce language was provided by Chuck Sams, a spokesman for the Confederated Tribes of the Umatilla Reservation.

136 "O Lord Jesus": Blanchet, *Historical Sketches*, 182.

136 on the ends of their ropes: *Oregon Spectator*, May 30, 1850.

136 "he got quiet": Victor, *The River of the West*, 496.

136 "a destiny too strong for them": Bancroft, *History of Oregon*, 2:99. This book was ghost-written by Frances Fuller Victor.

137 "satisfaction of the ladies": *New York Tribune*, August 21, 1850.

137 spectators got drunk: Rockwood, "Diary of Rev. G. H. Atkinson," 26.

137 "would never see another hanging": Campbell, *Autobiography*, 242.

138 state-funded murder: Benjamin Madley, "California's Yuki Indians: Defining Genocide in Native American History," *Western Historical Quarterly* 39, no. 3 (Autumn 2008): 303–32.

138 its residents lynched: Ken Gonzales-Day, *Lynching in the West: 1850–1935* (Durham, NC: Duke University Press, 2006), 27; list of those who were lynched, 205–28.

138 regardless of the individual's guilt: Gonzales-Day, *Lynching in the West*, 83.

138 testifying against whites: Gonzales-Day, *Lynching in the West*, 39.

138 chased most Indians out: Helen McLure, "What Dares to Style This Female a Woman? Lynching, Gender, and Culture in the Nineteenth-Century West," in Michael J. Pfeifer, ed., *Lynching Beyond Dixie* (Urbana: University of Illinois Press, 2013), 28–31.

140 a third of them were children: "Aftermath," U.S. Dakota War of 1862 (website), http://www.usdakotawar.org/history/aftermath.

140 largest white death toll: Scott W. Berg, *38 Nooses: Lincoln, Little Crow, and the Beginning of the Frontier's End* (New York: Vintage, 2012), 186.

140 "children are indiscriminately murdered": Berg, *38 Nooses*, 60.

140 "must be exterminated": Governor Ramsey, *Extra Session Message*, September 9, 1862, 12, online at Minnesota Legislative Reference Library, https://www.leg.state.mn.us/docs/nonmnpub/oclc18189672.pdf.

140 "killing with small-pox, poison, and kindness": Annual Report of Thomas J. Galbraith, agent for the Sioux of the Mississippi, January 7, 1863, in *Report of the Commissioner of Indian Affairs for 1863* (Washington, D.C.: Government Printing Office, 1863), 294.

140 the commission judged: Berg, *38 Nooses*, 38.

141 "condemned on general principles": Curt Brown, "In Little Crow's Wake, Horrors for the Dakota," *Minneapolis Star-Tribune*, August 16, 2012. Details and quotes in this paragraph come from Brown's stories, part of an excellent six-part series on the Dakota war, available at http://www.startribune.com/in-little-crow-s-wake-horrors-for-the-dakota/166163736/.

141 "anxious not to act": "The Trials and Hanging," U.S. Dakota War of 1862 (website), http://usdakotawar.org/history/aftermath/trials-hanging.

141 **not enough rope:** Brown, "In Little Crow's Wake."

142 **churchgoing farm country:** See Caroline Fraser, *Prairie Fires: The American Dreams of Laura Ingalls Wilder* (New York: Metropolitan Books, 2017), 14–24, for an excellent summary treatment of the Dakota War of 1862. The best book-length examination of these events is Berg, *38 Nooses*.

142 **"frontier favors an indiscriminate slaughter":** Major General S. R. Curtis to Headquarters of the Army, January 12, 1865, in *Report of the Joint Committee of the Conduct of the War* (Washington, D.C.: Government Printing Office, 1865).

143 **"committed on the white man":** Special Order No. 11, North Sub-district of the Plains, May 25, 1865, Ellison Papers, Denver Public Library, cited in Douglas C. McChristian, "Fort Laramie and the U.S. Army on the High Plains, 1849–1890," National Park Service Historic Resource Study, Fort Laramie National Historic Site, February 2003.

144 **transportation department of Clackamas County:** For a detailed and well-documented assessment of the possible burial site of the Cayuse Five, see James Nicita, "A Step Towards Healing: Repatriating the Cayuse Five; Author Offers Theory on Gravesite Location," *Clackamas Review*, June 13, 2018.

CHAPTER TEN: "Seeing That They Stood Alone"

145 **White settlers rushed:** The Donation Land Claim Act was passed by Congress on September 27, 1850. It was vague about what constituted "public lands," and settlers assumed that Indian lands included only those areas where Indians were actually visible. Whites began encroaching on land Indians had viewed as part of their traditional turf.

145 **Indians became a minority:** Theodore Stern, *Chiefs and Change in the Oregon Country* (Corvallis: Oregon State University Press, 1996), 2:365n29. The chart shows 10,000 settlers arrived in 1852, 7,500 in 1853, and 6,000 in 1854.

146 **"tribes have become so nearly extinct":** Quoted in Stern, *Chiefs and Change*, 244.

146 **"restrain our enterprising citizens":** Stern, *Chiefs and Change*, 271.

147 **"hindering the general growth":** George W. Manypenny, Letters to Committee on Indian Affairs, H.R. Misc. Doc. No. 38, 33rd Cong., 1st Sess. (1854), 2–3.

148 **"He hoped the removal":** Richards, *Isaac I. Stevens*, 178.

149 **"afraid to death of him":** Meg Stevens to her mother, February 18, 1855, Isaac Stevens Papers, University of Washington, as quoted in Richards, *Isaac I. Stevens*.

149 **"Americans are going to seize their lands":** Stern, *Chiefs and Change*, 273.

150 **"no land for sale":** A. J. Splawn, *Ka-ma-akin: The Last Hero of the Yakima* (Portland, OR: Kilham, 1917), 22. Scholars do not agree on the timing of this meeting of chiefs. There is some evidence it happened after they met with Stevens. But primary sources from the 1850s—letters and government reports—confirm that before the council with Stevens, many of the Columbia Plateau tribes were jointly preparing for war, if he demanded too much land.

150 **"uprising from every quarter":** Splawn, *Ka-ma-akin*, 22.

150 **"break up the Council":** James Doty, *Journal of Operations of Governor Isaac Ingalls Stevens of Washington Territory in 1855* (Fairfield, WA: Ye Galleon Press, 1978), 24.

150 surround Stevens and kill him: Granville O. Haller, "The Indian War of 1855–56 in Washington and Oregon," Granville O. Haller Papers, Suzzallo Library, University of Washington.

150 "I confidently expect": Stevens to James Doty, May 20, 1855, in Richards, *Isaac I. Stevens*, 200.

150 "plenty of water": Lawrence Kip, *The Indian Council in the Valley of the Walla-Walla, 1855* (San Francisco: Whitton, Towne, 1855), 27–28.

151 within what are now the city limits: "Treaty Council of 1855," Walla Walla 2020 (website), https://ww2020.net/history-websites/walla-walla-treaty-council-of-1855/.

152 smallest possible number of reservations: Kent D. Richards, "The Stevens Treaties of 1854–1855," *Oregon Historical Quarterly* 106, no. 3 (Fall 2005): 343–44.

152 "They were almost entirely naked": Kip, *The Indian Council*, 34–35.

154 they vehemently objected: Stern, *Chiefs and Change*, 244.

156 "unbroken friendship between the two races": Hazard Stevens, *The Life of Isaac Ingalls Stevens* (Boston: Houghton, Mifflin, 1900), 2:60.

156 "armed resistance was folly": Clifford M. Drury, *Chief Lawyer of the Nez Perce, 1796–1876*, Northwest Historical Series (Glendale, CA: Arthur H. Clark, 1979), 287.

156 "Red Judas" or "Uncle Tomahawk": Robert C. Carriker, review of *Chief Lawyer of the Nez Perce Indians, 1796–1876*, by Clifford M. Drury, *Historical Society of Southern California* 62, no. 1 (Spring 1986): 100.

157 "They were in gala dress": Doty, *Journal of Operations*, 26.

157 "in no cordial manner": Doty, *Journal of Operations*, 26.

158 "estimate our powers of resistance": Kip, *Indian Council*, 42.

158 "Nez Perces have evidently profited much": Stevens, *Isaac Ingalls Stevens*, 64.

158 no evidence of Sunday piety: These details come from Kip, *Indian Council*, 44.

158 "The haughty carriage": Stevens, *Isaac Ingalls Stevens*, 38–39.

159 "The Great Father has heard": Doty, *Journal of Operations*, 38.

159 "his red children": Doty, *Journal of Operations*, 39.

161 "for his white children": Doty, *Journal of Operations*, 42.

161 "land was not made for you alone": Doty, *Journal of Operations*, 51–52.

162 "Speak plain to us": Doty, *Journal of Operations*, 57.

163 "Listen to me you chiefs": U.S. Department of the Interior, Bureau of Indian Affairs, Certified Copy of the Original Minutes of the Official Proceedings at the Council in Walla Walla Valley, 1855, National Archives, Washington, D.C. Online at https://www.lib.uidaho.edu/mcbeth/governmentdoc/1855council.htm.

163 "an actual outbreak?": Kip, *Indian Council*, 48.

164 "I shall be sent to hell": Kip, *Indian Council*, 55.

164 "incensed against the Nez Perces": Kip, *Indian Council*, 69.

165 "came up and signed their Treaty": Doty, *Journal of Operations*, 30. There is disagreement between Doty's version of events, other official records, and tribal accounts as to precisely

when chiefs and headmen agreed to the treaty. The Confederated Tribes of the Umatilla Reservation observe treaty day events and celebrate a holiday on June 9, two days before the council at Walla Walla came to a formal end. Some records show that leaders of the Cayuse and Walla Walla tribes agreed to the treaty on June 8, the day Stevens offered them a separate reservation.

CHAPTER ELEVEN: Authentic Account

169 **"never felt at home":** Spalding to Rev. Selah B. Treat, Indian secretary of the American Board, October 1857, in Clifford M. Drury, *Henry Harmon Spalding* (Caldwell, ID: Caxton Printers, 1936), 371.

169 **ached to return:** Drury, *Henry Harmon Spalding*, 371. In the 1857 letter to Treat, Spalding wrote: "I have ever desired to return [to the Nez Perces]. . . . They have sent every year for me to return, have begged to have the mission renewed."

170 **"wholly unfitted in body and mind":** Rev. Elkanah Walker to Treat, December 1857, in Drury, *Henry Harmon Spalding*, 371.

170 **"appears to suffer":** Rev. Cushing Eells to Treat, January 1, 1855, WC Mss 103, Spalding Collection, Box 1, Whitman College Archives.

170 **"heart sickening & bloody butchery":** Spalding, "The Early Labors of Missionaries in Oregon," S. Ex. Doc. No. 41-37 (1871), 42. Spalding also claimed that priests instigated the massacre that claimed the lives of the Whitmans and of his wife, Eliza. Spalding to the American Board, April 22, 1870.

171 **"ought to be hung":** This accusation appeared in a letter from Spalding to Treat, October 14, 1850. It also appeared that year in the *Oregon Spectator*.

171 **"destitute of truth":** Millard Fillmore, letter to the editor, *Philadelphia Sun*, April 6, 1852, quoted in Drury, *Henry Harmon Spalding*, 365.

171 **"He felt it keenly":** Myron Eells, "Dr. Whitman and Oregon," *Morning Oregonian* (Portland), May 21, 1885, 6.

171 **not "sane on any subject":** Asahel Bush, *Weekly Oregon Statesman* (Salem), August 11, 1855, 2.

171 **"conduct of the Catholics":** Spalding to Lorinda Bewley Chapman, March 22, 1866, WC Mss 103, Spalding Collection, Box 4, Whitman College Archives.

172 **Spalding's unmistakable literary fingerprints:** The discovery of this unsigned obituary in the *Boston Recorder*—a reprint of an article in the *Chicago Herald*—was made by Sarah Koenig, during her research for a 2015 doctoral dissertation at Yale. See Sarah Elizabeth Koenig, *The Legend of Marcus Whitman and the Making of American History* (New Haven, CT: Yale University, 2015), 92–94. Koenig notes that the Presbyterian newspaper in Chicago in which the obituary first appeared was edited by college friends of Spalding's from Western Reserve College. She also explains that in 1848 "Spalding was the only surviving companion of Whitman's who had both the knowledge of Whitman's affairs and the connections to the Midwest to influence such an article."

172 **"Dr. Whitman made his last visit":** "Death of Dr. Marcus Whitman," *Boston Recorder*, June 16, 1848. The *Recorder* was a weekly newspaper of the Congregational Church.

172 **leader of the secret Supreme Order:** Henry H. Spalding Record Book, MS File Box 2, Pacific University Archives. The record book contains lists of Preble Wigwam members,

officers, dates of meetings, and locations. It shows that Spalding was a founding member of Preble Wigwam No. 38, organized April 11, 1855. By December of that year, he had become president. It also shows that most of the meetings of the group were at his house.

173 **in nearly every community in Oregon:** Malcolm Clark Jr., *The Eden Seekers* (Boston: Houghton Mifflin, 1981), 272.

173 **Know-Nothings elected eight governors:** Tyler Anbinder, *Nativism and Slavery: The Northern Know Nothings and the Politics of the 1850s* (New York: Oxford University Press, 1992), 1.

173 **"seven previous decades combined":** Anbinder, *Nativism and Slavery,* 3.

174 **most were Roman Catholics:** Anbinder, *Nativism and Slavery,* 8.

174 **steal away the western frontier:** Lyman Beecher, *A Plea for the West* (Cincinnati: Truman and Smith, 1836).

174 **"The Paranoid Style":** Richard Hofstadter, "The Paranoid Style in American Politics," *Harper's Magazine,* November 1964, 77.

175 **nuns behind convent walls:** Hofstadter, "The Paranoid Style," 80–81.

175 **"obey the priests in all things":** Maria Monk, *Awful Disclosures of Maria Monk as Exhibited in a Narrative of Her Sufferings During a Residence of Five Years as a Novice and Two Years as a Black Nun, in the Hotel Dieu Nunnery in Montreal* (London: Truslove and Bray, 1836), https://archive.org/details/awfuldisclosures00monkiala/page/n1.

175 **"probably the most widely read":** Hofstadter, "The Paranoid Style," 80–81.

176 **effectively kept Blacks out:** Greg Nokes, "Black Exclusion Law in Oregon," *Oregon Encyclopedia,* https://oregonencyclopedia.org/articles/exclusion_laws.

176 **whitest of America's big cities:** Among the fifty largest metro areas in the United States, Portland has the lowest percentage of nonwhite residents, according to U.S. Census figures. See "Race and Ethnicity in the United States," Statistical Atlas, https://statisticalatlas.com/United-States/Race-and-Ethnicity.

176 **largest Ku Klux Klan:** See "Brouillet's Account of the Murder of Dr. Whitman," Oregon History Project, https://oregonhistoryproject.org/articles/historical-records/brouillet39s-account-of-the-murder-of-dr-whitman/.

176 **would have shut down all Catholic schools:** Patricia Brandt and Lillian A. Pereyra, *Adapting in Eden: Oregon's Catholic Minority, 1838–1986* (Pullman: Washington State University Press, 2002), 92–93.

176 **declared unconstitutional in 1925:** *Pierce v. Society of Sisters,* 268 U.S. 510 (1925); see http://supreme.justia.com/us/268/510/case.html.

176 **"teacher of the Nez Perce":** Minutes of the Congregational Association of Oregon Annual Meeting, Salem, Oregon, September 1859, 7, Oregon Historical Society.

177 **"great numbers attended Mr. S's preaching":** J. W. Anderson, Indian agent, to Idaho Territory Superintendent of Indian Affairs D. W. Ballard, February 22, 1865, reprinted in Spalding, "Early Labors," 7.

179 **"outrage upon the red man":** Quotations from the generals are in Elliott West, *The Last Indian War* (New York: Oxford University Press, 2009), xv, xvi.

179 **"displayed a courage and skill":** Quoted in "Foreword," Big Hole National Battlefield, Nez Perce National Historical Park, National Park Service, https://www.nps.gov/parkhistory/online_books/nepe/greene/foreword.htm.

179 "I will fight no more forever": Chief Joseph's surrender speech in Report of the Secretary of War, 1877, H. Exec. Doc. 1, pt. 2, 45th Cong., 2nd sess., 630, as cited in West, *The Last Indian War*, 284, 373n2.

179 These eloquent words: See West, *The Last Indian War*, 283–88.

180 cause of death was sorrow: M. Gidley, *Kopet: A Documentary Narrative of Chief Joseph's Last Years* (Seattle: University of Washington Press, 1981), 66–67.

180 O'Neil had sacked Spalding: Spalding to O'Neil, November 17, 1856. In this churlish letter to O'Neil, Spalding asked why he had been dismissed. Letter in Whitman College Archives, reprinted in transcripts compiled by National Park Service ranger Richard J. Laughlin, on file at Penrose Library, Whitman College.

180 "a shameful disgrace": Spalding to Treat, November 15, 1865, letter quoted in Drury, *Henry Harmon Spalding*, 381.

181 "profess the purest principles": Rev. J. B. A. Brouillet, *Authentic Account of the Murder of Dr. Whitman and Other Missionaries by the Cayuse Indians of Oregon in 1847* (Portland, OR: S. J. McCormick, 1869), 3. This slightly revised version of the 1853 "Account of the Murder" is one of ten versions published between 1853 and 1925, according to George N. Belknap's exhaustive paper "Authentic Account of the Murder of Dr. Whitman: The History of a Pamphlet," *Papers of the Bibliographic Society of America* 55, no. 4 (1961): 319–46.

182 the U.S. Congress printed: H.R. Ex. Doc. No. 38, 35th Congress, 1st Session, 13–63, ordered printed January 25, 1858, 38; S. Exec. Doc. No. 40, 35th Congress, 1st Seassion, 13–64, ordered printed March 31, 1858.

182 "moved on by religious fanaticism": Brouillet, *Authentic Account*, 18.

182 "Mr. Spalding's memory": Brouillet, *Authentic Account*, 86.

182 "violent religious prejudices": Brouillet, *Authentic Account*, 91.

184 Spalding wrote it immediately: The letter was discovered and published in 1932. See Nellie B. Pipes, "Spalding Mission, 1843," *Oregon Historical Quarterly* 33, no. 4 (December 1932): 348–54.

184 "the consent of the board": Pipes, "Spalding Mission," 351.

CHAPTER TWELVE: Collaborate

186 "It kept us up late": E. Ruth Rockford, ed., "Diary of Rev. George H. Atkinson, D.D. 1847–1858 (Part III)," *Oregon Historical Quarterly* 40, no. 3 (September 1939): 270.

186 "urged him to write": Rockford, "Diary of Rev. George H. Atkinson," 271.

188 "future society is to be built": Atkinson to Spalding, December 10, 1849, WC Mss 103, Spalding Collection, Box 1, Whitman College Archives. Misdated in archive as having been written in 1832.

188 "burnishing of your armor": Atkinson to Spalding, January 12, 1851, WC Mss 103, Spalding Collection, Box 3, Whitman College Archives.

188 help secure his back pay: Atkinson to Spalding, May 24, 1851, WC Mss 103, Spalding Collection, Box 3, Whitman College Archives.

188 trust Atkinson's judgment: Spalding to Atkinson, September 1855, WC Mss 103, Spalding Collection, Box 3, Whitman College Archives.

188 "tremendous tirade of abuse": Spalding to Atkinson, October 27, 1855, WC Mss 103, Spalding Collection, Box 3, Whitman College Archives.

189 "great historical fact": Atkinson to Myron Eells, March 19, 1885, in *Morning Oregonian*, May 21, 1885, 6.

189 "rats and mice got in": Atkinson to Myron Eells, March 19, 1885, in *Morning Oregonian*, May 21, 1885, 6.

189 "saved Oregon to American interests": Atkinson to the American Board, November 20, 1858, quoted in William I. Marshall, *Acquisition of Oregon* (Seattle: Lowman and Hanford, 1911), 2:47.

191 "diligent and self-denying laborer": *Missionary Herald*, July 1848, 237.

191 "business of the mission": *Missionary Herald*, July 1848, 237. Four years before Whitman's murder, the *Herald* also wrote that his trip east was on missionary business. *Missionary Herald*, September 1843.

191 it made no mention of him: See Marshall, *Acquisition of Oregon*, 2:195–97. Marshall's exhaustive deconstruction of the Whitman legend unearthed these insights into the American Board's initial attitude toward Whitman.

192 Atkinson was the paper's Oregon editor: Spalding addresses a long letter in 1866 to "Rev. G. H. Atkinson, Oregon Editor of the Pacific." See Spalding to Atkinson, December 1, 1866, WC Mss 103, Spalding Collection, Box 3, Whitman College Archives.

193 "legs badly frozen": Spalding, *The Pacific*, October 19, 1865.

193 Spalding's own diary: Clifford M. Drury, ed., *The Diaries and Letters of Henry H. Spalding and Asa Bowen Smith* (Glendale, CA: Arthur H. Clark, 1958), 322. The diary of another missionary, Elkanah Walker, also confirms 1841 as the year the settlers arrived. See Marshall, *Acquisition of Oregon*, 2:85.

193 letter written by Whitman: Marcus Whitman to Greene, November 11, 1841.

194 "The great desire": Spalding, *The Pacific*, November 9, 1865.

195 Spalding sought a wider secular audience: Spalding to Victor, June 4, 1865, WC Mss 103, Spalding Collection, Box 4, Whitman College Archives.

195 "While East in 1865": Atkinson to Myron Eells, March 19, 1885, published in *Morning Oregonian*, May 21, 1885, 6.

196 "prejudice against the Jesuits": Atkinson to Eells, March 19, 1885.

196 "You can all rely upon him": Atkinson to Eells, March 19, 1885.

197 "Mr. Spalding is especially wanting": Eells to Treat, January 6, 1855, WC Mss 33, Box 1, Whitman College Archives.

197 regarded as "perfectly reliable": *Missionary Herald*, December 1866.

197 Eells was living in Walla Walla: G. Thomas Edwards, *The Triumph of Tradition* (Walla Walla, WA: Whitman College Press, 1992) 15–17.

197 "The single object of Dr. Whitman": Eells to Treat, May 28, 1866. The letter was reprinted in the *Missionary Herald*, December 1866.

198 Eells knew that Whitman: For two discussions of the evidence of Eells's mendacity, see Marshall, *Acquisition of Oregon*, 2:92, and Clifford M. Drury, *Marcus and Narcissa Whitman and the Opening of Old Oregon* (Seattle: Pacific Northwest National Parks and Forests Association, 1986), 2:464–66. The resolution Eells signed said that Whitman visited "the

United States as soon as practicable to confer with the Committee of the A.B.C.F.M. in regard to the interest of the mission."

198 "I have been an eye": Eells to Treat, May 28, 1866.

198 deeming it "entirely trustworthy": "Results of the Oregon Mission," *Missionary Herald*, December 1866, 370.

199 "It was not simply an American question": "Results of the Oregon Mission," 374.

199 "excited a great deal of interest": Treat to Eells, November 15, 1866, WC Mss 33, Box 1, Whitman College Archives.

199 "I will believe you": Atkinson, "Fruit of the Mission," *Missionary Herald*, March 1869, 79.

200 "gifts of a grateful people": Atkinson, "Fruit of the Mission," 82. Italics in original.

200 "benevolent may wish to bestow": Atkinson, "Fruit of the Mission," 82.

200 "for their exclusive use": "Treaty with the Walla Walla, Cayuse, Etc.," 1855, in James Doty, *Journal of Operations of Governor Isaac Ingalls Stevens of Washington Territory in 1855* (Fairfield, WA: Ye Galleon Press, 1978), 93.

200 "are being constantly annoyed": William H. Barnhart, U.S. Indian agent, Umatilla Indian Agency, July 25, 1868, in *Report of the Commissioner of Indian Affairs for the Year 1868* (Washington, D.C.: Government Printing Office, 1868), 114.

201 "great thoroughfare from all Oregon": J. W. Perit Huntington, Report on Umatilla Agency, August 20, 1867, in *Report of the Commissioner of Indian Affairs for the Year 1867* (Washington, D.C.: Government Printing Office, 1867), 67–68.

201 White neighbors grumbled: Robert H. Ruby and John A. Brown, *The Cayuse Indians: Imperial Tribesmen of Old Oregon* (Norman: University of Oklahoma Press, 1972), 267–68; also see Barnhart, *Report of the Commissioner of Indian Affairs*, and Huntington, Report on Umatilla Agency.

203 "welcome to use": Spalding to Gray, August 25, 1865, WC Mss 103, Spalding Collection, Box 4, Whitman College Archives.

203 seven chapters of a book: William H. Gray, *A History of Oregon, 1792–1849, Drawn from Personal Observation and Authentic Information* (Portland, OR: H. H. Bancroft, 1870).

203 "the most mendacious missionary": Hubert Howe Bancroft, *History of Oregon* (San Francisco: History Co., 1886), 1:196n16.

204 "his utter abhorrence of the Roman Catholic": Quoted in Malcom Clark Jr., "The Bigot Disclosed: 90 Years of Nativism," *Oregon Historical Quarterly* 75, no. 21 (June 1974): 122.

CHAPTER THIRTEEN: Brother Spalding Goes to Washington

206 "fearful power of this Romish": Spalding to *Missionary Herald*, April 22, 1870.

206 "throng the Indian country": Spalding to *Missionary Herald*, April 22, 1870.

206 "the murdering priest": Spalding to *Missionary Herald*, April 22, 1870.

206 publish his "manifesto": Spalding often used the word "manifesto" to describe his grab bag of claims, newspaper articles, testimonials, and endorsements. See Spalding, "The Early Labors of Missionaries in Oregon," S. Exec. Doc. No. 41-37 (1871), 43.

207   "the same kind of insanity": "Spalding's Lectures," *Albany Democrat* (Oregon), November 23, 1867, 2.

207   western edge of the American experience: Henry Harmon Spalding portrait, ca. 1860s, carte-de-visite albumen print, 2.5 x 4 in., Pacific University Archives.

208   "foul and libelous slanders": Spalding, "Early Labors," 49, 69.

208   "truthful history of the whole matter": Spalding, "Early Labors," 68.

208   "justice and patriotism of our request": Spalding, "Early Labors," 45.

209   "greatly to the benefit of Oregon": Spalding, "Early Labors," 23.

210   when it published Brouillet's writings: *Journal of the Senate Proceedings of the Legislative Assembly of Oregon*, Salem, OR., October 12, 1870, 373–78, HathiTrust Digital Library, https://hdl.handle.net/2027/njp.32101079832562?urlappend=%3Bseq=379.

210   "indefinitely postpone" any endorsement: *Journal of the Senate Proceedings*, 384.

211   "he would be in no fit state": Amelia Spalding Brown to Rachel Smith Spalding, October 26, 1870, Oregon Historical Society.

211   "a man of humble appearance": S. L. Humphrey, "An Evening with an Old Missionary," *Advance* (Chicago), December 1, 1870.

212   "unbounded sympathy & tender care": Spalding to Rachel Spalding, December 8, 1870, Spalding Collection, Oregon Historical Society. Details about his reception in upstate New York from Clifford M. Drury, *Henry Harmon Spalding* (Caldwell, ID: Caxton Printers, 1936), 338–91.

212   "wipe out this stain": Spalding, "Early Labors," 43.

213   promised his full cooperation: Drury, *Henry Harmon Spalding*, 390.

214   "the religion of our blessed Saviour": Quoted in Elliott West, *The Last Indian War* (New York: Oxford University Press, 2009), 103n19, citing "Report of Board of Indian Commissioners," in *Report of the Secretary of the Interior*, 1869.

214   religious takeover of reservation life: See Francis Paul Prucha, *The Great Father: The United States and the American Indians* (Lincoln: University of Nebraska Press, 1984). Also, Sarah Elizabeth Koenig, *The Legend of Marcus Whitman and the Making of American History* (New Haven, CT: Yale University, 2015), 117–19; and West, *The Last Indian War*, 100–105.

214   "oldest living Protestant missionary": Spalding, "Early Labors," 2.

214   early labors of missionaries: *Journal of the Senate of the United States*, 41st Congress, 3rd session, vol. 65 (Washington, D.C.: Government Printing Office, 1871), February 2, 1871, 205. Online at "A Century of Lawmaking for a New Nation: U.S. Congressional Documents and Debates, 1774–1875," American Memory, Library of Congress, https://memory.loc.gov.

214   promptly forwarded to the Senate: Parker to Department of the Interior, February 6, 1871, in Spalding, "Early Labors," 2.

215   write a long letter: In a letter to his wife, Spalding mentioned that Reverend Smith had written "a wonderful letter in commendation of my services as a missionary in the West and in defense of the truth. It will doubtless go to the Evangelist." Spalding to Rachel Spalding, February 12, 1871, WC Mss 103, Box 5, Spalding Collection, Whitman College Archives.

215 "his meek and quiet spirit": Quoted in Drury, *Henry Harmon Spalding*, 393.

215 "flat-footed contradictions": William I. Marshall, *Acquisition of Oregon* (Seattle: Lowman and Hanford, 1911), 2:172.

216 dealers of snuff and cigars: *Journal of the Senate of the United States*, February 9, 1871, 250.

216 "Dearest Wife: Glory to God": Spalding to Rachel Spalding, February 9, 1871, Spalding Collection, Oregon Historical Society.

217 "truth over calumnies": Spalding to Rachel Spalding, February 13, 1871, WC Mss 103, Box 5, Whitman College Archives.

218 his third involuntary departure: The details of Spalding's final employment at the reservation are carefully explained in Drury, *Henry Harmon Spalding*, 398–402.

218 "His work in Christianizing": Alvin M. Josephy, *The Nez Perce Indians and the Opening of the Northwest* (New Haven, CT: Yale University Press, 1965), 433.

219 Atkinson had been challenged: Atkinson to Spalding, March 17, 1873, WC Mss 103, Spalding Collection, Box 7, Whitman College Archives. The historian who doubted the report was Elwood Evans, a Washington State judge and historian who was among the first to use documentary evidence to challenge the Whitman myth.

219 contributed a testimonial to Spalding's manifesto: The statement by Evans appears in Spalding's manifesto under the headline "Whitman Not An Hour Too Soon—Hon. Elwood Evans's Testimony". In the text of the statement, Evans wrote, "There is no doubt that the arrival of Dr. Whitman [in Washington, D.C.] was opportune. The President was satisfied that the Territory was worth the effort to save it." See Spalding, "Early Labors," 23.

219 "systematic deception by ministers": Elwood Evans to William I. Marshall, August 11, 1882, Special Collections 4213, Box 2, Folder 6, University of Washington.

219 "What was Dr. Whitman's statement": Atkinson to Spalding, March 17, 1873.

220 renamed them Marcus and Narcissa Whitman: Drury, *Henry Harmon Spalding*, 415.

220 "Dr. Whitman's errand": Horace E. Scudder, *History of the United States* (Philadelphia: J. H. Butler, 1884), 348–50. Scudder changed later editions of his textbooks after learning of Spalding's lies.

220 "determined to save Oregon": Horace E. Scudder, *A Short History of the United States of America: For the Use of Beginners* (New York: Taintor Brothers, 1890), 200–201.

221 many other standard history texts: John Bach McMaster, *A School History of the United States* (New York: American Book, 1897), 322–24; D. H. Montgomery, *The Leading Facts of American History* (Boston: Ginn, 1896), 257–58; Allen C. Thomas, *Elementary History of the United States* (Boston: Heath, 1901), 290–98. In later editions of these books, after Spalding's story had been discredited, credulous accounts of Whitman's ride were changed or deleted.

221 regular fixture in Sunday schools: James G. Craigshead, *Story of Marcus Whitman* (Philadelphia: Presbyterian Board of Publication, 1895).

221 The story even appeared: *Encyclopaedia Britannica* (New York: Charles Scribner's Sons, 1884), s.v. "Oregon," 17:825.

221 "the finest in Oregon": E. J. Sommerville, Umatilla Agency Report, August 7, 1884, in *Report of the Commissioner for Indian Affairs for the Year 1884* (Washington, D.C.: Government Printing Office, 1884), 147.

222 killed "without cause": Sommerville, Umatilla Agency Report, 148–49.

222 A white jury acquitted: After the acquittal, in an early signal of the federal intervention that would help the tribes on the reservation in the twentieth century, a federal judge in Portland ruled that the U.S. government had jurisdiction over all crimes committed on an Indian reservation "by a white man on the property or person of an Indian." Barnhart and Anderson were then tried for manslaughter under federal law. See "An Important Decision," *Morning Astorian,* December 13, 1884, 4; *U.S. v. Barnhart,* 22 F. 285 (U.S.C.C. Or., 1884).

CHAPTER FOURTEEN: The Old College Lie

225 "no one seemed to believe": Stephen B. L. Penrose, *Whitman, An Unfinished Story* (Walla Walla, WA: Whitman Publishing, 1935), 144. Details about the school's financial problems, the failed presidency of James Eaton, and the rise of Penrose are taken from this book and from an authorized history of the college by G. Thomas Edwards, *The Triumph of Tradition* (Walla Walla, WA: Whitman College Press, 1992).

226 Penrose had excelled at Williams: The founder of Whitman, the Reverend Cushing Eells, was a Williams graduate, and from the beginning he tried to model the college after his alma mater.

226 a good college education: Penrose, *Whitman,* 144.

226 he stumbled upon: Penrose, *Whitman,* 145.

227 to give money to Whitman College: Penrose, *Whitman,* 145.

227 never raising more: Edwards, *The Triumph of Tradition,* 62.

227 "sorry that it ever appeared": Quoted in William I. Marshall, *Acquisition of Oregon* (Seattle: Lowman and Hanford, 1911), 2:339.

228 "grotesque distortion of the real facts": Edward G. Bourne, letter to the editor, *New York Times Saturday Review of Books,* February 22, 1902.

228 "inspiring story of pioneer devotion": Penrose, *Whitman,* 145.

228 "*hero enough to risk his life*": Stephen Penrose, *The Romance of a College,* pamphlet printed by Whitman College, 1894, WCA142, College Publication Collection, Whitman College Archives.

230 "then you do the talking": This account is from Penrose, *Whitman,* 147.

230 He became rich: Edward Franklin Williams, *The Life of Dr. D. K. Pearsons: Friend of the Small College and of Missions* (Chicago: Pilgrim Press, 1911), 44–45.

231 "seemed absurd under the circumstances": Penrose, *Whitman,* 145.

231 "a fatherly interest": Penrose, *Whitman,* 147.

232 "I'll lend you the money": Penrose, *Whitman,* 148.

232 forgave the entire debt: Williams, *The Life of Dr. D. K. Pearsons,* 202–3.

232 ranked his greatness: "Honor a Dead Hero: Services in Memory of Marcus Whitman," *Chicago Tribune,* June 29, 1895, 3.

232 To kick off the patriotic program: The account of the service at South Congregational Church is from "His Name Is Honored: Tributes to Marcus Whitman, the Hero of

Oregon, Story of a Patriot, Special Sermons in Many Congregational Churches," *Inter Ocean* (Chicago), July 1, 1895, 1.

234 "'the flag of the country they loved'": "His Name Is Honored," 10.

234 "under his helpful and practical wings": "The Whitman College Memorial," editorial, *Chicago Tribune*, February 2, 1895, 12.

235 "Nixon had but one": "Death of O. W. Nixon," *Whitman College Pioneer*, May 17, 1905, 1.

235 "in touch with the spirit of history": Oliver Woodson Nixon, *How Marcus Whitman Saved Oregon* (Chicago: Star, 1895), 5.

235 "depend on what was in the books": *A History of the City of Chicago* (Chicago: Inter Ocean, 1900), 324.

236 "unless I am authority": Nixon, *How Marcus Whitman Saved Oregon*, 5.

236 "years after they have rested": Oliver W. Nixon, "Neglected Hero," editorial, *Inter Ocean* (Chicago), November 29, 1895, 6.

237 "it is still being quoted": Clifford M. Drury, *Marcus and Narcissa Whitman and the Opening of Old Oregon* (Seattle: Pacific Northwest National Parks and Forests Association, 1986), 2:384.

237 format on Amazon: See https://www.amazon.com/How-Marcus-Whitman-Saved-Oregon/dp/1417965320, accessed July 12, 2020; https://www.amazon.com/Whitman-Patriotic-Christian-Devotion-Martyrdom/dp/1318067073.

237 "It was like a giant virus": Michael Paulus, interview with the author, Seattle, June 2018.

237 "most exciting of borderland romances": "New Literature," *Boston Globe*, August 24, 1896, 6.

237 "a triumph of show business": Joy S. Kasson, *Buffalo Bill's Wild West: Celebrity, Memory, and Popular History* (New York: Hill and Wang, 2000), 94. I rely on Kasson's book for details of the Wild West show in Chicago in 1893, and for the Columbia Exhibition in that city in the same year.

238 "great realism and thrilling effect": "Buffalo Bill's Wild West," *Inter Ocean* (Chicago), October 15, 1893, 29.

238 "talk Whitman, preach Whitman": *Walla Walla Union*, May 26, 1895, cited in Edwards, *The Triumph of Tradition*, 153.

239 "worthless and misleading book": Marshall, *Acquisition of Oregon*, 2:326.

239 "utterly untrustworthy as history": Edward Gaylord Bourne, *Essays in Historical Criticism* (New York: Charles Scribner's Sons, 1901), 47.

239 "noble-minded man": "Honor to Whom Honor Is Due," *Whitman College Quarterly* 1, no. 1 (1897).

240 "carried the audience by storm": "Pres. Penrose Address: Thrilling Account of Marcus Whitman's Famous Ride," *Worcester Daily Spy* (MA), April 21, 1896, 1.

240 "only college in a region": By 1896, the list of Northwest colleges included the University of Washington, Washington State University, the University of Oregon, Oregon State University, Gonzaga University, Willamette University, Pacific University, Seattle University, and Whitworth University.

240 glad to accept contributions: *Worcester Daily Spy* (MA), April 21, 1896, 1.

CHAPTER FIFTEEN: Skulls, Bones, Money

243 **well-preserved, nearly intact human skulls:** Penrose's bone-digging outing is described in the Whitman student newspaper: "The Whitman Remains," *Whitman College Pioneer*, November 1, 1897, 5–6; also in "Whitman's Bones: Relics of an Indian Massacre Fifty Years Ago," Associated Press Night Report, October 21, 1897; "At Whitman's Grave," *Walla Walla Union*, reprinted in *The Oregonian*, October 25, 1897, 3.

244 **"I felt it was Dr. Whitman":** Matilda Sager Delaney, *A Survivor's Recollection of the Whitman Massacre* (Spokane, WA: Esther Reed Chapter Daughters of the American Revolution, 1920), 45.

244 **bones soon found their way:** "Whitman's Bones," *Los Angeles Times*, October 22, 1897, 3; "Dug Up Their Bones," *Topeka State Journal*, October 23, 1897, 8; "Bones of Dr. Marcus Whitman, Killed by Indians 50 Years Ago," *Akron Beacon Journal*, November 1, 1897, 7.

245 **"showing no trace of gray":** Stephen Penrose, "College Notes," *Whitman College Quarterly* 1, no. 3 (October 1897): 32.

245 **"those miserable Cayuse fiends":** Edmond Stephen Meany, "In Memory of Marcus Whitman and Narcissa, His Wife," *Seattle Post-Intelligencer*, November 21, 1897, 24.

246 **"epoch-making in our country's history":** Text of Hallock's speech is in *Whitman College Quarterly* 1, no. 4 (December 1897): 4–28.

246 **festooned with flags:** "Grave of Martyrs: Memorial Exercises in Honor of the Whitman Massacre Anniversary," *Spokesman-Review* (Spokane, WA), December 1, 1897, 1.

246 **maximize the number of people:** Many of the details of the memorial exercises come from Meany, "In Memory of Marcus Whitman"; "Grave of Martyrs," *Spokesman-Review;* and G. Thomas Edwards, *The Triumph of Tradition* (Walla Walla, WA: Whitman College Press, 1992), 164–69.

247 **"deep regret to all":** Penrose, *Whitman College Quarterly* 1, no. 4 (December 1897): 54.

247 **"their royal entertainment":** *Whitman College Quarterly* 1, no. 4 (December 1897): 30–31.

248 **"a going institution":** Stephen B. L. Penrose, *Whitman, An Unfinished Story* (Walla Walla, WA: Whitman Publishing, 1935), 153.

248 **"would surely have perished":** Robert L. Whitner, "The Myth That Saved the College," address at Whitman College, February 16, 1982.

248 **the purchase of Alaska:** "In Memory of Dr. Whitman," *Washington Times*, November 29, 1897, 2.

248 **Whitman was the first to discover:** "Dr. Marcus Whitman," *The Outlook*, v. 57, December 4, 1897, 879, HathiTrust Digital Library, https://hdl.handle.net/2027/iau .31858033604038?urlappend=%3Bseq=885.

249 **"sudden luster beginning to glow":** "Whitman's Grave No Longer Unkempt," *Seattle Post-Intelligencer*, December 1, 1897, 1.

249 **"the brave and patriotic Dr. Marcus Whitman":** "How Oregon Was Saved," *New York Times*, November 29, 1897, column 1, 5.

249 **in the book pages of the *Times* itself:** "Books Received," *New York Times*, November 1, 1886, 2.

249 **save his job, not his country:** Hubert Howe Bancroft, *History of Oregon* (San Francisco: History Co., 1886), 1:340–45.

250 "untimely and pathetic fate": "Whitman Once More," *The Oregonian,* June 27, 1897. Frances Victor, in her letters, said she was a major influence on *The Oregonian's* skeptical editorial policy on the Whitman legend.

250 "patriotic martyrs of Oregon": George Ludington Weed, "When Dr. Whitman Added Three Stars to Our Flag," *Ladies' Home Journal,* November 1897, 9–11.

250 ahead of Meriwether Lewis: Henry Mitchell MacCracken, *The Hall of Fame: Being the Official Book Authorized by the New York University Senate as a Statement of the Origin and Constitution of the Hall of Fame, and of Its History Up to the Close of the Year, 1900* (New York: Knickerbocker, 1901), 58.

251 "seedy appearance": Edwards, *The Triumph of Tradition,* 510.

251 some of the money: Edwards, *The Triumph of Tradition,* 510.

251 "truth, justice, and American honor": *New Haven Evening Register,* February 19, 1901, quoted in Edward Gaylord Bourne, *Essays in Historical Criticism* (New York: Charles Scribner's Sons, 1901), 54.

251 "taken from their churches": Penrose, undated letter, ca. 1898, in Stephen B. L. Penrose Papers, WCA 38, Box 5 (Virginia Dox letters), Whitman College Archives.

252 Dox collected more cash: The official Whitman College history says she raised at least $100,000. Edwards, *The Triumph of Tradition,* 508. Obituaries in the *Hartford Courant* and *The New York Times* say she raised $250,000. *Hartford Courant,* February 15, 1941; *New York Times,* February 15, 1941, 15.

252 from ten to ten thousand: *Whitman College Quarterly* 3, no. 4, (December 1899): 17.

252 her adventures as a young missionary: "Ten Years with the Indians: Miss Virginia Dox Tells an Interesting Story of Her Work in the West," *News-Palladium* (Benton Harbor, MI), August 3, 1896, 3.

253 that Dox become financial agent: Penrose, *Whitman,* 148.

253 "It is faint praise to say": Penrose, *Whitman,* 150.

253 beaten an Indian child to death: Obituary, *New York Times,* February 15, 1941.

253 raise money for other missionaries: Edmund Lyman Hood, *The New West Education Commission, 1880–1893* (Jacksonville, FL: H. and W. B. Drew, 1905), 50.

253 "No other college": Dox to Penrose, May 18, 1906, Penrose Papers, WCA 38, Box 5 (Virginia Dox letters).

253 passion, conviction, and wit: *Hartford Courant,* February 15, 1941.

254 "this royal woman": "Miss Virginia Dox," *Inter Ocean* (Chicago), September 19, 1896, 3.

254 "He thinks I am a very wonderful woman": Dox to Penrose, March 26, 1898, Penrose Papers, WCA 38, Box 5 (Virginia Dox letters).

255 "ought to be behind bars": Dox to Penrose, March 3, 1898, Penrose Papers, WCA 38, Box 4 (Virginia Dox letters).

255 "I go from house to house": Dox to Penrose, July 4, 1898, Penrose Papers, WC 38, Box 4 (Virginia Dox letters).

255 "bitter and cruel things he said": Dox to Penrose, July 27, 1897, Penrose Papers, WC 38, Box 4 (Virginia Dox letters).

256 "a dreadful article": Dox to Penrose, January 9, 1901, Penrose Papers, WC 38, Box 4 (Virginia Dox letters).

CHAPTER SIXTEEN: "A Defenseless Little Western Institution"

258 **"more on the testimony of surviving witnesses":** Penrose to Bourne, December 15, 1900, Group 96, Series II, Box 12, Folder 100, E. G. Bourne Papers, Yale University Manuscripts and Archives.

258 **and utterly debunked:** See Joseph Rodman, "The Hatchet and the Cherry Tree," *The Critic* 44 (February 1904): 116.

258 **the story had been validated:** This point is made in F. H. Hodder, "The Marcus Whitman Legend," *The Dial*, January 16, 1902, 40–43. Hodder writes, "Everyone thinks he knows how Dr. Whitman undertook a perilous journey. . . . The various versions of this story differ in detail, but the burden of them all is that Whitman saved Oregon."

259 **"one of the most indefatigable old frauds":** Bourne to J. Franklin Jameson, editor of *The American Historical Review*, November 16, 1900, Group 96, Series II, Box 12, Folder 99, Bourne Papers.

259 **"I feel very well satisfied":** Bourne, diary entry, November 17, 1900, Group 96, Series II, Box 12, Folder 99, Bourne Papers.

259 **"More inaccurate invention":** Bourne to Jameson, November 17, 1900, Group 96, Series II, Box 12, Folder 99, Bourne Papers.

260 **"he liked to argue":** James Ford Rhodes, "Tribute to Edward Gaylord Bourne," *Proceedings of the Massachusetts Historical Society* 41 (1907–1908): 405. The description of Bourne's tuberculosis and his character come from Rhodes's obituary and from an obituary in the *Proceedings of the American Antiquarian Society* 19, no. 1 (April 1908): 18–20.

260 **traced to the *Mayflower*:** Bourne obituary, *Proceedings of the American Antiquarian Society* 19, no. 1 (April 1908): 18–20.

260 **little more than a "publicity stunt":** Henry E. Bourne, brother of Edward, in an undated document, Group 96, Series II, Box 12, Folder 99, Bourne Papers. Henry Bourne had access to his brother's diary and letters. He also quotes from a letter he received from Hutchinson describing the focus of his Whitman research.

261 **did not trust the student's research:** Henry E. Bourne, Bourne Papers.

261 **a "well-invented romance":** Frances Fuller Victor, "Did Dr. Whitman Save Oregon?," *Californian* 2, no. 9 (September 1880): 229–33.

261 **"ever have been raised but for me":** Victor to Bourne, May 21, 1901, Group 96, Series II, Box 12, Folder 101, 17, Bourne Papers.

262 **"I discovered so much falsehood":** Victor to Bourne, August 21, 1901, Group 96, Series II, Box 12, Folder 101, Bourne Papers. Victor continued to write long letters to Bourne after he published his paper in *The American Historical Review*. Bourne developed that paper into a longer essay published as *Essays in Historical Criticism* (New York: Charles Scribner's Sons, 1901). Bourne also thanked Victor in his paper for her scholarship and integrity. In a long footnote, he wrote, "It is but justice to say that Mrs. Victor enjoys the lonely distinction of being the only writer, so far as I know, who, having once published the legend, upon a more careful study of the evidence has had the open-mindedness to see and declare its legendary character." Bourne, "The Legend of Marcus Whitman," *American Historical Review* 6, no. 2 (January 1901): 288n1.

262 **"products of fancy develop":** Bourne, "The Legend," 276

262 "not only fictitious but impossible": Bourne, "The Legend," 287.

263 "will have to be torn out": "Marcus Whitman and His Great Ride: American Historical Society Makes an Exposure," *Los Angeles Times*, December 29, 1900, 4.

263 "almost from the start": *New York Tribune*, December 31, 1900, 6.

263 newspaper did not issue a correction: "Marcus Whitman," *New York Times*, January 5, 1901, 20.

264 "very critical and most exact": "The Legend of Marcus Whitman: Founded on Anti-Catholic Hatred," *American Catholic Historical Researches* 18, no. 2 (April 1901): 56–59.

264 "They can't hurt us": Nixon to Penrose, December 13, 1900, Stephen B. L. Penrose Papers, WCA 38, Box 9, Folder 6, Whitman College Archives. In this letter, Nixon quotes the remarks of his friend Pearsons.

264 "nothing they can do": Nixon to Penrose, December 5, 1900, Penrose Papers, WCA 38, Box 9, Folder 6.

264 "ignorant of or suppresses essential facts": Bourne, "The Legend," 276n1.

264 "Let us die with our armor on": Nixon to Myron Eells, December 31, 1900, Penrose Papers, WCA 38, Box 9, Folder 6.

265 "one can see the learned professor": Nixon, *Inter Ocean* (Chicago), January 21, 1901, 6.

265 "you will live to regret": Nixon to Bourne, January 8, 1901, Group 96, Series II, Box 12, Folder 99, Bourne Papers.

265 "grandest heroes who have lived": Nixon to Bourne, January 14, 1901, Group 96, Series II, Box 12, Folder 99, Bourne Papers.

265 "I am glad he has done so": "A Denial Is Made: Scholars Disagree Concerning Whitman's Ride," *Spokesman-Review* (Spokane, WA), January 2, 1901, 10.

265 "done much to hurt your work": Dox to Penrose, May 18, 1901, Penrose Papers, WCA 38, Box 4 (Virginia Dox letters).

266 "truth will in the end prevail": Penrose to Dox, May 24, 1901, Penrose Papers, WCA 38, Box 4 (Virginia Dox letters).

266 "attack a defenseless": Penrose to Bourne, January 26, 1901, Penrose Papers, WCA 38, Box 9, Folder 6.

266 "necessary to go outside of scientific": Myron Eells, *Reply to Professor Bourne's "Legend of Marcus Whitman"* (Walla Walla, WA: Statesman, 1902), 37.

267 a spiritual threat from Bourne: See *Homiletic Review*, July 1901, 21. For a much broader examination of this concern about Bourne's paper, see also Sarah Elizabeth Koenig, *The Legend of Marcus Whitman and the Making of American History* (New Haven, CT: Yale University, 2015), 270–80.

267 "moral incapacity" in Bourne: William Livingston Alden, "Assails Dr. Whitman's Fame," *Chicago Tribune*, November 18, 1901, 13.

267 "they turn to denying": Alden, "Assails Dr. Whitman's Fame."

267 "the only complete account in print": Advertisement for "Essays in Historical Criticism," *New York Times*, December 14, 1901, 36.

267 "is beyond dispute": Bourne, *Essays in Historical Criticism*, 100.

CHAPTER SEVENTEEN: Mephistopheles and the Original Sources

269 "far from being a wise": William I. Marshall, *Acquisition of Oregon* (Seattle: Lowman and Hanford, 1911), 1:17.

269 "third or fourth rate": William I. Marshall, "Marcus Whitman: A Discussion of Professor Bourne's Paper," paper delivered at the meeting of the American Historical Association, December 28, 1900, Ann Arbor, Michigan, after Bourne delivered his paper. *Annual Report of the American Historical Association for 1900* (Washington, D.C.: Government Printing Office, 1901), 232.

270 "utterly annihilate" their reputations: Marshall, *Acquisition of Oregon*, 1:56.

270 "extract pennies from Sunday school children": Marshall, *Acquisition of Oregon*, 2:338.

270 "constitutional & persistent liar": Marshall to William Mowry, June 20, 1887, Collection 4213, Box 2, Folder 6, William I. Marshall Papers, Special Collections, University of Washington.

270 dreaded and loathed Marshall: Nixon to Bourne, January 1901.

271 a successful living as a lecturer: These details come from a biographical sketch of Marshall written by his widow, Ellen Foster Marshall, in Chicago in 1909. Marshall, *Acquisition of Oregon*, 1:23–24.

271 "substantially true" when he first heard it: Details on the evolution of Marshall's thinking about the Whitman legend come from his letters, his principal book on the subject, *Acquisition of Oregon*, and published articles. The most detailed of the letters is Marshall to George H. Himes, August 24, 1888, Collection 4213, Box 2, Folder 4, William I. Marshall Papers, Special Collections, University of Washington. Marshall also mentioned some of this in "Marcus Whitman: A Discussion of Professor Bourne's Paper."

271 "I saw in it the material": Marshall to Himes, August 24, 1888.

272 "very great doubt" about the story: Marshall, *Acquisition of Oregon*, 1:10.

272 "no truth in the story": Marshall, *Acquisition of Oregon*, 1:10.

272 took it for granted that their lies: Evans to Marshall, August 11, 1882, Box 1, Folder 6, Marshall Papers.

273 "undertaken solely on missionary business": Marshall, *Acquisition of Oregon*, 1:11.

274 "Jack the Giant Killer": Marshall to Himes, August 24, 1888.

274 Nothing came of the offer: Marshall later learned that the then-president of the American Historical Association, William F. Poole, had personal reasons for not publishing Marshall's criticism of the Whitman legend. Poole had previously published an article under his name in the *Dial* magazine that endorsed the legend as historically correct. See Marshall, *Acquisition of Oregon*, 2:341–42.

275 "even tenor of the true historian": Leslie M. Scott, "Whitman Myth Exploded in Marshall's Exhaustive Book," *The Oregonian*, December 3, 1911, 45.

275 six times to look at documents: Marshall, *Acquisition of Oregon*, 1:65.

276 "its total falsity exposed": Marshall, *Acquisition of Oregon*, 2:342.

277 "I was sneered at": Marshall, *Acquisition of Oregon*, 2:342.

277 based it entirely on Marshall's research: William Marshall, "Marshall Attacks Story of Whitman," letter to the editor, *Inter Ocean* (Chicago), January 19, 1902, 12.

277 "Protestant gentleman for all these documents": The text is quoted by Oliver Nixon in a letter he wrote to Bourne. Nixon to Bourne, January 14, 1901, E. G. Bourne Papers, Yale University Manuscripts and Archives.

277 He was invited to address: *Chicago Tribune*, May 22, 1898, 2; *Inter Ocean* (Chicago), January 19, 1902, 12.

278 "not contain the name of Marcus Whitman": Marshall, "A Discussion of Professor Bourne's Paper," 229.

279 "a little swearing at the enemy": Marshall, "A Discussion of Professor Bourne's Paper," 230.

279 Bad blood between the two men: Nixon to Bourne, January 14, 1901.

279 "Our man Marshall": Nixon to Penrose, December 5, 1900.

279 "claims to annihilate the myth": Nixon to Penrose, December 13, 1900.

279 lies of Spalding: Marshall, "A Discussion of Professor Bourne's Paper," 235.

279 "Marshall was not there by accident": Oliver Nixon, "Bourne's Attack on the Story of Marcus Whitman," *Inter Ocean* (Chicago), November 25, 1901, 8.

280 "it would never have been": Marshall, "A Discussion of Professor Bourne's Paper," 222.

280 "the most painstaking examination": Edward Gaylord Bourne, *Essays in Historical Criticism* (New York: Charles Scribner's Sons, 1901), 51.

281 "it does not make you writhe": Marshall to Bourne, January 28, 1901, Folder 100, Bourne Papers.

281 "harrowing up the old gentleman's soul": Marshall to Bourne, January 7, 1901, 4, Folder 100, Bourne Papers.

281 "establish the facts of history": Marshall to Bourne, January 26, 1901.

282 "exposing the true character": Ripley Hitchcock, "The Whitman Legend: Another Revival of a Curious Myth Concerning the Early Days of Oregon," *New York Times Saturday Review*, September 28, 1901, 17–18.

282 lists of tales debunked by science: For a more complete examination of the fall of the Whitman story into academic disrepute, see Sarah Elizabeth Koenig, *The Legend of Marcus Whitman and the Making of American History* (New Haven, CT: Yale University, 2015), 279–80.

282 "legend will die hard": Cited in Koenig, *The Legend of Marcus Whitman*, 279–80; J. Franklin Jameson, review of *Essays in Historical Criticism*, by Edward Gaylord Bourne, *American Historical Review* 7, no. 4 (July 1902): 745–47.

283 "more cheek than most any man": Myron Eells, diary entry, July 28, 1902, Box 2, Myron Eells notebooks, Whitman College Archives.

CHAPTER EIGHTEEN: Lost Cause

285 *The American Historical Review* said: Charles W. Smith, "Review of *Acquisition of Oregon*," *American Historical Review* 17, no. 2 (January 1912): 385–86.

285 **many good years ahead of him:** The Pacific Northwest's embrace of Whitman as a local hero was widespread and enthusiastic, but not universal. *The Oregonian,* the newspaper in Portland that had long been skeptical of Spalding's claims, continued to cast doubt, as did a number of scholars in the Portland area.

286 **More than seven hundred Confederate monuments:** "Whose Heritage? Public Symbols of the Confederacy," Southern Poverty Law Center, February 1, 2019, https://www .splcenter.org/20190201/whose-heritage-public-symbols-confederacy.

287 **"unparalleled knowledge of Northwest history":** Penrose to Henry Pritchett, April 8, 1920, Penrose Collection, Whitman College Archives; cited in G. Thomas Edwards, *The Triumph of Tradition* (Walla Walla, WA: Whitman College Press, 1992), 444.

287 **the eastern elitism of Bourne:** William D. Lyman, "Some Observations upon the Negative Testimony and the General Spirit and Methods of Bourne and Marshall in Dealing with the Whitman Question," *Washington Historical Quarterly* 7, no. 2 (April 2, 1916): 99–122.

288 **Whitman legend as established historical fact:** Edwards, *The Triumph of Tradition,* 493.

288 **"love for Whitman's fame":** *The Masque of Marcus Whitman,* presented by Associated Students of Whitman College, June 9, 1919, at Whitman College. Program for play in WC Mss 155, Box 1, Folder 18, Penrose Family Collection, Whitman College Archives; text of play in *Whitman Codex* 1, no. 1: 31, 35.

289 **"who saved this land of ours":** Stephen B. L. Penrose, "How the West Was Won: Program and Story," May 28–29, 1924, Whitman College Archives, https://arminda.whitman.edu /object/arminda29542.

289 **drawing similarly huge crowds:** Details about the pageant come from Penrose, "How the West Was Won"; Edwards, *The Triumph of Tradition,* 491–93; Homer A. Post, "Walla Walla to Have Big Pageant Depicting 'How the West Was Won,'" *The Gazette* (Cedar Rapids, IA), June 1, 1923, 2; "How the West Was Won," *Walla Walla Bulletin,* June 7, 1923, 1.

290 **"Gladly he rides towards home":** Penrose, "How the West Was Won," 16.

290 **old Whitman mission:** The 35.5 acres of the mission were purchased for $10,000, which had been made as profit from the "Wagons West!" pageant. See "$10,822 Profit on Centennial," *Spokesman-Review* (Spokane, WA), January 13, 1937, 3.

291 **"national memorial to Marcus Whitman":** An Act to Provide for the Establishment of the Whitman National Monument, H.R. 7736, 74th Cong., 2d Sess. (1936), at 2028.

292 **"tragic and pathetic":** Edwards, *The Triumph of Tradition,* 502.

294 **student body president:** G. Thomas Edwards, *Tradition in a Turbulent Age: Whitman College, 1925–1975* (Walla Walla, WA: Whitman College, 2001), 229.

295 **"this excellent publicity":** Whitman College President Winslow S. Anderson to Douglas, October 4, 1943, WC Mss 431, Box 9, Folder 49, G. Thomas Edwards Papers, Whitman College Archives.

295 **"Did Whitman's trip save Oregon?":** See Clifford M. Drury, *Marcus and Narcissa Whitman and the Opening of Old Oregon* (Seattle: Pacific Northwest National Parks and Forests Association, 1986), 2:350.

296 **"a complex of many forces":** William O. Douglas, address, May 22, 1953, *Acceptance of the Statue of Marcus Whitman Presented by the State of Washington* (Washington, D.C.: Government Printing Office, 1955), 58–59.

whittled down its Whitman reference: For an analysis of how the Whitmans have been viewed at the college, see Grace Fritzke, "Marcus Whitman as History and Myth: The Evolving Values of Whitman College," thesis (2015), Penrose Library Arminda Collections, Whitman College, https://arminda.whitman.edu/object/arminda30318.

 two sentences about the Whitmans: "History of the College," Whitman College website, https://www.whitman.edu/about/whitman-hallmarks/history-of-the-college.

 "care even less": Jenifer Crabtree, "Administrative History," Whitman Mission National Historic Site, 1988, https://www.nps.gov/parkhistory/online_books/whmi/adhi/adhi7b.htm.

 "Whitman was gone as a presence at the college": Skotheim, interview with the author, May 23, 2019, Port Angeles, Washington.

 "as far away from the campus as possible": Dennis Crockett, email to the author, September 12, 2018.

 "The strangest part": Author phone interview with Kate Kunkel-Patterson, June 12, 2019.

 "It is up to us to decide": Quoted in a placard that was part of "A Proper Monument?," an exhibit at Whitman College in 2018.

 includes the three stars: The seal can be found online at https://www.whitman.edu/alumni/be-connected/whitman-traditions/college-seal.

CHAPTER NINETEEN: Predators

 "self-sustaining at an early day": Superintendent Indian Affairs, Portland, Oregon, October 1, 1860, in *Report of the Commissioner of Indian Affairs for the Year 1860* (Washington, D.C.: Government Printing Office, 1860), 177.

 "in constant fear": W. H. Barnhart, U.S. Indian agent, Umatilla Indian Agency, U.S. Office of Indian Affairs, *Report of the Commissioner of Indian Affairs for the Year 1866* (Washington, D.C.: Government Printing Office, 1866), 87.

 "It is hardly to be expected": W. H. Boyle, Indian Agent, August 15, 1870, in *Report of the Commissioner of Indian Affairs for the Year 1870* (Washington, D.C.: Government Printing Office, 1870), 548.

 Senate ratified 376 Indian treaties: Francis Paul Prucha, *American Indian Treaties: The History of a Political Anomaly* (Berkeley: University of California Press, 1994), 1.

 Congress halted treaty making: Congress decided to end Indian treaty making in 1871. Prucha, *American Indian Treaties*, 17.

 Congress had unilateral power: *Lone Wolf v. Hitchcock*, 187 U.S. 553 (1903). See https://supreme.justia.com/cases/federal/us/187/553/.

 "unlike that of any other people": Quoted in Prucha, *American Indian Treaties*, 1–2.

 allowed them to vote: "Voting Rights for Native Americans," in "Elections . . . The American Way," Presentations and Activities, Classroom Materials, Library of Congress website, accessed July 5, 2020, https://www.loc.gov/teachers/.

 the art of behaving like whites: Alexandra Harmon, "Indian Treaty History," *Oregon Historical Quarterly* 106, no. 3 (Fall 2005): 360.

309 **"it gave us a chance":** Antone Minthorn, interview with the author, Umatilla Reservation, Oregon, August 9, 2018.

310 **"the terrible crime will have passed forever":** Stephen A. Lowell, "The Indians of the Whitman Massacre," *Whitman College Quarterly* 2, no. 2 (June 1898): 23–24, 26.

310 **2.3 pounds of salmon:** Estimates of the Indian salmon catch and consumption in Charles F. Wilkinson, *Crossing the Next Meridian* (Washington, D.C.: Island Press, 1992), 185; Allan T. Scholz et al., *Fishes of Eastern Washington: A Natural History*, 1 (Biology Faculty Publications, Eastern Washington University, Cheney, WA, 2014), 86.

310 **"shall be set apart":** Treaty text in James Doty, *Journal of Operations of Governor Isaac Ingalls Stevens of Washington Territory in 1855* (Fairfield, WA: Ye Galleon Press, 1978), 93.

311 **"expulsion of the Indians":** William H. Barnhart, U.S. Indian agent, Umatilla Indian Agency, July 25, 1868, in *Annual Report of the Commissioner of Indian Affairs for 1868* (Washington, D.C.: Government Printing Office, 1868), 77.

311 **"all these useless and unproductive people":** "Umatilla Indian Reservation: A Public Nuisance That Ought to Be Abated," *Weekly Oregon Statesman* (Salem), June 12, 1875, 1.

311 **"a few worthless Indians":** *East Oregonian*, December 22, 1877, 2, cited in Robert H. Ruby and John A. Brown, *The Cayuse Indians: Imperial Tribesmen of Old Oregon* (Norman: University of Oklahoma Press, 1972), 279.

311 **twice its surveyed size:** After the Walla Walla Treaty of 1855, the original size of the Umatilla Reservation was to be 512,000 acres, but it was soon surveyed and legally established to be 245,699 acres. In years to come, it would continue to shrink because of pressure from surrounding whites and actions of the federal and state governments.

312 **"productive of great agricultural wealth":** *Memorial of the Legislature of Oregon, Asking the Passage of an Act to Extinguish the Title to the Umatilla Indian Reservation,* January 25, 1875, S. Misc. Doc. No. 43-53 (1875), 1.

313 **half the best farmland:** Charles F. Luce, "The Beginning of Modern Tribal Governance and Enacting Sovereignty: Part I, The Early Years," in *As Days Go By: Our History, Our Land, Our People,* ed. Jennifer Karson (Seattle: University of Washington Press, 2006), 151.

313 **"denuding these lands of the timber":** Charles Wilkins, U.S. Indian agent, "Report of Umatilla Agency," *Annual Report of the Commissioner of Indian Affairs for the Year 1898* (Washington, D.C.: Government Printing Office, 1898), 262.

313 **a conspiracy in 1908:** *United States v. Raley*, 173 F. 159 (1909).

313 **"common goal of assimilating":** Prucha, *American Indian Treaties*, 362.

314 **"no permanent [water] rights":** Letter from E. S. Parker, commissioner of Indian Affairs, May 16, 1870, quoted in Karson, *As Days Go By*, 102n28, 143.

314 **"usual and accustomed stations":** Treaty of 1855, Article 1, in Doty, *Journal of Operations*, 93–94.

314 **"United States promised the river twice":** Paul Koberstein, "The Umatilla River Blues," *The Oregonian*, October 6, 1991, B1.

315 **"rules governing ownership":** Blaine Harden, *A River Lost* (New York: W. W. Norton, 1996), 106.

315 "not the preservation but the remaking": Wallace Stegner, *Where the Bluebird Sings to the Lemonade Springs* (New York: Penguin Books, 1992), 85, 88.

315 a historian for the Bureau: Eric A. Stene, "Umatilla Project," Bureau of Reclamation, 1993, online at https://www.usbr.gov/projects/pdf.php?id=202.

316 "the fish can walk": Antone Minthorn, interview by Clark Hansen, July 25, 2000, "Columbia River Dissenters," Center for Columbia River History Oral Histories, SR 2783, 26, Oregon Historical Society.

316 "away from home and family life": Institute for Government Research, *The Problem of Indian Administration* (Baltimore: Johns Hopkins Press, 1928), 403.

316 "violation of the children's personalities": Institute for Government Research, *Problem of Indian Administration*, 403.

317 unemployment hovered at around 50 percent: Details in this paragraph come from Luce, "Beginning of Modern Tribal Governance," 151–53, and from *Comprehensive Plan, Confederated Tribes of the Umatilla Indian Reservation* (Pendleton, OR: Confederated Tribes of the Umatilla Indian Reservation, 2010), 36–37.

317 Almost all Indian-owned farmland: Luce, "Beginning of Modern Tribal Governance," 152.

317 last fluent native speakers of the Cayuse language died: Chuck Sams, communications director, Umatilla Reservation, interview with the author, July 6, 2018. Sams and other tribal leaders note that tribal language revitalization is happening on the Umatilla Reservation and across Indian Country, so there will probably be fluent Cayuse language speakers again.

317 still hated by white people: Bobbie Conner, director, Tamástslikt Cultural Institute, Confederated Tribes of the Umatilla Indian Reservation, interview with the author, August 8, 2018.

317 until after World War II: Sams interview. Sams said the U.S. Army promised to pay his great-grandmother Mary Sams $160 for a hundred horses it hauled away during World War I, but the money wasn't paid until the 1950s, and without interest.

318 round up reliable Indians: Luce, "Beginning of Modern Tribal Governance," 152.

318 white ranchers were taken care of: Luce, "Beginning of Modern Tribal Governance," 152.

319 worked in Washington as a law clerk: Dennis Hevesi, "Charles F. Luce, Ex-Chief of Con Ed, Is Dead at 90," *New York Times*, January 29, 2008.

321 sometimes express disapproval through silence: See Laurie Arnold, *Bartering with the Bones of Their Dead* (Seattle: University of Washington Press, 2012), 57, 107, 161n39.

321 by just 9 votes: Luce, "Beginning of Modern Tribal Governance," 157.

CHAPTER TWENTY: Broke

322 "there were no jobs": Antone Minthorn, interview with the author, Umatilla Reservation, Oregon, August 9, 2018.

323 About half of the country's 1.4 million: C. Matthew Snipp, "The Size and Distribution of the American Indian Population," in *Changing Numbers, Changing Needs: American Indian Demography and Public Health* (Washington, D.C.: National Academy Press, 1996), online at https://www.nap.edu/read/5355/chapter/4.

323 "the city made us new": Tommy Orange, *There There* (New York: Knopf, 2018), 8–9.

325 "end their status as wards": H.R. Con. Res. 108, 83d Cong. (1953).

325 Termination legislation would strip: "Land Tenure Issues," Indian Land Tenure Foundation, https://iltf.org/land-issues/issues/.

325 "try to absorb Indians": David Treuer, *The Heartbeat of Wounded Knee* (New York: Riverhead, 2019), 254.

325 "these white man tendencies": "The Indian Tribes Speak," *Princeton Daily Clarion* (Princeton, IN), August 15, 1954, 8.

327 "almost impossible to win this war": Harry S. Truman, "Rear Platform Remarks In Idaho," June 7, 1948, Harry S. Truman Library collection, public papers, online at www .trumanlibrary.gov/library/public-papers/119/rear-platform-remarks-idaho.

327 if one gargantuan concrete plug: "Dams: History and Purpose," Northwest Power and Conservation Council, https://www.nwcouncil.org/reports/columbia-river-history /damshistory.

328 at high risk of extirpation: Carl Segerstrom, "Courts Can't Keep Columbia and Snake River Salmon from the Edge of Extinction," *High Country News*, September 26, 2019.

329 They never did: See Blaine Harden, *A River Lost* (New York: W. W. Norton, 1996), 165, 268n3; Harden, "Nuclear Reactions," *Washington Post*, May 5, 1996; Michele Stenehjem, *On the Home Front: The Cold War Legacy of the Hanford Nuclear Site* (Lincoln: University of Nebraska Press, 1992), 113–30. Also Steve Olson, *The Apocalypse Factory* (New York: W. W. Norton, 2020), 180–84.

331 "rushes with great impetuosity": Alexander Ross, *Ross's Adventures of the First Settlers on the Oregon or Columbia River, 1810–1813* (London: Smith, Elder, 1849), 130.

332 "a white man's club": Charles F. Luce, "The Beginning of Modern Tribal Governance and Enacting Sovereignty: Part I, The Early Years," in *As Days Go By: Our History, Our Land, Our People*, ed. Jennifer Karson (Seattle: University of Washington Press, 2006), 165.

333 "do the future generation some good": "Umatilla Judgment Funds: Hearing on S. 2357 and H.R. 9477 Before the S. Subcomm. on Indian Affairs," 91st Cong. (1969) (statement of William Minthorn).

334 chose full per capita payouts: The $1,800 per person payment is in William Johnson, "Sovereignty of the CTUIR," in Karson, *As Days Go By*, 181.

334 "swamped with alcoholism": *Comprehensive Plan, Confederated Tribes of the Umatilla Indian Reservation* (Pendleton, OR: Confederated Tribes of the Umatilla Indian Reservation, 2010), 39.

335 "no reasonable expectation to believe": "Self-Determination and Recovery," in Karson, *As Days Go By*, 198. This chapter of the tribal history was written by Michael J. Farrow, a Cayuse and director of the tribes' first natural resources department.

335 "a Slum with Land": Allen L. Nacheman, Associated Press, July 5, 1970. His moving story touched a nerve; it was printed in newspapers in nearly every state.

335 "broke and completely disorganized": *Comprehensive Plan*, 38.

CHAPTER TWENTY-ONE: White People's Money

336 "intermittent remorse and prolonged failure": Richard M. Nixon, "Special Message on Indian Affairs," July 8, 1970, Public Papers of the Presidents of the United States, 564–67, 576; James M. Naughton, "President Urges Wider Indian Role in Aid for Tribes," *New York Times,* July 8, 1970, A1; Nick Martin, "Indian Country Deserves a Better Hero Than Richard Nixon," *New Republic,* October 21, 2019.

337 "last progressive Republican": John Aloysius Farrell, "The Operatic Life of Richard Nixon," *The Atlantic,* January 9, 2013.

337 "Abraham Lincoln of the Indian people": Sean Stroh, "Setting Precedent for Native American Progress," Nixon Foundation, https://www.nixonfoundation.org/2013/07/setting-precedent-for-native-american-progress/; MacDonald quoted in Len Garment to Nixon, November 20, 1970, in executive files, Box 1, White House Central Files, Nixon Presidential Materials, National Archives, in Joan Hoff, *Nixon Reconsidered* (New York: Basic Books, 1994), 339n31.

337 "goal of any new national policy": Nixon, "Special Message on Indian Affairs."

338 "That word 'massacre' implies": Antone Minthorn, interview with the author, Umatilla Reservation, Oregon, August 9, 2018.

339 There was money for many tribal members: "Self-Determination and Recovery," in *As Days Go By: Our History, Our Land, Our People,* ed. Jennifer Karson (Seattle: University of Washington Press, 2006), 195.

342 "All we want": *Seattle Times,* September 11, 1978, 14.

343 "polluted sink of sewage": Paul Koberstein, "The Umatilla River Blues," *The Oregonian,* October 6, 1991, B1.

343 long and expensive court battle: Peg Herring, "Uniting the Umatilla," Fall 2006, Oregon's Agriculture Progress Archive, Oregon State University, https://oregonprogress.oregonstate.edu/fall-2006/uniting-umatilla.

343 "not pay lawyers to fight": Herring, "Uniting the Umatilla."

344 began to show significant results in 1994: Christopher W. Shelley, "The Resurrection of a River: Re-watering the Umatilla Basin," Center for Columbia River History, 1999, 6.

344 "few times in my public life": Associated Press, "Hatfield Hails Umatilla Basin Water Project," *Statesman Journal* (Salem, OR), February 8, 1988, 5.

347 "staff, staff, staff": Les Minthorn, interview with the author, June 19, 2018, Umatilla Reservation.

347 "need you back at our rez": Bill Johnson, interview with the author, Umatilla Reservation, Oregon, August 9, 2018.

347 "one of only a few tribal courts": Gregory S. Arnold, "Hon. William D. Johnson, Chief Judge, Umatilla Tribal Court," *Federal Lawyer Magazine,* April 2015.

348 "very urgent needs": *A Quiet Crisis: Federal Funding and Unmet Needs in Indian Country* (Washington, D.C.: U.S. Commission on Civil Rights, July 2003), 4.

349 supported a casino: John David Tovey, "Casino Tribes Realize the American Dream," *Seattle Post-Intelligencer,* January 9, 2003.

351 reductions of smoking: Randall K. Q. Akee et al., "The Indian Gaming Regulatory Act and Its Effect on American Indian Economic Development," *Journal of Economic Perspectives* 29, no. 3 (Summer 2015): 185.

351 "simply the most successful economic venture": Akee, "Indian Gaming Regulatory Act," 196.

351 "local concentration of tribal gaming's benefits": Akee, "Indian Gaming Regulatory Act," 203.

352 "Doctor should be killed": A display in the museum at the Tamástslikt Cultural Institute quotes Teweutoyakonemy, the daughter of Tomahas, one of the convicted killers of the Whitmans, as saying this.

EPILOGUE

357 "viewed as imperialistic and destructive": Nicholas K. Geranios, "Scrutiny mounts of legacy of pioneering Northwest missionary," Associated Press, June 1, 2021.

358 "thirst for justice": Tom Banse, "Billy Frank Jr. in, Marcus Whitman out as part of U.S. Capitol statue swap," KUOW Radio, Seattle, April 14, 2021. Lynda V. Mapes, "Inslee signs into law bill to put statue honoring Billy Frank Jr. in U.S. Capitol," *Seattle Times*, April 14, 2021. The swap of the statues did not occur with passage of the law. A statue of Frank had to be made in a foundry and shipped to Washington, D.C. The swap was expected to take as long as a couple of years.

358 "This guy is a colonizer": Grace Jackson, "Statues are for Heroes: School clubs rally for removal of Marcus Whitman statue," *Whitman Wire*, Whitman College, Walla Walla, Washington, April 29, 2021.

359 removal became a priority: Jessie Brandt, "Narcissa Whitman monument outside Prentiss quietly removed," *Whitman Wire*, February 18, 2021.

359 "foundational violence of dispossession": Brandt.

359 Whitman College has never seriously: Gina Ohnstad emails to the author, September 2021.

360 full scholarships to five tribal students: Ohnstad emails to the author.

360 "very much open to increased involvement": Steve Thede phone interview and emails with the author, September 2021.

361 Sams who suggested to Whitman College: Chuck Sams conversations with author, September 23, 2021.

361 "cast serious doubt on the guilt": City of Oregon City staff report on Cayuse Five Tribute, Oregon City, Oregon, September 15, 2021, 1.

362 "change the way we talk": Thede interview and emails to the author.

363 "we are deeply troubled": Letter of apology to the Nez Perce Tribe from the Presbytery of the Inland Northwest, June 16, 2021.

363 "the journey will be long": Reverend Sheryl Kinder-Pyle emails to the author, September 2021.

BIBLIOGRAPHY

Allen, A. J. *Ten Years in Oregon*. Ithaca, New York: Press of Andrus Gauntlet, 1850.

Anbinder, Tyler. *Nativism and Slavery: The Northern Know Nothings and the Politics of the 1850s*. New York: Oxford University Press, 1992.

Arnold, Laurie. *Bartering with the Bones of Their Dead*. Seattle: University of Washington Press, 2012.

Bagley, Clarence B., ed. *Early Catholic Missions in Old Oregon*. Vol. 1. Seattle: Lowman & Hanford Company, 1932.

Bancroft, Hubert Howe. *History of Oregon*. Vols. 1–2. San Francisco: The History Company, 1886–88. Scholars believe this book was written by Oregon-based author and historian Frances Fuller Victor.

Barrows, William. *Oregon: The Struggle for Possession*. Boston: Houghton and Mifflin, 1883.

Belknap, George N. "Authentic Account of the Murder of Dr. Whitman: The History of a Pamphlet," *Papers of the Bibliographical Society of America* Vol. 55, No. 4 (Fourth Quarter, 1961), 319–46.

Berg, Scott W. *38 Nooses: Lincoln, Little Crow, and the Beginning of the Frontier's End.* New York: Vintage Books, 2012.

Blanchet, Francis Norbert. *Historical Sketches of the Catholic Church in Oregon During the Past Forty Years.* Portland: Oregon Catholic Church, 1878.

———. *Notice and Voyages of the Famed Quebec Mission to the Pacific Northwest: Being the Correspondences, Notices, etc., of Father Blanchet and Demers.* Portland: Oregon Historical Society, 1956.

Bourne, Edward Gaylord. *Essays in Historical Criticism: The Legend of Marcus Whitman, etc.* New York: Charles Scribner's Sons, 1901.

Boyd, Robert. *The Coming of the Spirit of Pestilence: Introduced Infectious Diseases and Population Decline Among Northwest Coast Indians, 1774–1874.* Seattle: University of Washington Press, 1999.

———. "The Pacific Northwest Measles Epidemic of 1847–48," *Oregon Historical Quarterly*, Vol. 95, No. 1 (Spring 1994), 6–17.

Brandt, Patricia, and Lillian A. Pereyra. *Adapting in Eden: Oregon Catholic Minority 1838–1986.* Pullman: Washington State University Press, 2002.

Brouillet, Jean-Baptiste Abraham. "Protestantism in Oregon: Authentic Account of the Murder of Dr. Whitman, and the Ungrateful Calumnies of H. H. Spalding, Protestant Missionary." First published in *New-York Freeman's Journal*, installments from February to May 1853. Published at least nine times in various locations in the Pacific Northwest until 1932. Complete reprint in Bagley, *Early Catholic Missions in Old Oregon*, 151–238.

Burns, Ken, and Stephen Ives. *The West*, eight-part documentary, September 1996, PBS, https://www.pbs.org/weta/thewest/program/.

Carr, Sarah Pratt. *Narcissa: The Cost of Empire, Libretto for the Opera.* Seattle: The Stuff Printing Concern, 1912.

Cebula, Larry. *Plateau Indians and the Quest for Spiritual Power, 1700–1850.* Lincoln: University of Nebraska Press, 2003.

———. "The Bigot Disclosed: 90 Years of Nativism." *Oregon Historical Quarterly*, Vol. 75, No. 2 (June 1974), 109–90.

Clark, Malcolm, Jr. *Eden Seekers: The Settlement of Oregon, 1818–1862.* Boston: Houghton Mifflin, 1981.

DeVoto, Bernard. *Across the Wide Missouri*. Boston: Houghton Mifflin, 1947.

Doty, James. Edward J. Kowrach, ed. *Journal of Operations of Governor Isaac Ingalls Stevens of Washington Territory in 1855*. Fairfield, Washington: Ye Galleon Press, 1978.

———. *Chief Lawyer of the Nez Perce, 1796–1876*. Glendale, California: Arthur H. Clark Company, Northwest Historical Series, No. 14, 1979.

———, ed. *The Diaries and Letters of Henry H. Spalding and Asa Bowen Smith Relating to the Nez Perce Mission, 1838–1842*. Glendale, California: Arthur H. Clark Company, 1958.

———. *Elkanah and Mary Walker: Pioneers Among the Spokanes*. Caldwell, Idaho: Caxton Printers, 1940.

———. *Henry Harmon Spalding: Pioneer of Old Oregon*. Caldwell, Idaho: Caxton Printers, 1936.

Drury, Clifford M. *Marcus and Narcissa Whitman and the Opening of Old Oregon*, Vols. 1–2. Seattle: Pacific Northwest National Parks and Forests Association, 1986.

———. *Marcus Whitman M.D.: Pioneer and Martyr*. Caldwell, Idaho: Caxton Printers, 1937.

———, ed. *On to Oregon: The Diaries of Mary Walker & Myra Eells*. Lincoln: University of Nebraska Press, 1963.

———, ed. *Where Wagons Could Go: Narcissa Whitman and Eliza Spalding*. Lincoln: University of Nebraska Press, 1997.

Edwards, Thomas G. *Tradition in a Turbulent Age: Whitman College 1925–1975*. Walla Walla, Washington: Whitman College, 2001.

———. *The Triumph of Tradition: The Emergence of Whitman College 1859–1924*. Walla Walla, Washington: Whitman College, 1992.

Eells, Myron. *Marcus Whitman: Pathfinder and Patriot*. Seattle: Alice Harriman Company, 1909.

Emmons, Della Gould. "Marcus Whitman," a play. Script among Della Gould Emmons papers, unsorted boxes, Tacoma Public Library, Tacoma, Washington.

———. *Northwest History in Action: A Collection of Twelve Plays Illustrating the Epochs of Northwest History*. Minneapolis: T. S. Denison & Co., 1960.

Fisher, Andrew H. *Shadow Tribe: The Making of Columbia River Indian Identity.* Seattle: Center for the Study of the Pacific Northwest with University of Washington Press, 2010.

Fraser, Caroline. *Prairie Fires: The American Dreams of Laura Ingalls Wilder.* New York: Metropolitan Books, 2017.

Gonzales-Day, Ken. *Lynching in the West 1850–1935.* Durham, North Carolina: Duke University Press, 2006.

Gray, William H. *A History of Oregon, 1792–1849, Drawn from Personal Observation and Authentic Information.* Portland: Harris & Holman, 1870.

Harden, Blaine. *A River Lost: The Life and Death of the Columbia.* New York: W. W. Norton, 2012.

Hofstadter, Richard. "The Paranoid Style in American Politics." *Harper's Magazine,* November 1964.

Howe, Daniel Walker. *What Hath God Wrought: The Transformation of America, 1815–1848.* New York: Oxford University Press, 2007.

Hulbert, Archer B., and Dorothy P. *Marcus Whitman—Crusader,* Vols. 1–2. Denver: Stewart Commission of Colorado College and Denver Public Library, 1938–1941.

Hunn, Eugene S., with James Stern and family. *Nch'i-Wána "The Big River": Mid-Columbia Indians and Their Land.* Seattle: University of Washington Press, 1990.

Jeffrey, Julie Roy. *Converting the West: A Biography of Narcissa Whitman.* Norman: University of Oklahoma Press, 1991.

Jessett, Thomas E. *The Indian Side of the Whitman Massacre.* Fairfield, Washington: Ye Galleon Press, 1985.

Josephy, Alvin M. *The Nez Perce Indians and the Opening of the Northwest.* New Haven, Connecticut: Yale University Press, 1965.

Karson, Jennifer, ed. *As Days Go By: Our History, Our Land, and Our People: The Cayuse, Umatilla, and Walla Walla.* Pendleton, Oregon: Tamástslikt Cultural Institute & Oregon Historical Society Press, with University of Washington Press, 2006.

Kasson, Joy S. *Buffalo Bill's Wild West: Celebrity, Memory, and Popular History.* New York: Hill and Wang, 2000.

Kip, Lawrence. *The Indian Council in the Valley of the Walla-Walla, 1855.* San Francisco: Whitton, Towne & Co. Printers, 1855.

Koenig, Sarah. *The Legend of Marcus Whitman and the Making of American History,* doctoral dissertation. New Haven, Connecticut: Yale University, 2015.

Lansing, Ronald. *Juggernaut: The Whitman Massacre Trial, 1850.* San Francisco: Ninth Judicial Court Historical Society, 1993.

Laughlin, Rick, ed. Missionary Correspondence Transcripts, letters to and from Oregon missionaries and the American Board of Commissioners for Foreign Missions. Whitman College and Northwest Archives.

Lepore, Jill. *These Truths: A History of the United States.* New York: W. W. Norton, 2018.

Limerick, Patricia. *The Legacy of Conquest: The Unbroken Past of the American West.* New York: W. W. Norton, 1987.

Luce, Tamara J. "Excavating First-Person Accounts of the Whitman Massacre," *Nebraska Anthropologist,* Vol. 27 (2012), 112–36.

Lyman, William D. "Some Observations upon the Negative Testimony and the General Spirit and Methods of Bourne and Marshall in Dealing with the Whitman Question," *Washington Historical Quarterly,* Vol. 7, No. 2 (April 2, 1916), 99–122.

Marshall, William I. *Acquisition of Oregon and the Long Suppressed Evidence About Marcus Whitman.* Vols. 1–2. Seattle: Lowman & Hanford Co., 1911. Digitized by the HathiTrust, http://hdl.handle.net/2027/uc2.ark:/13960/t5bc40r2d.

————. *History vs. the Whitman Saved Oregon Story.* Chicago: Press of the Blakely Printing Co., 1904.

————. "Marcus Whitman: A Discussion of Professor Bourne's Paper." Ann Arbor, Michigan, December 28, 1900. *Annual Report of the American Historical Association for 1900.* Washington, D.C.: Government Printing Office, 1901.

McCoy, Genevieve. "Sanctifying the Self and Saving the Savage: The Failure of the ABCFM Oregon Mission and the Conflicted Language of Calvinism," doctoral dissertation, University of Washington, Seattle, 1991.

McMurtry, Larry. *Sacagawea's Nickname: Essays on the American West.* New York: New York Review Books, 2001.

Miller, Christopher. *Prophetic Worlds: Indians and Whites on the Columbia Plateau*. New Brunswick, New Jersey: Rutgers University Press, 1985.

Morrison, Dorothy Nafus. *Outpost: John McLoughlin and the Far Northwest*. Portland: Oregon Historical Society Press, 1999.

Mowry, William A. *Marcus Whitman and the Early Days of Oregon*. New York: Silver, Burdett and Company, 1901.

Nixon, Oliver W. *How Marcus Whitman Saved Oregon: A True Romance of Patriotic Heroism, Christian Devotion and Final Martyrdom*. Chicago: Star Publishing Company, 1895.

Nokes, R. Gregory. *The Troubled Life of Peter Burnett: Oregon Pioneer and First Governor of California*. Corvallis: Oregon State University Press, 2018.

Olson, Steve. *The Apocalypse Factory: Plutonium and the Making of the Atomic Age*. New York: W. W. Norton, 2020.

Orange, Tommy. *There There*. New York: Alfred A. Knopf, 2018.

Palmer, Joel. *Journal of Travels: Over the Oregon Trail in 1845*. Portland: Oregon Historical Society Press, 1993.

Penrose. "The Romance of a College," pamphlet printed by Whitman College, 1894. Whitman College and Northwest Archives, WCA 142, College Publication Collection.

Penrose, Stephen B. L. *Whitman: An Unfinished Story*. Walla Walla, Washington: Whitman Publishing Co., 1935.

Prucha, Francis Paul. *American Indian Treaties: The History of a Political Anomaly*. Berkeley: University of California Press, 1994.

———. "Two Roads to Conversion: Protestant and Catholic Missionaries in the Pacific Northwest." *Pacific Northwest Quarterly*, October 1988.

Richards, Kent D. *Isaac I. Stevens: Young Man in a Hurry*. Pullman: Washington State University Press, 2016.

———, ed. "The Isaac I. Stevens and Joel Palmer Treaties 1855–2005." *Oregon Historical Quarterly*, Special Issue, Vol. 106, No. 3 (Fall 2005), 342–491.

Rockwood, Ruth, ed. "Diary of Rev. G. H. Atkinson 1847–1858, Part V." *Oregon Historical Quarterly*, Vol. 41, No. 1 (March 1940), 6–33.

Ruby, Robert H., and John A. Brown. *The Cayuse Indians: Imperial Tribesmen of Old Oregon*. Norman: University of Oklahoma Press, 1972.

Ryan, Mary P. *Cradle of the Middle Class: The Family in Oneida County, New York, 1790–1865*. Cambridge, UK: Cambridge University Press, 1981.

Sager, Catherine, Elizabeth Sager, and Matilda Sager. *The Whitman Massacre of 1847*. Fairfield, Washington: Ye Galleon Press, 1981.

Scott, Leslie M. "Indian Diseases as Aids to Pacific Northwest Settlement." *Oregon Historical Quarterly*, Vol. 29, No. 2 (June 1926), 161.

Spalding, Henry Harmon. "The Early Labors of the Missionaries in Oregon," U.S. Senate, 41st Congress, 3d Session, Ex. Doc. 37. Washington, D.C.: Government Printing Office, 1871. Reprinted in 1903.

Stegner, Wallace. *Where the Bluebird Sings to the Lemonade Springs*. New York: Penguin Books, 1992.

Stern, Theodore. *Chiefs & Change: Indian Relations at Fort Neʒ Perces 1818–1855*. Corvallis: Oregon State University Press, 1996.

———. *Chiefs & Chief Traders: Indian Relations at Fort Neʒ Perces, 1818–1855*. Corvallis: Oregon State University Press, 1993.

Stevens, Isaac Ingalls. Darrell Scott, ed. *A True Copy of the Record of the Official Proceedings at the Council in the Walla Walla Valley 1855*. Fairfield, Washington: Ye Galleon Press, 1996.

Tobie, Harvey Elmer. *No Man Like Joe: The Life and Times of Joseph L. Meek*. Portland: Binfords & Mort for Oregon Historical Society, 1949.

Treuer, David. *The Heartbeat of Wounded Knee: Native America from 1890 to the Present*. New York: Riverhead Books, 2019.

Victor, Frances Fuller. *The Early Indian Wars of Oregon*. Vol. 1, *The Cayuse War*. Corvallis, Oregon: Taxus Baccata, 2006, based on the original published in 1894.

———. *The River of the West*. Hartford, Connecticut: Columbian Book Company, 1870.

Walker, Deward E., Jr. *Conflict and Schism in Neʒ Perce Acculturation: A Study of Religion and Politics*. Pullman: Washington State University Press, 1968.

West, Elliot. *The Last Indian War*. New York: Oxford Press, 2009.

White, Richard. *It's Your Misfortune and None of My Own: A New History of the American West*. Norman: University of Oklahoma Press, 1991.

Whitman, Narcissa. *My Journal*. Fairfield, Washington: Ye Galleon Press, 1985.

Wilkinson, Charles F. *Crossing the Next Meridian: Land, Water, and the Future of the West*. Washington, D.C., Island Press, 1992.

IMAGE CREDITS

INDEX

Page numbers in *italics* refer to photographs.